A History of the Jews

A History of the Jews
Ancient and Modern

Ilan Halevi

Translated by A.M. Berrett

Zed Books Ltd.
London and New Jersey

A History of the Jews was first published in English by
Zed Books Ltd., 57 Caledonian Road, London N1 9BU, UK
and 171 First Avenue, Atlantic Highlands, NJ 07716, USA,
in 1987.

First reprint 1988

Originally published as *Question Juive, La Tribu, La Loi,
L'Espace,* © 1981, Editions de Minuit, Paris.

Translation copyright © Zed Books Ltd., 1987

Cover design Andrew Corbett

Cover picture shows a detail from *The Descendant of the
High Priest*, an oil painting by Isidor Kaufman.

Photograph copyright © Sotheby's, Inc.

Printed in the United Kingdom by The Bath Press, Avon.

British Library Cataloguing in Publication Data
Halevi, Ilan
    A history of the Jews, ancient and modern.
    1. Jews – History
    I. Title   II. Question Juive. *English*
    909'.04924   DS117

    ISBN 0-86232-531-5
    ISBN 0-86232-532-3 Pbk

Contents

1 The Tribe

It is doubtless an outcome of the histories involved rather than of the geography. For whatever reason, Palestine seems doomed, from time to time, to be cast in the role of frontier, fulcrum, limit. Several times in its history it has found itself caught between antagonistic, or simply rival, worlds – as if it really were at the very centre of the world. And today again, Palestine, the place now called Israel, in a dispute that is about far more than mere words, finds itself obliged to crystallize within itself, even if only ironically, the great contradictions of a universe that it does not comprehend and of which it knows nothing.

Which is heads and which is tails on this strange coin?

Here, the original and the "copy" endlessly mirror discordant reflections of each other's self-assertions. Established cleavages are disproved and reformed, the most startling alliances are made, conceptual frameworks turn against those who conceive them. A whole series of lessons of history clash and dissolve themselves in the service of mutually exclusive practical choices, and these lessons are themselves all the more incompatible in that they draw on the same symbols and are expressed in the same language.

Throughout the last hundred years, the twin processes of the expulsion of the Arabs and the settlement of the Jews have forced a community which drew the conditions and forms of its existence from an ancient and continuous implantation in the soil and space of Palestine, to assume the negative heritage of a history in which it had, on the whole, played no part: the history of European anti-Semitism, from the medieval persecutions to the tsarist pogroms and the Nazi genocide, by way of the Dreyfus affair.

The immigration of several hundred thousand European Jews into Palestine, starting from the end of the last century, the establishment of the State of Israel, accomplished through the expulsion of several hundred thousand Palestinians and the immigration of several hundred thousand Jews from Africa and Asia, introduced the "Jewish question", hitherto essentially a European question, into the heart of the tragedy of the Arab people of Palestine dispossessed of their space. From this irruption there arose the "Palestinian question".

Questions depend on who is asking them, as well as on those to whom they are addressed. It is extremely unusual for a people, a society, or even an individual to constitute a question, or problem in his own eyes. So the Palestinian question, the reluctant heir of the Jewish question, and like it the privileged locus of a "mythopoeic ideological delirium",[1] is only raised by its protagonists for their respective opponents, and for the world: interpellations with which each endeavours to cover the tumult of the other.

In the tangles of these endlessly distorted definitions, universal interpretations of history are also called into question; not simply because some other, equally unequivocal interpretation is preferred, but because they can now, at last, be objectified, and reduced to an apologetic function.

The Jewish question necessarily emerged prior to the Palestinian question since the latter is only the result of the attempt to settle the former by transplanting it. While this transplantation failed to settle it, it did transform it, and it is the trajectory of this transformation that we are going to examine.

Until the First World War, the word Palestine (land of the Philistines) was used to describe a region integrated into a larger whole – Syria, the Ottoman empire – which was at the same time divided into administrative units in a way that militated against any idea of unity. It was thus a region, not yet a question. However, the Palestinian question is not only the child of the transplanted European Jewish question. While it did emerge from Jewish colonization, it is also, in its way, the heir to what 19th century Europe called the "Eastern question".

Only a few years separate Marx's pamphlet *On the Jewish Question* (1844) from the short work published, in 1860, by Ernest Laharanne, Napoleon III's aide-de-camp, entitled *La nouvelle question d'Orient: empires d'Egypte et d'Arabie; reconstitution de la nationalité juive.* But the Jews involved in the European "Jewish question" were the ones living in Europe, not the Jews of Africa and Asia to whom Bonaparte addressed an appeal in 1799, calling on them to "rebuild their ancient homeland", under the protection of French arms. At that time, no one thought that the two questions could be linked, let alone become one and the same issue.

The Eastern question was perceived by the Western states as a policy problem, an enigma blocking their expansion. From the beginning of this century, the objective was clearly defined: the execution, hypocritically disguised as euthanasia, of the Ottoman state, "the sick man of Europe". The question was how best – from the British and French viewpoint – to hasten the disintegration of this enormous body and promote the rearrangement of its parts in an order compatible with the new imperatives of bourgeois freedom and industry?

Gradually, the Jewish question became a part of the Eastern question. Chronologically, the first factor in this process was the existence of a Jewish community in Palestine, and, in general, the existence of Jewish communities in various parts of the Ottoman empire. It was only in a second phase, during the last four decades of the 19th century, that the immigration of several tens of thousands of Jews from the Russian empire and the most backward areas of the Austro-Hungarian empire was grafted on to the issue and eventually became its overbearing aspect, a transformation rooted in the emergence, at the beginning of this century, of political Zionism, the vision expressed in Herzl's *The State of the Jews* (1896) and the Basel congress (1897). It was this conjunction which established the link between the Zionist movement and "governments" – the great powers of the day. On the basis of already accomplished facts and of processes already underway, it convinced the European states, especially Britain, to resolve in one stroke the question of Europe's Jews and the question of European domination over the East, by transferring the Jews to the East.

How ideologically omnipotent this first conceptual framework was! One has to stop and look closely, in order to see the imagery and the myth behind the satisfying equation.

In the formulation of this tripytch "Eastern question – Jewish question – Palestinian question", one can distinguish the interaction of distinct problematics on a given ground; but one can also see in it the prologue to a series of reductions, each of which dissolves into the next and all into one. The Arabs, the Jews, the West; or the Ottoman empire, Zionism, imperialism. Or a thousand other formulations. The essential thing remains that none of the three terms can be reduced to one of the two others, that none can be wholly explained by the other.

What, precisely, characterizes most explanations is that this triple play is reduced to a bipolarity: one of the three terms is unmasked – it is the second one in disguise. Such a reduction responds to numerous ideological and practical needs. It can serve every thesis: Zionist as well as anti-Zionist, conservative or revolutionary. The Zionist reduction of Arab nationalism to a variant of anti-Semitism corresponds to the radical reduction of Zionism to a mere function of the system of Western domination over the Arab East, an analysis in which the presumed agent of history is itself presented as a puppet, and Zionism is finally shown to be no more than a forgery, a fabrication, in the false reflection of an anti-Semitism that is itself unreal, a lying alibi for competition and reaction or even a distorted discourse on the class struggle.

Without attempting to go into great detail about the heretical and sacrilegious connections that this reductionism brings out on either side, one must note the silent convergence which emerges from the invective, and what is at stake: imperialism and nationalism, for example, appear as exclusive, antithetical hypotheses. Supposedly, a movement cannot belong to one sphere without inevitably excluding itself from the universe of the other. Yet on reflection this incompatibility is far from self-evident.

The European states, in general and individually. The Ottoman state, its structure, its state of health. Arab nationalism, the Jews of Palestine, the European immigrants, the crisis of the empires in eastern Europe, Zionism, the role of the great powers: it is easy to sketch an outline of the themes and subjects of this genealogy of the Palestinian question. And one can already sense the danger – the temptation – of letting one or two of these abstractions fall by the wayside in order to construct a neat little Manichaean psychodrama out of those which remain.

The attempt must therefore be made to read this history differently. In doing so, there is no need to invent, indeed scarcely any need to discover anything new. It is enough to have forgotten nothing, to censor nothing, to compare the omissions and convergences, to cross-check and illuminate.

We could approach this effort of memory from an unusual angle, one altogether in keeping with the urgency of the issue. We could start with the Jewish communities in the Arab world, and particularly in Palestine, in the days before they served as bridgeheads of Zionist penetration, before political Zionism, and even before the first wave of immigration from eastern Europe, the "Lovers of Zion", with their not yet secularized Messianism, who flocked to Palestine from the 1860s.

This was a time when the Ottoman empire was breaking up under the impact of the successive Capitulations granted by the Porte; the Napoleonic conquest had been a taste of things to come, and a fatal blow – even though the agony was to last more than a century.

Was Bonaparte's appeal at Gaza in 1799 simply whimsy? In any case, it was a legacy which became part of the foreign policy of his successors.

Whimsy? In London, in 1800, the very Christian James Bicheno – about whom there is no reason to suspect that he was a Bonapartist – published an essay on *The Restoration of the Jews*, followed in 1804 by an essay by Thomas Witherby, *An Attempt to Remove the Prejudices concerning the Jewish Nation*, by Byron's *Hebrew Melodies*, George Eliot's novel, *Daniel Deronda*, and many others.

And what is to be said of the strictly political decisions that followed this literary outpouring? In 1838, Lord Shaftesbury called for the establishment in Palestine of "a Jewish settlement guaranteed by the great powers". In the following year, as British troops took control of Aden, Palmerston gave the British vice-consul in Jerusalem special instructions concerning the "protection of the Jews". In 1840, while France was engaged in the military conquest of Algeria, it sent an expeditionary corps to Lebanon to defend the Maronites against the Druzes. In the same year, Moses Montefiore paid a visit to the viceroy of Egypt, Mohammed Ali. He was accompanied by Adolphe Crémieux, the future French minister who was to give his name to the decree making the Jews of Algeria French citizens, and by the German Jewish scholar Solomon Munk, who used the occasion of the visit to found the first modern Jewish school in Alexandria. Before long, Britain would send an expedition to Damascus to protect the Jews there, accused of ritual murder by the Christians. It was on this occasion that Sir Moses Montefiore addressed, in the name of Great Britain, his "co-religionists" in Damascus calling them "my brothers".

The widespread practice of "consular protection" consisted in removing an Ottoman citizen, or group of citizens, from the jurisdiction of the tribunals of the empire, obliging the Ottoman state, or any other plaintiff, to turn to the "judgement" of the European consulates in any dispute involving a "protected person". All the European powers were involved, each extending its protection to the confessional communities of its choice. The documents of the German consulate in Jerusalem from 1843 onwards[2] reflect a permanent intervention, not only at the level of inter-communal relations, but in the everyday life of the communities themselves. The "protection of the Jews" even in their own community projects was at that time one of the key aspects of German imperial policy in the region. And, while the modern-day Templars embarked on a classical form of agricultural colonization (here and there, in Palestine, one can still see the remains of this German colonization which preceded the Zionist one), the Churches and the Christian missions made a fortune in property, and, after the 1858 agrarian reform, even in property speculation.

The first half of the 19th century, which saw the crystallization of the basic features of the question posed by the East to the powers of modern Europe, was a time of general turmoil in empires, heralded by the Napoleonic hurricane. The triumphant bourgeois revolution was exported, but the low price of its goods was not always its only weapon. In 1830 France had embarked on a long and bloody conquest of the Algerian province of the Ottoman empire; Britain, meanwhile, was transforming its domination of the states of India into occupation pure and simple, and had established a bridgehead in southern Arabia by force.

It was, however, another thirty years before the Suez Canal was opened. This was because, in the meantime, the Sultan had had to deal with the Wahhabite revolt, the first of the "Arab revolts" of our times. The revolt constituted a theological challenge to the Islamic legitimacy of the Ottoman state; a demand for sovereignty over the Holy Places of Islam; centrifugal "feudalism" of the Bedouin tribes that were permanently struggling against the encroachment on their ancient freedoms by the central government, on the march at the least sign of weakness. Wahhabism represented all this and more. It was also a threat to which the Porte, with its orthodoxy under challenge, had to react as to a heresy with quite incalculable consequences. Mehmet Ali, the janissary-general, an outstanding product of the nurseries of soldiers into which the sultans put the young children of their Albanian slaves to make them into professional soldiers, sent by Istanbul to crush the Wahhabite rebellion, took advantage of the opportunity to carve himself out a kingdom. He became Mohammed Ali, king of the Arabs, using the Wahhabite threat as a lever to obtain the viceroyalty of Egypt and Syria, where his son Ibrahim Pasha pursued the dynastic work between 1832 and 1840: Arabization, but above all modernization. It was a short but decisive episode. In Egypt it served to destabilize the last elements of the old system still capable of offering resistance to Western penetration, while at the same time creating the infrastructure – the modernization of the irrigation system which re-vitalized the ancient dependence of the Egyptian peasant on the central government – which served to place the people of the Nile valley at the service of the British cotton industry. In the East, it demonstrated the vulnerability of the "sick man", and the fragility of its ancient institutions, and above all it stressed its internal contradictions, just as European military conquest and the national revolutions in the Balkans were threatening its rule from all sides.

Throughout this period (1799: Bonaparte's appeal; 1850: Laharanne calls for "a Jewish state from Smyrna to Suez") only the Jews in the East were directly involved. The European Jewish question, which the young Marx disputed with Bruno Bauer, had not yet undertaken to transplant itself. But, before their wretched co-religionists in eastern Europe, along with their influential co-religionists in western Europe (Montefiore, Crémieux, Munk and the leading figures in agricultural colonization, Rothschild and Hersch) took them up, as it were, the Jews of the East themselves were scarcely the centre of the Eastern Question. Until 1850, it was not the Jews, but the Christians who were the main object of the solicitude of the European powers: for, in the Balkans, the vast majority of the peasant population and the urban élite were Christian. The wave of "national democratic" revolutions that swept over Europe in 1848 took on the character of a confessional struggle. Here, the romanticism of bourgeois emancipation linked up with the imagery inherited from the Crusades. The stories, published in the West, about young Greek Christian girls raped by the Saracen soldiery deeply shocked a Europe which was discovering liberating and progressive imperialism, the highest stage of Christianity.

In Europe, where the creation of Christian states on the ruins of Ottoman rule rested on real social forces, and on an altogether standard demand for self-determination, "de-Ottomanization" was accomplished in a "revolutionary" process: certainly supported and inspired by the West, but nevertheless articulated on violent local contradictions. In North Africa, where Islamic history had not allowed Christian communities to survive, de-Ottomanization was accomplished by French military conquest.

In the East, the Ottoman empire, reduced to Turkey and the Arab Mashrek, was not yet vulnerable to military occupation. In fact, the rivalry between the French and the British, which also involved the Germans, Russians and even the Italians, meant that control had to be imposed by every available indirect means: trade, diplomacy, brief armed incursions here and there, philanthropy, provocations, interventions. This was the regime of the Capitulations, by which, since the Renaissance, the Ottoman state had first mortgaged its Treasury, then its monopoly over tax collection, then bit by bit all the elements of sovereignty. States, churches, great companies, charitable bodies and even the utopian phalansteries, all means were good to hasten the decay. For several decades, the Ottoman government collaborated in its own suicide.

The forces tearing the Empire apart took many forms, some of which might even appear contradictory: not surprisingly, as they were often pulling in different directions, as were the various contending powers. Yet they all converged on the same final solution to the Ottoman problem: the reduction of the empire to Asiatic Turkey. But this was not to happen until the First World War; the Jewish question in Europe then played a role, if not a determinant one, in the practical implementation of the solution. A century earlier, it was the Christians in the East who provided the West with its main channel for penetrating and destabilizing the Ottoman system.

In order to understand the strategic importance of such channels, it is necessary to grasp the mode of operation (if not of production) of the old system. It is necessary to understand the nature, at once despotic and fragile, of the link binding the communities in the countryside to the central government, in particular in the case of Palestine: tribes and clans of peasants were ruled by their customary law but were obliged to pay tribute for their autonomy to the extortionate soldier-state. It is necessary to understand the triangular relationship which came into being between the countryside, Turkish rule and the ruling classes in the towns, made up of Arab aristocracies proud of their military origins, although urbanized through and through, belonging to the dominant Muslim sect (Sunni throughout the Mashrek); merchants and artisans, among whom were a growing proportion of members of minority groups – Eastern Christians, but also Greeks, Armenians, "Latins" and "Jews". The peasantry itself was divided into communities that functioned like tribal groups but were defined as confessions: Shiite peasants in southern Lebanon, the Bekaa Valley and Syria; Druze peasants in the Chouf, Galilee and the Golan Heights; Maronite or Orthodox Christian peasants in the mountains and hills of the Anti-Lebanon as far as the Dead Sea. Not to mention the tiny communities of Samaritans in Nablus, clinging to their mountain for three thousand years, or the Circassians in Ghor, etc.

These communities, whose origins often went back to sectarian splits within a common religion (Shiites, Druzes), were closed groups. Membership of them was not a matter of belief. The inter-confessional clashes in the 19th century had nothing to do with religion or religious wars as Westerners understand the term today. It was not conceptions of the world or theologies that were at issue, but an inter-community balance of power whose equilibrium was upset by the direct or indirect intervention of the Western powers. Each confession constituted a framework for social identification: loyalty was to the group, to a mini-nation within the state, or to a tribe, it was no more a matter for choice than is one's country of birth or mother tongue.

In theory, the only movement possible was that of members of minorities towards the dominant Islam. Islamic law guaranteed the "Peoples of the Book", Jews and Christians, freedom of worship, but it forbade them to engage in any missionary work. It even provided for the Islamization of non-Muslim orphans looked after by the state. In practice, the Porte signed a thousand and one capitulations, each a retreat from this principle, but it was only in the second half of the 19th century that European missionaries could expand their work. While the agents of the (European but private) Ottoman Public Debt administration took the place of the state in the direct collection of taxes in the empire, the missions and legations opened schools, hospitals, and even a few orphanages where little Muslims were taught Christianity. But these were extreme cases. The efforts of the missions became directed towards strengthening the existing Christian communities, not towards an impossible missionary preaching among the members of other faiths. For the vast majority of the inhabitants of the Middle East at the time, confessional membership was an objective fact, involuntary, and with no ideological character. And, still today, one is Druze and socialist, Maronite and existentialist, Sunnite and atheist, Shiite and Communist, just as one can be Maronite and fascist, Druze and anti-Communist, Shiite and Muslim fundamentalist, Sunnite and Nasserist, Orthodox and Communist. One chooses one's party and one's ideology. Nowadays, one can (in some cases) even choose where one stands, but one cannot choose one's community.

The Ottoman political system, heir to the multinational Islamic state, was based on this equilibrium; the state, as arbiter and protector, guaranteed the coexistence and prerogatives of the multiplicity of *millets* – legally recognized communities each enjoying civil autonomy, collectively responsible for the payment of taxes and the maintenance of order.

In the countryside, the time-consuming burden of agricultural labour, the relative homogeneity of community lands, and the absence of communications made friction rare. The certainty of military intervention in the event, for example, of invasion of the lands of the neighbouring community, had long sufficed to maintain the balance of coexistence. In the urban areas, however, this balance, put to the test by competition and trade, could only be maintained so long as everyone continued to recognize the protector-state as the supreme arbiter of their disputes. By successive capitulations, the Porte had ended up mortgaging this role: as soon as Christians or Jews were involved in a dispute, even if it was only a purely commercial one, the consuls would intervene. And, as soon as the incidents became even slightly more serious (clashes between Jews and Christians in Damascus, violence between Maronites and Druzes in Lebanon), there would be a military expedition. Gunboat diplomacy was being applied with depressing regularity throughout the world: the bey of Algiers' slap, or the "insults" of the Chinese Governors to the officers of the British navy, were deemed to legitimize great wars of conquest and rapine. In the Middle East, the British and French simply cast themselves as philanthropists, only intervening to maintain the order that the Ottoman authorities were no longer able (and for good reason) to enforce, and to protect the minorities from the capriciousness and fanaticism of the populace.

The Hebrew newspaper *Sha'arei Tsiyon* (The Gates of Zion) described an ordinary incident in 1877 as follows:

> For eight days, three German warships and one Italian one have been anchored off Acre. The reason for their arrival is not known, but it is understood that they have come to protect the colonies of the Wurtemberg Templars.[3]

Another Hebrew newspaper, also published in Palestine although significantly entitled *Ha-Levanon* (The Lebanon), reported in 1880 an "ordinary" clash in Haifa between two processions, one Muslim and the other Christian, which degenerated into armed confrontation:

> There was a great disturbance in the town and the news was immediately telegraphed to Beirut and Cyprus. Very rapidly, two warships carrying British troops appeared off the coasts of our city to calm the disturbances. The government so informed Istanbul by telegraph, and from there the reply came that clearing up this matter would be entrusted to the British government.[4]

The Jews were altogether peripheral in this controversy: they were few in number and less prosperous than their Christian neighbours, less directly identified with the Christian powers of Europe. Neville Mandel estimates that, in 1855, the Jewish community in Palestine numbered 10,000 souls.[5] In 1882, after the first wave of immigration by the Lovers of Zion, there were 24,000 Jews in Palestine, some six or seven per cent of the total population. In 1864, the Hebrew paper *Ha-Megguid*, published in eastern Europe, deplored the fact that among the many Jews in Jaffa, most of them poverty-stricken and starving, there were only three Ashkenazi Jews, from central and eastern Europe. In 1871, according to the Hebrew periodical *Ha-Havatselet* (The Lily), published in Jerusalem, there were about 100 Jews in Haifa, and 150 in Acre.

The old *Yishuv* (settlement), the Palestinian Jewish community, was almost entirely concentrated in the four holy cities: Jerusalem and Hebron, Safed and Tiberias. Jerusalem was the site of the Wailing Wall, which the Jews called simply "The Western Wall"; a length of wall below two mosques (al-Aqsa, and the Dome of the Rock, called the Mosque of Omar) identified by tradition as part of the outer masonry of the Temple which stood there in the time of Herod and Jesus. In the quarter of the old city close by the wall several hundred pious Jews, mostly artisans, had been living for centuries. In Hebron, where the Mosque of Abraham, the tomb of the common patriarch, constitutes one of the great holy places of Islam, a small Jewish community lived, until the beginning of this century, without incident or friction. In Safed, beside the tomb of rabbi Shim'on Bar Yohaï, doctor of the Law in Roman times and the inspirer of medieval kabbalistic mysticism, as at Tiberias, the burial place of the holy rabbi Me'ir Ba'al Ha-ness (Master of the miracle), the most ancient core of the community, the best established, the only one economically independent of community charity, traced its establishment to the Muslim reconquest of the Crusader kingdoms. The Crusaders had driven the Jews out of Jerusalem, and it was Salah Eddin (Saladin), the Kurd, who had brought them back. The Jewish community in Jerusalem is said to have been founded in the 13th century by rabbi Moshe Ben Nahman, who came from Barcelona. In any case, and despite the proven presence of two or three Jewish families in Galilee which appear never to have left Palestine, this community identified itself as "Spanish": Sephardic, *Sephardim Tehorim*, "Pure Spanish", as its leaders liked to sign their letters and statements. And until the 20th century some of these families which had immigrated several hundred years earlier continued to speak among themselves the Judaeo-Spanish language that those expelled from Christian Spain in 1492 had also retained in the Balkans and in Turkey.

Around them collected small communities of Jews from the Maghrib or Egypt, Arabized like them, and others from farther away, who had come from Persia or Bukhara. Like them, whole communities of foreign Muslims, from Morocco or Bornu, gathered round the Holy Places, gradually creating their quarters in the pilgrimage cities open to visitors. This form of migratory pietism was a factor that brought Jews and Muslims together, rather than separating them: it was linked to the related concepts of *hajj* and *aliyah*,[6] which sanctify displacement. It also perpetuated a sense of the international space inherited from the trading civilization established by Islam between the 9th and 11th centuries, from Spain to Persia and India.

Thus, this Jewish community in Palestine, as "Arab" as those of Aleppo or Baghdad, was distinguished by the relative lowliness of its status, but even more by its holiness, which later became extremely important. It attracted towards it, beyond any economic logic, successive waves of pilgrims filled with all sorts of messianic hopes in which the idea of the central importance of Palestine, and of a "special link" with Eretz-Israel, was constantly affirmed. "There", Samuel Usqves wrote of Safed in the 16th century,

> any Jew may renew his inner life, change condition, reject erroneous habits and teachings, abandon practices that he has been forced to follow because of persecutions by the Nations[7] among whom he lived in exile. At Safed, each Jew receives the grace of the Lord, since there He gives him the freedom to repent.[8]

This "repentance" refers to the Marranos, who fled the persecutions they thought they had escaped by embracing the faith of the Spanish inquisition and, in their Italian or Ottoman exile, "returned" to Judaism. Repentance in Hebrew is *tshuva*, "return". The hospitality and tolerance shown by the Turkish masters of Palestine towards the Jewish and Marrano refugees from Spain and northern Italy had once again made this land the chosen country of all these returns.

Safed and Tiberias, in Galilee, were part of the *wilayet* of Sham, that is Syria, while Jerusalem and Hebron, because of the Muslim holy places, formed a spearate *sanjak* where residence taxes prevented the poorest people from settling. Hebron was a town without Christians, where Jews lived a stable existence. In Jerusalem the multitude of Muslim and Christian institutions made the Jewish community a negligible quantity with a very modest status. It was thus in Galilee, among places holy only to them, that, generation after generation, these few hundred families of "Spanish" Jews caught in the tide of the "return" gathered to live. At Safed, in the 15th century, for example, among the "Kabbalists" who speculated on the advent of messianic times, a certain Moshe Cordovero (the Cordovan) set up an "Association of Friends of Cordovero", which laid down the rules of community life and study: members were required to use the Hebrew language, for "at least one hour a day, for profane subjects".

This holiness was also, in its way, a business. But while, among the Christians, the pilgrims were customers of inns and a source of income, the Jewish pilgrims who came to swell the Jewish community, from the beginning of the 19th century, were for the most part very poor. Many of them came from Europe, and internationalized the practice of *haluka* (alms-giving): this was no longer simply the mere distribution of alms through which rabbinical law institutionalized the coexistence within the community of wealth and poverty, by humanizing it. It was now a matter of alms collected within the Jewish communities of Europe, for the benefit of learned beggars and pious parasites who went to end their days in Palestine.

Perhaps this is what distinguished this community from those of other regions of the Arab West (Maghrib) or East: the Palestine of the "Four Cities" was a meeting point with an Ashkenazi, northern Jewry whose crisis was soon to spill over beyond the borders of the Russian empire.

The repercussions of this crisis swept over Palestine and ended up by completely disrupting the system of relationships established between the old *Yishuv* and the other communities.

In the 1870s, in order to escape pursuit by their Muslim creditors, the Ashkenazim in the old city of Jerusalem "disguised themselves as Sephardic Jews". After 1929, it was the Jews of the old settlement who left their quarters and their houses to "take shelter" in the colonies founded by Zionist immigrants from Europe. Between these two dates, colonization had disrupted everything, and the Jews of Palestine were absorbed into the society of the Zionist "new pilgrims".

This process seems to be identical to that by which the Maronites in Lebanon detached themselves from the Arab society of Syria and moved into the orbit of French imperialism. But there was no colonial settlement in Lebanon. Perhaps it should be compared to the process by which the autochthonous Jews of Algeria officially became foreigners in the land of their birth and their roots, with the sole purpose of being able to live there as settlers. But the Jews of Palestine did not gain any privileged position in the new social order, nor the choice of opting for a new model-nationality.

Quite the contrrary: as "Arab" Jews, they were the object of truly colonialist contempt from the majority of the European immigrants. But, as the "old *Yishuv*", an almost anachronistic remnant of a past history, were they not the perfect witnesses for the militant anachronism of the Lovers of Zion? We have seen that the very idea of Jews of Palestine titillated in Christian – and especially Anglican – sensitivity, some strange sentimental nerve, some aesthetic nostalgia which fitted in perfectly with the strategic and economic interests of European states. Among the earliest Lovers of Zion who discovered the Jews in Jerusalem, there was indeed delighted amazement at the wealth of traditions, and the purity of the Hebrew language preserved in the liturgy and in learning. Above all there was the springboard provided for the immigrants by the fact the Jews under Ottoman rule had acquired rights: the recognized autonomy of the Jewish community as such, with its official chief rabbi, *hakham bashi*, and his prerogatives. Age gave this community, faced with the newcomers, a particular status.

The gradual detachment of this community from Palestinian Arab society throughout the first 30 years of this century was slow: during the 1920s, many Palestinian (and Syrian) Jews were violently opposed to Zionism, which they later came to accept. Moreover, they remained attached to their traditional vocation of state officials. Some of these families, the earlier generations of which had occupied posts in the civil service under the Ottoman administration, continued to serve in the British mandatory administration, and then the Israeli one. In 1978, the State of Israel even gave itself a Palestinian, if Zionist, Jew as President, in the person of Yitzhak Navon.

But what is important, from the point of view of this community, is that – unlike French or British imperialism – Zionism did not beckon them to turn to some new metropole but offered to build them a state in their own home: a state built in their name, but conceived, inhabited and ruled by foreigners who called themselves brothers; who indeed were brothers according to the rules and criteria of confessionalism, be they Ottoman, Islamic or Jewish, but who were nonetheless foreigners. This alienness did not arise from their European citizenship (did not all the Jews and all the Christians in the East, not to mention the Muslims, aspire to being protected by some power that would make the Sultan's law bend in their personal favour?) but from the culture which united them, of which the Yiddish language was the expression, which separated them by light-years from the world of the Palestinians. And this dispossession of a certain sense of their identity that the Jews of Palestine experienced collectively, as the European Jews moved in, foreshadowed one of the features of the future confrontation between Zionism and Arab Judaism.

Legend has it that the Hebrew poet Bialik, born in Russia and a poet of Zionism, summarized the negative nature of this confrontation in a sally full of implications. When someone asked him the reason for his dislike of Arabs, he is supposed to have replied: "It's because they remind me of Oriental Jews!" Here, as we can see, there is no sentimentality in the encounter; each attributes to the other the image of himself that he least wants to identify with.

What distinguished this domination fundamentally from the European one, was first of all that it took root. When he became a Frenchman at the end of the last century, the son of the Jewish artisan in Algeria would become acquainted with France and the French: he was no longer Algerian, Arab or Ottoman, but French. If things turned bad, he would return to his new motherland, like his "brothers" the Pieds-Noirs. By choosing France, he declared himself foreign to Algeria. When he chose to identify with the colonial power as a Jew, like the Jewish notables of Oran who wrote to the King of France in 1829 begging him to come and free them from the Ottoman yoke, he effectively declared his Jewishness to be that of an exile and a foreigner. He wanted now to be French and Jewish.

For the Jews of Palestine, on the contrary, the taking of power by European settlers, happening without them particularly wanting it, implied an opposite process. The "Pure Spaniard" was now called on to turn away, not only from Palestinian society, but also from his attraction towards England and France, and to identify himself with this foreign horde that despised him in the name of Europe and modernity, while declaring itself more autochthonous than life itself, rooted by four thousand years of clerical archaeology in the land of Palestine and Hebrew identity.

In Istanbul, Beirut, and Constantine, European civilization and tribal tradition were in competition. The temporary alliances they made did not eliminate their basic opposition. In Palestine, on the contrary, the settler society pushed the indigenous Jews back into an abstract glorification of the confessional group.

The "barons" of the assimilated Jewish bourgeoisie in France, the Rothschilds, had thrown themselves into the agricultural colonization of Algeria: their vineyards flourished on the lands stolen from the peasants by the French army. At the same time, they retained the positions that their parents and grandparents had acquired since the Revolution: lay community notables representing the Jews of France – and of the French empire. It was in this charitable capacity that, in the middle of the century, they founded the Alliance Israélite Universelle, a philanthropic Jewish organization whose main activity was the management of a network of primary and secondary schools, homes and vocational training centres for Jews in all the countries of North Africa and the Levant. The declared aim of the Alliance was to win all these people over to French culture. The Alliance's political programme, in harmony with French imperial expansion, was assimilation.

Yet, in Palestine, things were to happen differently. Certainly, the same Rothschilds bought land in Palestine, and planted vines there. They even opened schools there. But a variety of factors, essentially linked to immigration from eastern Europe, were to give their vine-growing and philanthropic enterprises an altogether different character.

In Algeria, the Muslim, Arab and Berber peasantry, expropriated by the occupying power, was transformed into an agricultural proletariat on Borgeaud's plantations and Rothschild's vineyards, while the Jews, emancipated by the Décret Crémieux and educated by the Alliance, took up positions in the administration and the liberal professions. In Palestine, the Ottomans still ruled, France was not the master, the administration was conducted in Turkish, and in the Alliance's schools, Hebrew and above all agriculture were taught. For the influx of European Jewish immigrants could not and did not seek to transform themselves into a stratum of administrators, intermediaries between the foreign government and the productive work of an indigenous society. Zionist immigration sought to dominate the Arabs not in order to exploit them, but to replace them. And, while throughout the Orient, including Palestine, towns were growing at the expense of the population of the villages, the immigrants founded, one after the other, agricultural colonies: the country had to be held, taken over, through and through, from end to end.

Subjugated by the newcomers, the Jews of Palestine were to witness the paradoxical intensification of their own confessional identity by assimilation, just as their own birthplace itself became the idealized metropole, and work on the land the source of a new hierarchy.

This process continued with the other Arab Jewish communities, as they came into contact with Zionist society, especially with the Yemenites, the main community of Oriental immigrants before 1948; then with the Moroccans, Egyptians, Iraqis and others after the establishment of the State of Israel.

While the Jews of Palestine were granted some respect, even if only because of their social status, the Yemenite or Moroccan Jews, whom the Ashkenazim called purely and simply "Blacks", were perceived by the mass of European immigrants as a negligible human quantity. The immigrants were engaged in the quest for an archaeo-biblical identity that would enable them to throw off the real identity that their European history had forged, and they overvalorized the traditional heritage of the Jews of the East at the same time as they ignored and denigrated it in practice.

Yet, the Zionist need to reconfirm the Oriental Jews in their Judaism reflected above all a very real concern, linked, precisely, to agricultural colonization. Only the Oriental Jews, stressed Dr. Thon of the Jewish Agency in 1908, were capable of working like Arabs, for Arab wages, while participating in the conquest of "Hebrew labour" and the removal of the Palestinian peasantry from lands bought from absentee landlords. It was on the basis of this good doctor's recommendation that the executive of the Jewish Agency sent an emissary to Yemen in 1910: the socialist Zionist Warshevsky, disguised for the occasion as "rabbi Yavni'eli", went off to preach religious Zionism and announce to the Jews there the coming of the Messiah.

Doctor Thon's report was based on observation of the situation as it existed in 1908, after two waves of spontaneous "messianic" immigration had brought several thousand Yemenite Jews to Palestine, essentially in the area around Jerusalem:

> If we could ensure that the Yemenite families settle permanently in the colonies, we would accomplish something else: Yemenite women and girls would work as maids instead of the Arab women and girls who are at present employed as servants by almost every family of colonists, for exorbitant wages of over 20 or 25 French francs a month![9]

Yavni'eli travelled all over Yemen, everywhere announcing the coming of the Messiah – of which the return of the Jews to the Land of Israel was one of the signs – and promising fortunes to all those who would "ascend" to the Holy Land.

In 1912, the Jewish Agency decided to cut its losses: there were too many immigrants. In that year alone, several hundred Jewish families had left Yemen to come and work on Jewish farms in Palestine. The Hebrew press in Palestine testified, in 1913, to the way in which these immigrants were exploited:

> When the well-off and rich peasants saw these faces lined with poverty and hunger, wearing turbans, hanging around in the barns and stables, they realized that here was material to be exploited. They secretly set a minimum wage not to be exceeded. They even attempted to make it a rule that every Yemenite worker would be tied to his masters and would not be allowed to go and work elsewhere without written authorization from his previous masters. When the question arose of building accommodation for the Yemenites, the farmers demanded that this quarter be built as far away as possible, so that the Yemenites would not be inside the colony.[10]

This refusal to mix with the Yemenites had already manifested itself in Jerusalem at the end of the previous century, when the Jews in the Old City had refused to make room for the first Yemenite pilgrims, who eventually settled in the Muslim village of Silwan, outside the walls, where a *yeshiva*, a rabbinical secondary school, survived until 1929. The writer Ahad Ha'am, a great literary and political figure in the Lovers of Zion movement, remarked in the spring of 1912:

> Recently, too, Yemenite Jews have been coming to Palestine, settling in the colonies, and working as labourers; the Zionists are already proclaiming that the Yemenites will build up the land. But this is another experiment on which judgement cannot yet be passed. Many people in Palestine think that the Yemenites are not physically strong enough for hard work; and moreover, their level of culture and their mentality are so different from ours that the question invariably presents itself whether an increase in their number will not change the whole character of the settlement, and whether the change will be for the better.[11]

With the formation of this Yemenite Jewish agricultural semi-proletariat during the last two decades of Ottoman rule in Palestine, a new social problematic was in the process of taking shape, which was quite foreign to Palestinians of any and every confession. The virtual relations of slavery which developed between Ashkenazi colonist-pilgrims from Europe and Arab-Jewish proletarian-pilgrims from Yemen existed solely in order to exclude the latter from the colonists' domain. At the same time, this "material to be exploited", with its unparalleled vulnerability, introduced into the community social relations of a brutality previously reserved for inter-communal relations: the Arab servants were indeed gradually replaced by Yemenite Jewish women in the *Yishuv*, and the Yemenite labourers were totally dependent on the settlers who employed them.

The complaints of Yemenite labourers of the time express already what was to become Zionism's major social dilemma. "We want to get out of this colony", wrote the Yemenites of Hadera in 1913, "because, with them [i.e., among the European Jewish settlers], they prefer Arabs to Hebrews." In other words, they pay Arab labourers more than their Yemenite servants. The Oriental Jews, after having enriched Rothschild's farmers and the settlers, were to serve the immigrant Zionist Workers as shock troops in the struggle for "Jewish labour"; against Arab workers, but also against their Jewish employers.

For the Oriental Jews in Palestine, Zionism – not as an ideology, but as a social and political fact that was imposed before it was assumed – was to play the role of a colonialism. But, whereas everywhere in the Mediterranean world colonialism opened up to the Jews, to varying degrees, the doors to embourgeoisement and Westernization, Zionism threw the Oriental Jews back on their tribal-confessional identity for the sole purpose of subjecting them to the most brutal proletarianization.

At the same time, Zionism displaced them outside Arab society in order to reintegrate them as proletarian-settlers. This displacement, which might take the physical form of moving home, had no other function than to eject the Arabs in favour of a European Jewish society. It was nevertheless to have, even more than Ahad Ha'am could imagine in his time, vast consequences for the future of the *Yishuv*. For Oriental immigration, restricted throughout the period of the British Mandate, was to become massive, by a political decision of the Zionist leadership, with the 1948 war and the violent expulsion of the Arabs. By radically altering the relations of force between the communities, and transforming social practice within the new entity, this immigration profoundly modified the character of the community.

The Oriental Jews could be manipulated, as we have seen, just like the Oriental Christians, for the defence of European interests. The Algerian experience was conclusive in this respect. But this love-match with imperialism usually went with a dowry: the status of super-citizen, increased rights and privileges, freedom to get rich and rise up the social ladder. While by entering into the orbit of Zionist colonization, the

Oriental Jews gained only the certainty of bartering their acquired social positions for that of modern proletarians.

It is true that, at the time of the massive exodus of Arab Jews, after the 1948 war, the Israeli leaders did everything they could to move the Jewish communities in Arab countries to Palestine. Numerous Moroccan Jews, in particular, still carry the bitterness of having been deceived by the Zionist emissaries. The deception was not to have talked to them of a chimerical nation and kingdom, but to have promised them fortunes and given them the assembly line and the building site; to have promised messianic justice and given them the iron law of the market, to have promised fraternity and given racism.

Of course, one must always be wary of conspiracy theories of history. It is unthinkable that whole communities should have left their countries of origin where they had been living for centuries solely because of a plot so Machiavellian that they were unaware of it, thinking they were leaving for other reasons: hundreds of thousands of men could not possibly have simply uprooted their lives by pure inadvertence. Can we really believe that they were naïve playthings of the Warshevsky-Yavni'elis, who let themselves by led by the nose by the Zionists and their lies? The explanation is all too pat: if a society packs its bags for the first false prophet who comes along, it is surely a sign that it is undergoing a profound crisis. And so the question must be asked: these Yemenite Jews who were already in Palestine even before Dr. Thon noticed them, what pulled them and what pushed them?

Religion? This is the reason classically invoked. In anti-Zionist historiography, a categorical, and often mechanical, distinction is made between religious Jewish immigration and political Zionism.

The Yemenite Jews, the first wave of whom arrived in Palestine in about 1874, and the second during the first years of the century, were not Zionist – meaning, not organized by the Zionist movement, either in its Herzlian state and Western branch, nor in its spiritual branch, in the manner of Ahad Ha'am and the Lovers of Zion; that is, they were strangers to the political and cultural universe of Europe. And it is also undeniable that they were profound believers and involved in the practice of their faith. It is thus natural that their motivations should be expressed in religious terms. But is it not true that the religious ideologies also expressed, by mediatizing them, the projects, hopes and interests of particular human groups in given situations? When one speaks of messianic currents sweeping through this or that community, is it not clear that these currents express – even if by the murky detour of eschatology – the crisis in this community, the rupture of its equilibrium and the social and political contradictions running through it?

The most positivist minds seem to consider religion as an ethereal domain on the threshold of which analysis respectfully comes to a halt. For religion, decreed once and for all to be a form of alienation, is the enemy of reason: there is therefore no need to seek any logic in it. Thanks to the explanation of religion, one can explain collective behaviours while deeming them to be rationally inexplicable. Thus, the Jews of Yemen are said to have come to Palestine at the end of the last century, when it was scarcely in their interest to do so, as what followed was to show, simply because they were subject to their own irrational beliefs. Later, the Zionists are said to have made them come to their settlements to work there, playing on their religious feelings. In 1948, virtually all the Jews still remaining in Yemen were airlifted to Palestine: they had been deceived, being told that the third kingdom of Israel had arrived. And, religious as they were, they sang in the plane: "David, David [Ben-Gurion], king of Israel!"

The first wave of Jewish immigrants from Yemen arrived in Palestine a few months after the fall of Sana'a to the Ottoman armies. In 1839, when the British conquered Aden, half the Jewish population of Sana'a left the capital to place themselves under the protective umbrella of the occupier. Collectively, the Jewish community of independent Yemen – the "Za'idite" imamate founded in 1629 when Kassim drove out the Ottomans who had been established there since 1546 – had been dubiously loyal to a state where the goodwill of the prince often counted for more than the principles of law and custom. The Jews had supported the Turks in every confrontation between the Porte and the Imam, and has been agents of Mehmet Ali during the episode of the Egyptian conquest, all without the least intervention, or even interference, either by the Western cancer, or by the Zionist devil. We must try and understand the reasons for all this, not just because of some subjective interest in the particular history of this community, but because it expresses the essence of the problematic of Arab Judaism in the imperialist age.

The Jews of Palestine were at the other extreme from the Europeanized Jews of Algeria or the Levant who expressed another aspect of the same problematic. What made them special was that they alone, or almost so, throughout a whole period, prefigured what has subsequently become the lot of many communities: the village communities which the Zionists were to transplant, implant or even simply abandon in the desert, as at Dimona in 1951, with no buses to go back in. So many Moroccan, Aramaean ("Kurdish"), or Indian rural communities; but also so many Arabic-speaking urban communities, from the Maghrib to Egypt, from Aleppo to Baghdad, the heirs of a prestigious civilization: all these were to be put through the same grinder in order to turn them into worker-soldiers and even peasant-soldiers. So much for the Messiah. The fervour died, but they remained.

Each community was to adapt to this situation in accordance with its character, its history and its own position: it is these attributes, specific to each, that explain why different communities had different fates. Why did some communities leave while others stayed, only to abandon later, at another turning in this trajectory, the land where they had lived for centuries? How did the various communities divide, some members going to one place, others to another, others again staying? Why did some communities, like the Yemenites, not even wait for the Zionists to come and fetch them to ascend to Palestine, while others, like the Iraqis, literally had to be driven out with bombs?[12]

We have seen that the European states had envisaged manipulating existing confessional-communal differences to their own advantage, including those involving the Oriental Jews, long before the beginnings of European Jewish immigration and Zionism. Zionism was later to capitalize on the gains made during the imperialist period that preceded the establishment of settlers. Yet, we have seen that some communities moved directly from their traditional way of life to its freely accepted demolition in the Zionist enterprise. Explaining this as something they did by mistake, or out of credulity (religious credulity, of course), or at any event without rhyme or reason, seems to me to partake of an attitude that can only be described as . . . religious.

What was there then, in the inter- or intra-communal relationships, to make them choose a destiny that, even if dreamed in the rosiest colours, implied pulling up deep roots and the will, spoken of by Samuel Usqves, "to change life"?

In that uplifting imagery which obliterates and replaces historical memory, nothing ever happens except the endless confrontation of good and evil. About Arab Jews, only two contradictory tales are admitted to this mythology: the anti-Zionist myth of the perfect integration of all Jews in all Arab societies at all times, and the Zionist myth of the permanent persecution of Jews under Islam. The truth, of course, lies in the actual functioning of society: the totality of the concrete relationships and contradictions between the various communities and the authorities.

Islamic law legitimized and consecrated the existence of Jewish and Christian communities while imposing on them a number of more or less symbolic restrictions, applied in very varied forms in different times and places. Fundamentally, their status as *dhimmi*, protégés of the Muslim state, guaranteed them against any infringement of their life or property, and they paid a special tax for their exemption from the armed service of Islam. This exemption, as it was understood, amounted to a prohibition on carrying arms. In a society still largely subjected to the law of the clan, the vendetta and the military autarky of the tribes, the impact of such a restriction is easy to imagine. But it must be pointed out that these barriers gave way occasionally, and often for long periods, thanks to a friendly ruler or liberal customs: as witness General Farhi who commanded the "Turkish" army of Egypt against Bonaparte at Acre.

In practice, the status of Jews and Christians in Muslim states fluctuated enormously. In the Maghrib, the five hundred years' war between the Cross and the Crescent – from the Crusades to the Spanish *reconquista* – left no Christians in the land of Islam and no Muslims in Christendom. On both sides, the Jews were the sole religious minority faced with the dominant faith. In the East, on the contrary, most of the minorities were Christians and belonged to churches that had always fought Rome. Even the

Crusaders did not recognize them, putting these schismatics on the same footing as Muslim infidels and Jews, and accepted into the City of God only the Armenians and Maronites who were tiny minorities in the sea of the Orthodox. Politically, the Oriental Christians had been unstable allies for the West: the Monophysites, a Christian sect persecuted by Byzantium, had opened the gates of Jerusalem to the armies of Islam, and the "Greeks" had signed a treaty of protection and understanding with the Caliph Omar.

A priori, the loyalty of the Jews to the Muslim state was even less suspect. Certainly, they maintained permanent relations with their co-religionists in the Christian world, but they were on the whole little inclined to plot on behalf of the Inquisitors and the mediaeval churches, those great organizers of *auto da fés* where heretics, witches and Jews were burned with great pomp and ceremony, especially as these persecutions in Christendom were occurring at a time of prosperity for the Jewish communities in Islam, between the 8th and the 12th centuries. This was the Andalusian golden age, what the Israeli Orientalist Goitein called, "the Judaeo-Arab symbiosis". From Iraq to Spain, the Jews had flourished in this civilization, producing not only merchants and bankers but also a host of doctors, mathematicians, philosophers, poets and mystics.

The symbiosis had survived, but the golden age was over: in the clashes that accompanied this decline, whether they were political (power struggles), social (Bedouin against the cities, tribes against states), or national (Berbers, Iranians, Turks or Mongols against Arabs), the status of the Jews became uncertain. It is not possible always to be everybody's friend and, when thrones collapsed, their favourite allies went through a bad patch. The history of the Jewish communities of the Muslim world is full of examples of these turnabouts: in 1762, rabbi Shalom Araki, a Minister at the court of the Imam of independent Yemen, was imprisoned by the heir to the throne, al-Mahdi Abbas ibn al-Mansur Hussein. The new Imam ordered the demolition of all synagogues in Sana'a, together with buildings that were "too high" in the Jewish quarter.[13] At the beginning of the 11th century, the Fatimid caliph al-Hakim, the heir to the most enlightened of dynasties, protector and defender of Jews and Christians in Egypt, was seized with a rage to persecute non-Muslims in 1012: churches and synagogues were destroyed, property was confiscated, discriminatory measures were taken, etc. Seven years later, everything was withdrawn, everything was calmed down again. But already, half the Jewish communities in Egypt had fled to Iraq or Yemen.

The communities were social entities, organized political bodies. They were persecuted or protected for political reasons. In the 11th and 12th centuries, the Almoravids and Almohads, who were to drive Arab Islam out of Spain and Morocco and institute their own form of Berber Islamic fundamentalism, inaugurated a policy of persecuting Jews which, here too, led to the massive emigration of the Jews of Morocco to Egypt. This persecution was not religious in the sense that it was not the faith that was under attack. It proceeded from a political vision of the forces making up the enemy front: internally, the corrupt Islam of the caliphs (and of their Jewish and even Christian protégés); externally, the Roman enemy. This persecution was only religious in the sense that the socio-political entities aimed at defined themselves in terms of religion. It was of course not racial. The concept of race, isolated from the concrete characteristics of the nation, the tribe or the community, did not exist before 19th century Europe invented it. And the traditional concept that was closest to it, the idea of the blood community implied by the assertion of a common tribal origin, precisely united Jews and Muslim Arabs: both in fact subscribed to the dogma of their cousinhood, not only as remote descendants of Shem, but also as Ishmaelites and Israelites, sons of Abraham, the common patriarch.

The minority communities were dependent on the power that protected them, which might abandon them, or collapse. On the whole, and for very long periods, the Jews enjoyed under Islam a *de facto* status which was often more liberal than the tolerance of Koranic law with regard to them. But this status preserved them as a community: it did not affect them as individuals. This preservation was never perceived as a ghetto, but rather as a franchise, an autonomy of the community as such. In times of crises, religious revolutions, wars and invasions, these communities – Jews, Christians, and also schismatic or sectarian Muslims – were often victims of oppression or riots, pillaging or persecution. However, writes Goitein, "I believe it is correct to say that as a whole the position of the non-Muslims under Arab Islam was far better than that of the Jews in Medieval Christian Europe".[14]

The vulnerability of this mode of inter-community articulation created among the minorities a propensity to accumulate guarantees, or multiply the number of protectors. Among the Jews of the Muslim world as elsewhere, the stock response to crisis was emigration. Often temporary, "until things calm down", this emigration was not an individual affair, but community-based. It was the advice that Maimonides – born at Cordova in 1135, died in Cairo in 1204, and the most illustrious example of the Judaeo-Arab symbiosis – gave the victims of persecution in his *Epistle to the Jews of Morocco*: it is a sin for Jews to remain in a country where they are maltreated. Faced with oppression, one neither yields nor struggles, one neither resists nor dies. One goes to seek asylum in the nearest "liberal" Muslim state – where the Jewish community will be once again protected.

That obviously presupposes that such states exist: in the political and territorial division of the Islamic empire which accompanied its decline and break-up, such states were always to exist. It also presupposes a sense of and means of inter-regional communication. They existed at the time of the Islamic commercial revolution in the 9th century; they were to be retained among certain sections of urban dwellers right down to contemporary times. A paradox? The sense of communications operating between the various Jewish communities in the Arab world was one of the most living testimonies to the mediaeval Arab unity that linked together the towns of Spain and Egypt, Syria and Yemen.[15]

Long after Maimonides, the Muslim philosopher and historian Ibn Khaldun also experienced this migration: born in Tunisia of Yemenite parents, he grew up in Spain where his political career obliged him to go into exile. After a secret stay in Morocco, where he hid for a time with the Jewish mathematician Khalluf el-Maghilli,[16] he too finished up in the haven of Mamluk Egypt, the last island of past greatness. Between the imperatives of Mediterranean trade and the religious obligation of the pilgrimage to Mecca, with the major economic activities associated with it, the post-mediaeval Arab world refused to be broken up, and the towns perpetuated the memory of the former unity. For the peasant population, of course, their settlement on the land, which was earlier than and often at odds with this unity, made practically any movement impossible. Until modern settler colonization, nothing would make the *fellahin* move from their land. But there were very few Jews engaged in agriculture, and their community institutions were predominantly urban: whence their structural capacity to emigrate, in a orderly manner rather than in panic.

We are here touching on what was specific about the Jewish communities in the functioning of post-mediaeval Islamic society: the geography, not only subjective, but practical, of their dispersion, their cosmopolitanism. For, while the integration of the Jewish community into the *millet* system raised no more problems of a political nature than the integration of the Christian and dissident Muslim confessional communities, the community identity so recognized straddled the frontiers of Empire: no liturgical or theological schism set the Jews of the Maghrib against the Jews of Spain who had come under Christian rule. On the contrary, throughout the Ottoman period, Arab Judaism can be seen, as in Palestine, blending into and uniting with the Spanish-Marrano diaspora that spread all over the Mediterranean, where it acquired a material power and a religious and intellectual authority which transformed the local communities into its power base. Thus, the Jewish community was not simply dispersed in the space of the Abbassid golden age. It saw itself, in its practice of travelling, business and marriage, in its religious life and internal controversies, as being part of a Jewish whole not all of which was embraced by Islam. The very Hebrew books which the Jews used for religious observances were for centuries printed in Italy, and beyond Pisa and Leghorn began another Jewish world.

The fact is that the Jew under Islam was not simply a creation of the state; he pre-existed it. Of course, the communities were subjected and often saw the capriciousness of a ruler or of the mob thwart their own aspirations, but they did not derive their vocation or their sense of collective identity from this state, even though they depended on its protection.

It is, therefore, this older stage of community organization and identity that we must look at. For, if the ups and downs of Arab Judaism relate to Arab society as a whole, the reactions and behaviours of the Jews faced with these events relate to Judaism: not to a metaphysic, but to a system of law, underpinned by a consensus, with its own courts, its institutions, its schools, its assemblies and its representatives. This law, older than Islam, which was weakened under the new conditions without however disappearing, contained the self-definition of the community: not such as it was, but such as it imagined itself to be. And it is this law, having made its separate way among the Ashkenazi Jews, which was to return from overseas or from beyond the Caucasus, transformed, unrecognizable.

Notes

1. Maxime Rodinson, "From the Jewish Nation to the Jewish Problem", in the preface to a new edition of *La Conception matérialiste de la question juive*, by Abraham Léon (Paris, E.D.I., 1968), translated in *Cult, Ghetto, and State* (London, Al Saqi Books, 1983).
2. Mordekhaï Eliav (ed.) *Ha-yishuv ha-yehudi be-Erez-Israel bi-re'i ha-mediniut ha-Germanit, 1842-1914* (The Jewish community in Palestine in the mirror of German policy, 1842-1914), an annotated collection of the documents of the German consulate in Jerusalem [in Hebrew, 2 vols.] (Tel Aviv, Hakkibutz Hameushad Publishing House, 1974).
3. Extract from an anthology of the Hebrew press in Palestine from 1857 to 1914 compiled and edited by Shlomo Sheva and Dan Ben Amots, entitled *Erets Tsiyon Yerushalayim* (Land of Zion Jerusalem) (Tel Aviv, Zmora-Bitan-Modan Publishing House, 1973).
4. Ibid., p. 36.
5. The figures from various sources seem to approximate those provided by Neville Mandel in "Turks, Arabs, and Jewish immigration into Palestine, 1882-1914", *St. Antony's Papers*, no. 17 (*Middle Eastern Affairs*, no. 4) (London, Oxford University Press, 1965): 10,000 Jews in Palestine in 1855, 300,000 inhabitants in Palestine in 1875; 24,000 Jews in 1882, 50,000 in 1895; 500,000 inhabitants in the country in 1900, 689,000 in 1914, including 85,000 Jews.
6. The *hajj* is the pilgrimage Muslims make to Mecca. The *aliyah*, literally "ascent", originally synonymous with pilgrimage (*alyat-reggel*, ascending on foot), has twice shifted its meaning: by the Middle Ages, the term only referred to the pilgrimage to Palestine, and the Zionists, today, make it synonymous with "Jewish immigration".
7. The word "Nations" (in Hebrew: *Goyim*) is often translated as "Gentiles". Used in the Bible to refer to the Hebrews themselves in the ordinary sense of "people", it gradually became synonymous with "non-Jew" from the Middle Ages onwards.
8. Quoted by Guy Casaril, *Shimeon Bar Yohaï et la Cabbale* (Paris, Editions du Seuil, 1967).
9. The key sections of Dr. Thon's report are reproduced in Alexandre Bein, *History of Zionist Colonization* [in Hebrew] (Tel Aviv, Massada Publishing House, 1970). Quoted by Haïm Hanegbi in "Les Yéménites", *I.S.R.A.C.*, no. 6, December 1971 (Paris, Maspéro).
10. *Ha-Ahduth* (Unity), paper of the Lovers of Zion, 1913. Reprinted in S. Sheva and D. Ben Amots, *Erets Tsiyon Yerushalayim*.

11. Ahad Ha-Am, *Ten Essays on Zionism and Judaism*, (London, 1922), p. 152, n. 1.

12. The facts about the Israeli terrorist provocations in Baghdad in 1950, published for the first time in Israel by the weekly *Ha-Olam Hazeh*, on 20 April and 1 June 1966, are now widely known. Faced with the unwillingness of Iraqi Jews to enrol on the lists for (legal) immigration to Israel, the Israeli secret services twice launched grenade attacks against Jews. The second attack, on the Shem-Tov synagogue, killed three people and wounded dozens. One of the members of the network, arrested by the Iraqi police, led them to some 15 caches of weapons from Israel, and implicated several Israeli figures in the affair. The facts were reported in detail by Kokhavi Shemesh in the Black Panthers' journal, no. 4, August 1972. They were confirmed by the journalist Barukh Nadel in a questionnaire sent to Mordekhaï Ben Porat through the Tel Aviv high court on 7 November 1977; see the account in the daily *Yedioth Aharonoth*, 8 November 1977. See also the eyewitness account by Wilbur Evaland, an employee of the United States embassy at the time, in *Ropes of Sand,* quoted by the *Sephardic Center for Social Research*, Berkeley, 1980.

13. Yassef Tubi, *Yehudei Teiman be-me'a ha-teisha' 'essrei* (The Jews of Yemen in the 19th century) [in Hebrew] (Tel Aviv, Afikim Publishing House, 1976).

14. S.D. Goitein, *Jews and Arabs, Their Contacts through the Ages* (New York, Schocken Books, 1955), p. 84.

15. For a detailed description of the material and intellectual life of Jews in the mediaeval Muslim world, there is no substitute for the studies that have emerged from the deciphering of the Cairo *Geniza* (old document cupboard), an inventory of which is to be found in Goitein, *A Mediterranean Society – The Jewish Communities of the Arab World as Portrayed in the Documents of the Cairo Geniza* (Cambridge, Cambridge University Press, 1967).

16. Muhsin Mahdi, *Ibn Khaldûn's Philosophy of History* (London, George Allen and Unwin, 1957).

2 The Law

"I learnt that the Law revealed by God to Moses was merely the law of the individual Hebrew state, therefore it was binding on none but the Hebrews, and not even on Hebrews after the downfall of their nation."

Barukh Spinoza[1]

Can we reread the letter of the myth, not so as to immerse ourselves in it as people used to in other times, but so as to extract from it – as resin bleeds from a tree while leaving it whole – the oblique and specific sense in which the law evolves? Throughout the biblical story, and throughout the tribulations of the practical power of the law, a law proclaimed as ideal acted as a banner for struggles to transform the law. This "law of the individual Hebrew state" that Spinoza talks of, however, was made up of many layers, and there is a big difference between the law of Moses and the declarations of the rabbis who nevertheless claimed to follow it. The Talmud (*Pirkei Aboth*), which mediaeval Judaism raised to the rank of "oral law", says: "Moses received the *Torah* at Sinai and transmitted it to Joshua, Joshua to the Elders, and the Elders to the prophets and the prophets to the men of the Great Synagogue." This is a simplified genealogy of those stages – fundamental revolutions within the very language of faithfulness to the old law – where the meaning of the same words is transformed and reversed: between Joshua and the Assembly of Sages in Sassanid Mesopotamia in the 4th century AD there was much more than the Elders. There were all the stages codified in the structure of this law, whether mythical or historical: the law of Moses in the desert; that of Joshua during the conquest of Canaan by the tribes of Israel; that of the Judges, the last of whom, Samuel, was to be the first of the prophets. Then came the kingdom: David, Solomon, the Temple, the state. A second cycle of the Law was born of the divorce of prophecy and government, after the division of the kingdom, war, and intrigues. With the fall of the kingdom of Judah and the exile of its leaders to Babylon, this second prophetic cycle came to an end. A third stage, that of the return to Zion under Persian protection, the rebuilding of the Temple and the rule of the priests, began, and it is only at this time that one can begin to talk of Judaism, among the exiled Judaeans, when Judah – the state – was no more. But again this adapted law underwent the vicissitudes and the metamorphoses of the protecting powers on which it henceforth depended. The Temple protected by the empire was opposed by the peasants and men of war who dreamed of restoring the kingdom of David. The empires passed and remained, the kingdom was indeed dead: after rebellions and revolts the Temple itself was to pass. Only then would the oral law of the rabbis begin, in several apocryphal stages of codification.

It was a system of law, and a system of political power: a state, or a state-that-was-not-yet-a-state, an emerging state which marked itself off from the natural, clanic, organization of inequality. A state that sprang from the pores of tribal law to dominate and violate it, to challenge and replace it. Or again, a state-that-was-no-longer-a-state: a protected law, withdrawn into its autonomy. And then again, a "deterritorialized" law, the law of the dispersed ethnic group. Where there is law and judgement, where there is power, there is an internal social problematic: its phases and mutations are what this rereading is about.

The anthology of sacred literature that Jews call the *Tannakh* (a contraction of the initial letters of *Torah-Nevi'im-Ktubim*: Pentateuch-Prophets-Scriptures) and Christians the Old Testament is both tendentious historiography and irrefutable evidence. It involves a complex reading, which requires cross-checking and finding points of similarity using a highly empirical approach. It involves a "paranoid" reading too, which endeavours to isolate a single meaning from the text, indicating the mechanisms and wellsprings of power – priestly, monarchical, scriptural, clerical, rabbinical. All in an attempt to grasp at each stage of the destiny of the people-myth, the internal structure of its servitude, its civil law, its quasi-state.

The third book of the Pentateuch, Leviticus, takes the form of a series of speeches and recommendations made by God to Moses in the Sinai desert, on the eve of the conquest of Canaan. God speaks to Moses, who speaks to Aaron, the high priest, who speaks to the people: he sets out for them the rules of sacrifice which have just been institutionalized in the Ark (*Ha-mishkan*), also called the Tent of the Meeting or of the Vocation (*Ohel Mo'ed*[2]). From this detailed and repetitive text there emerges a coherent political, social and economic vision, which is filled out by the statistical and military information contained in the following book, Numbers.

One thus needs to read several times. First, in order to doubt the apocryphal rewriting of history: the earliest versions are more than two thousands years later than the events reported. And these texts themselves – the *Septuagint* of the Greeks, the *Mikra* of the Massoretes ("Traditionalists") – refer to a complete recasting of older traditions, written and oral, a thousand years earlier, by the scribes of the First Return. Then, one needs to read in order to confront this story with two or three confirmed historical facts; and finally, in order to discern the mind of the redactor and the politico-juridical ideal that guided this rewriting that falsified the past.

The deciphering of the Scriptures is not an exact science, whatever experts in the subject may say. For it would require being able to measure in complete detail the extent of old falsifications, manipulated transmissions, or authentic and ancient forgeries. The fifth book of the Pentateuch provides a good example of this. It was a forgotten book, which existence was unknown to the people, and the priests "discovered" it most opportunely: did it not recapitulate all the earlier books, unifying them in a single reading that just happened to coincide with the understanding and projects of the lucky discoverers of the unknown texts?

Even the books whose main parts were indeed transmitted orally, from generation to generation, and guaranteed by the musical memory of the community before being committed to paper, were not protected from rewriting, censorship and falsification. Often, they were only written down because of the need to exorcise this memory and falsify it. So, before seeing them as precise historical or sociological documents, it is necessary carefully to pick out in them what Freud called the "distorting tendencies" – those that embellish out of a concern for apologetics, magnify out of a concern for the dramatic, and denigrate out of political preoccupation – and the projections through which the redactor modernized the text: anachronisms by which the scribe betrayed his contemporary obsessions. It is true that, in his *Moses and Monotheism*, Freud only illustrates his intention *a contrario*: he only brings out the distorting tendencies of the biblical narrative in order to replace them with his own fantasies. We shall try not to follow in his steps; our intention is more prosaic. We are not concerned here with laying bare the essence of the religion, but only with analysing what the texts tell of the legal organization, the genesis of "the law of the individual Hebrew state".

Perhaps this is because familiarity with the original documents and their traditional commentaries – several centuries of distorting and apologetic exegesis – inspires prudence. But this knowledge and other disciplines have given us a few basic certainties. With all these reservations in mind, it remains that the biblical story and its successive re-readings – Jewish, Christian and Muslim – testify uniquely to this chain of events: a tribal odyssey which runs through antiquity and acts as a model for the preservation of Jewish communities, and at the same time serves as the benchmark and principal backdrop of the two derived traditions – Christianity and Islam.

Year Zero

The West counts time from Christ: in this it acknowledges itself as the heir of the second Roman empire which made His cross a banner and His ordeal the end of prehistory. For with His word, say his followers, the Messiah was proclaimed to all the Nations and the era of Redemption began.

The reality was decidedly different: the Christian state was the political outcome of this messianism, the institutionalization of the upheavals that had preceded its advent.

In mediaeval Europe, the imbrication of the new religion and the new social order; the role of the papacy, the Church, the Inquisition, the crusades, the Reformation; all that gave the West reason to feel itself the child of the "Christian revolution" in the Roman empire. Perhaps, in order to be more exact, the new calendar ought to have been dated from the Council of Nicaea, or from some other event with more immediate institutional consequences than the Passion of the crucifixion: but the Christian sects, whatever their rivalries, all counted time from Jesus. For those, like Saint Paul, alias Saul of Tarsus, a Hellenized Jewish patrician, who had lived the old Judaic law, the Christian era marked the end of a world. By becoming the official religion of the empire, Christianity became the master of time, endowed with the power to count it in its own image. Before, after; BC, AD. The break was absolute, cutting off memory around a single great turning point: year zero. This was the end of the first movement, and the beginning of the second act, ours.

The Muslim world counts time from the *Hegira*, or the Emigration: this was the time when the prophet Mohammed and the handful of the first adherents of Islam left Mecca for Medina. From there, seven years later, they returned in triumph to their city, before setting out on the conquest of the world, starting with Jerusalem.

For the Arabs, but also for the whole settled population of the Fertile Crescent, and later of an empire that would link Persia to Spain, Islam inaugurated a new era: accomplishing – in some places through conquest, in others through administration, in others again through trade – a social, economic, political and cultural revolution unprecedented in the history of these peoples.

The Islamic state too was the institutionalization of the turbulent aspirations that had given rise to it, and it was the concrete expression of the new order born of the break-up of empires and the rupture of traditional balances on the Roman periphery. The time of Islam, the era of the Hegira, is the cycle of history inaugurated by the Islamic political revolution, which restructured and unified Byzantium, the desert and Persia, before turning to the conquest of the West. Before. After. The Sumerian epic of Gilgamesh, the pre-Islamic Arab saga of Antar and 'Abla, the Pharaohs, the Jews, the kingdom of Sheba, the Christians and the Medes; then the Koran. Year zero.

The French revolution, in its megalomaniac enthusiasm, introduced its own calendar: did it not inaugurate the new era of Liberty and Reason? What revolution since then has not been tempted by this pretension to reorder time?

Jews, on the other hand, count time . . . from the creation of the world! Certainly, it seems today naïve indeed to imagine, as rabbinical dogma asserts, that the world was created precisely five thousand seven hundred and forty-one years ago. There is no need to show that this mediaeval calculation, which was made more than a thousand years after the biblical rewriting, is false. What is important is that Jewish tradition does not count time around a precise event, does not place between the most distant past and the present some turning-point, some event articulating the before and the after of a new time. This calendar, which has no age other than the Stone Age, this philosophical commitment to the palaeolithic quite obviously constitutes the site of the expectation of the Messiah: nothing has yet come, the grammatical time of prophecy is the future.

Is there then no before or after in Judaism? Of course there is. But, precisely, none of the countless political revolutions in the existence of the Israelite tribes, or later of the Judaean nation, its diaspora or the restored establishment, founded a state order that was sufficiently lasting to proclaim itself the beginning of another history. None of these revolutions, except precisely those schisms, dissident movements and sects that were to give birth to Christianity and Islam, concerned an imperial space where other peoples would have been affected by the rearrangement. This single and linear time is thus cut up into numerous episodes where the destiny of the people, and not of the world, divided and deviated.

Such a detached perspective on history, reduced to the level of being the history of others, was not however pure expectation, since there was Law. The revelation of the Law constituted the turning-point, the unacknowledged Year Zero of that memory. But that year of the face-to-face meeting between Moses and the Cloud on the sacred mountain, the exact date of which the rabbis claim to know, did not mark the beginning of a new calculation. Nor did the departure from Egypt that had preceded it, nor the various stages of the conquest of Canaan, nor the establishment of the kingdom, nor the inauguration of the temple of Solomon, nor its destruction by Nebuchadnezzar's armies. Nor did the return to Persian rule, the episode of the Hasmonaean kingdom born of the revolt of the Maccabees, the destruction of the Temple under Vespasian and the opening in Palestine of the first rabbinical *yeshiva*.

But there is an undoubted turning-point, although a covert one: the Year Zero, not of the revelation of the Law, but of its rewriting.

Babylon, 538 BC. A proclamation of Cyrus, the new conqueror of the former Assyrian empire, orders the rebuilding of the Temple of Jerusalem destroyed fifty years earlier by Nebuchadnezzar.

Babylon, 458 BC. The scribe Ezra (Esdras) and the prophet Nehemiah are associated in the work of restoration. Nehemiah, it should be said, a Judaean prophet and priest, was no less than the governor of Judaea duly appointed by the emperor of the Persians.

This was the time when the Bible as we know it was redacted: rewritten, codified, expurgated, annotated, completed. The ancient Hebrew alphabet – the one the Samaritans of Nablus have retained down to the present day in their liturgy – was abandoned in favour of the square alphabet of the Aramaeans, with which Hebrew is written today. It is easy to imagine the possibilities of distortion opened up by this wholesale transliteration from one alphabet to another: this was when the whole of previous history, from the creation of the Persians to the fall of Judah, was summarized and reinterpreted. This vast manipulation of the text was to leave, standing out like crystals, a few fragments of the older telling retained in the collective memory of the people, and which were evidence against the new interpretations: whence this insistence in the "definitive" text on repeating several times over the same story in divergent versions. It was then, at this particular moment in history, which lasted almost a century, that Judaism was invented. This moment marks a turning-point: separating the before from the after. But for the text itself, it was only the present time of the reading.

The invention of Judaism: the law of Moses, given to the twelve tribes of Israel on the eve of the conquest of Canaan, had become the law of the kingdom of Israel, under David. But the kingdom had split: ten tribes out of twelve, rejecting this law, had followed the wicked kings who had had engraven on the ramparts of their palace in Samaria: "I do not recognize the God of Israel, and will have no part of Him." The anti-Mosaic kingdom thus established, however, was called Israel. It was the small rival state, bearing the name of the tribe of Judah, whose rulers took the Law as its banner, which inherited the "law of the individual Hebrew state". And it was this tribal name, describing at that time a territory and a kingdom, that soon came to describe, in exile, the Judaeans, the Jews.

Rebuilding of the Temple, restoration of the priesthood, return of the exiles. All backed by proclamations of the emperor of the Persians: not a whim, but a policy, as evidenced by the constancy of Persian "Judaeophilia", from Cyrus to Artaxerxes I, by way of Cambyses, Darius and Xerxes. Five generations of kings of kings based their Judaean policy on this alliance: not simply towards the mountain fief of southern Palestine, but with regard to the diaspora of the Judaeans throughout the empire. For, from 597 BC, and the first fall of Jerusalem, the majority of the Judaean aristocracy, both military and priestly, had been deported to Babylon, according to the normal custom of conquerors at that time.

In Babylon, priests and aristocrats had rubbed shoulders, formed the community, and continued the "class struggle" in which Judaean rule had torn itself apart: while the priesthood of Judaea operated officially, sanctioning the royal power and guaranteed by it, the prophets had long since been in opposition, if not in the armed subversion. Had not the prophet Jeremiah, a "revolutionary defeatist" before his time, encouraged the Syrian army, the "rod of the anger of the Lord", from the top of the walls of Jerusalem under siege, to overthrow this corrupt and criminal kingdom?

For their part, the ordinary people, the Hebrew peasantry of the kingdom of Judah, did not experience the honours of exile. They remained where they were, undone, like the people of the northern kingdom of Israel, after its fall before the Nineveh a hundred years earlier; integrated by the ties of inter-ethnic marriage and the adoption of local pagan cults into what the tradition calls '*Am ha-Arets*, or "people of the land", which the Talmud uses as a synonym for illiterate. All these people, that is the overwhelming majority of the "children of Israel", the Hebrews, ceased to be part of the history of Judaism. Later, many of them were to become Christians. Later again, many were to become Muslims. The Palestinian Arabs of today are no doubt the direct descendants of these ancient Hebrews, as well as of the "Canaanites", and the Moabites, the Jebusites and the Arabs.

Babylon: exile of the notables. The Judaeans in "Babel", says the text, were powerful and melancholic, and this "class character" was to colour the entire evolution of their doctrine.

Forty-nine years after Jerusalem, while Judaean high society was ruminating on its exile and its past greatness on the banks of the Euphrates,[3] it was the turn of proud Assyria itself, the inventor of civil codes, the power that had seized Palestine from the frontier of Egypt, to collapse under the blows of Cyrus. It was a dramatic turn of events. The new Persian conqueror was an absolute stranger to the civilization he inherited. He was an enlightened despot, and he freed the nationalities and ethnic groups which the conquered empire had crushed.

But there was no question of restoring a sovereign kingdom, even a tiny vassal one. First, because no mini-crown must tarnish the splendour of the grand unifying plan of the king of kings; but above all because it was a matter of managing not simply the autonomy of Judaea, but the civil autonomy of the Judaeans scattered to the four corners of the empire. The Persian imperial instructions are clear evidence of this concern; they gave the injunctions of Judaism force of law for all Jews, as far away as the Judaean military colony at Elephantine, in Upper Egypt, and subjected the whole of the diaspora to the spiritual and fiscal authority of the restored Temple.

It was the particular priestly organization of the Judaeans, the very existence of a caste of priests, that allowed the emperor to give concrete form to this alliance in which the new law was forged. When this Babylonian Judaism of Ezra and Nehemiah, of Persian protection, and of the rebuilding of the Temple was invented, the whole history of the Hebrews was the subject of a partisan rewriting: for the restorers, it comes as no surprise, were from priestly families; and, thanks to the Persians, the priests had just recovered power in the conquered community.

Thus, the second temple of Jerusalem was not, unlike the first, to symbolize the consecration of the state, and the territorialization of the Law. This satellite theocracy had no army: only a religious police which collected taxes and administered corporal punishment to members of the community who contravened the ritual prescriptions.

The history that the Babylonian narrator reread and gave out – from the creation of the world to the fall of Jerusalem – was thus entirely reworked to serve the thesis of the redactors: that the fall of the state followed inevitably from the very choice of the monarchy and that only the rule of the priests was compatible with the Law. Thus the Judaean priests reappropriated – irreversibly, it might be said – the meaning of the past. They defined for the nation in exile a separate destiny: a sect-people, a "nation of priests", with no other vocation than to apply its private law. This was the eminently political project that the tradition calls Return to Zion: the restoration of the rule of the priests and institutions of the Temple under the aegis of the Persian conqueror. The law of Moses, a tribal prophecy providing the basis for a conquest and a kingdom, had become Judaism: the assertion of a particular vocation to exist, as a dispersed community, "among the Nations".

Significantly, it was in Judaea itself that this separation of Israel from among the Nations had to be accomplished: the bulk of the population of Judaean territory was excluded from the process of restoration. It might well, of course, supply the servile manpower, but it could not be part of the "Assembly of Israel". The text records the census and the exclusion of the offspring of "foreign women". For, during the generations of the exile, the compiler of the book of Nehemiah records, scandalized: "Jews had married wives of Ashdad, of Ammon and of Moab: And their children spake half in the speech of Ashdad and could not speak in the Jews' language."[4] The exclusion of the "half-castes" marked the development of a code wholly inspired by the determination to isolate the ethnic group from the surrounding society, in order the better to mobilize it in the service of God, meaning: in order the better to subject it to the rule of its priests. And it was thus that the Nazi drafter of the 1933 Nuremberg laws wrote cynically in the preamble to them: "The model that I have kept constantly in front of me throughout the drafting of these laws is that of the laws of Ezra and Nehemiah, the first laws ever decreed for the protection of racial purity." The need to exclude the "people of the land" inspired a fanaticism in matters ritual, strengthened the obsession with food purity, and gave rise to a thousand and one practices of self-segregation.

A pattern thus emerged that was to be repeated: each time, in the subsequent history of Judaism, that the power of the priests was reformed, it would develop this renovation through a cunningly slanted repetition (*mishnah*) of the events of the first cycle. From this time, each stage of Hebrew law, then of talmudic law and later again of rabbinical law, was to express itself in commentaries, exegeses, parables and tractates that were always tied to the letter of the text, to the law of Moses. By the Middle Ages, this construction found its graphic representation in the careful lay-out of the pages of talmudic literature: one or several verses from the Bible, in Hebrew, would be written in large letters in the centre of the sheet, while on each side, in smaller letters in different sizes, would be the various levels of the commentary – in Aramaic – of the successive generations of the scholars of the Law. The first stage was that of the Palestinian *tannaim* whose teaching constituted the subject matter of the *mishnah* and the first Talmud: the second was that of the Mesopotamian *amoraim*, commentators and legislators whose opinions were entered into the enormous Babylonian Talmud. Then came the anonymous codifiers of the *targumim* (translations) in which the sages elucidated to the people the hidden meaning of the texts, in its profane Aramaic language.

From this Law, decked with all the levels of fable (*midrash*) and "completion" (*gemara*), of exegesis (*perush*) and additions (*tosefta*), the Talmuds would extract, adapting it to the conditions of mediaeval society in the East (Palestine and Mesopotamia from the 1st to the 6th centuries) a codification of the personal, family, economic and social life of the diaspora, which would serve for centuries as the legal model for the survival and organization of Jewish communities.

The ideal model of this law, the *Torah* of Moses, was thus, for Judaism, not the rule of real life: that was defined, from age to age, by the rabbis who commented, interpreted and amended. But the law of Sinai, revised and corrected by the scribes (*sofrim*) of the Restoration, contained the essence and spirit of it. To this we must now turn.

The law of the desert

Nehemiah, the prophet-governor, and Ezra, the writer: they concealed the novelty of their clerical project behind the law of Moses whose mantle they claimed. They claimed to continue the prophetic tradition which had fought against the monarchical order of Judah in the name of this ancient law. This was the major distorting tendency of the rewriting: it attributed to Moses and the prophets the desires of the redactor. This pretension to legitimacy was, of course, the basis for the claim to the priestly inheritance, and contained the theological justification of the priests' monopoly of power.

It also contained the assertion of the terrorism of the Law: the traditional imagery suggests that Moses was an irascible and infallible ruler, the spokesman for divine jealousy and vengeance. As supreme and superhuman leader of an undisciplined horde, he came back from his terrifying and solitary face-to-face meeting with an unnamable God of fire, holding in his hands the Tables of the Covenant. Ten commandments, six hundred and fifteen obligations: a Constitution, a civil code, a penal code, a medical code, ordinances and decrees, recommendations and a political programme for a century.

The absolutism of Moses, whom the tradition calls *rabbeinu*, "our Master", was based on the permanent rebellion of the people against the Law. Scarcely had the leader gone up to seek the inspiration for lawmaking than the tribes erected a pastoral and monetary idol: a golden calf. Then there were the rebellions in the desert: "leftist" mutinies by those who were impatient, or defeatist revolts by sceptics, not to mention individual delinquency and intrigues. "So, let's change people!" Moses suggests to the Almighty. "Let us continue with this one, since it is the one we began with", pleads the Lord. The Pentateuch, particularly the recapitulation in Deuteronomy, thus established the fundamentally guilty relationship between the people and their living God. A people reprieved, in constant breach of their contract with the God of hosts who makes and unmakes nations and kingdoms. A people of whom it is said they must be holy or not exist at all, and who determinedly persist in existing in the abominable forms of profane being.

Is this a paradox of this construction, or the survival of the collective memory? The people no more began with the Revelation than did time, and yet the Revelation offered them a covenant, the promise of being, in Canaan, a "great nation". But, just as the decimal military organization described in Numbers remained internal to the tribes and did not fuse them into a single army, so the new holy people retained or imagined an ethnic ancestry prior to the departure from Egypt, prior even to the entry into Egypt. "Our forefathers worshipped foreign Gods", "Our fathers worshipped idols, on the other side of the river . . . ". This admission of ethnic continuity is too insistent not to express an imperative: both on the part of later redactors inspired by their own ethnocentric project and also by the crumbs of oral memory that the reordered texts could not deny without losing credibility. Egypt or not, desert or not, the tribes of Israel federated by the Law and united in the military conquest of Canaan claimed that they had migrated over a journey from Chaldaea to the Syrian Houran and to Hebron, in Canaan. This legendary genealogy served not only as an argument for the conquest of the territory where the first act of the Covenant with the patriarchs Abraham, Isaac and Jacob occurred: it also linked the Hebrews to the patriarchs, and we know today that among the Canaanites of Tell Amarma these patriarchs are identified with the founding figures of the City.

It seems established today that while some Hebrew group or other – apart from the priestly tribe of Levi, which was manifestly Egyptianized – had indeed at some point been subjugated by the Pharaonic state on its frontiers,[5] the main body of the confederated tribes came together later: in the deserts of Sinai and Transjordan. The itinerary of the patriarchs' wanderings thus allowed clans of very diverse geographical origins to claim for themselves common descent from the great regional ancestors.

The invention of family links, through the invention of an eponymous common ancestor, was for a long time the necessary corollary of any alliance. For tribal society rests on the balance of deterrence formed by blood vengeance. Setting the bounds of the family, the clan, the tribe and the "race" – however mythical it might be – is thus fundamental: it defines precisely the field of military responsibility. In West Africa, two tribes that federated would establish a treaty of perpetual peace between them; through the conciliation of the wise men and elders of the two tribes it would be opportunely discovered that their respective great ancestors were brothers. In less definitive alliances, they might be discovered to be half-brothers, heirs to ancient blessings and curses; or cousins, in which case blood relationship does not exclude disputes. And, since what is done can always be undone, it is also possible to declare foreigners groups that are related to one another, but rivals. The manipulation of genealogical trees

takes the place of historiography and diplomacy. "I and my brother ⌐
the outsider, I alone against my brother", as the Bedouin saying has it. In
the vision of the *Torah,* humanity is a family: father, mother and the
children. Adam knew Eve, who begat Cain, then Abel, whom Cain killed.
Cain built the first town and his descendants invented civilization: cattle-
rearing, music and metal-working. But all those people were to perish in the
Flood. The sole survivors, through Noah, were the descendants of Seth, the
third son of Adam and Eve. Thus, on the summit of Mount Ararat, the
great zoological ark of the sole father of our humanity was shipwrecked,
and everything began again.

The division into three lineages, Shem, Ham and Japhet, which was for a
long time considered an ethno-linguistic classification of the human
families, inspired the slave-trading racism of Christian Europe and
America, the racist pseudo-linguistics of the 19th century, and even the
genocidal racisms of the contemporary period. This mythical division,
which ignores the vastness of the world and the multiplicity of peoples and
civilizations that the ancient East was unaware of, is borne out neither by
history nor by linguistics: the common origin, in any case, of the so-called
Semitic languages and so-called Hamitic languages is today no longer
disputed. Quite clearly, the function of this classification was to
legitimize in advance, in the desert, and, *a posteriori*, in Babylon – a
complex system of alliances and non-aggression pacts with peoples decreed
to be cousins, and of rivalry and enmity with the inhabitants of the lands
coveted, and their rulers and protectors. These accursed lineages, which
were precisely those against whom the Israelite tribes intended to wage war,
were thus excluded from the blood ties: as hereditary enemies, it was right
to exterminate them and seize their property.

From all the genealogical erudition of the biblical redactor, not a single
genealogical certainty can be drawn: we know today that languages move
from one ethnic group to another, and that the existence of a linguistic
community is not evidence of common origins, nor of the reverse. But,
what one can find in it is an illustration of the system of alliances and
enmities into which the federated tribes inserted themselves when they
settled in Palestine: "Those you shall not touch", said Moses, "for they are
the second cousins of What's-his-name, the brother of the half-sister of
Abraham's great nephew. Those, on the other hand, descend directly from
the evil Ham, who mocked his drunken father fifteen hundred years ago.
Burn their cities and put their inhabitants to the sword!"

No ethnic essence separated the good from the bad. It was the
geographical demands of conquest that made the sedentary populations in
the region enemies, and the nomadic tribes surrounding them potential
allies and clients.

The racial theorizing in which the text excels, however, was not enough
to legitimize the anathema. Here and there, peoples well known to be
cousins stood athwart the frontier of Israelite expansion: they were in the
end consigned to the exterminating wrath of the God of Hosts. But the

morality of the projected conquest – the morality of the ideal conquest such as the lawmaker planned it – derived from the very nature of the contract made between God and Israel: the destruction of Canaanite civilization is presented as a work of divine cleansing, the agrarian and urban cults of the ancient East as abominations in the sight of the Lord. But one does not simply exterminate people just like that, with the sole aim of enjoying life in their place. The promise was conditional on the terms of the Covenant: if the people remained faithful to the Law, its internal justice would preserve the country; otherwise, they would lose it.

Leviticus sets out the Law in detail: sacrifices of animals and offerings of agricultural produce. Quantities, qualities, methods, rates and seasonings. The people sacrifice and the priests eat. Cattle are sacrificed for any and every purpose: collectively for feasts and rituals, individually to expiate minor transgressions."Part is burned on the altar, it is a perfume agreeable to God." The rest is "reserved" for the priest, "that his sons and his daughters may eat".

To speak of twelve tribes is a euphemism. There were eleven tribes and the Levis, that English has transformed into Levites: a sacred tribe, a tribe devoted to "the services of the Tabernacle". It was the tribe of Aaron the high priest, to which Moses, saved from the waters and brought up in the house of Pharaoh, claimed to belong. A tribe devoted to administration: priests and officials, policemen and judges, a ruling caste in every way. It was a tribe-class, whose rule was the basis of the state. When the conquered country was apportioned, each of the eleven tribes received a territory. But the tribe of Levi had no inheritance: the Levites received as inheritance only four cities in each of the territories, forty-eight cities "of refuge", with their farming suburbs.

In this organization, in which the bureaucrat-tribe imposed its religious and police services on populations nomadizing between pastoralism and agriculture, the extraction of surplus value was achieved through sacrifice. The sacrificial relationship that subjugated the tribes of Israel to the tribe of Levi constituted the dominant social relationship.

Sacrifice was obligatory. From the text it emerges that every consumption of meat involved ritual slaughter and sacrifice: state control and fiscal levy in kind. The Levite state intervened in the food consumption process of society: people ate only through, and with, the priest. Lawbreakers were put to death.

The rationality of this domination was not, as in the classic manner, linked to the direct exercise of organized force: it was the men of the tribes who made up the army. But here the political commanded the military; conscription was obligatory for all men over twenty years of age, except the Levites themselves, since they served the Ark of the Covenant – the moving temple. This power was sacrificial; medical, and scientific. By exercising police administration of the supervision of meat and the cleanliness of life, the tribe of Levi officiated the ritual of its hegemony.

Sacrifice, then, established a social-ritual order in a formation that remained clanic. Since war was conducted by clansmen, justice could have remained tribal, governed by blood law and blood solidarity: brother would avenge brother and so on, up to war or peace. The twin necessity of maintaining the federation against each and every centrifugal tendency, and of establishing Levitical hegemony as a substitute for the slowly withering older form of social organization inevitably resulted in the sacred state usurping power previously diffused throughout the community, and gradually monopolizing the use of force. State interference in the customary blood law was responsible for the establishment of cities of refuge: if one man killed another, he would take refuge there. The Levites would then decide whether the killing was accidental or premeditated. In the former case, the killer would remain in the city where he would be protected. Otherwise, "he shall be handed over to the avenger of the blood". This growth of the priest-state in the pores of tribal law rested on another institution: the putting to death of offenders by collective stoning. This was not pure and simple lynching, since there had been a judgement. It was a question of the sentences being carried out by "all the community of Israel". Thus the tribesmen and women entered into a blood relationship that superseded the blood law at the same time as it enabled the state apparatus to wash its hands of it.

It was one of the characteristics of this state, whose formation is described in the last three books of the Pentateuch, that it denied, obscured and concealed its own repressive role. As a state-of-God, it claimed to be the state of the whole people, compelling the mass of the people to take responsibility for the use of force by the state. The war militia composed of tribesmen had only a mission of conquest, and no role in the maintenance of order. In these conditions, who assured the enforcement of the law?

To judge from the silence of the Babylonian redactor on this point, it would seem that the fear of God was enough to impose obedience. Contradictions within the group would thus be settled by simple ideological control, without recourse to the executive arm of the state.

When a man of Israel infringed one of the laws that set out his social obligations (theft, adultery), hygienic obligations (laws relating to sexual cleanness and uncleanness, and food), or ritual-fiscal obligations (obligatory sacrifices and offerings), he was condemned, according to a detailed scale, to a whole series of punishments: from the fine in kind – a tenth for the nostrils of the Lord, the rest to feed the priest's family – to temporary isolation (*quarantine*) and the death sentence.

The death penalty was prescribed not only for a whole series of sexual offences (adultery, incest, bestiality) but also for all infractions involving a rebellion against the state: blasphemy and subversive talk, and above all the private, unsanctioned slaughter of animals. Refusal to perform the concrete act of sacrifice, which consisted in feeding the Levites, was always identified with rebellion and punished with death.

Executions were not restricted to circumstances laid down in advance by the law, which made no provision for collective rebellion, and envisaged only individual crimes. But the text mentions numerous revolts, both individual revolts and organized ones: these rebellions were crushed and all the rebels were put to death.

How? The fire of God carried them off, consumed before the whole community. What was the fire of God? Had Moses and Aaron set up an electric chair in front of the Ark of the Covenant? Did the priests have a militia of executioners that tradition haloed with a divine cloud, like the *Anyota,* the leopard-men of ancient Kongo? We do not know. But we can understand the allusive character of the Babylonian redaction: for it needed to show both the effectiveness of the law and the needlessness of a real state. Here, the obscuring of the role of the executive served the redactors' project of a satellite-theocracy: the violence in it came from God, and from the people, never from a particular social category.

The basic model of this type of priestly power is well known. It is Pharaonic Egypt. We are aware of the many hypotheses that have been advanced on the subject of the Egyptian origin of Moses, perhaps even of the Egyptianness of the whole tribe of Levi; on the relationship of Moses to the monotheistic reformation of Akhenaten; on the possible coincidence between the Exodus and the counter-reformation of the clergy of Ammon. What is certain is that the influence of the Egyptian model decisively shaped the spirit of Mosaic law. But, in Egypt, it was the king who was God, and the priests were in the service of his state. In the wilderness, the state of God became the state of the Servants of God. In both cases, the priest – doctor, initiate, administrator and judge – exercised his power thanks to his monopoly of the rituals and practices deemed indispensable to survival.

The text suggests, in fact, through a mass of technical details, a wide cultural gap between Moses and his lieutenants on the one hand, skilled in a thousand and one sciences, particularly those to do with the manipulation of consciences and crowds, and, on the other hand, the mass of the tribesmen possessed of a religious respect for these supermen. Their knowledge is of course attributed to divine inspiration, but the text provides a number of indicators linking it to the Egyptian – and probably priestly-royal – origin of Moses. Elsewhere, mention is made of Moses' initiation by his father-in-law Jethro, the high priest of the Midianite Bedouin in Sinai.

Neither Moses nor the generation of the wilderness born "in the house of bondage" were to see the promised land with their own eyes. Only men and women who had not known the old society, who were born and grew up "in the camp" during the forty years in transit between Egypt and Canaan marked by the gift of the Law, only they were worthy of entering it and building there the order that God, through the mouth of Moses, had ordered to reign there – legislation, *a priori,* proclaimed before the conquest and settlement.

The historical books (Judges, Samuel, Kings and Chronicles), of diverse redaction, are at one in stressing – in order to deplore it – the considerable gap between this ideal legislation of the wilderness and the practical and historical reality of its implementation: its place in the social practice of the Hebrews during sedentarization and under the kingdoms of Israel and Judah. There can be no doubt that this law of the wilderness was never implemented anywhere, or at any time, in the precise form that the Babylonian redactors gave it, and which is evidence above all of their own ideal. In rebellion and secession, in corruption and abomination, the people, massively, rejected the Law. We have already seen that ten tribes out of twelve solemnly abandoned it in the third generation of the kings of Israel; but this rejection was to be slow and tortuous. On the death of Moses, it was Joshua, son of Nun, who became the leader. He led the Hebrews in the conquest of Canaan, and set up the so-called rule of the Judges. This degenerated rapidly: two of the four sons of Aaron, the great sacrificer and Moses' (adoptive) brother, Nadab and Abihu, had already, although priests, had to be put to death, even before crossing the Jordan, while Moses was still living. Corrupt, and shamelessly exploiting the privileges of their hereditary offices, the text describes them indulging in the forbidden pleasures of private appropriation of the public patrimony and fiscal fraud (consumption of meat without ritual sacrifice).

With sedentarization, the autonomy of the tribal structures became more accentuated. Instead of unfolding in the prescribed exterminating climate, settlement in Canaan took place, for many, in the framework of forbidden alliances with the peoples whom the Law had condemned to be massacred. There followed rebellions by the "stiff-necked people" which led to the establishment of the kingdom: rebellions against the Judges, rebellion by the bad priests against the Law, wars between tribes (such as the episode of the Benjamites of Guibea at the end of the Book of Judges), and finally the popular rebellion demanding the monarchy.

Then came Samuel, the last of the Judges, an upright Levite and inspired priest, who took back the initiative: to fight against the corruption of his caste and preserve the credibility and legitimacy of priestly supremacy. With a thousand reservations, by way of tortuous political zigzags, he established, as it were despite himself, the monarchy over Israel. He anointed king before the people a great gangling youth with no personality whom he chose because of his height, as if the better to deride the desire of the Israelites to have a king "like all the nations". Denouncing the monarchy even before it was introduced, by his own good offices, he set out the "right of the king" in overwhelming detail. On the pretext of explaining the monarchical constitution to the people, he described the bondage that awaited them under this despotic regime, stressing for the last time the merits of the priestly organization of the Judges to which he was putting an end: "And he will take your daughters to be concubines and servants and your sons to be cooks and to be bakers.... And he will take your menservants and your maidservants." For in his eyes, the God-King was the only figurehead the social organization and the power of the priests required; the demand for a monarchy was itself a rebellion against the Law.

So Samuel anointed Saul, and then started to plot with the military leaders of the tribe of Judah to overthrow the anointed one. The House of David, a Transjordanian Moabite through his grandmother, made an alliance with Samuel against the legitimate king of Israel, by which the kingdom would be his. Civil war and foreign war followed: David, pursued by Saul, fled to the Philistines, sea invaders of the southern coast of Palestine, Cretans and Cypriots, whom the Bible calls "peoples of the islands of the sea". He stayed with the Philistine king of Gath (near Gaza) for several years, and only the mistrust of the other Philistine princes prevented him going to war with them against his Hebrew "brothers". He finally returned and, in a process combining *coup d'état* and civil war, he took power with the support of Samuel and the politico-religious leadership. It was then that David embarked on the construction of the Temple in Jerusalem, which territorialized the Law on the frontier of Judah and Benjamin, the rebellious tribe in the last chapter of Judges.

A tribal split then became inevitable: ten of the twelve tribes seceded. They retained the name of Israel, and the fertile north of Palestine, as far as the Mediterranean coast. In the south, the desert and mountain kingdom of Judah chose to shelter in the shadow of the Law and the protection of Samuel, the prophet of the hour and the miracle-worker of the Levites and priestly class. It was a short-lived choice. King David, supposed author of the Psalms, singer, musician and dancer at the same time as Machiavellian statesman, became a lascivious and criminal old man, who had the husband of his mistress Bathsheba murdered. After the death of his son Solomon, the builder of the Temple, poet, philosopher[6] and diplomat, whom tradition did not forgive for having introduced pagan ceremonies in Jerusalem in honour of his Canaanite concubines, the kingdom split for good. Soon, Judah itself was governed by avaricious and criminal kings who "did evil in the eyes of the Lord": in particular, they persecuted the priests, who foretold their fall and denounced their misdeeds.

Prophecy and priesthood

With the emergence of the monarchy – even though draped in the folds of the Law – the state became profane, if not secular. Under David and Solomon, it was Samuel, the man of the transition, who retained a spiritual authority amounting in practice to a right of veto over royal decisions. However, this authority, which flowed from the decisive role played by the prophet in the establishment of the kingdom, was purely personal. Certainly, the administration of the Temple remained, as the avenue for priestly careers, but it seems that the people, before resuming the forms of worship of their indigenous neighbours and cousins, were largely concerned with their own secular activities and conflicts. For sedentarization was a source of new inequalities, of upward social mobility based on the spoliation of widows and orphans, and of power and palace intrigues. It was all very well for the state to proclaim itself sacred, and claim it was theocratic; the law of Israel now served as an argument only in foreign wars. Hebrew civil society flouted it every day. Soon the kings themselves renounced it. When monarchical rule became wicked, the most conscious elements of the priestly class went over into opposition. These were the prophets.

The phenomenon of prophetism is complex, and cannot be contained in a reductionist sociological-type explanation. Moreover, the phenomenon is not limited to the people of Israel alone, or to the area where Semitic languages are spoken alone, even though it is true that it proliferated most abundantly there. But perhaps this is because this region had long experience, without ever being able to overcome it, of the permanent crisis of the oldest forms of social organization: an interminable crisis, since these forms continue to exist, even if only in group consciousness. For prophets sprout all the more where civilizations clash and collapse, where there seems to be no end to political upheavals except in the end of the world, in the burial of the old and the decadent, and the birth of a new order which is often only the restoration of an older ideal. Prophetism, in this sense, linked to the messianic framework, is indeed the morality of history thrown in the face of politics. It emerges at times when masses of men are torn by the history of empires from their traditional modes of existence and representations without being integrated into the new political-ideological order.

If we leave aside the nature of prophetic inspiration (is it metaphysical, or clinical?), and concentrate on its social significance, it is its "street preacher" character that stands out, except that it is an essentially rural occurrence. What makes the prophet is not preaching the future, but preaching in public. He preaches the end of the world. He does not simply predict the fall of the Kingdom; he lovingly describes the violence and atrocities that will accompany the downfall of the proud. He proclaims that they richly deserve it and prays for the advent of their last day. He says it out loud; he addresses himself to the people, and becomes the symbol of the hatred that the people feel for the tyranny and capriciousness of the great. The prophets of Israel appeal to the public opinion, to the good sense, morality and anger of decent people. They brandish the old Law only as evidence of betrayal and abandonment.

Prophets were seditious people. They destabilized the established regime, and enjoyed in "propaganda and agitation among the masses".[7] They promised wicked rulers every suffering on earth and in hell; to the upright who listened to them and followed them they promised the blessings of paradise on earth. Seeing the external enemies of the ungodly state as simply the instruments of divine wrath, they prophesied their victory and the crushing of Judah. In short, they were revolutionaries.

In this extreme denunciation of the existing government, the prophets mobilized, among their listeners, every aspiration, conscious or repressed, for a freedom whose only real model was the autonomy of the clan in the old tribal society. The prophetic rejection of the state, even when it was expressed in terms of the days of the Messiah, that is of a new time, still rested on the nostalgic exaltation of the old tribal egalitarianism. This was the limit and ambiguity of this anti-monarchism: for the only possible political synthesis of the prophetic critique of social inequality and poverty was precisely the theocratic state, the state obedient to the word of the prophet, where the prophetic function would abdicate and return to priestly management.

The fact is that the great prophets of Israel, the succession of whom seemed like a dynasty parallel to that of the wicked kings of Judah, were not down-and-outs or inspired marginals as the modern Western imagination likes to picture them. They were all Levites and priests, aristocrats from good families and old lineages; in short, all pretenders to the exercise of priestly power, all artisans of the Restoration. That is no doubt the reason why prophecy fuelled more *coups d'état* – on the pattern already tried and tested by Samuel imposing David against Saul – than revolts.

It was thus not simply Moses and the Law of the wilderness, but also Samuel and all the prophets, great and small, of Israel and Judah, whom the scribes in the Babylonian exile rewrote. They thus laid claim to the heritage of sixteen generations of prophetic opposition: a real gold-mine of partisan memory in which resistance to the monarchical state and its practices merged with the fundamentalist denunciation of the moral jungle of the kingdom.

There was, however, a moment of prophecy which escaped them: a moment when the prophetic inspiration went beyond the priestly claim to legitimacy and issued in an absolutely, almost purely, negative demand. Thanks to the refusal of the prophet to countenance, even by a prudent silence, the injustice of Judah, and the corruption of the kingdom and the official temple serving it, all the rebellious spontaneity of the people, which had previously operated against the Law, could now be mobilized in its favour. But rebellion and revolt also seized the mind of the prophet. And the particular rejection borne by this *élan* transcended its social, ethnic and historical particularism to become a literally crazy rejection of injustice in general, alienation and death: an apocalyptic messianism in which the birth pangs of the new era announce the end of classes and nations, the end of creeds and gods. An ancient version of what Marx called "the end of the prehistory" of man, the moment when he "re-appropriates the essence of things". By popularizing this utopian and highly subversive vision, the prophets of Israel became the spokesmen of a demand that went far beyond the mere aspirations for a restoration held by the class from which they came. The clinical evidence of the prophetic language testifies to this taking over of the prophet by the prophecy: as the voice of God, with bones crushed, the prophet acted like a person possessed. In his visionary trance, he voiced the rebellious subconsciousness and the repressed violence of the whole society.[8]

It is this nihilist dimension of prophecy that conferred on it the universalism that Christianity and Islam, and, later, secular humanism were in turn to lay claim to. "Hear the word of the Lord, ye rulers of Sodom", Isaiah cried to the kings and people of Jerusalem and Judah:

> To what purpose is the multitude of your sacrifices unto me? saith the Lord: I am full of the burnt offerings of rams, and the fat of fed beasts; and I delight not in the blood of bullocks, or of lambs, or of he-goats... Bring no more vain oblations; incense is an abomination unto me; the new moons and sabbaths, the calling of assemblies, I cannot away with; it is iniquity, even the solemn meeting. Your new moons and your appointed feasts my soul hateth: they are a trouble unto me; I am weary to bear them. And when ye spread forth your hands, I will hide mine eyes from you: yea, when ye make many prayers, I will not hear: your hands are full of blood... How is the faithful city become an harlot! it was full of judgement; righteousness lodged in it; but now murderers... The princes are rebellious, and companions of thieves.[9]

Faced with the absolute perversion of the priestly system, the prophet turns to spiritual accents that make him the ancestor of the Christian, Jewish and Muslim mystics of the Middle Ages, and even of the moralism of the Reformation, perhaps even the anti-clericalism of modern social movements.

It is easy to show that at no time did the prophets of Israel really go beyond Israelite ethnic particularism and national pride: "For out of Zion shall go forth the law and the word of the Lord from Jerusalem".[10] It is easy to stress the theocratic finality of the language: "And I will restore thy judges as at the first, and thy counsellors as at the beginning: afterward thou shalt be called, the city of righteousness, the faithful city."[11] It still remains the case that the prophets initiated the literature of the outsider, of the downtrodden and of the man persecuted by the king's police, and that across the pages and the centuries the irrepressible breath of their hatred and their hope comes down to the men of our time: "They shall beat their swords into plowshares, and their spears into pruninghooks: nation shall not lift up sword unto nation, neither shall they learn war any more."[12]

Here we can see how little room for manoeuvre the Babylonian manipulators of the text had. The prophetic books were certainly the object of oral recitations, and were perhaps also written down in ancient Hebrew. So that the unifying and edifying mould imposed by the censors on the biblical anthology could only superficially alter the prophetic message: it comes through even behind the square letters of the Aramaic alphabet.

Here we are then, in Babylon. The diaspora is restructuring itself under the combined pressure of Persian rule and the awakening of the priests. Not without conflicts or tragedies, with ups and downs, the Temple was rebuilt, sacrifice re-established, and the priesthood restored to its privileges. Backed by the very real state of Cyrus and Darius, the ordinances of the new clergy had the force of law throughout the dispersed nation: its capital was Jerusalem, but its main centre remained Babylon. Right from this early stage, the majority of Judaeans chose to remain in this exile. Only a minority returned to participate in the reconstruction of Zion. But the essential thing is that the Temple served as a centre for the diaspora in Persia and Egypt, while the historical myth of the priestly state and the prophetic inheritance fuelled the language of the new clerics. The whole theocratic edifice suggested by the biblical rewriting had reached its logical conclusion; but it was neither the piety of the people nor the strength of the priests that imposed it. It was the policy of indirect rule pursued by the Persian emperor.

Thus the second Temple was not the centre of a state, but of an extra-territorial confessional dominion. A pattern was in the process of being fixed, which was to become the implicit structure of all later forms of Jewish community organization. Between the protector state and the community was a clergy that reminded the people of its peculiar destiny: to have neither territory nor state, but nevertheless to remain impervious to other peoples. The Judaism that was invented at this time was not a pure ontological choice. It reflected a dual project: that of Persian imperialism, and that of the Jewish clergy. From their alliance, what was Law, *Torah,* became religion, and Hebrew had to borrow a word, *Dath,* from the Persian language, to describe it.

Very soon, the satellite power of the Temple itself became the seat of struggles and intrigues. The patrician and priestly factions clashed over the power attached to the sanctuary, while the "people of the land" – who had been mostly excluded from the process of reconstruction – sometimes revolted against the new Establishment. Within the people, "the Jebusean and the Ammonite, the Hittite and the Canaanite" rubbed shoulders. It may be estimated that at least half the population of the countryside in Palestine at the time of the second Temple lived outside institutionalized Judaism, whatever its ethnic origin.

Statistics are lacking, and there is not enough documentation to draw up an exact picture of the actual social and economic relations in Palestine at that time. But it seems likely that the Judaeans absorbed part of the former Hebrew peasantry, while re-establishing, with Persian imperial support, their "feudal" domination over cultivated lands. Here, it was a matter for the most part of ransoming the peasants, by establishing clientage and protection relationships with their non-noble clans. Elsewhere, this appropriation of the land was accompanied by various forms of renting and serfdom. Slavery, which was universal in the imperial civilization of the time, was very widespread, but was essentially of a domestic sort, and was marginal in the agricultural production process before Roman times. There is evidence, on the other hand, for wage labour, which the Gospels translated as "hired labour", as early as Babylonian times. According to the Pentateuch, it was already being practised at the time of the conquest of Canaan. However that may be, at the time when Roman military might was established over Palestine, all the wage-workers, slaves, share-croppers, clients, day labourers, poor and indebted peasants, beggars, thieves and prostitutes lived outside the jealous statutes that the Assembly of Exiles had established over the community of Israel. Everywhere, the mass of ordinary people in the countryside and towns limited and threatened the legalistic vision of the priests, and made observance a luxury of the privileged, a caste prerogative.

Exit Artaxerxes, enter Alexander the Macedonian. The whole of the East succumbed to the fascination with Hellenism: the new civilization was cosmopolitan and city-based, its learning open to all.

Although priestly, the ruling classes in the Judaean protectorate now added to their love of power the adoption of foreign values. They became Hellenized says the Book of Maccabees, inventing a neologism to describe colonial acculturation. Within some of these sectors, imitation of the Greek model went as far as aesthetic surgery: "And they built a place of exercise in Jerusalem according to the laws of the Gentiles; and they made themselves uncircumcised."[13] To this cultural alienation of the urban élites, which fuelled the touchy nationalism of the rural chieftaincies, corresponded the triumphant universalism of the conquering wisdom. Among the Seleucid heirs of Alexander, kings in Antioch and rulers of Palestine, this triumph would soon brook no rival. Between the temple of Zeus, with its pomp and ceremony and its dues, and the temple of the God of Hosts sited in Jerusalem, rivalry soon raged, sharpened by the financial demands of their respective treasuries. It took only an intolerant Greek tax collector and an obstinate Jewish family head, to unleash an ambush, an armed incident, a guerrilla war, an uprising.

The questioning of the clerical protectorate under the empire marked the failure of the Temple. As the defeat of the kingdom had legitimized the priestly restoration, so the failure of the clergy now opened the way for monarchical messianism. Once the struggle with the empire was engaged, the military logic of war took over: and it was indeed for independence, for the restoration of the kingdom of Israel that the Maccabees were to fight. It was the Davidic model of the state, theocratic, but sovereign, that inspired them.

The Hasmonaean revolt of Judas Maccabeus and his sons restored the independence of the kingdom together with the function of the Temple. It was a reaction that was both rural-social and traditionalist, and it won the support of the party of pious men, the first *Hassidim,* scholars from good families, breaking with Hellenization. Their adherence illustrates the new history, in which the kingdom and the Temple, as in the past, were no longer on opposite sides. In the kingdom of Judah that they had restored, the sons of Judas Maccabeus proceeded to the systematic cumulation of monarchical and priestly functions. Kings and high priests: with the use of methods of government whose debt to Hellenistic civilization has been stressed by Vidal-Naquet,[14] the old Egyptian model of sacred monarchy was brought into being again – with the one major theological difference that the Hasmonaean king was a high priest and not God. This monarchism, however, was now only incidentally ethnic: feverishly territorial, it imposed Judaism on the "people of the land" – forced integration, but integration nevertheless.

The Hasmonaean kings succeeded in turning the clock back only briefly. Caught between the great powers, their state became the site of the same clashes and underwent the same evolution that had preceded – and to a large extent legitimized – its advent in the eyes of the people. Against the Greeks in Antioch and the Seleucid armies, the Hasmonaeans appealed to the Romans. These came running, delighted with such a stroke of good luck: a military intervention at the request of the local government! They were not to leave the country until the advent of Islam. Thus, the new kingdom of Judaea, which ruled an area larger than the old state of David, served as a state and a springboard in the rivalry of empires. At the same time as it re-established the privileges of the caste of priests, it launched itself into a series of military adventures to enlarge its territory, no doubt unaware that it was working for the entrenchment of Roman rule over the region.

With the exception of the sole woman ever to have reigned over Israel, Alexandra, the widow of Alexander Yannai, the sons of Judas Maccabeus soon transformed themselves, like their remote predecessors, into persecutors of the righteous, and bloodthirsty megalomaniacs. For several centuries, this unstable equilibrium between the Temple recognized by the empire and the permanent temptation of the Kingdom, marked by rebellion and war, went hand in hand with the disintegration of the ancient networks of practical and ideological loyalties.

This "new prophetism" constituted by monarchical messianism was exacerbated by the revolts that marked these centuries: Maccabees in the 2nd and 1st centuries BC; Zealots in Jerusalem in the 1st century AD; Bar-Kokhba's revolt in the 2nd century. Here the rejection of Graeco-Latin civilization was articulated on many social interests. The Maccabees were mountain peasant people who refused to pay tribute to the state. But they were also descendants of priestly families formerly associated with the administration of the Temple. However, while messianic nationalism took on the hue of popular anti-imperialism, it never involved the whole of the diaspora. Only the Palestinian *Yishuv* was affected by these upheavals, and often only a single region. One had ended at Massada, on the arid fortress in the desert of Judaea, opposite the Dead Sea, in the collective suicide of the fighters. The last revolt was that of the "sons of the stars," Bar-Kokhba. Isolated, the Messiah who minted coins bearing his name in his besieged kingdom, was railed at by the Jews who called him "Bar Koziba", son of lies. From Alexandria to Sephoris in Galilee, the Jewish communities in the diaspora collected funds and sent volunteers to fight against him and support Rome.[15]

Sects and schools

In the gap between the Temple-state and the actual functioning of post-Hasmonaean Judaean society novel forms of opposition and resistance arose, the many-sided prophetic and scriptural heritage feeding them all. Military messianism was one form of this, constantly asserted. The sects were another.

The community and monastic currents could lay claim to ancient traditions. As early as the 9th century BC, under the wicked kings of Israel, Jonadab Ben Rechab and his disciples, the Rechabites, "left the world in order to save it",[16] banning the consumption of alcohol and living in houses. Similarly, the practice of the Nezirate, codified in the Law of the desert: a mysticism of abstinence freely consented to for a period of six years, combined with celibacy and wandering. In the circumstances of Roman rule which followed the wave of Hellenization, these sects proliferated in Palestinian Judaism. They went hand in hand with the renewal of prophetism among the people, which attracted to it pell-mell all the *déclassé* strata, all those without a lineage and the urban semi-nomads of the new social periphery of the empire. The sects announced to them the only possible "good news" (Gospel): the end of the rotten world and the advent of a new age. The classical prophetism codified several centuries earlier, when it served the cause of priestly legitimacy, now served as a model for the root and branch rejection of a discredited Temple and priesthood. The prophetic reference to a justice and morality higher than ethnic loyalty, and apocalyptic messianism, with internationalist overtones, thus prepared the genesis of two great revealed religions.

But most of these sects remained within the orbit of Judaism. They were inspired and led by Judaeans, and they continued to conceive their opposition as a political and ideological – legal and ritual – struggle within the community of Israel. This was quite open in Palestine, where the community felt itself attached to the Temple even though it detested the party in power and its administration. It was less so in those areas where the Judaeans did not form the largest group. In Mesopotamia, where the largest and most prosperous community had lived since well before the destruction of the second Temple, these sects constituted pressure groups and groups expressing secular opinions, currents of ideas gathered round masters in the manner of the philosophical schools of the Greeks. Between the closed sects – community and priestly phalansteries – and the open schools – politico-theological opposition parties – there was a complex exchange of ideas and cleavages. Parallel with the decline of the official Temple, it marked the break-up of Judaism into contradictory currents: nationalist messianism, ritual formalism, opposition to Hellenism, Hellenization of worship and understanding of the Law, ethnocentric legalism and universalist spiritualism, but also missionary ritualism and national spiritualism.

From this "molecular" proliferation of religious activity two poles emerged. On the one hand, the sects, led, like that of Qumran, by priests and masters: they turned their backs both on the Temple and on the kingdom, and celebrated in study and piety the expectation of the messiah. On the other hand, the schools: their masters were for the time being no more than master-thinkers, writers, and teachers, who influenced the daily life of their contemporaries and the fabric of civil society. Paradoxically, the sects spread like wildfire among the Greek-speakers: their rites were learned and the teaching abolished everyday considerations. The schools, meanwhile, based themselves on the resistance of the "Syrian", that is Judaeo-Aramaic, milieu to Hellenization.

When, against a background of civil war in Jerusalem, in the 1st century, the Temple finally fell, the priesthood was suspended, and teaching of the Law by the scholars replaced sacrifice: in the shift that took place, the former priests went over to the sects and the masters of the schools replaced the Temple in the leadership of the protected community. But, against a background of nationalist uprisings and the marking out of the new imperial domain in the wars between Rome and the Parthians, sects and schools drew in no more than narrow élites, and when the Law itself, with the *Shekhina* – the "presence" that the Temple sheltered – disappeared from Jerusalem, the sects of priestly inspiration were scattered. The Judaism of the messianic and missionary sects was soon to implant itself throughout the known world.

One Judaean sect, founded by a *rabbi* from Nazareth in Galilee, ended by deliberately and radically breaking with the nationalist mould, and became Christianity, which was to retain an inveterate grudge against its Jewish origin. But when it began, it had been quite prepared to adopt any legitimist claim, making Jesus an obscure, but direct, descendant of king David, and placing his birth, in conformity with messianic prophecy, in Bethlehem, far away from his native Galilee. Saul of Tarsus, become Paul, the representative of the synthesis of priestliness and Hellenism, decided to break away. But for centuries, Jewish or proto-Jewish sects continued to profess and broadcast biblical practices and beliefs that were half way between this rupture and the ethnocentric conservatism of the great interpreters of the Law.

Another expression of religious dissidence arising out of the disintegration of the Temple-state can be found in those schools whose masters were almost all offspring of great priestly families, but who disputed the legitimacy of the administration of the Temple. *A priori,* what was at issue here was only an opposition internal to the problematic of the protected Temple-state, bearing on questions of rites, law and persons. But these exegetists, who accused the priests of tempering the Law out of profane deference to their Greek and Roman protectors, and mocking it personally, established a new form of "closed" asceticism: without leaving the world or shutting themselves away in the desert, they preached piety by example and by outdoing one another in observance. They bound themselves to obey a thousand and one prescriptions, and subjected themselves to countless taboos, the basis for which they found in the exegetical reading of the text, and one of whose main functions was to separate them from the people; not only from the Gentiles, but also from the "peoples of the land", the ignorant. They, the exegetists, were the "members" (*Haverim*) of the Association of exegetists. Commenting and translating into Aramaic the Law, the Prophets and the Scriptures, they practised a sort of scholarly and well-bred prophetism based on the never clearly expressed idea that the Temple no longer had any *raison d'être*, that the time for sacrifice was over, and that the Law alone – and, of course, its interpreters – should govern the community. It is true that the Jerusalem Talmud insisted, at this time, on the differences between artisans (Baalei ha-melakha, "masters of work") and *writers* (scribes) and officials, these latter being identified with wickedness, immorality and injustice. But this respect for workers must not be taken for what it was not: it was an internal opposition, not only within the Assembly of Israel, but within the stratum of scholars itself and, more precisely, of the independent faction of this stratum (independent, that is, of the priestly public service and its Roman protectors, but nevertheless profoundly respectful of order). Even when faced with the most corrupt and the most "anti-national" administration, one that was the basest of Roman stooges, the scholars of the Law, who were beginning to be called sages (*Hakhamim*) and rabbis (*Rabbanim*), did not question the legitimacy of the institutions articulated on the Temple and the Sanhedrin. The fact was that they belonged to the same class as their Sadducean political and theological enemies: the scribes, the sages, the rabbis, that is, the masters. One group officiated in the Temple and even in the palace of Herod and the neo-Hasmonaean kingdoms that were puppets of Rome; hated by the people, reviled by the sects, refuted by the scholars of the Law; others denounced them and took the side of the "people". It was from these strata that the figures emerged who were to save Judaism after the suicide of the rebels and the failure of nationalist messianism.

The first sages, still disarmed and with no institutional structure to serve them, had carried out a "split", whence their name Pharisees (*Perushim*) which later became synonymous with exegetists. But, from this move into a democratic form of opposition – quasi-parliamentary, combining voting in the assemblies of priestly notables and campaigns to win over opinion among the educated sectors – they ended up forming numerous poles of ideological counter-power in the community. In the context of the weakness of the Temple-state, and the lack of legitimacy of the Idumaean dynasty that the Romans had installed on the vacant throne of the Hasmonaeans, these poles were much more powerful than the prophets of Judah had been in their time. Their influence and popularity, their social rank and scholarly authority made them practically invulnerable.

In this new type of preaching the separation of power and civil morality appeared, in the form of the "private territory" (*reshuth ha-yahid*) which was close to individual morality and was the basis of the legal criticism of official society by the rabbis. Among the priestly aristocracy excluded from the exercise of power, the rabbis were thus to constitute schools which were very tribally to take the name of "Houses" and which, for the most part, were also to be dynasties: sons followed fathers in officiating.

The most famous rabbinical Houses in Roman times, contemporary with the birth of Christianity, were those of the two rival scholars, Hillel and Shammai. Tradition has it that they parted company on the issue of the recruitment of pupils. Shammai, the Rigorous, demanded for his school an absolute selectivity, in accordance with his very strict (*le-humra*) interpretation of the Law. Hillel, the Clement, considered as the ancestor of pharisaism and, beyond, of talmudic Judaism as a whole, in his school advocated the open door and the outstretched hand to any pupil anxious to learn. It is reported that when an impertinent fellow asked him point-blank to "state the whole law standing on one leg", he calmly replied: "Do not unto others that which you would not have them do unto you. That is the entire Law!" Universalism? Hillel was also the author of another aphorism, more often quoted, which says: "If I am not for me, who will be?"[17] Above all, he accepted official functions in the Temple. Later, the first hereditary rabbinical dynasty, protected by Byzantium, that of rabbi Gamaliel, his descendant, still claimed to belong to his House. Whereas Shammai saw his influence wane and his teaching taken up by the sects, among which there soon appeared authentic armed parties, such as the Sicarii (dagger men), who distinguished themselves by becoming the most violent and suicidal faction of pharisaic Judaism during the four years of civil war in Jerusalem, between 66 and 70AD, which marked the end of the Temple and the beginning of a new cycle.

The New Concordat

Legend, corroborated by Josephus, has it that the first *yeshiva,* the first rabbinical academy, was founded at Yavneh, in the coastal plain of southern Palestine, by the famous rabbi Yohanan Ben Zakkai. By agreement with the Roman besiegers, the sage had left the citadel, where the nationalist rebels had barricaded themselves up, in a coffin, abandoning them to their bloody fate, and going off "modestly" to open a school so as to perpetuate in it, with the agreement and protection of Rome, the study of the texts and the Law.

The important thing in this legend is that the rabbinism whose beginning it marks presents itself clearly as beyond the illusion of a restoration, whether of the priesthood or of the monarchy. No kingdom, and no Temple. So rabbinism was as indifferent to territorial messianic temptations as it was to the missionary tendencies of the Sadocite sects. The new Hebrew law regulated the life of the dispersed community without the support of the symbolic quasi-state that the Temple represented – in Aramaic civil society, whose language would be that of the Talmud.

The attitude of the first rabbis, whose teaching constituted the subject matter of the *mishnah*, and later of the Jerusalem Talmud, the Palestinian *tannaim* of the 1st and 2nd centuries, with respect to the armed conflict is in this respect revealing. Before leaving, Yohanan Ben Zakkai had attempted to convince his compatriots to abandon the path of suicide and negotiate a compromise. Two generations later, rabbi Akiba, who had succeeded the founder as head of the *yeshiva* at Yavneh, went off to join Bar-Kokhba's armed revolt, and the headship of the *yeshiva* reverted to the lineage of Gamaliel, the House of rabbi Hillel. They were neither "collaborators" like some priests, nor "Hellenists" like many others, nor "fanatics" (*Qannaim*) like the Zealots, neither élitists like the priests, nor populists like the revolting nationalists. Men of the middle way, in solidarity with the people in their rebellion while continuing to demonstrate the folly of it, almost to the end, the rabbis created the structures of a community organization alternative to the discredited, and then finally destroyed, Temple-state.

Everyday law from which the jurisprudence of the rabbinical tribunals was woven, after the destruction of the Temple and the opening of the Yavneh *yeshiva,* concerned the whole of the dispersed community of Israel, whose political and spiritual centre of gravity moved slowly towards Mesopotamia, where the Judaeo-Aramaic ethnic group was prospering in the shadow of the heirs of Darius. The rabbinical tribunals, schools and academies where the Law was taught and studied, the synagogue, or "house of assembly" – the place for collective reading and exegetic debate – were places that replaced the Temple, by decentralizing it, while abandoning their function of sacrifice. These were the institutional pillars of this new organization. But the new "state" too, more diffuse and more immaterial even than the old satellite-theocracy, was also guaranteed, externally, by the power of the empire in whose domain the community lived and moved, and which protected it.

This law regulated the social and economic life of the community: marriages and births, circumcisions and burials, divorces and inheritances, loans and repayments, wages and allowances, ownership of slaves and modes of renting land. It restored the image of a society that preserved its cohesion in its law and its self-segregation from among the nations. With each economic upheaval that affected the society as a whole, this law would invent a new understanding of the old law. With each political cataclysm provoked in the history of the empires, it would develop a new interpretation of the Wisdom of the Ancients. What remained was that the community drew its cohesion from its law – imperial protection, clerical leadership, ethno-tribal consciousness. The classes that crystallized despite this arrangement, and in contradiction with it – whether it be the old aristocracies or the merchants in the Middle Ages – almost never openly revolted against it to the point of abolishing it. They could choose to leave the community, but they could not take power in it without transforming themselves – declaring themselves holy and securing for themselves recognition by the spiritual authority of the priests, the scribes and the rabbis who were the repositories of the history of the people. Through the social, cultural and economic changes to which rabbinical law later adapted itself, the basic structure of the institution of rabbinical power remained the model of internal rule in the autonomous and protected community. However, the tribunals and schools, the fasts and festivals, the ceremonies and commandments, the ritual obligations and activities associated with sacrificial functions (ritual slaughter and supervision of meats), all these elements could only operate to the extent that the community, although dispersed, was not dissolved. As if repeating the "racial" obsession of Nehemiah, rabbinical law barricaded the community in its ethnic uniqueness. The preservation of the Jews as separate from the Nations became a sort of cosmic mission, a holy waiting game. And the Law became – far more than at Babylon eight or ten centuries earlier – a codification of the diaspora. "We, in any case, do not ask for what the world calls rights. All that we need is the right for the people of Israel to organize its own life, in accordance with the Law of its God."[18] Such was this rabbinical Judaism protected by the empire, that had made its eschatological compromise with the world as it is, and aspired neither to the self-sufficiency of nation states nor to dissolution in new forms of rule: retribalized and, in its adherence to the preaching of Ezra and Nehemiah, racist.

But it was not without contradictions. For a long time yet, messianism and monarchism continued to cast a shadow over this peaceful reconstruction. For their part, the sects pursued their paradoxically missionary activity outside Palestine. One of them was soon to conquer the heart of the Roman empire, from the top and from the bottom. It was the only one to have opted decisively, unambiguously, to become the Law-of-the-Gentiles. But the emergence of Christianity as a separate religion was not an event with such well-defined historical features as is generally represented: the schismatic form inherent in the way in which the new faith was disseminated is inseparable from the break-up of Judaism into sects.

Study of the Qumran manuscripts has thrown a particular light on the activities of the monastic sect known as the Essenes: some have sought to see in them the precursors of Christianity. Yet this order, with its priestly rather than scholarly character based on study and asceticism, was altogether localized within Judaism, although it is true that, being "Sadocite", it was as far removed from the Sadducean administration of the Temple as it was from the Pharisaic intelligentsia steeped in rabbinism. Significantly, one of these persecuted "Ebionite" (*Evion,* in Hebrew: poor) communities founded in Damascus a "New Covenant": "New Covenant" is also the Hebrew name for the Gospels. In fact, the Christian sects appeared in a context where Judaism was subjected to a dual movement of disintegration and reintegration. Alongside the politico-theological parties that clashed around the apparatuses of protected community rule – the Temple, its administration and the collection of its taxes, sacrifice and the priesthood, then later the Great Synagogue and the Yavneh *yeshiva* – there were all the currents that displaced the site of the Law and the faith.

Whether it was an élitist withdrawal of the pure and the just behind the walls of their rules or, on the contrary, a missionary impulse heretically offered to the pagans and the Gentiles, the logic of the ethical protest and metaphysical reflexion that animated these sects led them to "denationalize" messianism.

It was not accidental that the Judaeo-Christian sect spread rapidly among non-Jews: Greeks, Syrians, Canaanites and other "peoples of the land". Paul, alias Saul, who sent epistle after epistle to the Greeks, the Romans, the Hebrews, knew the Law: he had studied it, and lived in its shadow. But, as a Roman citizen, he also knew the world, and he chose: "There is neither Jew nor Greek, neither slave nor free man; there is neither man nor woman, for you are all one in Christ Jesus." The radical nature of this choice, at the other extreme from the nationalism of the great rabbinical schools, must be placed in the context of the transition that followed the end of the Temple. The "miserabilist" sects such as those of Qumran and Damascus testify to the multiplicity of missing links between the Judaism that drew its strength from its private ethnic law and the missionary universalism of the Christian churches. On the periphery of the ancient world known to the Jews, some of these sects were to grow through proselytism involving a calling into question of the ethno-tribal *parti pris*. They disseminated among the Gentiles a poorly codified monotheism based on the prophetic tradition, in most cases preparing the ground for Christianity and Islam. It was these sects that, in North Africa, Yemen and around the Caspian, among the Turcoman Khazars, gave rise to the aborted "Jewish kingdoms" that were to be absorbed by triumphant Islam.

Henceforth, rabbinism concerned only a core, a bastion of community life: a major part of the earlier Judaic heritage, the very part recorded in the Old Testament, moved elsewhere, into the two systems of divine law that directly emerged from it, and which henceforth, by sharing the empire of the known world of the Jews, impressed their own logics on the survival of Judaism.

The concordat of Yavneh, by which Rome had recognized Yohanan Ben Zakkai as having the right to preside over his *yeshiva*, not only involved the rabbis taking ideological control of the community: it also supposed its institutional cohesion and survival as a distinct social entity. In this respect, the behaviour of the Roman government towards the hereditary presidency (*Nessiuth*) of the Academy was quite significant: immediately after the destruction of the Temple, Yavneh became the seat of the Grand Rabbinate, the supreme body of dispersed Judaism, where transactions with the government of the empire occurred.

The master's best pupil was Akiva, who went off to join the anti-Roman guerrilla movement of the "false Messiah" Bar-Kokhba. The tradition suggests a sociological explanation for this desertion: born of "the people of the land", an illiterate, a shepherd until the age of forty, he studied the

Torah in order to be worthy of his employer's daughter, before going on to become the equal of the greatest scholars of his time. He is credited with the saying: "Do not dwell in a city, at the head of which are scholars!" (*talmidei-hakhanim,* literally: pupils of the sages) and the confession: "When I was not learned I used to say: give me a rabbi, that I may break him in pieces!"

After this episode, the hereditary presidency returned to the House of Hillel, symbolizing the continuity between the opposition of the Pharisees to the administration of the Temple and the new rabbinate. The heirs had neither the qualities nor the stature of the founders: Byzantium encouraged them to extend their administrative, fiscal and material privileges at the expense of the whole social category of sages and scholars. The Jerusalem Talmud gives enlightening indications about the struggles that the latter waged against the increased prerogatives of this central authority, judge and collector of taxes of all the Jews in the empire. There we learn that a Byzantine emperor had offered president Gamaliel IV a praetorian guard made up of... Gothic slaves! The presidency was only abolished in 429, when Gamaliel VI died without a male heir, under the twin pressure of the rabbinical class and the Christian opposition. The institution had lasted three centuries, the time of the Jerusalem Talmud. During the whole of this time it constituted, for the greater satisfaction of the Roman conquerors, what Mikhaël Avi-Yonah describes as "a factor of moderation, containing the thrust of extremist and fanatical elements."[19]

The Talmud

Gradually, there came to be an interplay between the constants and the variants in this history. The appearance of new rabbinical institutions marked a turning-point in the formation and representation of power in the community. Once again the break was denied, wrapping itself in the mantle of fidelity to the old law, but it was nevertheless a new pattern that was coming into being.

By codifying the diaspora, the new science of the Law kept up the idea of the survival of the people outside political-state forms of national existence. By making observance the basis of this survival, it not only assured the social supremacy of the rabbis; it also obscured the external origin of this internal power. By transforming the power of the dominant state into an expression of metaphysical necessity, it helped to reify the other, the non-Jew, and to crystallize a feeling of irreducible otherness between the collective Judaic "we" and all the rest of humanity as a whole – the Nations, the *Goyim.* Primitive exaltation of the tribe was here transformed into superiority, all the more compensatory because it occurred at a time of the most blatant political decline: occupation, deportation, enslavement, dispersion and persecutions. The territorialization of the Law, the Temple, had kept alive fatal messianic and military illusions of national restoration; the Romans had understood this, when they authorized the opening of synagogues at the very time when they decreed the expulsion of the Jews from Jerusalem.

No more Temple; no more *Shekhina,* divine presence, in the world. The era of prophecy was closed. Since the fall, says the Talmud, the gift of prophecy had been reserved for children and mad men. Now the time for piety, study and expectation had come.

From Palestine, when Byzantium became Christian and protection ended, the whole debate, like the community, was moved elsewhere: to Mesopotamia, which eight centuries earlier had fallen under Persian rule. And, when Persia became Muslim, the era of the compilation of the Talmud was to be considered finally ended, the second Babylonian compilation terminated and a whole new stage in the understanding of the Law begun.

Let us look at the chronology of this turning-point: rabbinism began with the Christian era. The talmudic schools flourished in Palestine until the 3rd century, before flowering in the sun of Aram of the two rivers. And the advent of Mohammed marked the end of the era. Chronologically, the Talmud codified Judaism between Jesus and Islam: first the Palestinian *tannaim*, then the Babylonian *amoraim;* then the scribes and the traditionalists – the Massoretes – codified and redacted it all, dotting the 'i's and crossing the 't's.

The compilation, which both selected and corrected, determined the limits of orthodoxy. The retroactive manner of writing the talmudic tractates transformed the contradictory rabbinical debate into a legal system. But one must be careful not to see the whole process as a linear one: the opinions of the sages written down in this way were divergent, and it is distance which made these polemics look like a system. These opinions, and the schools that supported them, in reality competed with far more numerous opponents than the tradition acknowledges: Christians, reviled by the Talmud, to whose existence reference could only be made accompanied by a host of curses; false messiahs and local prophets, and, above all, the whole range of ascetic and missionary Jewish sects which perpetuated the ancient heritage of the Rechabites and Essenes. It was precisely among the former that the greatest traditionalists were recruited – grammarians and lexicologists of the *Torah* and the Prophets – who advocated the study of the old Law and ignored its accretion of rabbinical commentaries. From the vast and changing world of these sects there emerged, in the early days of Islam, the Karaite schism.

Historians have tended to under-estimate the significance of this schism in the development of mediaeval Judaism. Yet it strikingly illustrates its hidden face. At a time when talmudic orthodoxy was formed, rabbinism was only one form among others of religious activity among Jews, both in

Palestine and in Mesopotamia. Karaism occupied a central position between the nationalist élitism of the Talmud, and the Christian break with the tribe. But, until the compilation of the Talmud was completed, Karaism did not exist: at most, there were tendencies and currents, sects and schools, that stressed the study of the *Torah* and the Prophets more than that of the scholars of the Law. These tendencies which opposed the rise of rabbinism and disputed the validity of the oral law in the very name of the written law were not then clearly distinct from the whole body of scattered Judaism. They consolidated in reaction to the growing absolutism of the Mesopotamian rabbinical academies at Sura and Pumbedita, and remained in permanent doctrinal counterpoint. Besides studying and copying the ancient Hebrew texts, in opposition to the Aramaic exegesis of the rabbis, they called for personal reading (*kria*) of the sacred text (*mikra*), which gave its name to the movement. Making reading a personal matter shortcircuited the spiritual, exegetic and legal authority of the rabbi, by a sort of Reformation *avant la lettre* in which the body of the separated community was dissolved.

Whereas rabbinism, faithful to the essence of the arrangement of Persian protection to which it had returned, united and strengthened the defences of the dispersed community, the pre-Karaite sects preached in the community and distributed ancient texts with no concern for the frontiers of the tribe. They were missionaries of a biblical prophetism simplified for the use of the Gentiles. Persecuted by the rabbis and their protectors, the missionary sects moved to the periphery: in the west as far as Tunisia, where the Berber Kahena struggling against Rome adopted their principles as its rallying point; in the south as far as Yemen, where king Dhu Nowas declared himself Jewish on the eve of the advent of Islam, persecuting, in the name of this extra-talmudic Judaism, the Christian Yemenites allied to the Coptic kingdom of Ethiopia. It is here, and not only in Christian ideology, that we must see the heritage of the implicit or explicit universalism of the prophets; and it was this mode of superficial dissemination of the foundations of the biblical tradition that accomplished the maturation of the collective ideological memory from which Islam was soon to emerge.

But the Karaite movement only structured itself as a schism, that is, as an open rebellion against the authority of the rabbis, under Islam: for Islamic prophecy itself unified the periphery of the ancient East on the basis of a universalist vision of the biblical tradition, in which the generosity of a moral message could inspire the expansion of military hegemony. Christian Rome and Umayyad Damascus were already confronting one another for the redivision of vast and distant lands of unknown Barbarians. Between these two camps and the ethnocentric conservatism of the rabbis, the domain within which the missionary sects moved narrowed dramatically. When Islam, the unequalled protector of rabbinical Judaism, installed a *gaon* – grand rabbi and supreme magistrate – over all the Jews in the caliphate, the only alternative left was revolt. And when the *gaon*

Natronai, in the 8th century, proclaimed that "whoever dares to dispute any of [his] decisions is like one who rebels against God and his Torah", the revolt that started in Baghdad inflamed the Jewish communities of Persia and Egypt, provoking the furious denunciation of the rabbis: everywhere, with the help of the Umayyad state or Christian bishops, Karaism was persecuted. In some places it merged into Christianity, in others into Islam, elsewhere it was recuperated and reintegrated in the body of talmudic Judaism, and it only survived as a marginal sect of archaeological interest, like the Samaritans clinging to their mountain at Nablus.

Rabbinical historiography, inevitably hostile to Karaism, traces its origin back to the colourful figure of Anan Ben-David. Imprisoned in Baghdad, he is said to have proclaimed himself the preacher of a new faith in order to get himself freed, building up hastily a convenient doctrine with the help of his companion in captivity, the schismatic and disputatious Muslim theologian Abu Hanifa. The legend is significant in so far as it brings together the two elements of the rabbinical accusation against the Karaites: that they mixed with non-Jews and that they disturbed public order. This was substantially the accusation once made against Jesus.

For the social order of the community as for the stability of imperial protection, the ethno-tribal cohesion of the Jews was indispensable. The missionary and universalist vocation of Karaism was perceived as a mortal threat: it amounted to the abandonment of loyalty to the group at the same time as it threatened the institutional and cosmic order that separated the Jews from others. The prophecy of Abu Issa el-Isfahani, a Persian Jew in the early days of triumphant Islam, who asked for Jesus and Mohammed to be recognized as prophets of Israel, and who is generally considered a precursor of Karaism, is a good illustration of this dilemma in that it united everyone against it, on all sides. For the talmudic system aimed at the preservation of the Jewish social entity: its law affected the Jew without touching his non-Jewish neighbour, and imposed on all the communities a single rule of life, paying no heed to the variety of environments. But this legal theory guaranteed by the (non-Jewish) empire was never transformed into an ethic of personal salvation. When it was de-territorialized, it did not replace the tribe-state by empire but by the autonomous community. This insurmountable ethnic boundary of rabbinical Judaism related to the global socio-political theory of those who possessed knowledge and authority within the community. The implicit philosophy of the Talmud, taking up the old argument of the scribes, linked the promise and election in the contract between God and his people with the renunciation of the ordinary forms of freedom. The dispersion, the condition of both rabbinical power and imperial protection, had become a virtue, albeit a negative one.

Thus, the power of the rabbis, even after the abolition of the Temple and the death penalty, was not simply the power of ideology. It affected the whole set of social, sexual, family and economic practices within the community. In the event of rebellion, the community might have recourse to exclusion. In the event of disorder, it was the empire, the "law of the kingdom" (*dina-de-malkhuta*) which, according to the talmudic saying, had the last word.

On the eve of the advent of Islam, the majority of Jews lived in Mesopotamia and southern Persia, under the protection of the Sassanid rulers: this protection, like the throne that dispensed it, had some serious shortcomings, which, for the Jews, led to riots, revolutions and massacres in the 5th and 6th centuries. The crisis, whose development can be measured in the decline of the institution of the Exilarch (*Resh-Galutha*) and the ending of the talmudic output, seemed bound to lead to schismatic breakaways. By becoming an empire on the ruins of the protecting states, Islam was to transform everything.

Notes

1. *Tractatus theologico-politicus* (The Hague, 1665); English translation by R.H.M. Elwes in *The Chief Works of Benedict de Spinoza*, 2 vols. (London, George Bech, 1882) vol. 1, p. 8.
2. "Free" translation in both cases.
3. "By the rivers of Babylon there we sat down, yea, we wept, when we remembered Zion. We hanged our harps upon the willows in the midst thereof. For there they that carried us away captive required of us mirth, saying, sing us one of the songs of Zion. How shall we sing the Lord's song in a strange land? If I forget thee, O Jerusalem, let my right hand forget her cunning. If I do not remember thee, let my tongue cleave to the roof of my mouth; if I prefer not Jerusalem above my chief joy." Psalm 137.
4. Nehemiah, XIII, 23–24.
5. The Hebrew name for Egypt, *Misrayim*, from which the Arabic *Misr* is derived, means "the straits", and also "the frontiers". It refers to the land of Goshen, the eastern edge of the Nile delta, nearest to the Sinai desert.
6. In addition to the Song of Songs and the Book of Job, Solomon is credited with the authorship of Proverbs and Ecclesiastes.
7. Mao Tse-Tung, *Combat Liberalism*.
8. This experience of the prophet physically possessed by his prophecy is analysed by André Neher in *Jérémie* (Paris, Plon, 1960).
9. Isaiah, I, 10, 11, 13, 14, 15, 21, 23.
10. Isaiah, II, 3.
11. Isaiah, I, 26.
12. Isaiah, II, 4; Hosea, II, 20; Zachariah, IX, 10; Psalm 46, 10.
13. Maccabees, I, 14, 15.
14. Especially to the Spartan model. See Pierre Vidal-Naquet's work, especially his preface to Josephus' *Guerre des Juifs* (Paris, Editions de Minuit, 1977), and the historical essay on this period in the collection, *Les Juifs, la mémoire et le présent* (Paris, Maspéro, 1981). See also Elias Bickerman, *From Ezra to the Last of the Maccabees – Foundations of Postbiblical Judaism* (New York, Schocken Books,

1947), and the article by Morton Smith, "Palestinian Judaism from Alexander to Pompey", in Pierre Grimal (ed.) *Hellenism and the Rise of Rome* (London, Weidenfeld and Nicolson, 1968).

15. Maxime Rodinson, "From the Jewish Nation to the Jewish Problem"; see note 1, chapter one in present work.

16. André Neher, *L'existence juive* (Paris, Editions du Seuil, 1962) p. 147.

17. The saying thus reported is incomplete, as Léon Poliakov rightly stresses in *Le Nouvel Observateur*, 25 May 1981. But Poliakov launches an unfounded attack on Maxime Rodinson when he accuses him of having "grossly cut" the talmudic quotation for the sole purpose of making it express more national egotism than it contains. First, because Rodinson only reported the aphorism by citing Pinsker, the Zionist theorist of the last century: it is Pinsker, who wanted to enclose Hillel in nationalism, not Rodinson. Furthermore, because the translation given by Poliakov of the phrase missing in Pinsker (and in Rodinson) – "And if I am only for myself, who then am I?" – is closer to exegesis than to literal translation – "And me, by myself, who am I?" – Maxime Rodinson explained all this himself in *Le Nouvel Observateur*, 27 June 1981.

18. Martin Buber, *For the Sake of Heaven. A Chronicle* (New York, Atheneum, 1969).

19. Mikhaël Avi-Yonah, *Biyemei Roma ou-Byzantion – Ha-historia ha yehudith shel Yehudei Erets-Israel lemin mered Bar-Kokhva vead reshith ha-kibbush ha-aravi* (Jerusalem, Mossad Bialik); English translation: *The Jews of Palestine. A Political History from the Bar-Khokhba War to the Arab Conquest* (Oxford, Basil Blackwell, 1971).

3 The Domain

A world was about to die, deprived of its centre by the advent of a new domain. For the ancient East, where, at the end of the 6th century, the Christian era resembled a final episode, history held its breath as Year Zero approached. We can sketch out the uncertain outlines of this new birth.

First, its geography: from the far West (*al-Maghrib al-Aqsa*) to the Afghan borders of China; from the Caucasus to Ethiopia; from the marches of India to Sicily. Before the curtain rises, two empires of unequal power are disputing this world domain: Byzantium, eastern Rome, with, behind it, western Rome and the new Christian kingdoms of Europe; and confronting this vast and divided world, Zoroastrian Persia, the heir of Cyrus, the last imperial avatar of that cycle of pre-Hellenistic civilizations with which the name of Babylon had been associated. Behind it, an inexhaustible reservoir of "Turkish" peoples: when Islam broke through this rampart, the grandchildren of the builders of Peking would come and camp before Damascus.

Two superpowers, we would say today. Each with its discourse, its ideology: its religion. The military balance of forces which enabled the Persians to repel Byzantine incursions, and even to make a few advances here and there, is misleading: the Persians were at the end of their tether. But Byzantine was weakened by its own division, torn by the permanent sedition of the Eastern Churches against the Latin yoke.

In the clash of the two empires, the desert separating Palestine from Mesopotamia became a frontier secured by the military presence of the Lakhmid and Ghassanid tribes: the former, Nestorians, served Persia; the latter, Jacobites, patrolled the desert for the Byzantines. This wall had a vital function: to close off the Arabian peninsular by holding the northern desert and thereby prevent the penetration of Arab tribes into the territory of the two empires.

There was nothing natural about the enclosure of the Arabs in the desert of Arabia. It interrupted and cut across very ancient lines of communication, which had made camel-rearers the natural navigators of the sandy oceans. They knew not only the urban islands scattered over it but also the civilizations whose shores it bathed: they were sailors, not fishes. Since earliest antiquity, the desert, bounded on the south by the fertility of

Yemen, had poured over the fertile valleys of the north – the Nile, the Jordan, the Tigris and the Euphrates – numerous waves of migration that had been absorbed one after the other by cities and empires. The most recent of these waves was Nabataean, but the ancient settlement of the Israelite tribes in the land of Canaan itself can be considered as one of those demographic alluvia deposited by the desert on the valleys of the Fertile Crescent. The peoples already rooted in the region before them spoke languages related to theirs, and the frontier was less an ethnic one than a social one, between the city-dwellers or agriculturalists of kingdoms and the free men of the tribes.

The linguistic structure of the region reproduced this stratification: Latin among the Catholics, Greek among the Orthodox, Syriac (Aramaic) among the Eastern Christians, the Jews and the ancient populations of Mesopotamia today dominated by Farsi-speaking dynasties. Aramaic, the "Babylonian" language that had given Hebrew its alphabet and in which the Talmuds had been compiled, had already for centuries been the *lingua franca* of the whole civilized East, that is, that part of it subject to the established authorities in the cities. It was a language half-way between the truly foreign languages of the empires (Persian, Greek, Latin) and the localized popular dialects, related in system and structure to Aramaic, which included the idioms which came together to develop into Arabic.

Writing, in Arabic, in the 12th century, the Jewish philosopher Musa Ibn Maimun, rabbi Moshe Ben Maimon, whom the Christians call Maimonides, justified himself thus: "Anyone who knows the three languages – Hebrew, Aramaic and Arabic – knows that they are only three branches of one and the same language." But there were other languages as well. The Nabataeans, for example, were Arabs who, by settling in the Negev and the Jordanian desert at the time of the Roman conquest, created a remarkable agricultural and urban civilization, and one that was altogether Hellenistic in its urbanism which flourished for nearly two hundred years. The pagan Nabataeans became Jacobite Christians, and the word *Nabati*, in Arabic, came to describe by extension any peasant in the Middle East speaking Aramaic. Aramaic was not only a language; it was also a socio-political level of regional communication. One moved from a localized tribal dialect to Aramaic as one moved from one area of civilization to another: from the primitive anarchy of the clans and their relative mobility between territories, to the territorialization of sovereignty and subjection to the urban order. All the ancient languages of this region – Phoenician, the languages of Canaan, Hebrew, Aramaic, Arabic – belong to the same family. The common linguistic structure of the region, which is evidence of ancient contact if not of unity, makes it easier to understand the speed and depth of the Arabization that was to follow the establishment of the Islamic state.

This linguistic unity is not evidence of ethnic unity. It was, on the contrary, the result of contact, mixing, exchange and acculturation. It did not form the basis of any racial unity other than that which made all the populations of the Middle East, in varying degrees, the result of ancient and continuous mixings. Neither genealogical myths, on whose credibility the Bible provides some striking evidence, nor the linguistic crytallizations that emerged from this common base, give any credence to the idea that these populations or the nations of this cultural area constituted a race. Yet, the diffusion of biblical, Judaeo-Christian and Christian beliefs had popularized throughout the Aramaic domain – that is, among the Gentiles of the ancient "Semitic" world – the legendary genealogy of peoples and human families contained in the *Torah*. Christianity, the heir in its way of the Old Testament, had taken over and enlarged the audience of this ethnographic saga marked by several centuries of Judaean partisanship. The missionary sects based their explanation of the world on this science of the past and the origins of nations, just as the rabbinical Jewish communities saw in it the basis of their peculiar destiny. Moreover, many of these biblical genealogical and historical myths projected by the messianic outburst of Judaism to the four corners of the Aramaic periphery themselves integrated features of traditional knowledge borrowed from other civilizations: from Egypt, and above all from Assyria at the time of the epic of Gilgamesh, but also from the Persians and others. Indeed, in the oral exchange and the non-institutionalized transmission of opinions and beliefs disseminated in the domain of imperial disintegration, the common "Semitic" origin of the peoples of the region faced with Persian and Greek foreigners was accepted as self-evident. The Latin-speakers saw in them alternatively Syrians or Arabs, depending on whether they were city-dwellers and merchants, or nomads and warriors. The peoples themselves gradually absorbed an ethnic genealogy that peddled the assumptions and vocabulary of altogether forgotten cleavages: they gradually learned to think they remembered what they had been told. Just as the ancient Hebrews had borrowed their founding patriarchs from the common myths of their Canaanite cousins, so the masses who nomadized between urban serfdom and the independent poverty of the desert saw, in the Christians and Jews, in the hermits and missionary preachers, Abraham's family album. And, as they looked at each of the pictures, they were told: "You see, the little one, there on the left, that's you!"

In the meanwhile, the closing of the two empires to the free movement and sedentarization of the Arab tribes, now bottled up in the peninsula, was to precipitate the Arab-Islamic explosion of the 7th century: from this third world arose, borne by a popular legitimacy previously unknown in the history of states, the concrete force that was to sweep away both Persia and Byzantium. One must picture this international problematic: the encirclement of Arabia by Christian states, the interplay of two blocs, the internal division of Byzantium, the Persian empire and its protected Judaism, and the missionary sects on the fringes of the desert.

There are no precise statistics about the number of Jews dispersed in the Arabian peninsula. Surrounded by regions that had known strong concentrations of Jewish population or influences, Arabia was subject to

Jewish and Christian influences which were contradictory in their claims, but claimed the same credentials. It seems that the major Jewish centre of Khaybar, in the north of the Hejaz, was established by refugees fleeing the massacres in Persia during the reign of Kawwaz. In any event, the presence of Jews in central and northern Arabia is attested to in several places and at several periods before the appearance of Islam, notably at Yathrib, which the Jews called, in Aramaic, *Medinta*, "the City", and which was to become the "City of the Prophet", Medina.

In his biography of the Prophet, Mohammed Essad bey writes:

> Legends tell us that the Amalekites came from the North, and that their chief Yathrib, discovered a few water sources there and built a number of clay huts to which he gave his name. The legendary Amalekites were followed by the Jews, who settled in the country in order to carry on trade in the wild, bare deserts. In ancient days, three Jewish tribes ruled over Yathrib: the Banu Nadir, the Banu Qainuqar and the Banu Quraizah. The tribes waged war, rivalled one another and did not differ very much from the heathen tribes of the country.

Different or not, we know that these Jewish tribes occupied a dominant position at Yathrib, and that they were more or less the owners of the palm plantations cultivated by the tribes of Yemenite immigrants with whom infant Islam was to ally. These tribes already struggling against the Jews of Medina to seize their hegemony over the city were to involve Islam, almost from its birth, in an ambiguous conflict with the Jews of Medina and, through them, with Judaism.

When the core of Islamic doctrine was being developed at Mecca, with Mohammed Ibn Abd Abdallah, Ibn Abd al-Muttalib and Ibn Hashem, the Koreishite, the new doctrine proudly claimed its Judaeo-Christian descent. The prophet and the earliest Muslims prayed facing Jerusalem. It was to Jerusalem that the Messenger of God was transported in a dream, and it was from there that he began his mystical ascent. For the Islam of the Revelation, the truth formed an unbroken chain from Abraham to Moses, from David to Nehemiah and from Jesus to Mohammed, the seal of the prophets and the confirmation of previous prophecies:

> And the Jews say the Christians follow nothing (true), and the Christians say the Jews follow nothing (true); yet both are readers of the Scripture. Even thus speak those who know not. Allah will judge between them on the Day of Resurrection concerning wherein they differ. . . . And they say: Be Jews or Christians, then you will be rightly guided. Say: Nay, but (we follow) the religion of Abraham, the upright, and he was not of the idolaters.

The next verse provides the key to this Abrahamic orthodoxy running through the Word of the Koran:

> Say: We believe in Allah and that which is revealed unto us and that which was revealed unto Abraham, and Ishmael, and Isaac, and Jacob, and the tribes, and that which Moses and Jesus received, and that which the Prophets received from their Lord. We make no distinction between any of them, and unto Him we have surrendered.[1]

It was not just a matter of simply, and ecumenically, lumping together all the stages of the prophecies, Israelite, Jewish and Christian, by declaring them all valid and identical in substance, despite the aberrant quarrels between Jews and Christians. God, here, through the word of His Messenger, re-established the biblical genealogy and restored Ishmael, Abraham's eldest son, to the first place in the prophetic chain: the eldest son, the first heir to the "testament of God", the chosen repository of the Revelation and the Covenant. This claim, and the version of the facts that underpin it, are crucial.

In Genesis, Ishmael, whom the Israelite tradition identified as the "ancestor of the Arabs", and of whom pre-Islamic Arabia seems to have been entirely ignorant,[2] was the eldest son of Abraham by his wife's Egyptian maidservant. However, the whole story of Hagar and Ishmael in the biblical account makes many admissions: that the patriarch is common to very many peoples moving about in this area for millenia and that the hereditary Covenant did not concern only the Israelite tribes; that God made a special covenant with Hagar and her son Ishmael, in which the submission to Sarah had to be rewarded, since the Lord was to make of the descendants of Ishmael, "a countless nation" and of Abraham himself the father of a "multitude of nations".

The word of the Koran denies the disinheriting fable suggested by the submission of the Egyptian maid to the "lady" who Abraham had brought from her native Chaldaea. It simply re-establishes the natural order and the right of the first-born. The text thus illuminates a basic aspect of the Islamic attitude towards the earlier Jewish and Christian revelations: the affirmation of the divine truth that they contain and the serene refutation of their partisan formulations. The core of concordant authenticity in this unitary "Abrahamism" of Islam concerns not only ethics and metaphysics, or the organizational principles of the City of God: it also concerns a certain, profoundly biblical, conception of the history of the empires and peoples of the region, a conception that was itself rooted in the philosophical tribalism of the nomadic clans. By tirelessly correcting Christian and Jewish "errors" and "falsifications", Islam confirms the very substance of the Israelite story, the law of Moses and the prophetic books; especially, the "favours that God bestowed on the children of Israel" at the time of their piety, from Moses to David and Ezra; especially the promise tucked away in Genesis to make the Ishmaelites – that is, the Arabs, according to the definition given by the Jews and, following them, the Christians – a great nation. Thus, the Jewish myth of the Ishmaelite origin of the Arabs became, with Islam, the myth of the Arabs themselves. The Word of God made this myth its own foundation, it wanted no other, and claimed no other heritage than that of Abraham and Ishmael, and the ethnic cousinship with those famous, fallen aristocrats, the Jews. Poor relations in Jewish tradition which knew them only as Ishmaelites, the Arabs who submitted themselves to the divine Law – the *Muslimun* – insisted on the kinship, in the name of which they were to abolish the poverty. Islam here discovered the articulation of Israelite tribalism and the Hellenized multinationalism of the Christians, and reconstituted its own genealogical tree of the Covenant; the contract made, on an individual basis, with Abraham because of his solitary justice, renewed with his descendants and accomplished in the kingdom of David and the temple of Solomon, had, as the Jews themselves recognized in all their scriptures, been cancelled by God on the grounds of unilateral breach and corruption of the Law. A new Jewish prophet, Jesus, then arose to extend the Covenant to the whole of humanity. But Rome and the Churches had distorted his message, and the Ishmaelites, like millions of men, continued to live in idolatry and ignorance of the true Law. God had then chosen Mohammed, an Ishmaelite descendant of Abraham, a cousin of the Jews, to proclaim the City of God to all the Infidels.

That is, to the pagans; not to the Jews or the Christians. As "Peoples of the Book" (*Ahl al-Kitab*), these latter were recognized and respected, protected in their faith and their worship, confirmed in their identity and even in their claim to the privilege of age. Hearing a quarrel between Aisha and Saffiyah, his eleventh wife, whom he had brought back from an expedition against a Jewish tribe, the Messenger said: "Saffiyah, say to this woman 'My father's name was Aaron, my uncle was Moses, and who were your fathers? Heathens!' "[3]

Such was the respect that the Islamic Revelation showed to Judaism and its claims – in theory, that is before the "taking of power", *a priori*, that is at Mecca, where there were neither Christians nor Jews, except perhaps scattered in the crowd of pilgrims who supplied the sacred tourist industry of the Kaaba. But the first Islamic state was to be built at Medina, where precisely the Jews were numerous and powerful, and were actively to oppose the rise of Islam.

At Medina the core of a major contradiction in the formation of the Islamic order came into being: the new Law clashed with well-defined and localized Jewish groups, not on the ground of theology, but on that of politics, that is of armed tribal alliances. It had to put its declared Judaeo-philia to the rude test of Medinan civil wars. The first *sahifa* regulating the relations between the Meccan emigrés and the five Medinan tribes (three of which were Jewish) is evidence of these favourable dispositions: the Jews are mentioned by name in it as an integral part of the "community of Believers", that is the Islamic social order. No restrictions were imposed on their citizenship: the Jewish tribes were armed and expected to contribute on a footing of equality to the armed defence of the community.

It seems that the Prophet must have believed that the Jews of Medina would recognize Mohammed's revelation as "Abrahamic" proselytism, and that they would accept Muslim rule over the town. He was to be rapidly disabused, and soon promulgated a whole succession of measures against the Jewish tribes of Medina – but never against Judaism itself. In the wars that followed, the three Jewish tribes of Medina, one after the other, lost everything: two of them, in turn, took the road into exile, leaving behind their property and their lands. All the men in the last one were beheaded, after the defeat of their coalition with the Meccans, preferring death to submission.

The Koran and the Tradition of the Prophet, his Sayings (*Hadith*), show this evolution. In the beginning, the war was strictly ideological: it was a battle for minds. The Jewish poets railed against the Prophet of Islam. This latter then had a few of them killed; or, if one prefers, some of his most zealous supporters avenged his sullied honour in the blood of the satirists. Then, after a minor incident in the market, a Muslim killed a Jew: a fight followed, in which a Muslim died. The Jews involved were, exclusively Qainoqas: artisans, goldsmiths and blacksmiths – the weakest of the Jewish tribes in the city. The Muslims laid siege to their fortress, and the defeated survivors took the road to Khaybar. Then a complicated series of events began, in which the Meccan merchants in coalition against Mohammed, the two Jewish tribes remaining in Medina, the Sceptics (*Monafikun*) among the Aws Yemenites in Yathrib, and the Qainoqa and later Nadir exiles who had taken refuge among the Jews in Khaybar, failed in each of their attempts to prevent the establishment and strengthening of the Muslim state. The Prophet waged the struggle on every front and, as befits a statesman, he hesitated before nothing: king David himself, whom Muslim tradition made into a prophet, had not hesitated, in the intrigues surrounding his climb to power, to conspire and assassinate his opponents. Right from the time of the first great pitched battles between the Koreishite armies and the supporters of Islam who had withdrawn into Medina, the fighting was bitter, and the Medinan opponents who had close links with the enemy were accused, often justly, of collusion with them.

The property confiscated from the expelled Jews was distributed to the emigrés, and – with one exception – only to the emigrés, putting an end to the economic dependence of Mohammed's adherents on the Medinans, that is on the Aws and Khazraj Yemenites. Legislation was drawn up to deal with the Jewish opposition. The decisive point was the ban on Jews taking part in the battle of Ohod, which excluded them from the Medinan army and revoked the original undertaking of the *cahifa*: it formed the basis of later Islamic legislation on the fundamentally disarmed status of the *dhimmis*, the Protected ones. As they moved from plot to defeat, and from hesitation to failed *coup d'état*, the Jews were expelled or killed, until not one remained in the city of the Prophet. The survivors of the tribe of the Quraizah (except the women and children, reduced to slavery) were massacred; executed in front of a great ditch at the entrance to the city, Ali himself cutting off the heads.

One may wonder about the reasons for this bloody separation. But one thing is certain: it did not arise from a theological dispute with Judaism by Islam. Quite the contrary, it could be said, for it is quite clear that, in the eyes of the Prophet, it was not Judaism that he was fighting by exterminating his Jewish enemies in Medina, but pagan resistance to the practical Law of the State of Believers. Islam in no way aspired to convert

Judaism. When they arrived in Medina, the emigrés had adopted a whole series of Jewish customs and behaviours: they adopted Jewish-style headdress, which was not that of the people of Mecca; they prayed facing Jerusalem and they obeyed a simplified version of Jewish dietary laws. However, some of these measures were revoked as the Medinan conflict got worse.

While the murderous intransigence of the young Islamic state does not explain the opposition of the Jews, it did make it irreversible. Yet, at no time in these successive wars against the Jewish tribes of Medina had the Prophet fought against either the Jewish faith, or against the three tribes at once. And, conversely, what is perhaps even more noteworthy is that at no time did the Jews of Medina wage their struggle either in the name of their faith, or in a united front.

Certainly, the Jews of Medina resisted Mohammed's claims to prophetic orthodoxy: ignorant of the letter of the Hebrew scriptures, the Messenger did not formulate his messages according to the codified rules and axioms of literal biblical scholarship. There can be no doubt that

> the Jewish intellectuals [of Medina] were extremely unwilling to endorse the validity of the revelation received by Muhammed. It was to them, as the repositories of the ancient scriptures, that people turned for a verdict on this new message and whether it conformed to the criteria of divine inspiration accepted by experts. Even if they had been well disposed towards the new movement, it was not easy for them to sanction what in their view were the incoherent ramblings of an illiterate...[4]

It is true indeed that the wording of the Koran introduced significant modifications into the biblical story, and, just like the Judaean scribes in the past, manipulated the contradictory features of memory and tradition by subjecting them to its distorting tendencies.

Perhaps another motive for reticence should be added: the precedent of Christianity and generally rabbinical Judaism's hatred of the missionary sects. The Judaeo-messianic language of Islam was bound to remind Jews of the misfortunes that had befallen them from the fact that the Christians claimed to mobilize their own scriptures against them. In this respect, the respectful non-interference of the pagans in the Jews' internal theological affairs was vastly preferable to the declared hostility of the Christians towards the law of Moses. However far removed they may have been from the Persian centre of rabbinical Judaism, the Jews of Medina and Khaybar were not unaware of the *de facto* alignment of the Jews and Persia against Byzantium. The Jewish tribes in the Hejaz might have had absolutely no perception of the regional alliances underpinning the survival of rabbinism, but it is not unreasonable to suppose that the global sympathies of the city-dwelling diaspora of the East also influenced their behaviour.

Yet, the confrontation in Medina in no way and at no time involved this diaspora, which would have continued to be unaware of it if the historiography of Islam had not made it into an event of cosmic dimensions. The massacres of 600 or 900 Jews of the Quraizah tribe is not listed in the rabbinical Jewish memory. The fact is that these killings, despite their appearance of martyrdom for the faith (strengthened by the image of those about to die preferring death to conversion), was part and parcel of an implacable law of tribal warfare: the war waged among the five Medinan clans, in fluctuating alliances with the power of the emigrés, was no exception. Mohammed's skill consisted precisely, after his withdrawal from the inter-clan rivalry in Mecca, in intervening in the unstable balance of the clans of Yathrib in order to subdue it and dominate it without ever becoming its prisoner. The fundamental importance of this clan functioning explains the initial alliance of the Khazrajites and the Muslims: did they not aspire to overthrow the power exercised over the city by the coalition of the Aws, who were Yemenite and pagan, and the Nadir, who were Arab and Jewish? It also explains the silence of the Nadir and the Quraizah at the time of the war against the Qainoqa and their expulsion: and the silence of the Quraizah at the time of the expulsion of the Nadir. It explains why the "sceptical" Aws chiefs fought to defend their Jewish allies.

This absolute integration of the Jewish tribes of Medina can be seen in another striking lacuna: in the story, there is no visible trace whatsoever of rabbinism within the Jewish society of Medina. Nothing in the lives of these warrior tribes suggests the existence or action of any particular Law: no synagogue, no assembly, no school, no rabbinate. They were armed clans, landowners with their strongholds, and their own clients: sovereign. Does this indicate the powerlessness, or the failure of rabbinism in this desert periphery where there was no imperial protection to guarantee the authority of the scholars of the Law? The Jews of Medina do not even appear to have been concerned about physical separation from the Gentiles: Kaab Ibn el-Ashraf, the murdered Jewish poet, was only Nadir, and hence "Jewish", through his mother. And, like the pagan poetess, also killed, Asma Bint Marwan, it was in Mecca where he had gone to make an alliance with the Koreishites, that he recited his odes against Mohammed: not to defend the law of Moses against falsifications nor to refute Islam in terms of bibilical theology, but to encourage the pagan troops of Abu Suffyan Ibn Harb, who later became the first Umayyad. Both what is recorded and what is not mentioned are at one in portraying a lightly worn if not formal Judaism, which did not make its believers stand out in their social practice. Were the Jews of Medina Bedouin formerly converted to Judaism, or former Jewish settlers who had come from Persia or Palestine? What we do know is that the three Jewish tribes and the two others that had come from Yemen "warred with one another regardless of religion. Jews fought Jews; Arabs fought Arabs. Jews allied themselves with Arabs to fight other Jews".[5]

It was in order to preserve their integrated and dominant position in this system that the Jewish tribes of Medina had opposed the party of

Mohammed and the Muslim state, not to defend a faith that no one was threatening, nor to preserve a community autonomy that had no *raison d'être*, in a place where the state did not exist and the clan was sovereign. In other words, the hostility of the Jews of Medina derived from their view of their secular political interests. By disarming and exiling them, Islam separated them, uprooted them from this tribal integration, and in many ways forced them back on Judaism, and delivered them over to rabbinism and Protection.

At the level of its own theory, Islam evolved between the extreme poles of the first charter and the campaigns against the Jews of Medina. The spirit of the *dhimma*, or Protection, which codified the rights and duties of the Peoples of the Book in the Muslim city, was inspired by the spontaneous Judaeo-philia of the Prophet, but its formulations reflected the Medina experience – particularly on the subject of the bearing of arms, where the exemption almost everywhere became a prohibition.

Significantly, it was in Jerusalem that one of the versions of the Ordinance of Omar gave concrete shape to one of the most flagrant failures to live up to the spirit of this protection. Jerusalem had fallen into the hands of Omar without a fight: the Eastern Christians, weary of the Byzantine persecutions, opened the gates of the city to the armies of Islam. Muslim tradition relates proudly that the caliph Omar refused to pray before the Holy Sepulchre, so as not to provide Muslims with an excuse, "after his death", to construct a mosque on the site of the church – thus showing admirable tolerance. However, this alliance had been negotiated and the Christians had set a condition *sine qua non* for their acquiescence: that the Jews not be permitted to return to Jerusalem. And the caliph had yielded.

But law, statutes, conventions, principles and verses are one thing: the actual practice of societies and of individuals in societies is another. Throughout the history of the Muslim world, the position of the Jews would vary – sometimes along with that of the Christians, sometimes separately. The basic tolerance implied by Protection would never be denied in theory; it would, on more than one occasion, be nullified in practice. It would often, over long periods, be overtaken by *de facto* tolerance and liberalism that were even less restrictive than the strict application of Koranic law on the subject. In any case, the Muslim supporters of this or that policy would be able to find, in the various episodes of the life and preaching of the Prophet, justifications and examples, sometimes of severity, sometimes of clemency. On each occasion, it is possible to trace the origin of these choices and see in them the action of social, economic and political factors.

Shortly after the stabilization of Islamic power in the largest empire that had ever existed up to that time, the Abbassid revolution inaugurated a period of exceptional clemency: in three centuries, this golden age was to transform the face of Judaism completely.

Andalusia: The Golden Age

> With the great Arab conquests following the rise of Islam, which converted all
> the countries between Spain and Persia into a single territory dominated by the
> new religion, and soon after by the Arabic language as well, the majority of the
> Jewish people of that time came under Arab rule. Thus began the long and great
> period of Jewish-Arab symbiosis... At the time of the Muslim-Arab conquest,
> the majority of the Jews were still engaged in agriculture and manual labour...
> The Jewish people, too, more or less, disappeared as an agricultural people
> during the seventh and eighth centuries, but, unlike other ancient populations,
> returned to life as a nation of merchants and artisans. This transformation was
> due to the great "bourgeois revolution" of the ninth century (which has not yet
> been sufficiently investigated[6]). Due to this revolution, the civilization of the
> Middle East during early mediaeval times was characterized by its commerce,
> industry and bureaucratic organization, at a time when western Europe was
> mainly agricultural and was dominated by knights and feudal lords. The Jews
> took their full share in this great Middle-Eastern mercantile civilization, in
> particular from the tenth to the thirteenth centuries; and it was at that time and
> in that part of the world that Judaism itself received its final shape.[7]

With this revolution which abolished, in practice, the restrictions placed on
the free movement of Jews in the geographical and social domain of the
new civilization, the Jewish communities of the Muslim world were to be
transformed and to flourish.

In the first place, they were confirmed by the Islamic state, both in their
confessional identity and in their unity. The state recognized the Jews, but
it recognized only one sort: there was to be no more sectarian
disintegration, no more dissident movements and prophetism. By
restoring, alongside the declining institution of the exilarch, the absolute
authority of the *gaon*, the caliphs imposed on all Jews the centralized
authority of a single rabbinate, mercilessly persecuting the missionary
heresies and Karaite counter-authorities. After this, there was no leaving
Judaism, not even to join Islam: while conversion was permitted, it was not
encouraged. There was no doctrinal imperative to convert the Peoples of
the Book to Islam and it deprived the state of the *jizya*, the tax that the
dhimmis paid in exchange for their exemption from the armed service of the
community. In Egypt, Syria and Iraq, where Jews and Christians
constituted a large part of the owning classes in the towns, the state had an
interest in preserving these considerable sources of fiscal revenues. But the
Islamic state equally banned the Peoples of the Book from engaging in any
missionary activity: there was no leaving Judaism, but there was no
entering it either. A diaspora that was in the process of losing its identity,
under the contradictory pressures of schisms and conversions, found itself
at the end of this process consolidated and redefined, structured and
guaranteed.

Next, the very geography of the Jewish dispersion was modified.

Concentrated in the far east of the old Egyptian-Babylonian world, the Jews followed the armies of Islam as far as the new West and remote Spain. Free in their movements and linked to one another by the unity of the Muslim world, the most remote communities entered into the common orbit, borne along by the current. While Islamic law homogenized them and enclosed them in their institutionalized tribal-confessional identity, these communities moved massively westward.

This resituating of the diaspora in the Islamic domain displaced the centre of gravity of Judaism from the frontiers of Persia to the western Mediterranean, that is, at the gates of the Christian West still plunged in pre-capitalist darkness. But this migration, which pointed the Jews towards a different history, was not based on the internal social or ideological logic of Judaism. It was neither the departure from Egypt nor the return to Zion, nor the expulsion from Jerusalem nor the conquest of the Promised Land. The migration westward proceeded from the general movement of society which was being structured on the frontiers of the caliphate: from the same movement that brought the Yemenite ancestors of Ibn Khaldun to Tunisia, with their artisanal populations of Jews and Christians. No doubt the capacity of these communities – institutionalized by rabbinical law – to maintain their social cohesion while moving within a domain where sovereignty belonged to the Other, made them highly receptive to this movement, probably more so than the Eastern Christian communities.

Goitein[8] has summarized the social transformation that accompanied this double movement, institutional and spatial, of talmudic Judaism and its ill-defined periphery towards the new Muslim world. The stability of agrarian relations which the Babylonian *Amora'im* of the 4th century had ruled on in their rabbinical tractates had long since given way to the insecurity born of the repeated convulsions that marked the end of the Sassanid empire, punctuated by riots and uprisings, revolts and invasions, wars and *coups d'état*. Jewish communities had fled as far as Arabia to get away from the upheavals of the confrontation between Rome and Persia. In Syria and Egypt, hated by the Greek Christians, protected, but only half-heartedly, by Byzantium, Jewish communities survived interspersed by Karaite sects more powerful in their midst than the rabbis of far-off Babel. In this dispersion, the land base which still underpinned the Law in Palestine and Mesopotamia – symbolized by the persistent reference in property and purely commercial contracts, at the end of the talmudic period on the eve of Islam, to plots of land situated, fictionally, in Palestine – was breaking up. So that by the 6th century the Jews were peasants, workers, slaves, slave owners, artisans, officials, bandits, merchants, judges and rabbis, doctors and ministers of pagan states, landowners and tenants, but above all ... soldiers: mere mercenaries or military officials of the Persian empire, and even in the armies of Christian states.

The Muslim state had confiscated the lands and weapons of Jews while undertaking to protect them as clerics, merchants or artisans. Tying the Islamized and later Arabized peasantry, to the land, it broke the last links attaching the Jews of Palestine and Mesopotamia to the world of agricultural production. By inaugurating the era of trading relations and commercial and banking activities, the Abbassid revolution opened the doors of secular power to the minorities. Thus, the expulsion of the Jews from their social positions took place upwards, towards the dominant society: towards the mercantile, manufacturing or intellectual bourgeoisie of the towns. This freely accepted displacement in social space was also, often, a migration, a conquest of the west: the Islamic state in the west was not, as it was in the east, tied down by old social relationships. Here, there was no charter, no local élite lukewarmly rallied in order to conserve its power, no heritage to constrain the Utopia. Islamized indigenes and emigrants formed together – as in Medina, but on an infinitely larger scale – the City. And here, unlike in Medina, the Jews played a particular role, the one that rabbinical Judaism claimed for them: disarmed and protected, "a people of priests" devoted to the study of its Law with no secular ambition, at the same time as being the real and prosperous ally of the imperial order. Hence, carried along by the general trend, the Jews became artisans and merchants, poets, doctors, bankers and philosophers, scholars and officials, courtiers and mystics. No doubt this transformation did not affect the most rural and peripheral communities, but it brought the Jews of the towns into contact with those caught in the wave of westward migration.

Contrary to what was soon to happen in Christian Europe, no stigma attached to this socio-professional specialization of Jews, in a society which remembered that Mohammed himself was a merchant. Far from setting the Jew apart, trade was the preferred ground of communication. The fact was that mediaeval Islamic society was not only the heir of Medina: it was also – as it was accused of being from the earliest days of Islam by the partisans (*Shi'ites*) of Ali, and by all the reformist movements in Islam, using various languages – the heir to the pre-Islamic Meccan society, whose patrons had become the champions of the prophecy that they had initially strongly opposed. This was the Mecca, where, in the court of the Kaaba, before Mohammed came and upset everything, every possible idol co-existed in the shadow of the stone sent to Abraham to guide him in his wandering. Pre-Islamic Mecca where, provided that business was good, "religion had nothing to say".

These physical transformations were accompanied by a complete cultural mutation, both linguistic and religious. The Jews of the Mediterranean who spoke Greek, Aramaic, Punic (that is, the Canaanite of Phoenicia, spoken from Tyre to Carthage) and even Latin, would henceforth all speak Arabic: "Arabic itself became a Jewish language and, unlike Latin in Europe, was employed by Jews for all secular and religious purposes, with the sole exemption of the synagogue service."[9] This Arabization ran deep: there was no Judeao-Arabic patois in areas where the Arabization of the Muslims themselves was consummated, but, on the contrary, a mastery of the language, and its peculiar logic and sensitivity, which produced a vast Jewish literature in Arabic between the 10th and 14th centuries.

Linguistic integration laid the ground for a vital intellectual osmosis: Muslims and Jews, from Spain to Iraq, were to join together in the discovery, study, imitation, defence and illustration of Hellenistic philosophy, Platonic and neo-Platonic, Aristotelian and neo-Aristotelian, in what Franz Rosenthal rightly called "the classical heritage in Islam".[10] The enthusiasm for dialectical reason created a new science of ideology called theology, designed to make Law and philosophy coincide: to rationalize the divine Revelation and so show that it was at one with logic and the natural order. Whatever their confession, the new social classes that grew up in the light of the bourgeois revolution in mediaeval Islam discovered the world from an unexpected angle, and they turned naturally to the Greek heritage to answer their quest for rationality. Ibn Sinna (Avicenna), Ibn Rushd (Averroes), al-Farabi... Hundreds of philosophers and translators, theologians and commentators, historians and geographers, mathematicians and linguists, doctors and jurists, poets and mystics... all arguing for several hundred years with Moses and Plato, Aristotle and Jesus, Mohammed and Socrates, and with one another... One has only to read any of the great works of this time to be struck by the astonishing freedom of movement of ideas that these texts imply, and amazed by their unbelievable modernity.

The Jews participated like the others in this rationalist flowering. Maxime Rodinson cites[11] the story reported by an Arab author and mentioned by Renan in 1883, of the pious Spanish Muslim shocked by the proceedings at a meeting of theologians (*mutakallimun*) which he had attended on his visit to Baghdad:

> At the first meeting I attended there were Muslims of all kinds, orthodox and unorthodox, and also Zorastrians (Mazdeans), materialists, atheists, Jews, Christians, in short all sorts of infidels. Each group had a leader to defend its views and whenever one of those leaders entered the room everyone stood up as a mark of respect and no one sat down again until the leader had taken his seat. The room was soon full to overflowing. Then one of the non-believers (that is, non-Muslims) took the floor. "We have met here to reason," he said. "You know all the conditions. You Muslims will not adduce reasons drawn from your book, or based on the authority of your Prophet, for we believe in neither. Everyone must keep to arguments based on reason." Everyone applauded.

From Cordoba to Cairo, Maimonides expresses this balance well. His works of Jewish piety were written in literary Arabic, but were printed in Hebrew characters by simple transliteration from one alphabet to the other in order to get round the Islamic ban on missionary activity by Peoples of the Book in Ayyubid Egypt where the *Rambam* (Rabbi Moshe Ben Maimon) died in 1204. It is known that, despite this device, his works were read and discussed by theologians of all faiths. In *The Guide for the Perplexed*,[12] he debated with Ibn Farabi and the *mutakallimun*, with Aristotle and the sophists, as well as with the Karaites whom he fought with all the authority of his rabbinical position. Enlightened though he was, Maimonides remained a talmudist for whom science was in the service of piety: he was politically opposed to the bourgeois revolution of the Abbassids and their materialist theologies, but was intellectually formed by them. Even his pietistic and traditionalist bias was expressed in the language of the dialectic, and was part of the general movement of philosophical ideas and culture of reason.

The Jews cooperated in this rationlist flowering, philosophizing Judaism according to the methods tried and tested by their Muslim friends in philosophizing Islam. They also took part in the reaction: the mystical and fundamentalist refutation of philosophy. And, there again, the harmony of thinking between Muslim and Jewish reactionaries is striking. The Jewish mystic Bahya Ibn Pakuda, a contemporary of al-Ghazali, the great master of Sufi mysticism, wrote, in Arabic, *The Duties of the Heart*: the application to Judaism of the Ghazalian concept of the Intention of the heart as a condition of prayer. In it he speaks particularly of the Righteous from among the Nations, virtuous non-Jews of whom Noah was the model. To illustrate the wisdom of these Gentiles, Bahya cites words – but he does not mention that the Muslim *Hadith* attributes them to . . . Jesus! Then there is the example of Ibn Gabirol; a well known Hebrew poet, he had written, in Arabic, a mystical work, *The Fountain of Life*. In the West, for a long time, only the Latin translation was known, and there was even one Pope who had made the *Fons Vitae* one of his favourite Christian readings. This was before it was discovered that Avicebron was not a Christian, nor a Muslim as was subsequently believed, but a Jew. The peculiar feature of this intellectual integration of the Jews in mediaeval Muslim civilization is that it did not lead to fusion, and the dissolution of Judaism in a unified discourse. In Muslim theology as in Muslim mysticism, classical Arab Judaism found the model of a Renaissance that Islam, in both its aspects, encouraged and cultivated. No one expressed this harmony better than Yehuda Halevi, the mystic, who codified in Arabic the grammar of Hebrew. While Jewish theology long continued to be written in Arabic ("It is", said Maimonides, "a richer and more modern language"), poetry in Hebrew was cultivated and developed. Maimonides' translator into Hebrew, his contemporary Yehuda Ibn Tibbon, explained in the preface, written in Provence, to his *Guide*, that all these great works could only have been written in Arabic, since they used Arab concepts for which no words existed in Hebrew. But, today, when Jews have been speaking Arabic for hundreds of years, and have become familiar with these concepts, new Hebrew words can at last be invented to describe them!

The reorganization renewed religious and community institutions: alongside the official rabbinical authorities whose decisions had the force of law, the merchants were now represented by the *Wakil* – in Hebrew: *Pkid ha-soharim*, the Employee of the businessmen – whose influence tempered that of the rabbis and foreshadowed the subordination of the community to the philanthropy of "assimilated" notables. A new *Mishnah*, a new stage of the Law, was launched and soon codified: a law of exemption, of How not to observe the letter of the archaic and inappropriate talmudic law while claiming to remain faithful to tradition.

In this symbiosis, Islam saved the Judaism of the Talmud from disintegration and gave it a new content, in the image of Islam and the image which Islam had of Judaism. The Judaeo-Arab cultural flowering which fed on this movement reversed the movement: at first, the Arabs had, with Islam, adopted and raised to new heights, the idea which the Jews had disseminated through their writings and their sects of a certain tribal history of the Law. It was now the Jews who learned to see themselves and think of themselves through the representation of themselves reflected back by the two aspects – dialectical or mystical – of dominant Islam and the Arab culture in which they participated.

Islam and Judaism

It is impossible to periodize the process of decline that dogged and nibbled away at this civilization. The politico-military decadence can be explained: civil and foreign wars, Christian and Tartar invasions, revolutions and counter-revolutions waged in the name of Islamic schisms, the centrifugal pulls of non-Arabized Muslim peoples, the weakening of the power of the towns over the countryside and the nomadic tribes . . . But one area would be still at its zenith when another was already ruined: and this fall itself contained its own limits.

The effervescence agitating North Africa by the 11th century, where Islam had performed an abrupt and radical historical mutation, produced the waves of Almoravid and Almohad "revolutionaries" that questioned the very bases of mediaeval Muslim liberalism. The Ismaili revolt in the East which shook the foundations of the Muslim states of Egypt and Iraq in the name of a Shi'ite Islam that was challenging and insurrectionary, led to a conservative reaction in official Islam which ended further debate.

The personal fate of Yehuda Halevi, the Toledan, illuminates the trajectory of this decay in which the Andalusian spring died. He was a court poet composing odes to the beautiful ladies and great lords who supported his art; he began by taking up theology, writing a book in Arabic "in defence of a vilified religion" in which he set out to refute in one blow philosophy, Christianity and Islam, in order to glorify Judaism. The military confrontation between Islam and Christianity fuelled an aristocratic and haughty neutralism in Yehuda Halevi which expressed itself in nationalist, or tribal, pride inspired by the best biblical and talmudic sources. Everything went into it: from the intrinsic superiority of the Hebrew language over Arabic (in which he wrote) to the chemical quality of the atmosphere in Palestine, which "made people intelligent". A racist, he considered that "If God had wanted men to be equal, he would not have created the Blacks." He mentioned the inhabitants of India only to declare that "one can give no credence to what they say, since it is well known that these peoples are liars".[13] But his very racism was related to his quality as a "civilized" Arab, and not only to his Jewishness: developing a hierarchy from the biblical genealogy, he put the Arabs in the first rank after the Hebrews, while the Christian barbarians in the north were worth no more in his eyes than the pagan barbarians in the south. Thus Jewish particularism still expressed itself unconsciously in terms of the dominant society. Yehuda Halevi was the author of numerous Jewish liturgical poems in Hebrew; legend has it that he made a vow of silence. He became a pilgrim, and is said to have met his death in the Holy Land, dying in the Old City at the Damascus gate, under the hooves of a crusader's horse. "Journey to the East":[14] a symbolic and disillusioned reversal of the rush to the west in the first centuries of the *Hegira*. With decline, the practical status of the Jews under Islam became uncertain, and as prosperity had affected them as Jews, so insecurity strengthened them in Judaism. In both cases, Arabization had profoundly changed them: but, each time, it was Judaism that was consolidated.

The Islamic city was not only the site of a contradiction between the mystical religiosity of the desert and the rationality of the Greek town. The theological problematic that occupied Jews and Muslims for several centuries was not only a verbal adhesion to the Law. The desire to reconcile reason and revelation proceeded from an existential rejection of the philosophy/religion dichotomy, an imperfection no doubt of the state, the tribute that it had to pay to the heritage of the "primitive democracy" of the Bedouin tribes which was as far back as Islam could trace its line of descent. Muslim and Jewish theology, and the parallel mystical and fundamentalist currents that followed it, all in their way expressed this retreat from the certainties of revelation and the tribe.

For the development of what Maxime Rodinson calls "a capitalist sector" was not a bourgeois revolution: this sector did not aspire, or at least did not do so consciously, to impose its exclusive hegemony on the whole of society, or to substitute its own rationality for that of the city as a whole. The Islamic state continued alone to think of society as a whole, by virtue of the fact that the plan of the *Hegira* integrated in advance the unknowns of the imperial domain. But the Islamic state only conceived itself in a definite relationship with the communities that composed it. While dominant, it never succeeded in occupying the whole domain alone. It subordinated the entities whose existence and interplay formed the social fabric itself, it did not dissolve or abolish them.

Between the Islamic state and Judaism, there was a sort of exchange, which went back to the idea held by Islam of its own relationship to the law of Moses and the impact of this idea on the behaviour of the Jews themselves. It was a history in which the Israelites, an old Arab tribe, had had the privelege of the first Revelation, laying the remote foundations of the City of God. It was the very manner in which the old aristocracies survived that made the abandonment of Judaism unthinkable, just as it was the survival of clanic modes of organization that made it useless.

This relationship raised to a higher level the rationality of the protection of the community by the empire. For Judaism had hitherto only known empires that were tolerant or ill-disposed. If the empire was tolerant, the community was protected, and called upon to obey its judges and its sages; if it was ill-disposed, Judaism had to suffer its misfortune in patience, or move its rabbinical lares elsewhere. But Islam went further: it based this guarantee on adherence to part of the intimate, private language of the community itself. It thus forced Judaism, on its own ground, to grant a partial recognition, albeit negatively, of the theological validity of Islam.

Whereas the *dhimma* constrained the Christians, who were fundamentally missionary, to observe what was for them an unnatural reserve that was to transform the heritage of the Byzantine sects into a mosaic of new tribes, for rabbinism it represented the realization of an idea as old as Ezra and Nehemiah. Thus it can be said that this civilization and Judaism were made for one another, and they found one another. Of course, this wonderment did not last, and does not fully do justice to the ambiguous and complex relationship that came and went between Judaism and Arab Islam and between Muslims and Jews. When insecurity came, it would become possible, as under al-Hakim in the 11th century, to flee Egypt and go and take refuge with Basil II in Byzantium. Yet it was under the decadent protection of the Ottomans that the Jews of the Arab world experienced the longest period of peace and security, if not of prosperity, in their history.

This decisive period in the formation of Judaism was imprinted on all the later forms of rabbinical organization. In the structural ambivalence of Islamic theory with regard to them and in the practical ambivalence of the Islamic state and community, there emerged a complex relationship of enmity and sympathy, of identification and alienation. And if Jerusalem played some obscure and symbolic role in all this, Palestine was not then the major site of this ambiguity, which was played out from Yemen to Medina, and from Almohad Morocco to Shi'ite Persia.

The most cursory look at the scene of this dialectic reveals the third actor, Rome-of-a-thousand-names, which, all this time, had been transforming itself, slyly, into the Christian West. The drama, of course, was being played out with three players, not two.

Christianity and the Jews

The centre of gravity of the Jewish world was in the process of moving towards Christian Europe, and Spain was the key area in this process. There, a section of the well-to-do Jews in al-Andalus decided to cling to Spanish soil after the *reconquista*: the Christian rulers had invited them to do so, promising the Jews protection and tolerance if they helped them to keep up the war against the Crescent. Few had accepted: the mass of Jews had moved to the nearest Muslim states. But the fits of ill-humour of these states, with their persecutions and revolts, had hardened the rabbinical communities which had long since absorbed these ups and downs into the reproduction of their tribalism. In the five hundred years of war that drew and redrew the map of Spain, the Jews became used to finding themselves on both sides of the front: for it was not only against Islam, but against their own lords and bishops that the Christian kings wanted to use the Jewish merchants, bankers and advisers. In the complex economic and diplomatic game that was played out between the powers of the two blocs – between the Genoese merchants of Acre and the traders of Venice, which was neutral in the Crusades – part of this Jewish bourgeoisie in Spain, but also of the ordinary people and its rabbis, found a place in the shadow of the Cross, where the Andalusian Jews met their brothers from the north, from Provence or Champagne, whom Rome had brought as far as the marches of Germany. For several centuries, from the 10th to the 15th, a diffuse and continuous process of emigration northward and eastward, punctuated by the rhythm of the expulsions that in turn emptied France and England, the states of Germany, and finally Spain and north Italy of their Jewish communities, concentrated the largest Jewish population in history in the middle of the European continent. In the west, however, short-lived symbioses had been worked out, between rabbinism and the Christian states: flowerings interrupted by massacres and migrations, the memory of which became the heritage of communities that had been several times exiled. The life and death of Judaism in Christian Spain, eliminated from the peninsula by the beginning of the 16th century, is an example of such transplants. The Jews there were as Hispanicized as their ancestors and cousins were Arabized, and the ones who fled Castille were to carry their Spain elsewhere: not only because they left with their rabbis and their books, but also because they took with them the Spanish language *as a Jewish language*, and were to continue to use it for several centuries in Turkey and the Balkans.

In the year that Columbus discovered America, the last Muslim stronghold fell to the Catholic rulers and, three months later, Ferdinand expelled all the Jews from Spain (except for those who accepted to become Christians, and for whom a new history began, that of the Marranos). A small number of the well-to-do bought a respite in Portugal, from where they spread to Holland, England and the New World. The majority turned eastward: from the Maghrib to Iraq, but above all from Italy to Turkey. The two routes crossed each other in Palestine, where the most fervent among them were attracted by the renewal of pietism that accompanied this exodus: this Spanish emigration to the Holy Land, which went back to Nachmanides,[15] reconstituted Palestinian Judaism while it continued to claim itself Spanish: Sephardic.

The brutal termination of this symbiosis, the horrors of the Inquisition and the persecution of the Marranos after the expulsion, made people forget how deep was the cultural appropriation represented by the persistence of Judaeo-Spanish. A flourishing rabbinical culture existed in the Middle Ages in the shadow of the Castillian princes, who made their Catholic, but also mercantile and centralizing, state play the same protective role as Islam, the heir of Cyrus. In this transition by way of Latinity, those who pushed as far as "gentle Provence" could still enjoy there the strategic position that made them the preferred middlemen in commercial and intellectual exchanges between the ancient East and the new West. There, for several generations, people would peacefully translate Aristotle from Arabic to Latin, one civilization into the language of the other, without the side-effects of the Crusades and the humiliations suffered elsewhere disturbing the peaceful course of the Rhône.

Yehuda Halevi, living in the 11th century in Muslim Spain, was already, although very timidly, lumping the Crescent and the Cross together. In the war between giants that the two were engaged in, he saw a different destiny for Israel than that of these worlds. Before redistributing their Jews all around the Mediterranean, the Christian states of still divided Spain had received the flows coming in the opposite direction, refugees from France and Andalusian artisans. There, the communities, having nothing to learn from their Christian masters about the things of the mind, fed on their own intellectual capital, accumulated in the talmudic and rabbinical literature of previous centuries. The Jews were isolated from the mass of Christians whose imagination associated the Jew alternatively with the devil or the pig, and they pursued their legal and scholarly debates like sleepwalkers, wholly occupied with their Law, and theologically resigned to their total powerlessness.

It was against the background of this passage through Latin Iberia that there appeared, towards the end of the 13th century, a literary work with a peculiar fate, which was to transform the intellectual and religious life of the Jews of Spain, and then of the whole of the Mediterranean and the East, and finally Europe: *The Book of Splendour* (*Sefer Ha-Zohar*), considered as the central work of mediaeval Jewish mysticism, the famous kabbala.

The Book of Splendour began to circulate in Spain at the beginning of the 14th century, on both sides of the moving line that separated the Christian kingdoms from the Muslim states. Fifty years later, although still in manuscript form, it had been widely distributed: since reading of it was not recommended at the time by any authority, its popularity might be said to have come from below.

Written in Aramaic, *The Book of Splendour* takes the form of a collection of sayings by the Palestinian *tanna* Simeon Bar Yohai, a great talmudic figure and a contemporary of Yohanan Ben Zakkai, the founder of the Yavneh *yeshiva* and also of institutionalized rabbinism. It is, however, likely that the *Zohar* was composed and prepared, or at least compiled and edited, by one rabbi Moses de Leon, in Christian Spain in the 13th century. There is no reason here to talk of forgery: from the Deuteronomy miraculously rediscovered in the ruins to the retrospective writing of the Talmuds, this fabrication (the same mechanism was at work in the compilation of the Gospels and in the anthology of the *Hadiths* of the Prophet Mohammed) typified the method by which the Law was updated. The mode of exposition of the *Book of Splendour* suggests, in the very manner of the apocryphal writing of the talmudic tractates, an absolute modesty on the part of the transcriber: it denies the possibility that the anonymous scribes, and not the scholars whose opinions are transcribed, were the true authors of it. But there was re-writing. The very tension that runs through the text, a thousand years later than the events it describes, gives it that third temporal dimension that marks the sacred compilations of the biblical and talmudic re-writings. The modesty of the recorder and his claim to write down only what was already known put the *Zohar* on the same footing as the known sacred texts: this traditional guarantee alone made possible and promised something new.

But the choice of language and of official author is unusual – and in this light so is the success of the book from one end of the Mediterranean to the other. For Aramaic at that time was no longer spoken except by tiny Jewish and Christian groups in the Mashrek, essentially in Kurdistan, and had never been spoken in the Muslim, nor, obviously, the Christian West. Aramaic came to Castille through the Talmud and went no further than the Talmud. A dead language in the East, unknown in the West, Aramaic had become the talmudic language par excellence. As such, it was studied, but no longer spoken. But here was a book that was a hit, not in translation, but in the original: the place from which it claimed to speak was 2nd century Palestine – before Islam, before Rome became Christian. This choice contained the essence of the new mysticism, in which the expectation of the Messiah smoothed out time and relativized kingdoms and empires. Here Christianity and Islam might as well never have existed, since every kingdom is vanity. How ungrateful history is! It was with the conceptual tools and the practical circumstances produced by the Muslim empire that Judaism had survived and moved to the west and that now it theorized the end of time.

The style of the *Zohar*, conversations between Bar Yohai and his companions,[16] are talmudically realistic. The form is in fact that of the *Midrash*: "homiletic commentary on the biblical text" which "appeals to the imagination and not to the strict literal meaning, using history, myth, apologetics and parables".[17] Moreover, one of the chapters of *The Book of Splendour* is entitled "The Secret Midrash", providing the basis for the work's claim to be no more than the late transcription of the oral teaching of Bar Yohai, passed down "by word of mouth" for a thousand years, through the unbroken chain of his disciples. But the architecture of the work and its mode of exposition are quite patently modern. Gershom Scholem sees in this the influence of mediaeval Christian scholasticism. But the infatuation with mathematics and the symbolism of numbers, the love of tabular formations and decimal constructions seem to betray the Arab-

Greek influence of nearby Andalusia. It is, in any event, a different work, committing to paper, not without some taste for the sensational, the "Secrets of the Law".

What makes the *Zohar* a decisive landmark in the Jewish representation of the world is the massive come-back of messianism in the area of oral law, that is of rabbinism and legal practice. Before the consolidation of talmudic Judaism, messianism had been closely bound up with suicidal military attempts to restore the kingdom. Based on a compromise with the empire and the renunciation of state forms of national existence, rabbinism had practically excluded from its language any reference to an invisible and remote end of time, which had no relevance for the here and now history of Jewish and non-Jewish humanity. In the detailed arrangement of everyday life, exile, the new crossing of the desert of peoples, was an unalterable fact for the immediate future. Expectation of the days of the Messiah, divine wrath and the Apocalypse became quietism: while waiting, man must live. By opportunely exhuming the *Zohar* in the manner of a new Deuteronomy, Moses de Léon was recopying, in his laboratory Aramaic, the messianic fervour and hope at the very heart of the talmudic tradition.

For several centuries this messianic fervour inherited from biblical prophetism had fuelled sectarian and missionary dissident movements, giving birth in turn to Christianity and Islam, which had taken up the theme of the Day of Judgement and the Resurrection of the Dead. Classical talmudism, forged in the struggle against these heresies as much as in obedience to the law of the kingdom – without however casting aside the language and prospect of the Expectation – regulated the exile through the notion of the End of Time. But the silence of the rabbis on this point could not eliminate a prospect that was both prophetic and universalized by the two derived religions: it was the ransom for the claim to perpetuate, over and beyond the hiatuses, the original Law. The rabbinical denial that there had been any qualitative changes in the prophetic message enabled the texts themselves to bear witness against oblivion, and, in the forced humility of the Latin yoke or the unease of the Berber-Islamic revolutions, to fuel a new hope of redemption. But the *Zohar* did better: it found the expression of an exacerbated messianism, scarcely differentiated from the military nationalism of Bar Kokhba, just beneath the surface, in the Palestinian *Mishnah* itself, the prestigious foundation of all later talmudic literature.

The total hegemony of the Talmud over the intellectual life of the Jews, based at least as much on the protection of states as on its own merits, had become such that religious opposition, innovation or transformation of practice were now expressed only in the very terms of the rabbinical debate. In this new model, in which the wars devastating the Mediterranean prefigured the apocalyptic wars of Gog and Magog, observance and study took on a new meaning: for in the world Good and Evil were waging a fight to the finish, the outcome of which was the coming of new times. Each small action, each commandment obeyed, each rite performed brought the Last Day closer. Each lapse postponed it. Thus, messianism and observance were no longer opposed to one another: they were mutually reinforcing.

This cosmic alchemy in which the Jews every day chose, in their actions and their shortcomings, the very destiny of the world, rested on an ancient science, but one that had hitherto not been widespread in the rabbinical world: the deciphering of texts. The whole Bible was seen as an enormous coded message (each letter of the Hebrew alphabet being provided with its own numerical value, from 1 to 10, then from 10 to 20, 30, etc., on to 100, 200, 300 and 400): discovering the right combinations of them would uncover the hidden meaning of the text. Old books emerged from oblivion: the *Book of Creation* (*Sefer Ha-Yezira*), the *Maassei Merkaba*, an apocalyptical allegory on the Vision of the Chariot in the Book of Ezekiel, *The Smaller Palaces* and the *Greater Palaces* (*Hekhalot Zutari* and *Hekhalot Rabbati*), new editions of tractates written in Byzantium or Persia, which had not been made part of the talmudic anthology. Schools were set up, artisans and traders studied feverishly, new tractates were written. The Kabbala – whose etymology evokes the Reception – was on the way to becoming the highest form of study of the texts and the only authentically popular Jewish religious literature from top to bottom of Jewish society, in which power – the Law – was the Book and books. In Morocco, Bar Yohai became a towering figure, almost equal to Moses in the chain of authority. In Yemen, the study of the Kabbala became an integral part of talmudic study. From the time of the opening, in Italy, of the first Hebrew printing presses at the end of the 15th century, kabbalistic books flooded the market, and messianism based on the new exegetic method became a permanent feature of the intellectual world of the Jewish communities on both sides of the Mediterranean.

The spread of kabbalistic study at the end of the Middle Ages assumed the proportions of a pietistic and messianic tidal wave which established new forms of counter-authority, and soon of intellectual power, in the Jewish communities of the Mediterranean world. This unacknowledged Reformation, which transformed the institutionalized rabbinism of its time – the mere manager and "amender"[18] of talmudic legality – by outdoing it in observance, is in some ways reminiscent of the rise of the pharisees against and within the assemblies of the Temple. Here, too, fidelity to orthodoxy served as a banner for the renewal of practice. But the democratization implied by the multiplication of small study circles and the passion for reading also reflected, where kabbalistic science best took root, the retreat of community, and even religious, life, into the narrow structures of the clan, or even, for the communities in the Latin West, of the family. This withdrawal into itself, in the image of the *Tsimtsum* by means of which, according to the *Zohar,* God is said to have created the world, constituted the well-spring of the Kabbala. It distanced it from any active rebellion, whether against the rabbinical order or against the kingdom, be it Christian, Muslim or pagan. It was a negative reflection of the partial or gradual withdrawal of Protection.

The relationship between the *Zohar* and later kabbalistic knowledge and orthodoxy is reflected in the very personality of its alleged author, Simeon Bar Yohai. In fact, talmudic studies had for a very long time been dominated by the opinions of Babylonian scholars: the Babylonian Talmud constituted a vast literature, the scale of which overwhelmed the Palestinian Mishnah and Talmud, which were preoccupied with legal and ritual questions. The Babylonian *amoraim*, scholars in a prosperous and stable community, had legislated its separate survival and the purity of its customs, providing the model of mediaeval rabbinism in the good years of Protection. However, the Mishnah of the Palestinian *tannaim*, like the tradition of the pharisees Shammai and Hillel, formed the basis of the *Pirkei Aboth* of the whole talmudic edifice. But 1st and 2nd century Palestinian rabbinism, unlike its Babylonian successor, was shot through with the double trauma of the end of the Temple and the bloody crushing of the hopes of the kingdom: the expulsion from Jerusalem and the Yavneh agreement. Akiva the shepherd had moved from academic teaching to anti-Roman guerrilla; Bar-Kokhba's revolt had split Jewry, and the split divided the closest sages. The Mishnah was the work, retrospective of course like every Judaic work, of rabbi Yehuda Ha-Nasi, the first hereditary patriarch of Yavneh, who took the title of *Nasi* (president) and was often called, among other titles, Our Holy Rabbi.

> He was famous for his piety, his humility, his great knowledge and his vast wealth. "From Moses until Rabbi" says the Talmud, "we do not find sacred learning and [secular] greatness [i.e., knowledge and rank] combined to such an extent in the one [person]." He was personally ascetic, but ran a princely household and maintained a sumptuous table. On terms of great intimacy with one of the Roman emperors of the Antonine family, he used his reputation on behalf of his nation. In a year of famine, he opened his granaries and distributed corn to the needy. He had a large number of disciples and maintained them with his own money. Using the advantages of his birth and high position, he encouraged the study of the Law and, in agreement with the sages of his time, drew up the code of the Mishnah, a work which was completed in 218. He prohibited teaching in public places. In another edict, he restored the *semikha* (ordination), a rule by which anyone who did not hold this right from the Nasi or the established religious authority, was forbidden to make doctrinal decisions and pronounce judgements.[19]

Yehuda Ha-Nasi was the pupil of Bar Yohai. Born after the crushing of the revolt of the messiah (*mashiah*: anointed, that is, king) Bar-Kokhba, his collaboration with the Roman government posed no problems for him, any more than it did for his friend Ishmael Bar Yossi: "The Roman government had made him responsible for the arrest of thieves, a task which he performed so assiduously that he was criticized."[20] But the figure of Bar Yohai whom the Mishnah of rabbi Yehuda Ha-Nasi restored – the known, "discovered Midrash" – was on an altogether different scale. Denounced to the Roman governor for having made anti-colonialist remarks, he hid with his son in the desert for twelve years before being amnestied. Later, in a move that took him as far as Rome, he went and asked the emperor to abolish anti-Jewish decrees.

The retrospective unanimity of the apocryphal codifiers of the Mishnah fails to conceal the upheavals of the divisions and disputes that set the Elders against one another, and contributed to the formation at Usha, in Galilee, of a rabbinical academy competing with the one at Yavneh. Nor could the ethnocentrism of the later talmudic masters conceal the fact that some of these scholars, precisely among the most nationalist ones, were converts, like Akiva, or sons of converts, like rabbi Meir. By choosing as their master the fascinating and complex character of Simeon Bar Yohai, the kabbalists undermined the Talmud in its own narrative claims. By imposing the idea of a wider, richer and more disputed oral law than the previously consecrated rabbinical anthology, the *Mekubbalim* ("Received"), they reopened, as it were, the rabbinical debate. On the one hand, the somewhat aesthetic and symbolic interpretation of observance for itself made the dissemination of their ideas a feature of public piety, and on the other hand, the new knowledge made possible a personal reappropriation of the understanding of the Law. In its spread, it benefited from its practical aspects: reading and study were within the reach of the humblest communities, and knowledge of the secrets of the Law excited the mystical curiosity of the faithful. A rather morbid romanticism had always surrounded the idea of secrets: the Talmud itself speaks of the Four who had wanted to visit the Vineyard (*Ha-Pardess*, Paradise) only one of whom (Akiva) had come back alive and well. At a more popular level, the secrets fuelled the trade in amulets, horoscopes and healers; at a higher level, people made careful numerical calculations to determine the date of the coming of the Messiah, heralded by cataclysms, epidemics and crusades. The messianic expectation of the kabbalists was, in fact, wholly expectation: it was simply a matter of purifying oneself, never of demanding or taking. But this expectation was a mental excursion outside present time and space, a permanent exercise in readiness. The Messiah will come, he is coming; when the Day of Judgement dawns, by the sole effect of our piety, the persecutors will be chastised and God will gather up Israel from among the Nations like a shepherd his scattered lambs. In the logic of this hope, hundreds of kabbalists went and settled in Galilee, near the tomb of Bar Yohai, so as to be in the front line on the Day of Redemption.

This messianism fed on persecution: humiliations, lack of security, explosions of violence and expulsions. It was the apocalypse of mediaeval Judaism that the Kabbala saw as the end of the world altogether. The population movement that mixed up refugees from Christian Spain and the heirs of Arab Judaism in the Mediterranean made this expectation into the ideological axis of a complex exodus from Protection.

The Kabbala was born in Christian Spain, although it claimed to be older than the law of Moses itself: for the chain of initiation, says the *Zohar*, led not only from Moses to the members of the Great Synagogue that Ezra himself is said to have founded. It led from primitive man (*Adam Qadmon*) – the man of the Garden before the Fall, having an innate knowledge of the world – to Moses, by way of the Egyptian priests and Jethro, his father-in-law. Yet, it was in Castille that this retrospective look at knowledge was formulated and it was in the Mediterranean that it became mixed with rabbinism. In this it was following the itinerary of the Sephardic diaspora, part of which was returning to the world of Islam.

Further north, other European symbioses of Judaism had also come into being. Some, like the one in Provence, survived modestly by producing literary and scholastic works of great value, and then died out peacefully. Others, like the French Judaism of the *langue de' oïl*, which had produced the great commentator Rashi, rabbi Salomon Isaac, of Troyes in Champagne, were to disappear without trace with the expulsions, dissolved into the neighbouring Judaeo-German Jewry. Yet, the commentaries of Rashi, the inventor of a "Gothic" Hebrew script based on the contraction of several letters and used in the writing of Judaeo-Spanish, were part of the rabbinical teaching all over the world. Gershom Scholem says:

> Rashi died at Troyes in the 12th century. He was born and grew up at Worms, in the Rhineland, where the language of the Jewish communities was not German, but French, since they came from Gaul. French was spoken in Lorraine and on the banks of the Rhine, and, in the Jewish communities, people spoke first Latin, then Frankish, then French, until the 13th century. When Rashi found a rare word in the Bible, for a plant for example, he translated it into Old French, so that his commentary is very important for knowledge of Old French, and also of the Bible, for philologists in general.[21]

In the Christian West, until the Expulsion, that is, for several centuries, the Christian rulers enacted and repealed, depending on the vagaries of their conflict-laden alliances with the three estates, a detailed legislation to expropriate the Jews, limit their rights and increase the burden of their obligations and ritual humiliations. The decrees imposing expulsion, forced conversion or expropriation were often revoked, but the refugees usually did not return and the lands were not restored. Expulsion from the land, which had the effect of virtually excluding Jews from the rural areas, was accompanied by the obligation to assume, from top to bottom of feudal society, the role of banker and usurer condemned by Christian morality but required by the mercantile development of capital.

Thus, a social transformation that was experienced by the Jews of the Muslim world as a betterment here took on the colours of disgrace. Already an outsider, a Deicide, and something of a Saracen, the usurer-Jew was transformed into a metaphysical figure of social evil: sin against Christianity and oppression of the Christian. A daemonic image of the child-stealer and the vampire, interchangeable in the mediaeval Western imagination with the Arab, the Turk, and the Gypsy, the Jew would survive in this domain only as irredeemably an outsider or completely absorbed. When the expulsion was completed, the Western cultural domain would be, to use the Nazi expression, "empty of Jews", and it was without malice that Molière, attentive to the way people actually think and speak, made one of his characters say: "What Arab, what Jew is there?"

For the Jews who survived by the grace of the prince in this Christian domain, protection covered no more than worship and private life. Community life withdrew into the structures of the family, while linguistic integration transformed worship into an individual religious denomination, not without difficulties and obstructions, but already outside the social problematic defined by rabbinical law, outside any contract by which the state would give a special position to the separate organization of Judaism. Protected as individuals, for material reasons, by states girded with the crusaders' sword, the Jews of the West were to cease, after the majority of them had left, to contribute to rabbinism.

It was in France, during the 14th century, that the cultural void came into being isolating the Jewry of the German linguistic area from the Mediterranean diaspora. The many-sided pressures on the part of the Christian states on the Jews living there caused the migrations to converge on the new frontier of the Tartars and the Slavs. As before, Jewry under threat emigrated and sought an equilibrium of survival on the periphery. Pushed by the same factors that had practically eliminated the Jews from France, the Jews of northern Italy and Bohemia, the Rhineland and Prussia flooded towards the kingdom of Poland, where the Catholic rulers offered them the terms of an unparalleled protection.

Notes

1. Koran, 2. 113, 135 and 136.

2. Cf. Maxime Rodinson, *The Arabs*, tr. A. Goldhammer (London, Croom Helm, 1981) p. 42.

3. Mohammed Essad bey, *Mohammed*, tr. H.L. Ripperger (London, Cobden-Sanderson, 1938) p. 217.

4. Maxime Rodinson, *Mohammed,* tr. A. Carter (London, Allen Lane, 1971) pp. 160–1.

5. Mohammed Essad Bey, *Mohammed*, p. 148.

6. S.D. Goitein wrote these lines before the appearance of Maxime Rodinson's *Islam et Capitalisme* (Paris, Editions du Seuil, 1965). Eng. tr., *Islam and Capitalism* (Harmondsworth, Penguin Books, 1974).

7. S.D. Goitein, *A Mediterranean Society*, (London, Cambridge University Press, 1967), pp. 6–7.

8. Former director of the School of Oriental Studies at the Hebrew University of Jerusalem, Goitein was still recently teaching Arabic at the University of Pennsylvania. Apart from his works on the Cairo *Geniza*, he has written the most comprehensive studies of the life of the Jewish communities in Yemen.

9. S.D. Goitein, op. cit.

10. Franz Rosenthal, *The Classical Heritage in Islam* (London, Routledge and Kegan Paul, 1975); original edition in German published by Artemis Verlag AG, Zurich, 1965.

11. In "L'Islam, doctrine de progrès ou de réaction?", in *Marxisme et monde musulman* (Paris, Editions du Seuil, 1972); Eng. tr. "Islam: Doctrine for Progress or Reaction?", in *Marxism and the Muslim World* (New York, Monthly Review Press, 1981) pp. 60–1.

12. Moses Maimonides, *The Guides for the Perplexed* (London, Routledge and Kegan Paul, 1947).

13. Judah Halevi's *Kitab al-Khazari*, translated into English from the Arabic by H. Hirschfield (London, Carlingold, 1931).

14. Ibn Khaldûn, *Le Voyage d'Orient et d'Occident* (Paris, Editions Sindbad, 1980).

15. The Christians call Nachmanides rabbi Moshe Ben Nahman, whom the Jews call Ramban. He was the victor in a "disputation" at Barcelona in 1263: he fled Spain and answered the appeal of Salah Eddin, settling in Jerusalem and renewing the life of the *Yishuv*.

16. Apart from Guy Casaril's little book cited above, see Gerhard Scholem (ed.) *Zohar, The Book of Splendor* (New York, Schocken Books, 1949).

17. Gerhard Scholem, *Zohar*, p. 12.

18. Since the time of the first scholars of the Law, the sages had pronounced *taqanoth*, or enactments, i.e., amendments, to adapt legislation to unforeseen circumstances.

19. M.S. Ullman, grand rabbi of the central Consistory, "Supplément contenant les noms propres mentionnés dans le traité d'aboth", in N.P. Sander and I. Trenel, *Dictionnaire hébreu-français* (Paris, Société de livres moraux et religieux, 1859); reprinted by Slatkine Reprints, Geneva, 1979.

20. Ibid.

21. "L'identité juive. Entretiens de Jean Bollack et Pierre Bourdieu avec Gershom Scholem", *Actes de la recherche en sciences sociales*, December 1980.

4 Europe

Ashkenazi in Germany

The adaptation of Judaism to changing conditions was a sign of an undeniable vitality and of the functional, working effectiveness of rabbinism as the social and political framework of the dispersed community, as it moved from one protection to another. This system of separate social relations, in which power and authority within the community mediatized and masked the nature and mechanism of the power of the state over it, remained dependent on two features, without which the entity risked disintegration or radical change: the protection of the kingdom, and the ideological control of the community by its rabbis, based on the loyalty of its members to the language of the tribe and the Law.

The breakdown of this understanding was often expressed in forced conversions, expulsions and massacres. But voluntary conversions, not only to the religion of the protectors, but to their civilization – Hellenism or modern secularism – were also typical expressions of it. For the Jewish society described by the Talmud and idealized by mediaeval rabbinism to survive, it was not enough that the state be well-disposed towards Jews as human beings: that was in fact quite useless. The kingdom – whether pagan, Christian or Muslim – had to grant the rabbinical organization a monopoly over the running of civil affairs and social control within the community. This was the basis of an objective alliance, and one that was not necessarily disinterested, between the protector and those protected: any confusion of roles being contrary to the very terms of the contract.

For the community to survive, the state therefore had to want to preserve it as such, either because it was useful to it – for example, against another social, national or religious group – or because it preferred to ensure its control through the medium of its own judges. This survival was thus dependence. But, without the conscious will of the non-Jewish ruler to protect, not the Jews, but Judaism, even this dependence became a subject of archaeological study, condemned to disappear. That is what happened, at the time of the Crusades, in western Europe, where the community life faded and became stunted, while the inhabitants of the ghetto awaited bourgeois emancipation at the gates of the national society of the countries of their birth. For the states which expelled and reduced Jewry in the Middle Ages were the very ones that were the first to emancipate them: strong, centralizing states, caught up in the process of mercantile and cultural unification from the Middle Ages, in which the nation was forged against all the old communities, under the jealous hegemony of the king-state.

There remained the weak states: peripheral zones where the indigenous social organization was subordinated to the military or economic needs of the neighbouring state or states. Mediaeval conditions were to some extent perpetuated there: in southern Italy, for example, where the Jewish community life expelled from northern Italy took refuge.

There remained too the multinational empires, the classic model of which in Europe had long since defined itself as holy, Roman and Germanic. It was a strong state and one that was strongly Christian, but one condemned to administering large numbers of scarcely evangelized Barbarians in the north and east, in a *de facto* multinationalism which was accentuated as the map of Europe was re-drawn, from the Spanish-Austrian Netherlands to the Austria-Hungary of the Hapsburgs: in the 19th century Prague and Galicia, Hungary and the Danube were all part of it. Here, the state endlessly manipulated complex social and national disequilibria: it not only played off, in the manner of the rulers of the West, the three estates of feudal society against one another, it also set peoples and nationalities against one another, not only within its own temporary frontiers, but also among its neighbours. It is easy to see that these structural features of the multinational empires were more conducive to the establishment of a contract for the protection of Judaism than the conditions of the nation-state in the West.

Germany, a piece of Empire that did not exist as a nation-state before the 19th century, constituted an extreme case in post-mediaeval Europe: neither a national state, nor a multinational state, Germany was an assemblage of bits of a nation scattered in several states.

Beyond that again there was the "new frontier", eastern Europe. The Polish state which came into being there was new, militarily strong and socially weak, and contained various dominated nationalities and minorities. Judaism was to flourish there for four centuries.

After the Crusades, the political division of the Mediterranean world nurtured a practical split in the Diaspora. In spite of episodic contacts that continued to occur over the centuries, and even migratory movements such as the return of the Jews from Spain in the 16th century, to Ottoman rule, the destiny of the Jewries of the Christian world and the lands of Islam henceforward followed two separate trajectories. In Christian Europe, where northern Judaism took shape, this autarky crystallized within the German-language area.

It was at the beginning of the 11th century, in Germany, that the Judaism that took the Hebrew name of Germany, *Ashkenaz*,[1] defined itself in relation to Arab and Mediterranean Judaism. The charter of this secession was, as it is only right, an act of rabbinical law: the Amendments (*taqanoth*) of *Shum*, that is of Spier-Worms-Mainz, promulgated on the very talmudic authority of rabbi Gershon of Worms. This new decree proscribed polygamy, in contradiction with both tradition and with continuing practice in Islamic countries. One vital detail: the separatist act that broke the monocephalism of legal authority constituted, by its content, a fundamental adaptation to the custom of Christian society; not only to its economic constraints and its monopoly of violence, but also to its ideology, its morality.

At this point, the breach was consummated. Until then, the Law had been drawn up for all the dispersions: it had been so at the time of the Talmud as under the Temple, and the Jewish *geonim* of the caliphs had aspired to do the same. With the legally autonomous constitution of Ashkenazi Judaism, a *de facto* and *de jure* situation emerged, which divided the world of the diaspora into blocs with precise and recognized, although changing, boundaries. In the 17th century, Jewish literature had five "rites" (*tqassim*) – Ashkenazi (German), Sephardic (Spanish), Italian, Babylonian and Yemenite – and an even larger number of communities (*'edoth*) defined according to the regions or states where they were dispersed.

In the German-speaking area, the political splintering enabled mediaeval Jewish society to move, as one expulsion followed another, with massacres and burnings at the stake, from one principality to another without leaving the German language area: a vast domain, carried by the Holy Roman Empire as far as Bohemia and Hungary, enlarged at swordpoint as far as the Baltic by the Teutonic Knights, extended by trade as far as the marches of Muscovy, in contrast to the political weakness of the German vassal princes of the Holy Roman Empire. However, the forced removals occurred within a single cultural domain, as was the case with the Judaeo-Arab migrations from Morocco to Egypt in the same period.

It was within this splintering that the linguistic synthesis occurred from which Yiddish emerged: at a time when German had not yet achieved its own unification, it was appropriated by the Jews of the 12th and 13th centuries as a Jewish language, much as the Aramaic of the Talmud and the Arabic of classical Judaism had been. Ashkenazi Judaism which, from the 13–14th century, formed a separate society within the kingdom of Poland, identified itself as German, and the survival of Judaeo-German (Yiddish) over several centuries spent among peoples speaking Slavic languages is striking testimony to this.

Given the spread of Yiddish among the Jews of eastern Europe, from Lithuania to the shores of the Black Sea, it seems that we are dealing with a linguistic migration comparable to that of Judaeo-Spanish in the eastern Mediterranean and the Balkans; fleeing Spain, the Jews had gone to be Spaniards among the Italians, the Greeks, the Bulgarians and the Turks. Even those who returned to the unbroken Judaeo-Arab synthesis continued to boast of their "Spanishness". Similarly, the Jews fleeing the

Germany of the Crusades and the massacres of the Black Death are said to have carried German with them as they moved east. Such a movement, in which the community engaged in an interrupted cultural synthesis, transported elsewhere its lares and its organization, was, as we have seen, rationalized by the theology of the Exile and rabbinical law. Moreover, the Polish founders of the Piast dynasty threw their kingdom wide open to the immigration of German traders of all faiths.

Such is the classic picture of the historiography of European Judaism, which conflicts with what appears at first glance to be a demographic enigma: the concentration of Yiddish-speaking, that is German-speaking, Jews, in eastern Europe, in numbers out of all proportion to the other communities. Indeed, even if it is undeniable that there existed in Germany and Austria, in Bohemia and the Rhineland, a dense and structured Jewish community network, it is not easy to see how the persecutions, epidemics and massacres could have transformed a few tens of thousands of German Jews into millions of Polish Jews. Now, whatever the statistical estimates used, by the 17th century there was a striking demographic disparity between the various Jewish communities: the Ashkenazi world of eastern Europe was soon to dominate numerically the whole Diaspora. At the end of the last century, when statistical methods were devised, the disproportion lay in a single figure: nine Jews in ten were then Ashkenazim, Yiddish-speakers or the children and grandchildren of Yiddish-speakers in eastern Europe. All the rest together – the assimilated ones in the West, the Marrano-Sepharadim in the Mediterranean, the Jews in the Arab world, Persia, India and Ethiopia – thus made up only one-tenth of the Jews in the whole world.

This numerical disparity made the Ashkenazi Jews the main, if not the sole, victims of the European Jewish question in contemporary times. For it was the Yiddish-speaking Jewish society of eastern Europe that engendered the massive emigration towards western Europe and America at the time of the industrial revolution: it was in that society that Zionism arose, and it was that society that was almost totally annihilated by the Nazi genocide. Thus the history of east European Judaism, in the eyes of Westerners, is confused with the history of the Jews as a whole. And, among the Ashkenazi Jews themselves, the demographic marginality of non-Ashkenazi Jews consolidated the feeling that Judaism meant *Yiddischkeit*: for, from the 14th to the 19th century, the most numerous Jewish population in history – several million souls at the end of this period – was concentrated on a single territory, unified by its institutions and speaking its own language.

We need to consider what were the circumstances of this concentration, how it came about and what it implied. The numbers, in the first place: how did these communities in central and eastern Europe become so numerous? How did the demographic and social centre of gravity of Judaism move from the Mediterranean to the shores of the Baltic, from Spain to the Carpathians, and from Italy to the Ukraine?

Various factors can be cited: the population crisis that affected the Mediterranean world in the 12th and 13th centuries; epidemics; the demographic explosion that affected Europe in the 19th century, except for the colonial countries where Oriental Jews lived. A comparison can also be made between the relative stability, prosperity and security of Judaism in ancient Poland and the migratory and quasi-clandestine uncertainty of Mediterranean Judaism. But it is impossible to avoid the idea that German Judaism as it moved eastward, was grafted on to human elements that already existed in the region, in numbers such they are in themselves sufficient to explain this proliferation.

It seems, in fact, that a distinction must be made between the German character of Jewish culture in eastern Europe and the physical origin of Ashkenazi Jews, the essential point being precisely that the various components were blended into a whole whose German language became, in Slavic lands, the distinctive mark of its Jewishness. For if the idiom was Yiddish, that is Jewish, the rabbinical society that spoke it defined itself as Ashkenazi, that is, German. But this society absorbed, quite obviously, a whole series of groups: individual converts by marriage or personal choice, and communities already established in the territory.

A fashionable theory in the West and in the Arab world since Arthur Koestler popularized it in his book *The Thirteenth Tribe*, sees virtually all the Jews of eastern Europe as the direct descendants of the Khazars of the Caspian, who are said to have adopted Judaism in the 8th century. These Turco-Mongol converts are said to have dispersed after the fall of their kingdom, like the other Tartar hordes in the territories of the Slavs, where they are said to have built the Jewish communities, learning German through contact with traders and settlers who had come from the west.

This attractive theory has provoked, here and there, an infatuation in which the passion for truth is at odds with the passion for descent, the pseudo-science of the genesis of nations explained by ethnic origin, which is one of the banal forms of the racist mentality. For this reason it is not out of place to discuss it a little.

There were certainly Jews in eastern Europe before Casimir the Great, king of Poland, opened up his territory in 1354 to "German" Jewish immigration, a large part of which came not from the west but from the south: from Bohemia and other regions of the Holy Roman Empire. From Roman times, isolated Jews had become involved in the commercial routes that led to these regions: Scythians and Thracians were the "Barbarians of the north" of the Greek world. Their continued paganism and their "primitiveness" had made them absolute slaves of the Roman empires, to the point where their ethnic name, *Slav*, had ended up replacing older names for slavery. Anyone in the eastern Mediterranean – Greek, Syrian, Jew, Christian, Muslim or pagan – who had been involved in the slave trade had some idea of the Slavs and their territories. In the Byzantine period, and even more after the advent of the Caliphate, Jewish, Greek or Oriental traders participated in commercial activities which turned Kiev and the

Danube valley into a key axis in the trade between East and West, before the crusades, Genoese and Venetian maritime trade and the development of the cloth trade in the West by-passed it.

> But, farther north, on the trails which joined Bavaria to the great market of Prague and thence by the terraces on the northern flank of the Carpathians, continued to the Dnieper, caravans passed back and forth, laden on the return journey with products of Constantinople or of Asia. At Kiev they met the great transversal which, running across the plains and from river to river, linked the riparian countries of the Baltic with the Black Sea, the Caspian or the rest of Turkestan.[2]

But

> from the end of the eleventh century Flemish cloth was sold at Novgorod. Little by little, the route of the Russian plains became hazardous and was finally closed. Thenceforward Scandinavia and the Baltic countries turned towards the West. The process of change which was thus set in motion was completed when, in the course of the twelfth century, German merchants took over the Baltic.[3]

Thus, the territories that were to be incorporated in reconstructed post-Tartar Poland, such as the Ukraine, where the first Russian state – the principality of Kiev – had flourished, had long been a known periphery of the Holy Roman Empire or Byzantium. In the year 1000, Jewish traders are found in Prague, and it is likely that there were Jewish settlements of various sizes scattered at various points along these highways that were doomed to become an anachronism. The Jewish settlements that were to be found in this region at that time (which must not be confused with those of the Sephardim in southern Europe, whose presence in Romania and Hungary simply testifies to the late retreat of the Ottoman frontier) were also certainly integrated into the dominant Judaeo-German social and cultural norms: the same phenomenon occurred in the Balkans and Turkey, and even – to a much lesser extent – in some regions of the Arab world, where the minority of "pure Spanish" newcomers imposed its own cultural and religious norms on the local communities whose leadership was taken over by these "fleeing lords". In the case of eastern Europe, however, the mechanism seems insufficient to account for the demographic disproportion and to answer the question: how did they become millions? This is where the theory of the Khazars comes in.

The Khazar Hypothesis

Since earliest antiquity, the mountainous deserts of central Asia had poured wave after wave of their nomadic populations, sometimes eastward over China which the Mongols controlled for several centuries, sometimes over Persia and the Caucasus, sometimes westward right into the heart of Europe: the West still remembers Attila's Huns, nomads who devastated as far as Gaul in the 5th century, before falling back into Hungary where they were joined five hundred years later by their Turco-Mongol "brothers", the Magyars, who gave their language to modern Hungary. As Fernand Braudel[4] shows, "the door of the conquered house closed" on many of these conquerors. The nomadic horsemen of the Gobi, settling down in conquered China, became "Sinicized". Soon the Turks alone would be carrying the banner of the old Caliphate, far from their Barbarian origin. This absorption of the conqueror by the conquered civilization is not at all surprising, given how frequently it happens in the history of civilizations. There have, however, been a number of striking cases: the Macedonians had become Greeks in all humility, the Persians had come to know Chaldaea and Assyria without unlearning Persian. The Germans had become Romanized without adopting Latin: the Seljuk Turks, though Islamized, did not become Arabized. The Magyars became Catholics, but continued to speak their Finno-Ugrian language. The "Brutish" Turks, also called Bulgars, adopted a Slavic language in the region that today bears their name, while those in the Urals retained their language. Some, then, of this string of Turco-Mongol tribes blended into the surrounding civilizations, while numerous others remained a permanent reservoir of dynamic and warlike demographic explosions tossed between the ebb and flow of these invasions. For a thousand years, the zone between the Baltic and the Urals, bounded in the south by the Danube, the Black Sea and the Caspian, watered by the Dnieper, the Don, the Dniester and the Volga, was the scene of a permanent invasion. There, until the 11th–12th century, the military transhumance of the peoples of the steppes did not have to face any state or empire able to stand in its way, no bloc of civilization comparable to Persia, Byzantium or Rome, or even to its last German avatar. And the Christian and Slav states which came into being in this area – the "Varangian"[5] principality of Kiev, the kingdom of Poland, the grand-duchy of Lithuania, the principality of Muscovy and the empire of the Tsars – were only forged in a continuous struggle, a thousand-year war against "Tartaria".

There was a multitude of these peoples: as horse rearers, they were naturally transporters, caravanners and traders, as much as horsemen and warriors. They spoke Turkic languages that were related but nevertheless distinct, and retained, so long as they did not settle down, their Shamanistic tribal and religious structures. The Mongol Golden Horde of Genghis Khan and Tamerlane was, until the 14th century, the last wave and the western high point of the vast and temporary migration that swept across Poland to the marches of Germany in the 13th century, transporting several million men from the heart of Asia to the centre of Europe, and leaving hundreds of thousands clinging to lands briefly conquered during its partial withdrawal eastward.

Until the Islamization of the northern marches of Persia, in the 8th century, these peoples were pagan, and moreover very tolerant. They gave a warm welcome, over the centuries, to all missionaries, both Christian and Muslim, and the nomadic horsemen of the steppes did not conduct their wars or their politics in the name of a faith: neither of the Shamanism of their ancestors, nor of the Christian or Muslim convictions that history and geography had led some of them, here and there, to adopt.

Some of these groups, however, took control, for considerable lengths of time, of major communication centres, establishing around them short-lived quasi-states which entered into contact with the neighbouring empires in complex relationships of clientage and suzerainty, essentially based on the imperial need for human barriers against the main body of the wave. For both Byzantium and Persia, the Ghassanid and Lakhmid Arab tribes had played this role of frontier guards against the tribes of the desert.

It was against this background that there appeared, in the 6th century, on the west bank of the Caspian Sea, the kingdom of the Khazars. Originally the term "Khazar" did not describe a particular ethnic group: it was a sort of generic name for all the Turco-Mongol peoples on the move in this region. It seems that the word itself derives from a Turkish root meaning "nomad": in which case it would be a Turkish equivalent of the Arabic *Bedu* (Bedouin) describing, within a multi-tribal language, not an ethno-linguistic group, but a sociological category, the occupation and way of life of whole populations and even, at the extreme, a value system based on the specificity of this mode of organization. Thus, the Khazars were called Kaissak in the Urals, and Kazakh on the borders of China and Afghanistan where the Russian revolution would establish Kazakhstan; from their name would come the name of the Cossacks and the English word "Hussar". But the Turcoman peoples of the Volga and the Caspian or the Crimea, whose own ethnic names were the Kalmyks and the Khirghiz, the Uzbeks and the Bashkirs, the Tatars called Tartars and many others, were, at the time of which we are speaking, Khazars on every criterion.

It is then one of these groups which, in about the 6th century, established the kingdom of the nomads, on the site of Itil, where the countless arms of the Volga pour into the Caspian. Kingdom is a word that might be confusing since it suggests both the defined unity of a nation, and the domination of one class over the whole of society through the mechanism of a state. But here it seems that there was prolonged domination – military control – of a region particularly sensitive in inter-regional trade through an alliance of clans and tribes, without, however, this grip on the delta of the great river implying either the formation of a distinct Khazar national entity deriving its identity from the territory, or the crystallization of a social conflict situation internal to this entity. This "kingdom" that served as a buffer and a rampart for both Persia and Byzantium, for both the Roman cross and the Islamic crescent, soon constituted, from the north of the Caspian to the Sea of Azov and the Crimea, a small settled military power which gave itself over to trade with some success. It was thus inevitable that the neighbouring empires would make contact with it in order to attempt to turn it into a vassal, or to make it into an ally.

Most of the mediaeval sources – most of which are Arab – assert that the Khazar kingdom, initially pagan, became a Jewish kingdom during the 8th century. The choice of Judaism as a state religion is said to have reflected a logic of positive neutralism between Byzantium and the caliphate, enabling the kingdom to preserve its independence *vis-à-vis* the two blocs without risking laying itself open to attempts at conversion by the two religions. However, the Arab geographers and travellers, who visited this kingdom before its fall in the 11th century, describe it as a place where a large section of the population was Islamized, and coexisted peacefully with the Christians, Jews and pagans. Certainly, these travellers say that "the Khazar kings are Jewish", but they report a picture of indifference and tolerance altogether incompatible with the jealousy of the sole God: a Mongol state without a state religion.

The Khazars in the east, that is, around the northern Caspian, were to be rapidly absorbed by the self-Islamizing movement of the conquering Turkmens, who turned these areas into the hinterland of Sunnite Turkey and Shi'ite Persia. Soon the whole region was absorbed by the Khanates of Astrakhan and Kazan. By the 9th century, the fief of the Khazars was reduced to the Crimea, or "Little Khazaria": *Gazzaria* is, moreover, the Latin and Italian name for the Crimea. The last kings of Little Khazaria were Christians and, at about the end of the 10th century, the Khazar kingdom of the Crimea collapsed in the face of the coalition between nearby Byzantium and the newly Christianized Russians, who moved from the ranks of the barbarians to the dignity of being soldiers of the Greek Orthodox Church. But, until the Varangian princes consented to abandon their nordic paganism (before becoming "Greek" Christians, they had already become Slavicized during their long march towards Kiev), it was the Khazar kingdom that acted as Byzantium's guardian against the Slavs. The conversion of the Khazar kings to Christianity was sealed, in accordance with custom, by a marriage, and there was one Byzantine emperor, Leo the Khazar, whose mother was a Khazar princess.

According to the Khazarist theory put forward by Koestler, based on the works of the American historian J.D.M. Dunlop, the Khazar king Bulan was converted to Judaism in 740, making his kingdom a Jewish state and leading to the conversion of his people. But Arab descriptions of the kingdom, a century or two after this "conversion", in no way corroborate the idea that Judaism had been the religion of the people. What we know of the pagan institutions of the kingdom, confirmed by the historians and geographers of the time, as well as by the Khazar experts themselves, suggests on the contrary the survival of the Mongol model illustrated elsewhere, including by the Golden Horde, especially the sharing of the kingship between the spiritual power of the *Kagan* and the military power of the *Bek*. The Khazar experts admit that they do not know whether "king" Bulan was Kagan or Bek. But they nevertheless claim that Judaism was the state religion at Itil. Even more, they claim that, when the kingdom changed religion, the east becoming Muslim and the Crimea Christian, the people of the Khazars remained faithful to Judaism and not to their kingdom. Fleeing persecution, they are said to have dispersed northward and westward, carrying in their Mongol wagons the Judaism which was to give birth to the Ashkenazi world.

The centrepiece of this argument is the famous "Khazar Correspondence": an exchange of letters between the Jewish chief minister of the Ummayyad caliph of Cordoba and the Jewish scribe of Joseph, the king of Khazaria, in the 10th century. "The authenticity of the correspondence has been the subject of controversy", writes Koestler. And it is indeed true that manipulation, or even forgery, in the transmission of documents of this sort cannot be ruled out. But analysis of the content of the "Correspondence" suggests that it is at least partly authentic to the extent that the letters themselves contradict the assertions of the possible forgers.

Let us leave aside the modern manipulations of Khazar experts, which are no more than digressions on the major creation, that of the correspondent himself, the diplomat, politician and "Court Jew" Hasdai Ibn Shaprut, the personal advisor of caliph Abderrahman III. It was he, as a high personality in the Islamic state, who took the initiative of making contact with the Khazar king Joseph and sending him a messenger. Hasdai Ibn Shaprut's letter, however, appears to be the personal message from an Andalusian Jew to a Jewish king at the same time as an examination of a rabbinical passage intended to determine whether the Judaism of the Khazars was authentic.

Ibn Shaprut, ambassador and minister of Christian affairs, that is, responsible for the relations between the caliphate of Cordoba and Byzantium and other Christian states, recalls how he came to be making his enquiry. Already, three years earlier, he says, he had wanted to get in touch with the king, but the messenger he had sent had been unable to reach Khazaria, the Byzantines having prevented him from doing so. "Understandably so: . . . it was certainly not in Constantinople's interest to facilitate an alliance between Khazaria and the Cordoba Caliphate with its Jewish Chief Minister."[6] He therefore sent this second message through two Jews who were members of an "embassy from Eastern Europe which had arrived at Cordoba".

The Byzantines and Persians were aware of the existence of a Khazar kingdom, and king Joseph's secretary, who replied, a few years later, to Ibn Shaprut's missive, boasted of the strategic role of his kingdom:

> With the help of the Almighty, I guard the mouth of the river [the Volga] and do not permit the Rus who come in their ships to invade the land of the Arabs . . . I fight heavy wars with them [the Rus] for if I allowed it they would devastate the lands of Ishmael even to Baghdad.[7]

The Cordoban's incredulity concerns the Jewishness of the kingdom: when he first heard of the existence of a Jewish kingdom in Khazaria mentioned by Jewish merchants from Persia, he says, he had not believed them. Having secured confirmation of the fact from the Byzantine ambassadors in Cordoba, he was now writing to reassure himself: "I feel the urge to know the truth, whether there is really a place on this earth where harassed Israel can rule itself, where it is subject to nobody."

The questions that Ibn Shaprut asks in order to know the truth revolve around two keys: the origin of the Khazar Jews, and the forms of their religious practice. For, for Hasdai Ibn Shaprut, as for all post-talmudic rabbinical Judaism, as for the Umayyad caliphs struggling against the Abbassids in the east, their sects and their schismatic theologians, the Jews were: 1) the descendants of the Israelite tribes; 2) those who observe the prescriptions of talmudic law.

On the question concerning observance, king Joseph's secretary is as discreet as possible and speaks of the tolerance of the kingdom that welcomes the sages of Israel; we know that the Jews were not the only ones to benefit from it, and that pagans, Christians and Muslims enjoyed it too. However, he claims that the Khazar kingdom gives the lie to those who say that the "Sceptre of Judah", as Ibn Shaprut said in his letter, "has forever fallen from the Jews' hand". But where the Cordoban doctor expected the story of an emigration, he received the miraculous account of a conversion: that of king Bulan, two centuries earlier.

Bulan's conversion is the subject of the major work by Yehuda Halevi, written a hundred years after the correspondence and four hundred years after "the facts", the *Kitab al-Khazari* (The Khazar Book, tr. Hirschfield, new revised ed., London 1931). In it, Halevi takes up the version of the reply to Ibn Shaprut in which this conversion is preceded by an oratorical and philosophical exchange between the supporters of the various monotheistic faiths. In this version, the rabbi triumphs over his opponents by reason, and Bulan decides to embrace Judaism. The Arab geographer Al-Bakri, in his *Book of Kingdoms and Roads*, gives another version of this conversion:

> Then the King asked for a Muslim, and they sent him a scholarly, clever man who was good at arguments. But the Jew hired someone who imprisoned him on the journey, and he died. And the Jew succeeded in winning the King for his faith, so that he embraced Judaism.

This religion, however, was not the Judaism of Ibn Shaprut, the rabbis and the *geonim*, but rather its absolute opposite, its schismatic and missionary *bête noire:* Karaism. Indeed, the Khazar experts recognize this, and Koestler writes:

> It seems highly probable that the conversion of King Bulan and his followers was another intermediary step, that they embraced a primitive or rudimentary form of Judaism, based on the Bible alone, excluding the Talmud, all rabbinical literature, and the observances derived from it. In this respect they resembled the Karaites, a fundamentalist sect which originated in the 8th century in Persia and spread among Jews all over the world – particularly in 'Little Khazaria', i.e., the Crimea, Dunlop and some other authorities surmised that between Bulan and Obadiah (i.e. roughly between 740 and 800) some form of Karaism prevailed in the country, and that orthodox 'Rabbinic' Judaism was only introduced in the course of Obadiah's religious reform.[8]

This "reform", on which Dunlop and those who think like him, such as Koestler, following Yehuda Halevi, base their theory, is not corroborated by any other evidence, except for the permission granted by Obadiah, the reformer, to the Jewish sages of Persia (the homeland of Karaism at the time of its spread) to open schools and synagogues in the Khazar kingdom. Travelling in the northern Crimea between 1170 and 1185, the Jewish rabbi Petachia, from Regensberg in Germany, denounced the heretical Karaite practices of the "Khazar Jews": "And the Rabbi Petachia asked them: 'Why do you not believe in the words of the sages?' They replied: 'Because our fathers did not teach them to us.' "[9]

We know that the religion of the Khazar kings – even more the religion of one of two simultaneous kings – was not necessarily that of the people. But we also have every reason to doubt that king Joseph himself, two hundred years after Obadiah's "rabbinical reform", had ever belonged to the sphere of talmudic Judaism: the very nature of the response of his secretary – who was yet concerned to affirm his "Jewish-ness" – to Ibn Shaprut's question concerning the origin of the Khazar Jews is proof of it. Joseph, in fact, does not at all lay claim to an Israelite origin. His secretary is categorical: the Khazar kings are the direct descendants of Japheth, Noah's third son, through his grandson Togarma, the ancestor of all the Turkish tribes: "We have found in the family registers of our fathers that Togarma had ten sons, and the names of their offspring are as follows: Uigur, Dursu, Avars, Huns, Basilii, Tarniakh, Khazars, Zagora, Bulgars, Sabir. We are the sons of Khazar, the seventh."

It is known that the missionary practice of the Karaites involved the adaptation of the tradition and liturgy to the cultural norms of the people to be educated. Their translations of the Bible into profane language carefully avoided restoring the anthropomorphic expressions and metaphors in the text, and they developed simplified rituals for the use of Gentiles.

The Talmud, on the contrary, only knows and institutionalizes individual and total conversion: this was the *guiur*, by which a Gentile became a "Convert", *guer*. The word in the Bible is synonymous with stranger, and conversion was based on the injunction of the Pentateuch: "The same law for you and for the stranger who lives under your roof." But where the Karaites read this as meaning the universalist principle of equality among men, censoring the ritual of ethnocentric allusions, the rabbis interpreted the obligation to oblige non-Jewish slaves to ritual observance like their Hebrew masters. This meant that the talmudic principle according to which "the text never escapes its literal meaning" (*Ein Mikra yotseh mid ei pesh peshutto*) was itself susceptible of interpretation.

Maimonides, who wrote hundreds of pages to debate with the Karaites and refute their views, was not aware of this polemic and its implications when he replied, in his *Letter*, to the convert who asked him if he also had to speak of "his ancestors", Abraham, Isaac and Jacob, in the prayers. "By entering into the Covenant", the Rambam declared, "you too have become the descendant of the Patriarchs, and you must say the prayers like everyone else." For the assumed descent was not conceived of as being solely spiritual. Even if only for the sole purpose of retaining the ritual unchanged and prohibiting any reform, it demanded adhesion to a genealogical fiction. By entering into the covenant of Abraham and Moses, the convert changed his ancestors. Those of the Israelites, the Bedouins in the Sinai, became his: he would adopt the system of tribal values and the national myth of the group which he joined.

Such conversions occurred in large numbers at several stages in the history of Judaism: under the Hasmonaean kings, conversion was often imposed on Canaanite customs; in Roman times, in Palestine, it proceeded from a voluntary assimilation of the converts within the culturally dominant Judaic society, and we have seen that some of the greatest and most nationalist of the *tannaim* of the Mishnah were converts. From the 4th century onwards, however, when the Babylonian academies took up the lawmaking role of the *yeshivoth* of Yavneh and Isha, the pre-Karaite Saducite sects adopted an actively missionary policy, which the rabbinical and Umayyad persecutions drove back towards the Barbarians on the periphery. For the most part, these persecutions prepared the ground for Islam and Christianity, but also sometimes for rabbinical Judaism. In some Jewish communities in the Caucasus, which are Turkish-speaking and non-Ashkenazi, and in those in Uzbekistan, Samarkand and Bukhara, one can see the descendants of these Mongols and Khazars converted by Karaite missionaries from Iran, later re-absorbed by the Orthodox Judaism of the caliphate and its Ottoman successor.

But it is certain that king Joseph, the Karaite ruler of a tolerant and multi-religious kingdom, at the other extreme from the Karaite "Jewish" kingdom of Dhu Nowas in Yemen, a great massacrer of Christians in the name of the *Torah*, would not have boasted of his Turkish ancestry if he had adhered to the obligatory ethnic fiction of rabbinical Judaism. The ultimate proof of this lies in the imminence of the subsequent conversions of the Khazars to Islam and Christianity.

The Karaites of the Crimea, however, as to whose Khazar origin there is no doubt, did not disappear after the collapse of the last Khazar state before the combined forces of the Rus and Byzantium. Little Khazaria was the home, until the beginning of the present century, of the largest of the last Karaite communities, which had spread out towards the Baltic: there were some in Kiev when the principality was being built there, there were some a few years later in "Hungary" in the principality of Halich, and in 1398, Alexander Vytautas, known as Witold, grand-duke of Lithuania, imported into his capital at Troki several hundred Karaite families from the Crimea, who were Turkish-speaking and soldiers by profession, as a garrison.

Moreover, the dispersion of the Karaites in eastern Europe involved not only the Khazars but also the "Kumans", another Turkish-speaking people migrating westward, noticed by all the chroniclers of this region because of the large proportion of ginger-haired people with very white skins among some of these tribes, and who were also marked by Karaite proselytism A regiment of them fought alongside the joint Polish–Lithuanian forces, against the troops of the Teutonic Order, in 1410, at the Battle of Tannenberg.

> The second continuator of the Lübeck chronicle says that, among the troops fighting the army of the Teutonic Order, there were also "Saracens". The chronicler says specifically that these came from the shores of the Caspian Sea where, he says, *Roden Juden* (red Jews) live. The north of the Caspian Sea is the main Khazar territory, and then Cuman, and these red Jews are most likely none other than the light-skinned and/or ginger-haired Cumans. Because of their beliefs based on the Bible, they were taken to be Jews.[10]

The settlement of the Karaites from the Crimea in Lithuania was linked to their military role: Witold distributed them according to a strategic plan, against the German knights. But the Karaites were not enough:

> In order to establish a second line of protection, some ten kilometres from Troki, in the Vaka valley, Witold created several villages of Muslim refugees from eastern Europe. This population which also lived in other regions of Lithuania, was descended from several Altaic, Finnish or Caucasian peoples, united by their religion. Formerly they were called *Muslims*, and later the name *Tatars* became usual. In eastern Europe, this word described the Muslim population of Asiatic origin.[11]

It is not inconceivable that some of these Khazar and Cuman populations who "were taken to be Jews" were assimilated to Ashkenazi Judaism that was coming into existence at the same period in Poland. It seems, indeed, that after the Union of Lublin between Poland and Lithuania, the rabbinical Jews attempted to impose their jurisdiction (and the collection of their taxes) on the Karaite communities. But the privileges "won by the bow and the sword" enjoyed by the Lithuanian Karaites as a military order, which gave them the right to own Christian serfs, were not the sort of privileges one gives up easily, especially as the union between Poland and Lithuania brought the Jews of Poland face to face with the competition of the Christian merchants of the Baltic, and marked the beginning of their troubles.

In conclusion, the very fact that Karaism in the Crimea and Lithuania was impervious to rabbinical Judaism argues against the theory of the Khazar experts: three centuries after their settlement on the shores of the Baltic, they were still speaking their archaic Turkish dialect, thanks to which, in the 16th century, they published the first translation of the Bible into Turkish; they were still practising the profession of arms and worked in the organizations that ransomed Christian prisoners sold into slavery from the Turks and the Tartars. It is possible that this imperviousness was not altogether total, especially in the Ukraine, where Muscovy was gradually nibbling away at Polish independence. But there is nothing to suggest a mass move of the Khazars and Karaite Turcomans to Judaism, and to explain in this way, as Dunlop and Koestler do, why there were so many Ashkenazi Jews in eastern Europe.

In order to account for the numbers and the obvious mixing of ethnic groups, it is necessary, therefore, to look at all the human inflows that inflated these communities from the 13th and 14th centuries onwards: Jews from Germany and France fleeing persecutions and massacres following epidemics; traders, such as the Radonites (from the Rhône) who, as early as the 11th century, were including Poland in their itinerary; northern Italians driven out of the Spanish states; artisans and traders from Bohemia and the Holy Roman Empire; Greeks and Byzantines from outlying regions, isolated Orientals and Persians; Judaized Slavs who were domestic dependents of, or married to, Jews, and, finally, Khazars and other Turcomans converted in stages. Not to mention the offspring of rebellious Cossacks whose Jewish mothers had been raped. Following the great anti-Jewish outburst of the mid-17th century, the rabbis in Poland deliberated on their case and decreed that they were the legal sons of their official fathers, since in the matter of Jewishness, the law was clear cut: only the mother counted! So the little children of mixed birth were Jews: so much for genetics! The concentration, preservation and multiplication of Jews in eastern Europe did not derive from some arithmetical or biological miracle, but from the exceptional conditions of protection, autonomy and prosperity that the kingdom of Poland offered Judaism – and the exercise of its genealogical fiction – over a vast territory, for more than three centuries.

Poland

This long excursion into the detail of the Khazarist theory will at least have served to bring us closer to the general movement of peoples and ethnic groups in the area where this unprecedented concentration of Jewish communities occurred. The elasticity of frontiers, made and unmade as wars and invasions followed one another, reflects here the displacement of groups but does not correspond to it. We have seen the Turkish-Mongol wave flood over the first Poland and withdraw in the 14th century, following the ebb of the Golden Horde. We have seen the Bulgars of the Danube become Slavs, the Khazars disperse, Russia come into being and grow in permanent confrontation with Asia... Poland struggling against the Teutonic Knights settled the mercantile bourgeoisie from Germany in its towns, while the grand-dukes of Lithuania created Karaite and Muslim Turkish villages. This geopolitics of nationalities, which underlay the construction and rivalry of states, was tied up with clashes that used religion as a pretext: Russia, from the principality of Kiev to post-Tartar Muscovy, was the pupil of Byzantium and the Greek Church; it was therefore Orthodox. Poland, like the Holy Roman Empire, was Catholic: thus the Russian expansion into the Ukraine was liberation for the Orthodox oppressed under the "Latin" yoke of the Poles. But, when the Russian Church imposed the reforms of Nikon, the Old Believers went and took refuge under Polish protection.

Two orders in this structure, whose function is generally poorly understood, enjoyed special autonomy: the Jews and the Cossacks.

There is no doubt that the word Cossack is derived from the word Kazakh, Khazar, etc., which in east European usage is interchangeable with Tatar, Tartar, Turkish, Mongol, Saracen and many other names. Yet, by the 16th century, it described groups and populations speaking Slavic languages and Christian by religion. How had this peculiar shift occurred?

In Poland and Lithuania, where a Karaite regiment served in the royal army until the 17th century, the Turkish-speaking Khazars were compelled, so we read, "to serve with the Cossacks, a sort of police force responsible for protecting highways and bridges, stopping bandits, carrying important official letters, etc."[12] And Simon Szyszman adds: "These Cossacks must not be confused with the Ukrainian ones; they had nothing in common with them, except the name." The question then arises: if they had nothing in common with them, why did they have the same name?

The Cossacks, writes Théophile Grol,[13] speaking precisely of those in the Ukraine, "were the descendants of enserfed peasants who had fled and settled on the frontier lands of old Poland and the endless steppes, on the banks of the Dnieper and the Dniester and in the Crimea". Like the Ukrainian peasants who had revolted and settled in the "Zaporogue" territory ("beyond the river"), they established there "a free Cossack republic, based on military principles. Every inhabitant was a soldier . . . At the head of the whole Cossack army was an 'Ataman'."[14]

The way in which this "republic" functioned, born as it was in the protection that the Muscovite princes, taking advantage of imperial rivalry, extended over it, explains the shift of language: the revolting peasants, nomads because they were fugitives, armed because they were rebelling, spontaneously recreated the apparent structure of the Horde, in the manner of the territorial autonomies of the Kalmyks and the Tatars who were there, and whose ancient freedoms the tsars only slowly chipped away. Did the revolting Ukrainian peasants proclaim themselves Cossacks first, or did the Polish nobles christen them so out of contempt? Was it not rather the nature of the new contract of vassalage that bound the Cossack "armies" to the Russian government – the "Cossack service" of the old Turcoman guards – that earned these former serfs who had become frontier guards such a name?

Peasant revolts were a sporadic feature of feudal society. In the West, however, the jacqueries were doomed before they started; the armed network of fiefs made it impossible for them to spread, their local rootedness meant their encirclement, and there were no longer any "virgin lands" between states. In eastern Europe, on the other hand, the far-off state vanished in the steppes: frontier lands, where real Tatars lived their nomadic existence, a no man's land before the khanate of the Crimea, Ottoman Turkey and Shi'ite Persia. There the revolted serfs took refuge and settled. At this stage they were still hunted bandits. But the weakness of the Polish state on whose frontiers the "Republic of the Zaporogue Cossacks" was established like the neighbouring "Cossack armies", enabled these sanctuaries of Slav "Jacques" to survive.

The oppression of the Ukrainian peasantry by the Polish feudal lords was threefold. As social oppression, it was unparalleled in its cruelty and brutality: the serf was *bydlo*, a beast of burden, and, at the least mistake, he would be punished with a thousand tortures and codified amputations in a disciplinary system in which cutting off the nostrils was the unit of measurement. As national oppression, it forced the Ukrainian peasant to address the lord in Polish. As religious oppression, it persecuted the Greek Orthodox religion and made Catholicism the law of the kingdom. Thus, the revolted peasants became the flag-bearers of many liberations, joined by malcontents of every sort, and soon by rebelling minor nobles: all Cossacks.

Tsarist Russia encouraged what it saw as a means of detaching the Ukraine from Poland and, when it later annexed it, it gave the Cossacks a statute guaranteeing them absolute sovereignty over their territories and the free distribution of "pay, salt and shot" in exchange for military service performed in a separate army. The Cossacks thus defended the Russian conquests on all fronts: the tsars moved them from one part of the steppes to another as their expeditions and wars demanded, both against the Turks and their allies and against the Tartars who resisted the Russian seizure of their lands. Later, in the 18th century, the persecutions against the upholders of the "Old Faith" and the centralizing endeavours of Catherine II provoked, much farther east, a revolt by the Yaik and Volga Cossacks against the Russian empire, in which the rebels joined up for several months with the Muslim peoples, the Bashkirs, the Kalmyks and the Kirghiz, against the backdrop of the Russo-Turkish war in the Crimea.[15]

In a second phase, the rebel serfs and the petty nobles who had taken to the *maquis* (to the steppe, one should say) became a military order with the status of an ethnic group. Grol speaks of "the formation of the Cossack people in the mid-16th century". Pugachev, the false tsar of the Ural Cossacks, himself a Great Russian Don Cossack spoke, in one of his manifestoes, of "the Cossack race". "The majority of the Cossacks", writes Pierre Pascal, "were Ukrainians in the case of the Zaporogues, Great Russians in the case of the Don and Yaik Cossacks; but among the former were numerous Tatars and among the latter in even larger numbers Kalmyks and Kirghiz."[16]

The first great Cossack revolt, led by the *Hetman* Bogdan Chmielnizcki against the kingdom of Poland between 1648 and 1658, notably saw vast massacres of Jews settled on the domains of Catholic Polish lords whose affairs they managed. These massacres heralded the crisis from which the modern European Jewish question would emerge. But the decisive role of the Cossack phenomenon in the history of this region underlines the vagueness, or the semantic shift, which affected the identification of socio-cultural and ethno-linguistic groups in eastern Europe; it also illustrates the entanglement of ethnic, religious and social determinations in the pre-capitalist structures of these states. Were the Cossacks a people? Against all historical and archaeological logic, certainly against all ethnic logic, Lenin at one time thought that the Cossacks too had the right to self-determination!

People, classes, orders, castes . . . So many approximations for shifting or incomplete formations, whose history and configuration altered according to the changing fortunes of war, and were no more than what they were at any particular point in time in these changing fates, whatever the idea they may have had of themselves.

It is vital to grasp the overall picture of which the history of the Slav countries was a part, in order to understand the fate of the Jews in these regions. It is necessary to see the dual movement of Germans eastward and Tartars westward, which underlay and informed the rival constructions of Poland and Russia and distorted their social problematics.

> Colonists from Germania in the broad sense (often from Lorraine or the Netherlands) settled east of the Elbe from the twelfth to the thirteenth century and even in the fourteenth, by means of political or social arrangements, and also by force. The newcomers built their villages in the midst of vast forest clearings, laid out their houses along the roads, probably introduced heavy ploughs with iron ploughshares, created farms and imposed German law on both these and the Slav towns – the Magdeburg law for the mainland and the Lubeck for the seas. This involved an immense migration.[17]

Not only did this movement of Germans eastward, periodically flooding over Poland, run up against the established network of Slav towns and peoples, it also counterbalanced the movement of Turkish-Mongol Tartars westwards. For the Golden Horde came and went in successive waves between Europe and China, as though attracted by the vacuum, taking advantage of the weaknesses of empires on which its transhumance fed. In the 16th century, the Russians took Kazan and Astrakhan, and this marked the beginning of their expansion into Asia: the Mongols retreated eastward and the nomads in the south of Russia reduced their pressure.

> In the course of this action, old Muscovy lost a number of its peasants, who fled from the strict authority of their lords. The lands they abandoned passed into the hands of new arrivals, peasants from the Baltic countries and Poland. The gaps this group left unoccupied were filled in their turn, and at the appropriate moment, by peasants from Brandenburg or Scotland. It was a sort of relay race. This is the view that two distinguished historians, Alexandre and Eugéne Kulischer, take of this silent history, this man-slide from Germany to China. Its currents run underground as though concealed beneath the skin of history.[18]

Ashkenazi Jewry in Poland was formed at the time that this reversal was happening, which was also the time of the Germans *Ostsiedlung*. And, while it is true that the Jews of Germany took over the leadership of communities partly made up of semi-Judaized Khazars and Cumans, it is also true that the formation of this Jewry occurred at the very crossroads of these two waves, participating in both, and definitely outside the process by which the Slavs set out on the conquest of their own domain and hegemony. The revolt of the Polish and Ukrainian peasants as well as the Russian colonization of the Urals, the Caucasus, the Crimea and Siberia, were part of this conquest, as was the creation of Christian Bulgaria. In its own movement eastward, Ashkenazi Jewry not only met remnants of Persian and Byzantine Jewry moving westward; it – quite unintentionally – carved out its own autonomous domain in the interstices of these flows. Jewish-German society, which was flourishing at the time of the Polish monarchy and feudalism, entered into crisis when its protectors began to yield ground: to the Christian merchants of their own towns and the clergy; to the Cossack revolt of the Ukrainian peasantry and, finally, to Russian expansion.

When Mieszko III (1173–1202) struck coins with inscriptions in Hebrew in his kingdom of Greater Poland, "the use of these coins was not related to any question of religion. They were minted because many of the Polish people were more used to this type of script than to the Roman script, not considering it as specifically Jewish".[19] The Hebrew alphabet for writing Polish may even have been a contribution of Karaite Khazaria, doubtless the result of the artisanal expertise of the Jews of Germany.

When Boleslav Kalitzky, of Halich, granted the charter of civil self-government and commercial freedom to Jews who settled in his principality, in 1264, this charter was absolutely similar to the charter of Magdeburg which regulated the self-government of German towns. Casimir Piast, called the Great, confirmed and extended the privileges that Boleslav the Pious had guaranteed to the Jews following the devastating episode of the Tatar conquest. While the German clergy and settlers, still dreaming of the Crusades and the fires of the stake in the West, provoked – on the basis of accusations, classic in western Europe, of ritual murders – the pogroms at Cracow and Poznan (1399) and even, in 1495, a short-lived expulsion of the Jews from Lithuania, the kings of Poland, almost without exception, continued both to encourage Jewish immigration and to guarantee the autonomy of rabbinism within the structure of the kingdom. In 1551, Sigismund Augustus, the last king of the House of Jagellon, endowed Polish Jewry with an autonomous Constitution: the rabbinical hierarchy was centralized, and ran a Jewish "parliament" composed of rabbis and lay notables, recognized by the state and upheld by its authority. This was the Council of the Four Lands (*Vaad Arba Aratsoth*): Lesser Poland, Greater Poland, Podolia and Volhynia. In 1623, the Jews of Lithuania inaugurated their own Council.

From the governmental point of view, the system was useful. It was upon the

Jewish community as a whole that there devolved the function of collecting the heavy taxes which constituted their *raison d'être*, and the function could not be performed efficiently if the communal authorities did not possess the necessary power to take proceedings against the recalcitrant.[20]

At the beginning of the 17th century, when the demographic centre of gravity of Polish Judaism had moved towards the Ukraine where the Jews were tax-farming and exploiting the estates of Catholic lords, it was this Council of the Four Lands that sent a letter "to the Jewish tax-farmers and overseers". "In it one can read that their 'gentle treatment' of the Ukrainian peasantry might lead to great misfortunes for all the Jews of Poland."[21]

The great misfortunes were not long in coming. The prosperity of Polish Jewry like that of the monarchy that protected it was to suffer the repeated blows of national, religious, socio-economic, ideological and ethnic contradictions as a result of which, by a series of partitions, Poland disappeared completely in 1815. As the contemporary Yiddish writer, Isaac Bashevis Singer, says with ironic eloquence:

> Once again the Cossacks attacked Poland, once again they massacred the Jews, at Lublin and in the surrounding areas. The Polish soldiers murdered many of the survivors. Then the Muscovites invaded the eastern provinces and the Swedes the northern ones. It was a time of troubles. Whole communities of Jews could breathe once again, they returned to Judaism. What else could they have done? Accept the religion of their murderers?[22]

In fact, it is quite clear that religion was not at all an issue in these relationships, except as a sign of recognition for groups that were both "nationalitarian" and social. In the Ukraine, which, between the 17th and the 19th centuries, moved from Polish rule to the empire of the tsars, this ethnic division of labour and space had an almost mechanical appearance: the landowners were Polish, the soldiers Cossack, the traders and artisans Jewish and the serfs Ukrainian. Each with its own language, and/or religion, occupying a particular niche in the socio-economic space; each in its own way, and not only the Jews, a "people-class".

A people-class?

The expulsion of the Jews of the West to eastern Europe, like that of the Jews of the Lithuanian towns towards the Jewish towns and villages in the Ukraine, went hand in hand with the rise of Christian commercial bourgeoises: after the flourishing era of mediaeval trade in which Jews "beyond the barriers" acted as a link between the most distant regions, the emergence of business and manufacturing drove them on to new peripheries.

Abraham Léon, in his *La conception matérialiste de la question juive* (English edition: *The Jewish Question*),[23] brilliantly, though no doubt rather too schematically, set out the thesis generally accepted by Marxists, that of a people-class. Taking up the most firmly based of Marx's insights on the subject, Léon claimed that it was the specific economic function of the Jews in the natural pre-capitalist mercantile economy of mediaeval Europe that explains the survival of the princely protections without which Judaism could not have survived. Since Marx, there has been a debate, between historians and philosophers of history, fuelled by the theses of Weber and Sombart,[24] on the sequence and interaction of causes and effects, economic and ideological, on both Jews and Christians, of this specialization of the Jews.

In his preface to the new edition of Abraham Léon's book in 1967, Maxime Rodinson shows the limits of the argument: contrary to the idea that Léon develops, of an essentially commercial dispersion of the Jewish communities of Europe before the Crusades, the specialization of the Jews came about very late. We have seen that it did not exist in the East before Islam. Léon, a former socialist-Zionist who became a Trotskyite when he was twenty years old in Nazi-occupied Belgium and died in 1944 in deportation, was determined to reduce the history of society to an economic mechanism, and this prevented him from understanding the national and political dimensions of this concentration of Jews in the functions of middlemen, of men in the middle. The economistic reduction made it possible to confer retrospectively on the process of protecting and then expelling the Jews a unity wholly contained within the history of capitalism. Describing the penultimate moment of mediaeval Judaism in the West, Léon writes that

> the system was one of grandiose simplicity. Jews despoiled the lords and the kings fleeced the Jews. But, in order to fleece them, it was essential to keep them there. That is why the kings protected the Jews and encouraged their ventures with all the means available to the throne.

However,

> the transformation of all classes of society into producers of exchange values, into owners of money, raises them unanimously against Jewish usury, whose archaic character emphasizes its rapacity. The struggle against the Jews takes on increasingly violent forms.

And thus "the Jews were progressively expelled from all the Western countries. It was an exodus from more developed countries to the more backward ones of Eastern Europe."[25]

When he opened up his kingdom to Jews from Germany, king Casimir had invoked "the principle of tolerance imposed by divine law"; behind this humanism, Léon sees the economic function of Jewish traders, artisans and usurers vital to what he calls "the natural economy". There is no doubt about the role played by Jewish (and also, and it is here that things become complicated, German) artisans and traders in the reconstruction of Poland after the Tatar invasion of 1240–41. However, it cannot be claimed, as Léon does, that Poland "which became the main refuge of Jews driven out of everywhere else", was at that time "plunged deep in feudal chaos"; on the contrary, the state that settled the Jews from Germany and Bohemia on its territory was a confident conquering monarchy, quite capable of holding out against the growing Christian urban bourgeoisie and the bishops. This Casimir Piast, whom the "feudalists" lambasted and had nicknamed "king of the serfs and Jews", was not ruling over a "feudal chaos", but was animated by a determination to transform Poland into a great "Western" power.[26] Feudal anarchy would come later. It is, moreover, significant that, when the monarchy weakened in the face of the Church and Christian merchants in the cities, it was under the protection of the feudal lords, on their estates, that Polish Jewry took refuge; and their socio-economic position then went far beyond the mere functions of exchange. Not only because the Jewish artisanat implied, in the conditions of social separation and community concentration, domestic production, but also because the economic prerogatives that the Jews of Poland enjoyed from the 13th century were absolutely not limited to those that the Jews in France and Germany had enjoyed, *de facto*, before the era of the expulsions. In the 12th century, writes Théophile Grol, "one finds Jews who are the owners of whole villages. In the archives of the 14th and 15th centuries, one finds villages with Jewish names: Zidovska Vola, Zidovska Vila, Kazhari, etc."[27] And Cecil Roth adds that alongside a small proportion of money-lenders, Jews were present

> in every branch of commercial activity... Wealthy Jews are found as tax-farmers; they administered the excise and tolls, they were frequently employed as financial agents for the sovereign. Some leased and exploited the landed property of the nobility, or the Crown domains... They worked the salt-mines, purchased standing timber, traded in furs, exported surplus agricultural produce into Germany. The Jewish *Randar (Arrendator)*, or innkeeper-taxgatherer, was familiar in the remotest villages.[28]

Dazzled by his economistic mechanism, Léon rather twisted the facts. Determined to reduce wars, persecutions and insurrections to struggles between economic forms and modes of production that successively displaced one another through violence (feudalism, commercial capitalism, industrial capitalism), he prevents himself from thinking about the inconsistencies of this way of seeing things. If, in the 12th century, one finds in Poland Jewish villages whose name is Khazari, perhaps we must, without falling into the excesses of Koestler and those who think like him, see the very existence of Jewish communities in this domain as an older phenomenon, and not blindly follow, as Léon does, the classical theses of rabbinical and later Jewish nationalist historiography as to the process by which these communities were formed. Above all, these communities were not simply economic abstractions but constituted a separate society, speaking its own language and possessing its own institutions; they did not occupy only one position in social relations. They also occupied – almost sovereignly – the geographical domain of their autonomy. And it was because of this depth that the Jews in Poland had become not only the middlemen in exchange, but also the direct intermediaries of Polish feudal exploitation, not "outside the barriers" or "royal serfs" like the Jews in the West, but on the contrary internal to the feudal order. And the fact that German-speaking Jews were inside the agrarian system of Polish Catholics was only possible because the serf himself was a Greek Orthodox Ukrainian.

Léon's shift is not accidental: it relates to the systematically obscured aspect of the concept of "people-class", the "people" aspect. The obscuring affects not only the internal social function of community power; it also disguises one of the main objective functions of the establishment of the Jews in Poland, and of their gradual displacement towards the Ukraine: that of creating a socio-cultural and demographic screen in a zone where sovereignty was threatened by vast population movements. It was a policy of colonization by an intermediary ethnic group, which might anachronistically be compared to the colonial logic of the Crémieux decree, in Algeria, in the late 19th century, granting French citizenship, at one and the same time, to indigenous Jews and to any Jewish or Christian European who agreed to settle on occupied Arab lands or towns. This system rested on the most brutal oppression. In the Russian empire, which was to annex most of the area where this occupation occurred, and which Lenin called "the prison of peoples", this *de facto* multinationalism was structured around violence. Each of the nationalities involved repeatedly attempted, either to recover its independence or to establish its hegemony over all or part of this domain. Except, precisely, the Jews: until the 19th century, their separate community life, articulated on the protection of the kings and lords and institutionalized according to its own rabbinical model, constituted in its entirety a function, and not a contradiction, of this system.

The juridical and religious life of the Jewish communities of eastern Europe, which flourished until the 17th century, reflected the functioning of the rabbinical social organization, which the Ashkenazi sages were to perfect in exceptional circumstances: "Nowhere, since the decay of the Jewish centre in Palestine, had so complete an approach to autonomy existed."[29] And, when this society entered into crisis, it was to be swept by new mystical and messianic currents, expressing its disruption in the very language of rabbinical debate: far from breaking down the traditional problematic of community identity and self-image, they would invest it with a renewed life and content, conferring an enhanced legitimacy on the institutions representing it.

This was because the spatial facts and demographic features of Ashkenazi Judaism in eastern Europe made for an unprecedented situation: several hundred thousands, and before long millions of Jews were now concentrated on a scattered but still continuous territory in which, in 1860, according to Nathan Weinstock, they constituted 70 per cent of the population.

What was, in fact, happening here was the emergence of the material conditions of nationalitarian existence. Yet, and so long as the social, legal, educational and family organization of rabbinical orthodoxy persisted, no national demand arose from this society, which only thought of itself through the prism of the messianic eschatology of the diaspora and exile.

The Shtetl: a mini-city

As Léon stresses: "in Poland royal protection took on unusual proportions in this epoch." In his *History of the Jews*, Graetz writes: "The general, political and economic conditions of Poland led the Jews to live as a state within the state, with their own religious, administrative and financial institutions. The Jews formed a special class there, enjoying a special internal autonomy." Describing the activity of the Council of the Four Lands, Roth specifies that:

> Apart from apportioning taxes, it would assist in enforcing royal edicts; it passed sumptuary laws, to enforce moderation in dress and social life; ... it supervised the system of education; it acted as a court of appeal, and decided on matters which were in dispute between one congregation and another, it exercised a rigid control over Hebrew printing... All its regulations, however trivial, could be enforced if the necessity arose, by the power of excommunication, backed by the authority of the State.[30]

Here, protection explicitly concerned the rabbinical organization of Jewish society. Defining by decree, in 1551, the autonomous constitution of Judaism in Poland, Sigismund Augustus laid down that "the coercive power of the State may be made available to it".

A direct consequence of the demographic factors mentioned above was the particular form of establishment of this autonomy over the territory: the social structure here differed fundamentally from everything that Judaism had known since the end of the Roman age. The community was not simply isolated by the frontier of the clan, as in Arab society, nor by that of status, as in the Christian West. The minority of Jews whose occupation put them in touch with the Gentiles, even if they acted as philanthropic benefactors to the community – redistributing to "charity" a part of their profits – and *chtadlanim*, intermediaries with the Polish government and spokesmen for the interests of their co-religionists, were not its effective leaders. It was no longer a matter here of representing a ghetto – the Jewish quarter of a Christian town – but of managing a society scattered over a vast territory. The basic unit of this administrative organization headed by its "councils" was the *kahal* (public): the physical form of the community, outside the large towns where it co-existed with Christians as in the ghettos in the West, was the exclusively Jewish small town. In Hebrew, *ayarah*, in Yiddish, *shtetl*, literally, "mini-city".

The whole zone whose geographical outlines we have sketched was thus dotted with exclusively Jewish towns and villages, self-governing and linked to one another by various central institutions. Protection here covered not only the legal and fiscal autonomy which ensured the social domination of the rabbinical caste in alliance with the assimilated notables who frequented the Polish government. It also meant, in practice, a *de facto* sovereignty over plots of the domain, the continuous and recognized usufruct of pieces of territory.

Such an exclusive occupation of pieces of the countryside was not only unprecedented in the history of post-talmudic Judaism; it survived in an absolutely closed cultural environment, which was ideologically hostile and often aggressive, but above all linguistically separate. At Yavneh, as at Babylon, on the eve of Islam, the language of the everyday life of Jews, the language of talmudic commentary, Aramaic, was common to Jews and others. It was the same later, with Arabic and Spanish. Judaeo-German itself, at the time when it was formed, testified to a cultural give and take between Jews and German society. Whereas the Jewish mini-city in eastern Europe, a discontinuous protectorate, did not speak the language of its neighbours. No Judaeo-Slav dialect, no acculturation emerged from this coexistence and juxtaposition. Here, a curtain of intellectual opacity gave physical form to the separation.

The legal and administrative autonomy of the Jewish protectorate could never have culminated in the ritual and despotic authoritarianism of the Ashkenazi rabbinical dynasties if the Jews, as a whole, in these regions had not been both united among themselves and isolated from others by the walls of a linguistic universe that was peculiarly their own. The totality of the perception of the world was thus refracted through the prism of a language that was as private as the Law, and as national as the institutions that governed the internal social order of the community.

However, the linguistic autonomy of the *Shtetl* (taken here, not in the sense of a particular small town, but of the whole of the society that was born of the interaction of the small towns and the cities) cannot be defined simply. For ideological reproduction – the cement of the global social order – passed through the channel of three languages: Hebrew, the language of compulsory religious schooling organized by the community, that is the sacred language; Aramaic, the language of the oral law and essential for study; and finally Yiddish, then exclusively a spoken language, confined to the purely material and personal domains of everyday life. This trilingualism was not simply skin-deep. It reflected the dual alienation of Jews in the *Shtetl vis-à-vis* their official identity, what Marx called their "chimaerical nationality": when they were Israelites in exile in Babylon, they were already bilingual, putting their Hebrew texts from one alphabet to the other, commenting on them and translating them for the people into Aramaic. Later, when they were "Babylonians" in exile in Germany, they were speaking Yiddish. And now they were in Galicia and the Ukraine, bearers of this triple heritage, rendered three times incapable of defining themselves in terms of the present of the place that tolerated them.

In addition, this trilingualism was altogether hierarchical, and the (late) Yiddish proverb stresses this, saying: "fish is not meat, nor Yiddish a language." When it is realized that the dietary prohibitions of the Law distinguish between meat – which must never be mixed with or come into contact with milk products – and fish, which is *parveh*, i.e., neutral – neither meat nor milk product, and able to accompany either the one or the other – we can see the importance of the distinction. Each of the three complementary languages corresponded to a given level of communication within Jewish society: none of them on its own constituted a complete and self-sufficient whole. The trichotomy among the sacred (Hebrew), the legal (Aramaic) and the private (Yiddish) ran through the social order by materializing the discourse that underlay it.

All the conditions were therefore present, in the 16th century, for the Judaeo-Ashkenazi society of central and eastern Europe to become the site of a peculiar experimentation of the rabbinical project, without being interrupted by some great expulsion or any tribal or commercial secularization. As if the ideal of Ezra and Nehemiah, revised and corrected by the sages and the rabbis, had waited for this Ukrainian winter, this Lithuanian tip of the world, to find at last the circumstances it needed. In the shelter of the objective conditions that we have just outlined, the *Shtetl* was to become, for several centuries, the domain of the application of the Law, the kingdom where orthodoxy reigned uncontested. But this orthodoxy was more absolute than talmudic and classical Judaism had been: the Mishnah fails to conceal the sharpness of the debates and contradictions between schools, the political options and social interests that divided the educated stratum. When the Babylonian academies in Mesopotamia legislated for the Diaspora, they lacked the means to silence either their learned opponents or the sects challenging them. And even when the Umayyads attempted to confer supreme legal authority on the *gaon*, the division of the Muslim world enabled the dissidents to take refuge with their Abbassid rivals; whereas Ashkenazi rabbinism henceforth saw only debates of the most formal kind. Of course, a large-scale social mutation had occurred between the two moments: the Jewish peasantry, the "people of the land", had been replaced by the non-Jew, the Gentile, the Goy. As the law of a caste, of a class, of a particular order, post-mediaeval Polish Judaism was no longer riven by the same social contradictions as in talmudic times. It replaced exegetic discussion and criticism by recitation and *pilpul*, the art of argument that consisted in making anything say anything: its acme of intellectual achievement, says Roth, was

> to establish an artificial analogy between different themes, to create elaborate distinctions between connected passages, to build up a syllogism between texts which had nothing to do with one another, or to treat the end of one tractate and the beginning of the next (relating to a different subject) as though they constituted a continuous text... To study the plain text was considered

elementary, and only a scholar who had proved his mettle in the intricacies of *pilpul* now counted for anything. The method was futile, wasteful, and from certain points of view even pernicious.[31]

This dogmatism was the basis for an exaggerated ritualism. Well before the diffusion of kabbalistic ideas, the Ashkenazi Judaism of southern Germany had made exaggerated observance a virtue. For generations, the rabbis of Europe were to explore the ancient texts to deduce new observances from them, new prescriptions, new prohibitions: in short, new ways of serving God. The more gratuitous they were, the more effective they would be. The more absurd they were, the more it was necessary to argue brilliantly to justify them. The method was admirably suited to the imperatives of the right of exemption, of which the casuistics of the Jesuits were but a pale reflection.

This hegemony determined in advance the forms that the internal reactions and contradictions of the system of community rule would take: they would be mystical and messianic, whether they were defeated and hence decreed heretical, or successful in blending into orthodoxy, by reforming it. But the new ideas on which these movements would build would almost always come from elsewhere: from the world outside the *Shtetl* represented by the Jewish communities of the Mediterranean world and the East.

Strictness and exaggeration in the performance of ritual prescriptions were not new in European Judaism. In the 13th century, the *Hasidim*, or "pious men", of Worms, claimed allegiance to Judah the Hasid (*Yehuda ha-Hasid*), who died at Regensberg in 1217. In France, at the same time, says Gershom Scholem, "some communities admitted members freed of all practical activity ... In mediaeval France they were called Hasidim (Pious) or *Prushim*".[32] But at that time it was an élitist and voluntary practice, like the Nazarenes or pharisees in Roman times: a moral aristocracy drawing its members from within the stratum of the educated raised itself by observance or asceticism above the ignorant populace. On the contrary, the Ashkenazi rabbis, who enjoyed an absolute authority over the community as a whole, henceforth imposed on all the adult males of the *Shtetl* strict observance of the whole Law perfected by their attention.

By the beginning of the 16th century, the jealous and tyrannical domination of the *halakha* – the rabbinical "custom" derived from the Talmud – and the hierarchy of power based on knowledge of the texts rested on the printing and diffusion of religious books. This literature gave rabbinical conservatism its letters of credence and strengthened its authority. But it also tended to break the cultural and mental isolation of the *Shtetl* by linking it up with the circulation of ideas and practices elaborated elsewhere: not among the Poles, the Russians, the Ukrainians or the Germans, but among the rabbis of Italy or the East. Of Palestine, particularly, of the "Land of Israel", from where the kabbalistic rabbinism of Spain was to spread to Poland.

It was in fact from Safed, in Palestine, where Spanish "pious men" had been expecting the Messiah since the 13th century beside the tomb of Simeon Bar Yohai, that there emerged, in the kabbalistic atmosphere in which Moses Cordovero had written his *Vineyard of Pomegranates (Pardes Rimonim),*[33] the leading work of orthodoxy, the *Shulchan Aruch* ("The Set Table") by Yossef Caro (1488–1575). The grand rabbi of Cracow, Moses Isserles (1520–1572), author of a detailed commentary on the work of the Hispano-Palestinian kabbalist Caro and the son-in-law of Shalom Shakhna, grand rabbi of Lublin and Lesser Poland, had it adopted as a practical manual of orthodox observance by the whole of Ashkenazi Judaism.

It was also at Safed, in the 16th century, that rabbi Isaac Luria Ashkenazi – Sephardic through his mother and Ashkenazi through his father – officiated in two synagogues, one Spanish, the other German. Historians of Judaism agree that he played a key role in the diffusion of kabbalistic ideas in central and eastern Europe.

The penetration of kabbalistic mysticism into the Ashkenazi world practically coincided with the end of the prosperity of the *Shtetl*: the Union of Lublin, which sealed Polish-Lithuanian unity in the 15th century, had marked the beginning of the withdrawal of Jewish privileges. Seeking a substitute for weakening royal protection, the Jews had gone and established their community life on the feudal estates in the steppes in the south and east, with the consequences that are well known: the 17th century was punctuated by the great massacres of the Cossack revolt, between 1648 and 1658, itself preceded by the "little massacres" of 1637. The coming of Russian protection for the Cossacks, in 1654, transformed the anti-Polish, anti-Catholic and anti-Jewish revolt of the peasantry into a permanent feature. Wars and invasions (by the Russians and the Swedes), and liberation movements such as that of Stephen Czarniecki against the Swedish invader were unfailingly accompanied by new massacres. There followed the return to Judaism of which Singer writes: the return to mysticism. As in Christian Spain, where the *Zohar* had seen the light of day, ritualistic quietism became transformed into millenarian and messianic anguish. As usual, persecutions and economic crisis heralded the end of time.

Two storms, a century apart, shook this universe, by materializing its capacity to let itself be drawn along by the first false Messiah to appear. Shabbetai Zvi in the 17th century, and Yaacov Frank in the 18th, both trained in the Kabbala, galvanized the hopes of redemption of the Jews of Europe in ephemeral flare-ups.

Zvi, a Sephardi from Smyrna, proclaimed himself the Messiah in 1665. The enthusiasm that he aroused rapidly spread beyond the borders of his community – to Italy, Holland, England and Germany – and even touched Polish Jewry. Indeed, the companion of Zvi and of the Palestinian Jew who served as his "prophet", Nathan of Gaza, was supposedly a Polish Jewish woman of whom it was said that she had only escaped the recent massacres by agreeing to be converted to Catholicism, before moving to Turkey and returning to the faith of her ancestors. In any event, the Sabbatian heresy precipitated a departure of Ashkenazi pilgrims to Palestine, where Zvi had promised them redemption and the restoration of the kingdom.

Then came the *coup de théâtre:* summoned by the Sultan to renounce his prophetic claims or die, Zvi converted to Islam, and with him several thousand of his disciples (the spiritual ancestors of the Turkish sect of the *Donmeh*). Yet, long after his death, and despite this spectacular act of apostasy, Sabbatianism remained influential. A century later, in Hamburg, rabbis Emden and Eybeschutz were still engaging in polemics about it, and the accusation of Sabbatianism featured in their quarrels.

It was, however, in Podolia, that is, in the Ukraine, that Jacob Leibowitz, called "Frank" appeared, in the 18th century. He not only claimed to be the Messiah; he also claimed to be the reincarnation of Zvi himself.

Even from the orthodox historiography of Frankism, which is allusive and calumnious, a few facts can be gleaned. The rapid spread of the new sect provoked a reaction on the part of the orthodox rabbinate. Meeting in Brody, a special rabbinical tribunal pronounced the *herem* – excommunication and banishment – on the members of the sect, using as a pretext their "loose morals". Frank and his followers then declared themselves Zoharists, claiming that the Kabbala annulled the authority of the rabbis and the Talmud. It was following this episode that the orthodox rabbinate prohibited reading of the *Zohar* before the age of forty. But the open dissidence of the Frankists against the authority of the rabbis, which, significantly, was directed against the Talmud, had to be taken before "the executive power of the state": summoned by the Polish Church to state their principles, the Frankists, faithful to the example of Zvi, declared themselves *en bloc* a Christian sect, and finally abandoned Judaism.

While Sabbatianism had shaken western and Mediterranean Judaism, it had barely touched the Ashkenazi world of eastern Europe. Whereas Frankism, less international in its spread, had had its main field of operations in the demographic centre of gravity of Polish Judaism. It had profoundly shocked the rabbinical classes and the urban notables, precipitating an anti-kabbalistic inquisition in which the spectres of Zvi and Frank acted as the main bogeys, strengthening even more the authoritarianism and élitism of the official leaders of the community.

But the concern and revolt of the civil *Shtetl* against the omnipotence of the scholars and the central institutions did not end for all that. While in the Mediterranean false messiahs continued to appear among the Sephardic and Marrano kabbalists of Italy, England and the Netherlands, Kabbalism, which had been a banner in the anti-rabbinical struggle, continued to spread in Poland virtually underground. Kabbalistic literature, rare and semi-illegal, was replaced by oral tradition whose mode of transmission systematized and simplified it to the extreme. Magic and the science of amulets, considered as "practical Kabbala", took on a new lease of life by grafting themselves on to the spontaneous rebellion of popular messianism against orthodoxy, and, in the new conditions of pietism and expectation, the power of the rabbis no longer had the legitimacy and authority that it had had at the time of prosperity and royal protection.

Hasidism

It was against this background that the *Baal Shem Tov* appeared, also born in the Ukraine in 1700, who founded the most important movement in European Judaism in modern times: Hasidism (*Hasidut,* in Hebrew: piety). This pietist, populist and supremely popular movement[34] aroused the passionate adherence of hundreds of thousands of Jews in eastern and central Europe, and was to survive in Europe until the Second World War.[35]

Unlike the messianisms of the same period, Hasidism was careful, while spreading its own conceptions, never openly to call into question either rabbinical orthodoxy or the authority of the Talmud. It never even directly claimed allegiance to the Kabbala. Yet it provoked what can only be described as a revolution in the religious practice of the Yiddish-speaking masses of eastern Europe. We must grasp the significance of the emergence of this movement in relation to the problematic that concerns us: the internal one – the relations of power within the community; and the external one – the relationship, real and imaginary, with the concrete power of the state. And, here again, we must attempt to unravel simple repetition from that which, within the many layered discourse of Judaic eschatology, bears the singular imprint of that time and place.

Israel ben Eliezer, whom his followers nicknamed "Master of the Good Name" (*Baal Shem Tov:* abbreviated as Besht) was, according to legend, a simple Podolian lime-digger. He became the idolized leader of a rapidly growing movement, and enjoyed "rare personal magnetism". He

> taught that piety was superior to scholarship, and that it was the prerogative of any man, however ignorant and however poor, to attain communion with his God ... On the other hand, there existed certain Righteous Ones *(Zodikim)* who were close to the Almighty, and whose intercession might sometimes sway His immutable Will ... After the founder's death, the conception arose that some families possessed a kind of special merit, which passed down by hereditary right from one *Zodik,* or Righteous One, to another, all designated to act as intermediaries between man and God. Dov Baer of Meseritz (1710–1772), the earliest scholar among the adherents of Hasidism, adapted the new doctrines to the taste of the more learned elements, amongst whom it henceforth began to make increasing headway.[36]

Sabbatian messianism erupted at the same time as the first great anti-

Jewish (and anti-Polish) uprising of the Ukrainian peasantry. Frankism, which had followed it, was destroying itself at the very time that Hasidism was flowering. As the renewal of messianic mysticism and pietism had accompanied the crisis of mediaeval Islamic society and the persecutions in Europe at the time of the Crusades, so the crisis of the old feudal world was gripping the Ashkenazi-Jewish world in a vice: in the west, the rising bourgeoisie and revolution were putting the emancipation of the Jews on the agenda, that is putting an end to the separate community order, while in the east the revolt of the oppressed nationalities of the two empires was reconquering first the socio-economic domain and then the territorial domain which the empires had granted to Jewish autonomy.

Hasidism in Poland emerged not only from an atmosphere that was propitious to messianism, but also from a climate in which false messianisms had already cut deeply into the very body of Jewish society. At the level of the crisis itself, Judaism had never been so threatened from within since the end of the Byzantine period. "Practical Kabbala" constituted the immediate background. From the calculation of messianic time and the numerical decoding of texts to prediction of the future and miraculous cures, was only a short step: that which separated the élite of scholars – the social basis of the rabbinical caste – from the multitude of the "ordinary people" of the community. Along with the development of the sects which gathered around these messiahs, true or false, there was an increase in semi-magical practices among the people. The *Baalei ha-Shem* (literally: "Masters of the Name") constituted a recognized category of itinerant preacher-healers, half-way between authentic rabbinical mysticism and these charlatans.

The "Name" that their appellation evokes is of course the Name of God, which rabbinical tradition surrounded with the most absolute secrecy. The letters YHWH – which Western transliteration turns into the form Yahweh or Jehovah – are never pronounced in Jewish tradition. They are deemed to constitute a sort of set of abstract initials to describe the Unnameable; they are replaced in reading by *Adonaï* (literally: "My Lord"), or more simply by *Ha-Shem,* "the Name". The complete taboo on pronouncing the name of God, from the talmudic period, could not fail to give rise to a whole "science" of the secret Name. Kabbalistic literature had contributed to this flowering by popularizing the idea that Moses, then Joshua, then the prophets, then the members of the Great Synagogue of Ezra, and, after them, a secret and unbroken chain of initiates, knew the Name of God – that is, the vocalization of YHWH – which they transmitted from mouth to mouth at the moment of their death. The enunciation of the Name was thus endowed with a sacred value: in popular language, meaning "with magical virtues". The "masters of the Name" seem thus to have been, at the end of the 17th and beginning of the 18th century, a growing phenomenon, reflecting both the decline of the Kabbala, the emergence of religious hierarchies outside the official rabbinate and the extreme attraction of the Jewish masses of the *Shtetl* for spiritual remedies: a metaphysical hypochondria already implicit in the traditional ritualism and pietism inherited from the Middle Ages, but exacerbated by the new features of this crisis: impoverishment and persecution.

The founder of Hasidism, the *Baal Shem Tov*, was thus a "Master of the Name"; but he was *tov*; good. Was it the Name that was good, or the master? The meaning of the Hebrew expression is too vague (it can also mean "man of good repute") to be of any help here. The founder of contemporary Ashkenazi mysticism was a healer but a "good" one. One can see in this an implicit disapproval of the doubtful character of other "masters of the Name"; in any case, there was the idea that the *Besht*, who died in 1760, was not a mere itinerant healer, exorcizing the possessed and selling talismans, but a mediator of a different quality. A later Hasidic legend tells how one of the faithful had asked the Righteous man for a word of intercession, thinking that the Master would write a magical secret formula. But, on a scrap of paper given to his client, the Master had written only his own name, a symbol of his personal intercession and his almost analytical taking over of responsibility for the need of the other.

The official rabbinical hierarchy had established a social hierarchy in the community wholly legitimized by talmudic learning. Here, to rabbinical ritualism was added a cult of exegetic study and erudition which recreated, within the community, the type of cleavage that had existed between sages and "peoples of the land" at the time of the Jerusalem Talmud. Thus, the glorification of knowledge could serve to institutionalize the ignorance of the ignorant. Protected by the ignorance of the humble and by the protection of the prince, the rabbinical caste could thus prosper in the shadow of the rich.

Hasidism appears first of all as a reaction of revolt against this élitism of book learning. By stressing devotion in observance and by sanctifying every corner of everyday life, this pietism expressed the pressure of practical forms of popular religiosity on rabbinical institutions and language. Herein lay the basic ambiguity of Hasidism, which put it on the same wavelength as the formation of talmudic Judaism itself: for the Hasidic movement was, in one and the same movement, to contest the existing hierarchy and its scriptural "class language", and to found, in the ideological enthusiasm of a sect transforming itself into a mass movement, a clerical hierarchy of a new sort, which was rapidly to transform itself into an obscurantist and miserabilist caricature of the old one. For rejection of the authority of the rabbinical establishment found its counterpart in faithfulness and devotion to the person of the Master, which limited the mental and spatial universe of his disciples, or pupils, to his "court" alone.

The "cultural revolution" introduced by Hasidism into the forms of power within the community, provoked, for a time, a decentralization of rabbinical power, hitherto structured around the *kahalim* and the regional councils, at the same time expressing the feudalization and ruralization of Jewish life in the Ukraine. The earliest Hasidic leaders came from small towns, unlike the orthodox rabbis concentrated in the large towns. And for a long time they remained restricted within an intra-community geography where the territory structured by the habitation and sovereignty of non-Jews was literally not seen, was denied. Similarly, the direct material upkeep of the Righteous One and his (often numerous) family by the pupils and their families, the direct dependence of the *zaddik* on the narrow community that peopled his court as well as on the pilgrims and visitors, constituted the inevitable counterpart of his independence of the official rabbinical hierarchy and the fiscal administration which linked it directly to the functioning of the kingdom of Poland.

By subjecting the faithful to the charismatic social organization of the court (less than the community, but more than a single family) Hasidism freed them from the rule of the rabbis only to subject them to an even more despotic domination. Moreover, the dynasties of the Righteous, often hereditary, which were to people the Hasidic movement during its two hundred-year expansion soon transported their courts into the large towns and transformed themselves into a new rabbinical establishment, sometimes through struggle, sometimes through alliance with the old one, to such an extent that, at the beginning of the 20th century, Hasidism would appear as the obscurantist-popular wing of Ashkenazi rabbinical Judaism.

It was not only the establishment of Hasidic ideas and practices that gave it this popular character. The sanctification of activities previously considered as profane, such as the imbibing of alcohol, ecstatic dancing, or even sexuality, represented an adaptation – a concession – to the actual way of life of the masses of the *Shtetl.* And the absolute subordination of women in the home in this model, based in theory on their exclusion from spiritual life,[37] epitomizes its obscurantist side as much as the refusal to study profane sciences, or the rejection of technological civilization.

As with all the previous stages in the actualization of the Law, Hasidic Judaism only innovated by clothing itself in the colours of true orthodoxy: indeed, it refused to organize a sect, i.e., a schism. The host of sectarian cells centred on the Righteous who rapidly transformed themselves into *wonderrebbes,* miracle rabbis, did not form a new church, but a current within rabbinism itself. That is why one feature of this evolution recurred: the real contradictions running through the communal society, even when they had their roots in transformations occurring in the outside world (that is, in the history of non-Jewish states and societies), were expressed in the language of tradition, in the conceptual framework of talmudic debate. Here again, as several times before in the history of Judaism, an archaic framework of thought reflecting conditions that had long since disappeared, was reinvigorated by the challenge that developed within it. The revolt did not, in fact, signal a disintegration of the whole whose organization it challenged; on the contrary, because the revolt conceived of itself as internal, it made for cohesion at a higher level. Nor was the Hasidic challenge to the power of the rabbis simply a sign of social contradictions within the community. It also testifies to the impact of rabbinical language on the civil society of the *Shtetl,* which elaborated its own response in the very terms used by the challenged forms of authority. Hasidism therefore marked an unprecedented taking over of pietism by the lowliest strata of Jewish society and was to impregnate the whole of the Ashkenazi world.

The ambivalence of challenge and fidelity in Hasidism is seen in the stormy history of its relations with orthodoxy. So long as the *Hasidim* limited themselves to adoring their Righteous One in the little town of Medjiboj, the rabbinical hierarchy of Poland ignored them. Between the pedlar healers carrying amulets and the itinerant kabbalists, the *Besht* aroused no anxiety. He preached piety, not the kingdom. His teaching could not be suspected, despite its kabbalistic undertones, of leading to Sabbatian deviations. Moreover, virtually illiterate in his preaching, he did not claim allegiance to either the Kabbala or any writing, which dispensed him from having to pronounce himself on the validity of other texts. So that the Talmud itself was never challenged: it was the practice of bookish study which was wholly downgraded in the affectivism of piety. Above all, the movement remained limited to Podolia, and spread among ordinary people, in places where the orthodox hierarchy of the northern and western towns was either absent or very remote. In a second stage, however, the movement spread rapidly; a "secret" meeting was arranged, at Vilna, in about 1772.

The Lithuanian town of Vilna, where the new sect established itself, cannot have been chosen by chance: it was the seat of rabbi Elijah ben Solomon, the supreme rabbinical authority in Poland at the time. He declared war on the new movement, and the *Hasidim* were officially condemned and excommunicated. The orthodox became *Mithnagdim,* the "Opponents", a term which illustrates well enough the defensive character of the talmudic cause, and its retreat in the face of the formidable spread of the new movement. As Roth writes: "When the din of battle died down, a new spirit had pervaded both sides. The *Hasidim* now recognized the importance of the traditional order of things, and counted Rabbis of outstanding learning and ability amongst their numbers."[38] For orthodoxy and Hasidism fought each other only briefly. The second generation of the Righteous Ones, under the lash of the *Maggid* (Preacher) of Mezeritz, embarked on the peaceful take-over of the rabbinical world of the educated and owning strata. Soon, in a Galicia which had come under Austrian rule, orthodoxy and Hasidism formed an alliance against a common enemy – the Enlightenment movement brought by the Napoleonic conquest.

Yet, the initial terms of orthodox opposition to Hasidism were those of an irreducible antagonism. The rabbi of Vilna had himself called *gaon,* like his remote predecessors in rabbinism under the Umayyad caliphs, guardians of the Talmud and persecutors of the Karaites. Since Lithuania was, moreover, one of the regions of eastern Europe where Karaite communities survived until modern times, it may be supposed that the *gaon* of Vilna and the supporters of orthodoxy were not unconscious of this aspect of the gaonite heritage, which inspired the failed persecution of the Frankists in the same period.

The ghost of the Khazars hovers again over this history. It is tempting to attribute to it a hidden, underground role in the resurgence of notions that were, in general, very far removed from the heritage of mediaeval Judaism. The stress put by the *Hasidim* on humility is in some ways reminiscent of the pauperism of the Ebionite: the cult of the Righteous One and community life is reminiscent of the rule of the Sadocite sects. It is tempting to find a Karaite coherence in the whole of the practices and ideas circulating among the masses of the *Shtetl* at odds with rabbinical orthodoxy. And, since Karaism in eastern Europe was, without any doubt at all, an offshoot of Khazaria, the followers of Dunlop and Koestler might see in the confrontation between the masses affected by Hasidism and the rabbinical caste an implicit revolt of indigenous Judaism against the Judaeo-German aristocracy. However attractive such a picture may be, it must face up to the paradox that it involves. The fashionable aestheticist, romantic and folkloric approach to Hasidism which has spread in the West, and which owes much to Martin Buber, at least in the United States, had in fact long been preceded among Western historians of Judaism (and Jewish nationalists), particularly in the 19th century, by the opposite tendency. Thus, the importance of Kabbalism in the culture of classical mediaeval Judaism, and the centrality of Hasidism in the history of the Jews of eastern Europe were systematically played down in attempts to make the social system of the ghetto and the *Shtetl* presentable.[39] In this denial of the mystical, magical and dynastic dimension of popular Judaism, the apologists of a rabbinism revisited in the light of emancipation have attempted to present Hasidism and the Kabbala as marginal, peripheral movements compared to the glorious course of talmudic logic, and above all as foreign to the Jewish cultural tradition. Some have seen in it the influence of Islam and even of Buddhism; the most subtle have seen in it Christian influence.

In fact, while it is true that the ideas of the dominant society have constantly imprinted their impact on the elaboration of official, written and institutionalized Judaism, the spread of Hasidism among the people, like that of the Kabbala in the Mediterranean several centuries earlier, proceeded by the same token from the fact that it had firm roots in the actual conditions of life. One pole of these conditions was the reality of the rabbinical social and institutional system, and the other the everyday experience of a persecution inflicted on the Jews as Jews. When the Cossacks and the Ukrainian peasants swept through massacring Poles, Roman Catholics (who spoke the same language as their tormentors) and Jews (a religious community with a language of its own, whose members were the essential intermediaries between Orthodox serfs and papist lords), they did not ask the Jewish farmer or artisan if he was not, by chance, the descendant of some Khazar convert or Karaite whom the nasty rabbis had conscripted into the talmudic enterprise: it was not talmudism that was being attacked, but the Jews as a group that was at once religious, ethnic and social. The idea that the Jews themselves had of their identity and the dialectic of this threefold determination was irrelevant to the reality of the global confrontation. Persecution made the question of the real or imagined existence of the persecuted group a bad joke. By definition, it existed, since it was being persecuted, and whilst it may be true that it was being persecuted by mistake, in that its own myth had been taken at face value, the fact remains that it had no other choice, as Singer says, than "to return to Judaism". The lack of choice facing the individuals making up this society confronted by the peasant revolt in fact bore no comparison with the heroic fidelity of the "martyrs" of mediaeval Judaism in the West, who could always have agreed to bow to adversity and become Christians, remaining, like the Spanish Marranos, suspected and despised, but at least saving their skins. The Ukrainian peasant, on the other hand, was not in the least interested in converting Jews. It was not their faith that he was attacking but their place in society, and the domain.

Thus, although the messianic fervour that prevailed when Hasidism appeared and developed challenged the élitist organization of official rabbinism which had functioned well in the good days, it had its roots in a movement of return to the community. The community state of emergency precipitated both an upsurge of loyalty to the group as a whole and the relative democratization of its internal hierarchy. And it did so well that Hasidism which downplayed book-learning – that is the study of Hebrew and Aramaic – in favour of oral narration – in Yiddish – extracted the eastern Judaeo-German idiom from the ghetto where its status as a profane language had confined it.

There is one area where Hasidism not only did not challenge orthodoxy, but outbid the rabbinical discourse: the crucial area of the cleavage between Jews and non-Jews. The eschatological justification of difference as essential Difference was one of the constantly recurring themes of rabbinical Judaism: Separation *(havdalah)* was a key concept. God separated Israel from among the Nations and this extraction was of an ontological nature: "Like day from night, like the sacred from the profane." Talmudic law pushed the horror of the mixing of species to the point of prohibiting any grafting of vegetable species. Kabbalistic literature was full of such expressions of national pride and messianic particularism. But the intellectual practice of the Mediterranean Kabbala could, through exegesis, lead to heretical questionings of this basic distinction, which cannot simply be reduced to the divine guarantee of the ethnic superiority of the chosen group. The rabbinical caste, indeed, was dependent on it for its good relations with the princely rulers and the stratum of intermediaries. The weight of this dual relationship tempered the cosmological tribalism of the Law. It had even, under the tolerant Islam of the Abbassids, allowed this tribalism to harmonize its language with the surrounding civilization, which was itself fascinated by Greek Reason.

Nothing like this, no modification of rabbinical ethnicism was at work in the universe of the *Hasidim:* the fact was that the persecution of the community was occurring in conditions that were unique in the history of this Law. The *de facto* separation of the *Shtetl* from the surrounding society, a separation that was not only religious and social, but also linguistic and spatial, found in this the theological weapons it needed to assert itself. While postponing to an indefinite future the hopes for a political messiah, Hasidism also expressed, by its outright denial of time and place, the historical subjectivism of the *Shtetl* which could later fuel the growth of Jewish nationalism.

The internal crisis of the *Shtetl,* whose roots are to be found in the crisis of Polish feudalism, was exacerbated and radically aggravated. The domain of Polish sovereignty was shrinking rapidly. A kingdom that had stretched from the Baltic to the Black Sea grew smaller and smaller as around it tsarist Russia, the Hapsburg empire and the German states grew larger and larger. The Polish question became the European question and centuries-old Polish Jewry saw its territory carved up among several states. Austria, which took Galicia, lightened the conditions of Jews there: but Russia, having seized the Ukraine and Byelorussia, oppressed them there, said Lenin, "more harshly than the Negroes". The Napoleonic conquest, short as it may have been, precipitated the disintegration, inducing a general upheaval in the empires of the centre and east. Following the French occupation, the whole map of the region was transformed. The new frontier of Austria and Russia, which shared the whole of what remained of Poland in 1815, cut the Ashkenazi world in two, divided the dynasties of Hasidic rabbis, and determined new sub-problematics. The sociological unity of Ashkenazi Judaism was beginning to fracture.

Notes

1. The term *Ashkenaz* to describe Germany only appeared at the beginning of the Middle Ages. In the Bible, it is the name of one of the sons of Japhet, and was later arbitrarily given to Germany, just as the name *Sarfat* – originally the name of the Phoenician town of Sarepta – was given to France at about the same period.
2. Marc Bloch, *Feudal Society* (Eng. tr. London, Routledge & Kegan Paul, 1961) p. 66.
3. Ibid., p. 70.
4. Fernand Braudel, *Civilization and Capitalism, 15th – 18th Century, Vol. I, The Structures of Everyday Life,* tr. S. Reynolds (London, Collins, 1981), especially the chapter entitled "Weight of Numbers".
5. The Varangian princes were, like the legendary Rurik, of Scandinavian origin, and had only become "Slavicized" during their long march southward, where they clashed with the Khazars and the Byzantines. By converting to the Orthodox faith, they secured a reversal of alliances from Byzantium and thus sealed the end of Khazar power.
6. Arthur Koestler, *The Thirteenth Tribe* (London, Hutchinson, 1976) p. 70.
7. Ibid., p. 76.
8. Ibid., pp. 74–5.

9. Ibid., p. 79.

10. Simon Szyszman, *Le karaïsme* (Lausanne, Editions l'Age d'Homme, 1980) p. 85.

11. Ibid., p. 90.

12. Ibid., p. 91.

13. Théophile Grol, *Grands moments de l'histoire juive* (Paris, Editeurs français réunis, 1980).

14. Ibid., p. 134.

15. On the revolt of the Yaik Cossacks, see Puskin, *Histoire de Pougatchov* in *Oeuvres* (Paris, Pléiade, Gallimard, 1973).

16. Pierre Pascal, *La révolte de Pougatchëv* (Paris, Julliard, 1971).

17. F. Braudel, *Civilization and Capitalism*, p. 100.

18. Ibid., p. 97.

19. A.N. Poliak, quoted by Koestler, *The Thirteenth Tribe*, p. 62.

20. Cecil Roth, *A Short History of the Jewish People* (London, East and West, 1959; first ed. 1936) pp. 292–3.

21. Théophile Grol, *Grands moments,* p. 135.

22. Quoted by Albert Memmi in *La libération du juif* (Paris, Payot, 1966) p. 70.

23. Abraham Léon, *La conception matérialiste de la question juive* (Paris, E.D.1, new ed., 1968); English edition *The Jewish Question. A Marxist Interpretation* (Mexico, D.F., Ediciones Pioneras, 1950).

24. Max Weber, *Ancient Judaism*, tr. H.H. Gerth and D. Martindale (London, Allen and Unwin, 1952); Werner Sombart, *The Jews and Modern Capitalism,* tr. M Epstein (New York, E.P. Dutton, 1914).

25. Abraham Léon, *The Jewish Question,* pp. 119 and 114–5.

26. Cecil Roth, *A Short History,* p. 290.

27. Théophile Grol, *Grands moments*, p. 96.

28. Cecil Roth, *A Short History,* p. 292.

29. Ibid., p. 294.

30. Ibid., p. 293–4.

31. Ibid., p. 294–5.

32. Gershom Scholem, "Entretiens", in *Actes de la recherche en sciences sociales.*

33. Written in Hebrew, the *Vineyard of Pomegranates* constituted the first systematic presentation of kabbalistic ideas. Cordovero, the leader of the association that bore his name, was the master of Yossef Caro, and one of the great Sephardim who contributed to disseminating the Kabbala and the mysticism of orthodoxy throughout the Jewish world.

34. On Hasidism, see Gershom G. Scholem, *Major Trends in Jewish Mysticism* (New York, Schocken Books, 1946), and Martin Buber's *Hasidic Stories,* as well as his novel mentioned above *For the Sake of Heaven.* On Hasidism in Galicia at the beginning of the century, see the testimony of the Prague writer Jiri Langer, *Nine Gates.*

35. Hasidism survives today mainly in Israel and the United States, and in the small community of emigrés from Hungary (Belz) whom Jacques Gutwirth has studied at Antwerp in *Vie juive traditionelle* (Paris, Editions de Minuit, 1979).

36. Cecil Roth, *A Short History,* pp. 334–5.

37. The everyday liturgy of rabbinical Judaism requires male Jews to say the morning blessing: "Blessed art thou, Lord, who made me neither Gentile, nor peasant, nor woman...", while Jewish women say: "Blessed art thou, Lord, who made me according to thy will..." A good description of the status of women in the Ashkenazi Jewish tradition is to be found in the book by the American-Israeli

Leslie Haselton, *Israeli Women, the Reality Behind the Myth* (Jerusalem, Eidanim Publishing House, 1978).

38. Cecil Roth, *A Short History*, p. 335.
39. Cf. Gershom Scholem, "Entretiens", *Actes de la recherche.*

5   The Crisis

Emancipation and Anti-Semitism

The redrawing of the frontiers separating the Ukraine from Galicia consigned the fragments of the *Shtetl* to different destinies. In the east, in tsarist Russia, the protector of the Cossacks, the old rabbinical order endeavoured to survive, when conditions of its survival were disappearing. In Austria-Hungary, on the other hand, the legal emancipation of the Jews, completed in 1867, but already under way in the 1820s, posed a series of novel questions to the traditional organization.

The movements of Jewish population across the new frontiers and beyond very soon made it wholly illusory to attempt to enclose this problematic in the closed framework of states. The Ukraine and Galicia, Prague, Alsace, Antwerp and London were becoming different facets of a single European question. The *Shtetl* itself, which had been an inward-looking and self-centred universe, became the locus of a provincial consciousness, henceforth defining itself by comparison: not any more with the indeterminate Other, the non-Jew, the *goy*, but with a world-wide hierarchy in which the West dominated the world. It was a slow and painful transformation, which gave birth to the contemporary Jewish question: assimilation and anti-Semitism, massacres and pogroms culminating in the Nazi genocide, Zionism and its consequences, both for the Palestinians and the Arab world, and for the Jews and the world.

While the Jews became concentrated, all through the Middle Ages, in central and eastern Europe, small communities had remained in the West, especially in Germany, where, despite expulsions, there were still to be found, here and there, Jews and even Jewish quarters in some towns. There were even more in Austria and Bohemia, but also communities in the Netherlands, France and England, where Spanish and Portuguese Marranos fleeing the persecutions of the Inquisition had settled in the 17th century.

The everyday domination that Christian governments had exercised over the small Jewish minorities that remained in the West had made the type of autonomy that governed the existence of the *Shtetl* in the east inconceivable. Here, freedom was restricted to a freedom of worship that was often hedged about with conditions. Enclosed in the domain of family and private life, Judaism was practically denied any social existence. With all community life thus reduced to religious life in the secular sense of the term, Judaism was to confront the new challenges posed by emancipation – in some places by dissolving, in others by reforming itself, in others again by going to seek elsewhere the conditions missing for the continued protection of the rabbinical system.

In stages, the emancipation that the Jews in the West awaited at the doors of the new society integrated them into the life of the nation-state. From the time of the abolition of the *ancient régime* of orders and privileges, of special statuses and estates, they were to enter wholeheartedly and often with no reservations, into the common civilization. In France, where the separation of church and state accompanied the spread of secularism and atheism, one could as soon be Jewish as one was Catholic or Seventh Day Adventist: one could choose to be Voltairian and rationalist, and one was then no more than of Jewish origin as one might be of Huguenot origin. One could, like Spinoza in Holland in the mid-17th century think philosophically about human society as a whole, in the light of both the classical heritage and the internal critique of the religion of the Hebrews.

In 1655, Cromwell had authorized the settlement of a Marrano community in London, and behind them, the Jews of the kingdom and from elsewhere had thrown themselves into this unheard of freedom. A century later, the American Republic, which was to perpetuate the enslavement of Africans for another hundred years (sixty years more than the "colonial metropole") endowed itself with a constitution and institutions free of any discriminatory concern with regard to the Jews, who enjoyed the same status as a church in the United States. The French revolution emancipated the Jews, and despite a few problems and doubts, only the Vichy regime, during the German occupation of France, was even, in practice, to call this emancipation into question.

Everywhere it happened, emancipation enabled the Jews to enter the city at the same time as it dissolved the authority of the community over its members. Where it was reconstituted or rather, where attempts were made to reconstitute an imitation of it, like the Empire with the Israelite Consistory of France, it was the better to ensure domination, no longer by the rabbis, but by the Rothschilds and other *chtadlanim*, who became by the same token the direct and philanthropic leaders of the communal Church.

Strictly, a distinction should be made among the various states, in order to trace in Italy and France, in England and Belgium the uneven periodization of this process, its local twists and turns and its special cases. However, the central case, both in terms of the numbers of people involved and in its implications, is that of a late, partial or abortive, erratic or simply temporary emancipation: Austria and the German states.

It was Napoleon who had brought to Europe, in the baggage of the Grand Army, the emancipation of the Jews: the Restoration and the Holy Alliances were to enable the German states to defer putting it into effect for over half a century, and tsarist Russia to refuse it until its dying day. For the emancipation of Jews had, in the meantime, become a litmus test of the new democratic order and suffered its vagaries. The social and cultural geography of European Jewry in the 19th century, with this gradation from east to west, from the *Shtetl* to the ghetto and democracy, gave way to a new distribution: the attraction of bourgeois civilization – or the desire to flee the pogroms – was immense, and led to great population movements. In fifty years, the mass emigration of "Jews from the east" to the west was to modify profoundly the demographic features of the Jewish question in Austria and Germany. The Jewish population of Vienna rose from a few hundreds to two hundred thousand: most of the new arrivals came from the Polish territories annexed to the Empire or to Prussia, and they constituted only the first wave of a migratory movement that involved several million *Ostjuden* moving to the west, the children and grandchildren of the civilization of the *Shtetl* in crisis.

This rural exodus which drained the inhabitants of the small Jewish towns to the great German-speaking cities might take the form of quite a short journey, from some small town in Galicia with its charismatic Righteous Ones to the modern society of Prague or Vienna. Elsewhere, it crossed the frontiers of states and continents. Between the rural Poland of the *Hasidim* and the industrial civilization that was beginning to transform the landscape, there was no official frontier, but two worlds continued for a while yet to mark themselves off. Soon, the two worlds, in interaction and in crisis, would co-exist over the whole of Europe.

Germany and Austria were the preferred places to which people emigrated in the westard movement. Their geographical position favoured this. But they were also, above all, states where German was spoken. In the ethnic geopolitics of pre-revolutionary Europe, the fact that Jews spoke Yiddish testified to their Germanness, which they laid claim to in their way by defining themselves as Ashkenazis and not as Poles or Russians. In terms of the rabbinical picture of the European domain, emigration to Germany was a return, not a leap into the unknown like America. In Germany, where the political patchwork made possible a multiplicity of statuses, the transition was more fluid: in one generation, people moved from Yiddish to German, from tradition to secularism or reform Judaism, from ancient mercantile and artisanal classes to the new bourgeoisie. The problem was, of course, that this movement did not affect everybody, and new ones kept on coming, fresh from their old communal universe. And everything had to be started all over again.

The immigrants from the east who flocked in their hundreds of thousands marginalized the already settled Jews. In the emancipated scheme of things that was beginning to emerge, there remained only degrees: the elasticity of frontiers had transformed Europe into the seat of a Jewish question in which places simply indicated numbers. Thus, at the very point when Jewish society was breaking up as an autonomous social system, disintegrating into a host of special social situations, the idea spread among Europeans as among the Jews of Europe, of a single Jewish question: a question which always went back, in the last analysis, to the idea that each had a Judaism in general. The idea: at the beginning of the 19th century, as, alas, much later, the "idea" of the Jew replaced the analysis and perception of concrete situations. It was an idea in which the Christian prism filtered and distorted observation. Emancipation inaugurated the era when the Jew looked at himself in the eye of the Western Christian, and integrated the vision of the other into his own representation of himself. The Jew, but not all Jews, and not straightaway.

A dramatic breach had thus occurred in the traditional perception of space and time: by breaking down the imperviousness of the old social barriers and the immobility of ancient statuses, and by giving rise to a gigantic social re-ordering against the background of the industrial revolution, the displacement of frontiers and populations posed the theoretical problem of emancipation even in the rabbinical imagination.[1]

This situation soon provoked reactions within German society: between 1815 and 1843, the massive immigration of Jews and their difficult integration into a society in which they did not always enjoy civil rights created a new *de facto* situation. It was then that Bruno Bauer, a Protestant theologian, a "left Hegelian" and former teacher of Marx, wrote *On the Jewish Question*, in which, going against the stream, he took up the question of the emancipation of the Jews, which he claimed was popular. It was thus that he provoked his pupil, the young Marx, to write a pamphlet as a response bearing the same title.

The polemic between Bauer and Marx is a good illustration of the limits of the Western emancipated perception of the question – limits common to both Bauer and Marx, implicit and inscribed in the convergence of much of what they say. Bauer's argument is relatively simple, and Marx himself summarizes it quite well. The Jews will only be truly emancipated, says Bauer, when the state is no longer Christian, and the Jews have renounced Judaism. For Judaism is itself a privilege and, as such, cannot reasonably demand the abolition of other privileges.

Marx does not respond to take up the defence of the Jews, but in order to attack Bauer's bourgeois idealization of the state, and his altogether theological propensity, to seek the essence of Judaism in its eschatology and its rejection of Christianity. Marx replaces this fetishism of political forms by examining social forms and their material roots: "We do not turn secular questions into theological questions. We turn theological questions into secular ones. History has long enough been seen in terms set by superstition, we now look at superstition in terms of history."

In this text by the young Marx the most penetrating insights and assertions are mixed up with the most questionable formulas. Criticizing the confusion Bauer makes between political emancipation and human emancipation, he writes: "We ask the converse question: Does the standpoint of political emancipation give the right to demand from the Jew the abolition of Judaism and from man the abolition of religion?" But later, when he states what remains the basic axiom of any materialist reflection on the question: "Judaism continues to exist not in spite of history, but owing to history", he embarks on a dissertation on "the basis of the Jewish religion" in which it emerges that "history" is nothing other than an economic and moral essence:

> What, in itself, was the basis of the Jewish religion? Practical need, egoism. The monotheism of the Jew, therefore, is in reality the polytheism of the many needs . . . Money is the jealous god of Israel . . . The bill of exchange is the real god of the Jew. His god is only an illusory bill of exchange . . . The groundless law of the Jew is only a religious caricature of groundless morality and right in general, of the purely formal rites with which the world of self-interest surrounds itself.

This is because, for Marx, "Christianity is the sublime thought of Judaism, Judaism is the common practical application of Christianity." In this the subjective and aestheticist theology of Bauer is not far away.

The source of this failure to understand the concrete dimensions of the question appears precisely when Marx attempts to bring Bauer back to consideration of the facts: "The Jewish question acquires a different form depending on the state in which the Jew lives." And he explains that there exist three typical cases: Germany, where there is no state, and where "the Jewish question is a purely theological one", France, where the question is one of constitutionalism, of the "incompleteness of political emancipation", and the free states of North America, where "the Jewish question loses its theological significance and becomes a really secular question". Not a word about eastern Europe, where the majority of Jews were still living and where for two centuries the conditions of the crisis which was to lead to the massacres and emigration of millions of men to the Western countries, had been ripening. The idea that Judaism could be anything other than a mere function of bourgeois society, *a fortiori*, that it could itself be the site of contradictions – that is, lacking a single ideological essence – no more crosses the mind of the young Marx than it does that of the old Bauer. Whence their shared and systematic use of the singular: "The" Jew. Whence Marx's idea that Judaism is a pure product of bourgeois society, and that it will disappear with it: an anti-historical, anti-Marxist idea if ever there was one.

The Bauer-Marx polemic enables us to assess this emerging Jewish question, by illustrating the European problematic of the emancipation of the Jews. A certain number of axioms emerge from it, which are commonly agreed: in particular, the identification of Judaism and trade, which takes up the mediaeval imagery of the Jewish usurer as a real figure in Western society, and the denunciation of religious formalism and talmudic hypocrisy in terms that call to mind the Christian critique of pharisaism. At the same time a new element is appearing: the critique of Christianity. Following Voltaire, Marx sees in Judaism the essence, and, in some way, the quintessence, of the worst Christianity. Thus, because the critique of religious alienation has no other object than Christianity, it only perceives

Judaism as a moment in Christian development, only through the distorted image given of it, for its own ends, by Christian theology. Thus, Christian anti-Judaism became paradoxically strengthened when it was transmuted into anti-Christianity, and one can already see converging the first outlines of what was to become modern European anti-Semitism.

However, for European discourse, whether theological or anti-religious, on Judaism to become an effective component of anti-Jewish ideology, it still lacked some essential themes: one of them was of a conceptual nature, and concerns the appearance of pseudo-scientific notions about race (developed in France and then in Germany during the years that followed the Bauer-Marx polemic). The others flowed from the conditions specific to the Russian empire: towards the late 1860s, anti-Semitism became a concerted policy of the Russian autocracy, and in particular of its police, as a safety valve and outlet for social discontent, while conservative discourse identified the Jews pressing for emancipation with subversion and revolution. The political crisis of Judaism in tsarist Russia and generally in the Austrian empire was to precipitate a flood of *Ostjuden* over western Europe that would make the Jews appear as symbols and agents of the destruction of the old world, whereas they were only its objects.

The anti-Semitism that developed in this situation was of course only anti-Semitic in the claim to see the Jews as a race in the sense that the racist theorists of 19th century Europe were giving this word. We have seen that this had no foundation. But we have also seen that Judaism had peddled and reproduced the myth of a tribal sort of ethnic unity, that is one based on blood ties. That is why large sections of the Jewish world, both in eastern Europe and among the *Ostjuden* recently settled in the West, came to accept, and even to claim, that they belonged to this imaginary "Jewish race": for it was one of the features of contemporary racism that it reformulated in a pseudo-biological, pseudo-genetic and pseudo-anthropological jargon the most primitive mechanisms of group aggressiveness, self-magnification and disparagement of others, the mythification of the collective self and the "diabolization" of the other.

This hatred that pedantically proclaimed itself anti-Semitism was practically aimed only at Jews. But it is undeniable that the anti-Semitic discourse was consciously inserted into the general racist discourse on Asia, on civilization and barbarism: and that by this token, it also affected the Arabs. More precisely, the term anti-Semitism tended to load onto the Jews not only their own ignominy but also the whole weight of "Asiatic barbarism". However, there were no Arabs in the European social landscape. While racist contempt for them did exist, it could only serve to justify projects for colonial expansion and domination "over there", that is, in areas where they were living. Whereas the Jews were present and highly visible in the everyday landscape of Germans in the second half of the 19th century. Hatred towards them was not part of an imperialist project to reorganize the world in terms of colonial internationalization or in the name of progress. On the contrary, the sudden appearance and social mobility of the Jews was denounced in the very name of the "good old times": the times of old hierarchies, old loyalties, old social relationships and the guaranteed statuses of the feudal order, and of that ethnic space that Nazi madness was to wish *judenrein*: empty of Jews.

Maxime Rodinson has analysed[2] the shift by which hatred of the Jews in the Graeco-Latin world and Christian anti-Judaism, having enriched the discourse (the "story", in Jean-Pierre Faye's expression) of the anti-Semites, found themselves provided retrospectively with an essence, defying epochs and societies: anti-Semitism thus came to be conceived of as an essential, and in some ways metaphysical, constant of non-Jewish societies, the symmetrical and absolute counterpart of the eternally bad essence of the Jews in anti-Semitic paranoia. Yet, modern anti-Semitism, born of the specific conditions of 19th century Europe, was as radically different from mediaeval Christian anti-Judaism as the emancipated Jewish society of democratic countries was from the Jewish ghettos and small towns of the Middle Ages. But what Rodinson calls ethnic "essentialism" was much too deep-rooted, on both sides, for this sort of generalization not to have soil where it could grow and reproduce itself. In anti-Semitic discourse the Jew became the very figure of evil, the devil, and, in this Manichaean Satanism, the occult and provisional master of the world.

It is necessary to grasp the speed with which this implicit history of History with a capital H unfolded, in the 19th century, when everything was tottering. The organized and official persecution of Jews in the Russian empire, reflecting popular and anti-Jewish peasant traditions, accelerated the movement of Jewish emigration westward. Arriving in the West, they discovered, as Weizmann was to say, that "they had brought anti-Semitism with them in their baggage", and that emancipation was like the burden of Sisyphus or the torment of Tantalus: as more and more tried to embrace it, so its object eluded them.

> The Jews of the Austrian empire received fully equal rights only in 1867. In Germany, some independent states emancipated their Jews quite early, but others did not; notably, Prussia was grudging and tardy in this matter, and final emancipation of the Jews in the German empire as a whole was only granted by Bismarck in 1871. In the Ottoman empire the Jews were subject to official discrimination until 1909, and in Russia (as well as Romania) until 1917. Thus, modern anti-Semitism began within a decade of the emancipation of the Jews in central Europe and long before the emancipation of the biggest Jewish community at that time, that of the Tsarist empire.[3]

While pogrom followed pogrom in the Russian empire, pushing the crisis and disintegration of Jewish society to its climax, the anti-Semitism that emerged as an ideological-political current in the West began to call into question the scarcely acquired emancipation, completing the forcible displacement of Jewish problematics and transforming the mental and intellectual world of assimilated Jews into a peripheral fringe of the scattered *Shtetl*.

In the space of two generations, the status and place of the Jews of Europe had thus undergone changes on an unparalleled scale: from the *Shtetl* to modern citizenship by way of all the transitional situations, from the pogroms of Byelorussia and the Ukraine to the theoretical anti-Semitism of the German right and some "lefts" in France (the famous "socialism of fools" of which Bebel speaks). The flight from tradition, emigration to the West of the Enlightenment, and, at the end of this road, the *Dreyfus* affair, the counterpart of the Kishinev massacres.

Israel Shahak rightly stresses that the whole of the intellectual and cultural characteristics that Westerners identify with Jewishness and consider to be the constitutive features of "being Jewish" – such as humour, criticism, liberalism, cosmopolitanism – were part of the culture of this crisis, and, mostly, of this rupture, and not of some traditional Jewish culture. But it is true that the continuous crisis and the virtual halt in the incomplete emancipation continued for over a century: long enough for this transition to become a world in itself.

But it is also necessary to grasp the social changes that accompanied this crisis. "There are countries and times", wrote Barukh Hagani in 1929,

> when the Jew, the oldest of Europeans and until then the most humiliated, appeared in the eyes of the least biased observer in the 19th century as the typical representative of the new man, the incarnation of business wealth as opposed to the landed wealth which had made the strength and pride of feudal Europe.

In central Europe, where the exchange between the two worlds occurred, the social situation of the *Ostjuden* who continued to pour in, knew every fluctuation and gradation: a section of the new immigrants became well integrated into the dynamic of the local bourgeoisie, becoming assimilated to the way of life, the social and economic customs and the mentality of the dominant classes in the nation-state whose citizens they became. But, alongside this successful integration, there was the whole small world of wheeling and dealing, in which a great number of middlemen eked out a living, as well as all those who sank into the wretchedness of wage labour or the endless toil of artisans. In a word, and even though the stereotype of the Jewish man of wealth made the most prosperous and ostentatious of the *nouveaux riches* symbols representative of the community, Jewish society no longer constituted, as it did in mediaeval times, a people-class endowed with a unique social character: on the contrary, this flashy embourgeoise-ment of a section of Jewish society had as its counterpart the proletarianization of the fringe at the other end of the scale, and was in fact a manifestaton of the disintegration of the separate Jewish social problematic.

In the Russian empire, where the social mobility of Jews was thwarted by the policy of the government as much as by the weakness of bourgeois processes in general, the embourgeoisement of a minority of Jews occurred in proportions radically different from those in Germany or France. For the vast majority, which continued to live in the Pale, it was the old mode of subsistence that was decaying on the spot, plunging whole strata of former artisans and middlemen into the most desperate poverty. And, for a proportion that was to grow after the 1870s (1868: emancipation of the serfs in Russia, "kulakization" of the communal lands), the sign of new times would be proletarianization. But the circumstances of territorial concentration and social cohesion of the *Shtetl* here made it possible for the division of labour to operate in a closed framework, in the absence of any possibility of assimilation. Thus, what happened was simultaneously the embourgeoisement of some and the proletarianization of others by the former: the capitalist exploitation of Jews by Jews. By the end of the 19th century whole branches of manufacturing and small-scale industry, linked to the transformation of the methods of production in activities traditionally widespread among Jewish artisans (hat-making, clothing) were in majority Jewish, both the bosses and the wage-workers. This temporary emergence of a Jewish proletariat, facing a Jewish bourgeoisie, gave rise to the *Bund*, a trade union organization of Jewish workers, which was transformed into a party working for the national-cultural autonomy of Jews in the framework of Russian social democracy.

Thus we see the old Jewish society, not only threatened and battered by persecutions and emigration, but also re-ordered in the image of the Europe to which the industrial revolution gave an appearance never before seen. In these circumstances, what happened to the traditional power of the Law and the ideology that underpinned it?

It is not difficult to imagine the decline and decrepitude of the old forms of authority once the material framework of their effectiveness had been disrupted. Here, a world which had become fixed and consolidated, found itself brutally carved up and subjected to the logic of unheard of transformation. The ideological crisis which was latent in it exploded.

The New Ideas

What distinguished this crisis from all previous ones (or what made it the final moment in their spiral), was that it exploded the ideological problematic – the theology – through the prism of which the Jews had hitherto rationalized their fate. The exodus of the Jews of Spain to the Levant, that of the Jews of Germany and Bohemia to Poland, like earlier displacements of the Law, had refashioned Judaism by re-ordering it. But, through the successive stages of rabbinism, mediaeval theology, the Kabbala, and Hasidism, each upheaval in the Jews' conditions of existence resulted in the confirmation, adaptation and strengthening of the talmudic pattern. The very influence of ideas and conceptions from the environment – Hellenistic, Babylonian, Islamic or Christian – was expressed in the terms of Judaic discourse, the transhumance of the priest-tribe through the desert of the Nations, its mirages and its manna, its wandering. Whereas here, because the civilization whose hegemony extended its shadow over the collective subjectivity of the Jews of Europe was questioning its own derived theology, transforming the people-witness into a pure ethnographic and religious anachronism, it was the very framework of Judaic identity that was fractured.

This explosion occurred in two stages: first in western Europe, then in eastern Europe. In the first, it took on the appearance of an evolution, in the second of a cataclysm. In western Europe, where the centralizing state had ended any administrative autonomy of the community at a very early date, it was Judaism itself that learned to conform to the intellectual order of the new world, by reforming itself. In eastern Europe, the community order cracked and resisted the sudden occupation of its own domain by states, especially by the Russian state in Poland, the Ukraine and Byelorussia.

Thus, the attitude of the Jews to bourgeois civilization took on altogether different forms and meanings as between the two areas. In the west, where this evolution occurred in the 18th century, it was an extension of the European movement of the Enlightenment. In central and eastern Europe, where the Enlightenment remained an ideal that was repressed and condemned to insurrectionary strategies for the society as a whole, the Enlightenment crystallized with the apocalyptic messianism of the *Shtetl* and fuelled the process of break-up. This wide disparity of situations at either end of the continent had led to a striking synchronism: at the very time when Hasidism was emerging in Poland, the reform of Judaism was getting under way in Germany. In the one, popular messianism at the service of rabbinical obscurantism, and in the other bourgeois science and reason in the practice and language of assimilation.

The synchronism had a precedent: it is enough to consider for a moment the whole of this domain of the diaspora, a century earlier, in, for example, 1655-65. In 1655 the Marranos settled in London; ten years later, Zvi proclaimed himself the Messiah at Smyrna. In 1656, the Russians took under their protection the Cossacks of the Ukraine in revolt against the Polish Catholics and the Jews. And, in 1665, Spinoza published his *Tractatus Theologio–Politicus*. The Marrano diaspora in the West, at the opposite extreme from the Ashkenazi Judaism of Poland and the Arab and Sephardic Judaism of the East, turned its back on the Old World, its eyes fixed on America. Zvi, who wanted to bring the Jews of London, Antwerp and Hamburg back to Palestine, looked in the opposite direction. In the 17th century, at the very time that the Ashkenazim who were suffering anti-Jewish peasant revolts "returned to Judaism", it was the two poles of the Sephardic universe that expressed the dilemma in a radical manner: the impossibility for the old Law of surviving in the new conditions.

The Marranos, the Jews of Christian Spain, most of them wealthy and "Court Jews", who had accepted the authority of the Christian law, preferred apostasy to exile or death. Some of them indeed succeeded in merging into the mass of Christians, joining the earlier waves of *Meshummadim:* a Hebrew and Judaeo-Spanish word which describes the Jews converted to Christianity by the name "Annihilated". Others, on the contrary, particularly after the expulsion of 1492, subjected to the suspicious jealousy of their neighbours and the persecutions of the Inquisition, secretly perpetuated a symbolic and sentimental Judaism under the cloak of the most ostentatious Catholicism. Here there was no synthesis, no syncretic schism in the manner of Frankism, but a double language, a double life, the coexistence of the most shameless submission and the most gratuitous resistance. This situation made the "New Christians", whom the Spaniards called *Marranos* (Pigs) and whom the courts endlessly accused of Judaic practices, the main victims of the repression orchestrated by the Jesuits. After having been converted by force, the Marranos were accused of insincerity: in these circumstances, the reality of their conversion became impossible to prove. So they ended up leaving Spain, and Portugal which eventually emulated Spain, although with some delay and a little less enthusiasm for lighting pyres of *autos da fé*.

In France, at Bayonne and Bordeaux, they settled as Christians, but soon returned to "the faith of their fathers": a Judaism reconsituted from Catholicism, without either Hebrew or the Talmud. Prefiguring reform Judaism and assimilation, their way of life substituted family worship and ceremonies, lived privately, for what rabbinism had codified as a social system. In Holland, where the Marranos settled as Christians, they were at first suspected of Spanish Catholicism. They held themselves out as victims of the Inquisition, and they were honoured: the Protestant bourgeoisie of the Netherlands gave the Jews their first secular status in the west. In Germany, the Lutheran academies at Jena and Frankfurt, and following them the Hamburg senate, authorized the settlement of Marranos: it was passing as Marranos that the first Ashkenazim fleeing the revolts and massacres in Poland returned to these areas that had been forbidden since the Middle Ages.

But it was in Italy, particularly under the tolerant protection of the grand-dukes of Tuscany, at Pisa and Leghorn, that the Marranos who flocked there performed a true return to Judaism: for there they joined up with earlier waves of expulsions and the domain of the Mediterranean diaspora: thousands of rabbis, talmudists and kabbalists. It was there that, around the Hebrew printing houses, the exchange among exiles occurred. It was there that Marrano scholars became mystics and visionaries; it was there that the refugees from the Ukrainian uprisings came to seek help; it was there that the groups organized to ransom from the Turks Polish Jewish captives who had fallen into the hands of the Tartars. At the beginning of the 16th century, in a Venice which was still neutral in the confrontation between Spain and Turkey, rabbi Eliahu Capsali had compiled a History of the Jews of Turkey (*Sefer Eliahu*), full of praise for the tolerance of the sultans and wishing them victory against the states of the Inquisition.

Baruch Spinoza (1632–77) drew from the new organization of the world, which could be especially well observed from Amsterdam, the most subversive of conclusions: in the light of the idea of freedom which oozed from every pore of the rising bourgeoisie, he called into question all the old laws of servitude, beginning with that of his co-religionists. But he did not become a Christian. On the contrary, he wrote in his *Tractatus Theologico-Politicus:* "Religious and political prejudices are the cause of all tyranny. As a negation of reasonable thoughts, the fruit of a terrible fear, prejudice obliges the people to believe blindly in the tyrant, to adore him as a God". So that he who would be called "the first official atheist in Europe" was banished in due and proper rabbinical form, excluded from his community and driven out of Amsterdam with the support of the Calvinist pastors whose intolerance towards dissident Protestant sects he had denounced.

The Jewish community that excommunicated Spinoza was at the same time shaken, from top to bottom, by a great surge of Sabbatian messianism. And the rabbis of Europe who pronounced the anathema against Spinoza only rejected Zvi after he had put himself outside the community by embracing Islam. In a word, Zvi, a Spanish Jew in a Greek Christian city in Ottoman Turkey, the son of the agent of an English business house, expressed the soul of the Marrano-Sephardic diaspora better than did Spinoza. But both spoke the crisis of Mediterranean and Western Judaism in this great centre where the Old World met the Atlantic: they were contemporaries and, in the 17th century, both precociously spelled out the tension and the anguish, the rift between return (to the old Law and the old Land) and departure: departure from the tribe and its private time, but also departure to the Americas where Marranos made their fortunes in the slave trade, banking or industry. One foot in the Kabbala, the other in emancipation. One foot in nationalist messianism, the other in Western rationalism.

The Netherlands, like England, illustrates a situation that was special in two ways: in the precociousness of these developments, and in the fact that the Jewish bourgeoisie that participated in it was Sephardic, or, as it identified itself, Portuguese. It was linked to the Spanish diaspora in Italy and Turkey, and also in Egypt and the East, and culturally isolated, in any case, from the majority Ashkenazi world of Poland. So that Zvi made some inroads among the Marranos of Europe obsessed by the idea of return, but only reached eastern Europe in echoes. As for Spinoza, who wrote in Latin, and whose name was cursed by the rabbis, his influence on the behaviour of the *Shtetl* was obviously non-existent.

It was from Germany, where a small Jewish community aspiring to political integration, had been reconstituted, on the Marrano model, that the response of Judaism to the challenge of emancipation went out: the Jewish movement of the Enlightenment, the *Haskalah,* and the reform of rabbinism. For Germany was to play for the Jews of the Yiddish-speaking *Shtetl* the role of new cultural metropole, where the threatened communal Judaism was transformed with emigration into a religious denomination inside modern nationality.

The Reform, and also the "culture of culture" that the *Haskalah* was, are linked with the name of Moses Mendelssohn. His philosophical work in German had such a tremendous influence on his time and later that Arthur Ruppin, a Zionist leader in Palestine in the 1930s, wrote, in 1911, in a book published in Berlin:

> If we are to believe the statements made in several Jewish histories, the revolution in the social and cultural status of the Jews must be ascribed solely to the fact that Moses Mendelssohn happened to be born in 1729, that he came to Berlin in 1743, that he there became the friend of Lessing, translated the Bible into German, and wrote a number of important philosophical works. It need hardly be said that such a view reveals a puerile view of history. The real cause of the so-called emancipation of the Jews is not to be found in the achievements of any single Jew, but in the sudden change of outlook, social and economic, which characterised the whole of the eighteenth century.[4]

It was the Berlin Voltarian Aron Gumhertz who had introduced the young Mendelssohn, a rabbinical scholar and a man who had taught himself European culture, into the circles where people read Montesquieu and Rousseau, and also Spinoza, and where he met Lessing. Fought by and excommunicated by the Orthodox rabbis, Mendelssohn openly preached the reform and "Germanization" of Judaism: an important advocate of philosophy of the Enlightenment, he wrote numerous works, both for the Jews and for his Christian fellow citizens. In his lifetime, his philosophical work had more influence on the Christians than on the Jews, but his German translation of the Bible, banned by the rabbis as a work of the devil, was the first element of a rationalist revolt within Jewish orthodoxy. Mendelssohn was a German philosopher, but he was also a Jewish reformer: he set up a network of "reformed" schools, in which Maimonides and the Talmud were taught in German alongside secular subjects. Grol stresses the conservative character of Mendelssohn's radicalism, and the bourgeois Berlin conformism that inspired his activity, denounced by all the rabbis of Europe, but supported by the rabbinate of Berlin.[5]

But this "Jewish Protestantism" that made the Jews of Germany Germans of the Mosaic faith was at one and the same time modernist, and the defender of what it saw as essential: the convergence of Judaism, Christianity and bourgeois reason. So it was normal that it should find illustrious antecedents in Greek-Arab-Jewish classical culture. Maimonides and the Golden Age of mediaeval Judaism became for the Reform the theoretical model of a Judaism that was enlightened and integrated, rationalist and religious, that is, in harmony with the dominant society. The parallel is arresting – which had caused Mendelssohn to be called the third Moses, after the Moses of Mount Sinai and Maimonides – between the reforming ideal of Mendelssohn and the theological vision of the Andalusian philosophers.

Significantly, Mendelssohn fought for the German language: he had himself translated (and criticized) Jean-Jacques Rousseau's treatise *On the*

Origin of Inequalities among Men and stressed, against the French-speaking world that dominated European democratic culture at the time, the importance of writing, speaking and teaching in "the language of the people".This linguistic concern was to become a basic feature of the German dilemma, the parameters of which Fichte, after the Napoleonic invasion, set out in his *Speech to the German Nation*. But the same infatuation with German (which is in some ways reminiscent of the linguistic narcissism of classical Arabic) inspired in Mendelssohn a hatred of Yiddish – a "jargon... of cooks and maidservants", a "misbegotten dialect of the German language"[6] – and the determination to develop the teaching of Hebrew. In 1783, Mendelssohn's friends, meeting as the "Society of Friends of the Hebrew Language", published the first Hebrew periodical, *Ha-Maassef (The Gatherer)*, which defended the Enlightenment and Reform.

The *Haskalah's* influence went out from Germany to the *Shtetl:* and since, by the 18th century, the Jewish masses of eastern Europe were beginning gradually to move westward, the link-up was soon made. There, rabbinical orthodoxy rose up as one man, *Hasidim* and *Mitnagdim* together, to denounce the Enlightenment: the confrontation between the Law and Reason, perpetuated by the feudal absolutism of the Holy Alliance, left no room for the reform of worship. Faced with orthodoxy buttressed by the *Halakha* and the old rabbinical order, the *Haskalah* became transformed into a banner for the secular struggle and a channel of social criticism. In the West, where the bourgeois revolution was irreversibly achieved, the Reform salvaged something. In the Austro-Hungarian and Russian empires, the Enlightenment and philosophy fuelled a challenge to tyranny: the tyranny of the state, and the tyranny of the rabbinical mini-state.

The reform directly inspired by Mendelssohn's ideas was only a beginning. A conservative movement was developing in the United States along similar lines, while the *Haskalah* itself penetrated, especially in Germany, the world of orthodox Judaism. The intellectual revolution thus initiated within Judaism, frozen for centuries in talmudic orthodoxy and rabbinical *pilpul*, was to engender a multitude of currents of ideas that were often contradictory.

In the West, the Enlightenment nurtured the Reform, but also, rapidly, assimilation: not only *de facto* integration into the dominant culture and society, but a philosophy in which the cult of Reason became the religion of Western civilization, to which Jews became converted with all the ardour of neophytes. The orthodox-Jewish caricature of reform-Jewish language: "The true *kipah* (cap) is not on the head but in the head, and the *sabbath* is Sunday" touches on this determination to conform and be respectable that characterized the middling Jewish bourgeoisie of the West from the time of the Reform. Here, the critique of tradition and the breach with the fate of the community combined the universalist and humanist upsurge with scorn – sometimes hatred – for the masses of the *Shtetl*. Love of Western civilization and progress came quite naturally to the notables attracted to power as by a magnet. This very proper and, in each country, patriotic assimilationism, spread particularly among those recently emancipated. In France particularly: the Second Empire and the assimilated Jewish notables exported it to the far end of the Mediterranean, where this ideology was a great success from Istanbul to Algiers, by way of Alexandria, among Jews drawn into the orbit of French imperialism. It can be said of this enthusiasm for the culture of the Other, in which there was an element of servility, but also of liberating revolt, what Memmi wrote of self-rejection, that it "can be a shabby trick, a final abandonment, an ignoble plea to get oneself accepted. But it can also be the first step towards revolt, the first gesture of the oppressed as he awakens, the angry rejection of what he has become in slavery".[7]

In eastern Europe, there was nothing like that. There, no assimilation was possible: not only was the general emancipation of society blocked, but Jewish society was linguistically separate and culturally foreign to the Polish, Ukrainian or Russian nation. Here, the Enlightenment fuelled a rejection of disintegration and decadence which became consciously integrated into the general challenge to the aristocratic order.

Once again, a distinction must be made between the degrees of this contrast: between the Austro-Hungarian empire in which Prague and Vienna coexisted with the newly annexed Hasidic small towns of Galicia, and tsarist Russia where, alongside a minority of privileged Jews who were accepted, subject to a *numerus clausus,* into secondary schools and universities, the majority wallowed in a decadent *Shtetl,* caught up in a brutal and backward industrialization, the target of the frequently murderous hostility of the peasants. In Austria, where the social and economic emancipation of the Jews had preceded their civil liberation, orthodoxy and Hasidism made an alliance against the *Haskalah.* In Russia, the *Haskalah* imported from the West was to play among the Jews the role European philosophy played in Christian society, while the obscurantism of the rabbis was the counterpart of the total political obscurantism of the Russian autocracy which banned the sons of the nobility from reading Fichte or Schelling.

Like the Jews and Muslims of the Middle Ages, who translated the Greeks into Arabic in order the better to appropriate them, the advocates of the Enlightenment, the *Maskilim,* translated – as Mendelssohn himself had translated. They translated the classics and the moderns, Jews and others, and before long they wrote. Poets, philosophers, novelists, journalists emerged from this flowering. The *Haskalah* promoted a true cultural rebirth, or perhaps simply a birth, in which the critique of the old rabbinical social organization constituted the departure point and the dominant ideological motive. The major anomaly of this output lay in one fact: the modern Jewish literature inspired by the Enlightenment after the second half of the 19th century, in eastern Europe, was written in two languages: Yiddish and Hebrew. The collapse of the hierarchical system that underpinned the multi-lingualism of the *Shtetl* opened up a new linguistic dilemma for civil Jewish society, which was to divide the Yiddish-speaking world for several decades. But it must be stressed here that the literature inspired by the penetration of democratic ideals within the *Shtetl* was neither Russian nor Polish, neither Romanian nor Ukrainian, but Jewish (although secular): whether in Yiddish or Hebrew, was, so to say, an internal debate, once it was clear that this literature was addressed solely to Jews, and that it did not reflect the least integration into the surrounding culture, but on the contrary, the renewal and regeneration of the *Shtetl's* own culture.

The new philosophy that fuelled this nationalism, which was initially cultural, prepared the ground for political nationalism in the following generation. In the West, the enlightened Jew, whether he had reformed his Judaism or had simply cultivated it, whether he had rejected the authority of the rabbis in the name of divine Reason or in the name of secularism, became a citizen of the nation-state whose language he spoke. In Poland and Russia, the nation-state did not exist, nor did citizenship, and the Jews did not speak the language of their neighbours. So long as impoverishment was added to insecurity, persecutions and arbitrariness, Judaism, far from reforming itself, became ever more deeply sunk in messianic pietism and clerical feudalism, in an atmosphere of the end of the world.

In order to grasp the movement and the new type of conflict involved in this situation, it is necessary to have a clear idea of the interplay between the emigration of Jews from Poland and Russia to Austria and Germany, and the constant displacement of the frontiers of Prussia eastward. The fact that it spoke Yiddish made the Jewish world of the Russian empire, as Herzl stressed to Kaiser Wilhelm in 1903, an element of "the sphere of influence of German culture". The *Haskalah* could also be considered as the specific contribution of the enlightened Jewish bourgeoisie of Germany to the civilizing conquest of the "Slav" east: the Berlin metropole of the *Haskalah* preparing the integration of the Jews, that is, the disintegration of the rabbinical social system, and their Germanization. The *Haskalah* was born in the very German movement of the Enlightenment: not in the least revolutionary (had not Napoleon shown the horrors that were bound to arise from revolutionary disorder?) and tremendously civilizing with regard to the east, obsessed with the homogenization of the German-speaking area and the defence and illustration of the German language. The German origin of the Jewish religious organization of Poland, the memory of mediaeval migrations, and the reality of the reverse movement from the time of the Napoleonic conquest gave this construction, in which the Jew was not a category of man but a category of German, a formal coherence. Thus Mendelssohn and the "Master of the Good Name", at the two extremes of the Ashkenazi universe, experienced, like Spinoza and Zvi a century before them, and in an infinitely less radical manner, the dilemma and the challenge of emancipation, and did so in two geographically contiguous areas – from Berlin to Lithuania – but in cultural times zones that were virtually impermeable. Not entirely impermeable, however, and not for long: the intermingling of people from different areas soon created a situation where the *Haskalah* and Hasidism coexisted in the same towns. In the new Jewish bourgeoisie, people learned to be Czech, Hungarian, Polish, and even Russian... of Mosaic faith, on the German model of Mendelssohn. And everywhere the *Haskalah* would serve as the impetus and the vehicle for internal revolt against the rabbinical model of protection.

This was the expression of a real harmony between the Ashkenazi world and the geopolitics of its diaspora. In the West, Judaism became democratic and European: in Russia it remained obscurantist and despotic in the image of the government. The ideas of the Republic of the rights of man, which, in the West, had gone hand in hand with the legal emancipation and effective assimilation of Jews, had become in the "prisons of peoples" constituted by the two multi-national empires, founding mothers of numerous nationalisms – Polish, Czech, Hungarian, etc. Everywhere dominated peoples took up for themselves the idea of freedom, they turned it into nationalism against the "feudal" – but above all foreign – tyrannies that were crushing them. As it moved east, the spirit of 1848 and the European democratic revolution fuelled a touchy nationalism in which the modernism of the insurrectionary intentions was articulated on the determined traditionalism of territorial demands and discourse about the nation. This explains why many of these "revolutionary" movements had no other programme than to restore ancient monarchies, that had sometimes disappeared centuries before, as symbols of the historical continuity of a homeland in which ethnicism and confessionalism draped themselves in partisan historiography. It is in this context that one must understand the emergence, from 1860 onwards, of various Jewish nationalist schools of thought in the Russian empire: the defeat of Protection given concrete form in the recrudescence of pogroms and the impoverishment of community life, against a background of wars and revolutions in which the Jews, because of where and who they were, always got a few blows, engendered a rebellion which came first from the most Westernized sectors, the ones most enlightened by the German *Haskalah* (but also by the European Enlightenment which Peter the Great had adopted as the guiding light of his attempts to modernize Russia). In the Hebrew culture born of the *Haskalah* and the rejection of Yiddish, there emerged a generation of poets, writers and new leaders of thought in revolt against the order of the *Shtetl*. They demonstrated their acceptance of Western civilization by projecting on to that order the language of the Slavophiles about the Russian people, or of Fichte about the language of the ancestors. In the polemics and disputes that these schools waged against one another, the echo of this national problematic can be heard, obsessed by the West even when it claims to reject it. Alexander Koyré described this tension among the Russian Westernizers and Slavophiles in the 1820s and 1830s in terms that can easily be applied to the situation of

Ashkenazi Judaism, and indeed to that of all the other nations dominated by the West. Intellectual élites were torn between "the deliberate and servile imitation of the external forms of Western civilization, its customs, dress and even language", and "the need to oppose the West and preserve the intimate heritage of national life"; they were also in reality opposed to "the narrow traditionalism of the old believers, opponents of Peter the Great's reform" and modernism. This dilemma led, throughout 19th century Europe and later throughout the world, from imitation of the West, and particularly of France, to "the laying of the foundations of this very. national civilization".

> Westernizers and Slavophiles were both equally Westernized, deeply admiring of the civilization of Europe, and even close examination indicates that the Westernizers were not the most Westernized. No doubt the latter thought themselves closer to the West, because they admired it more, but... the interpretation of Western ideas that they offered to Russia was often only a very Russian transposition. The Slavophiles, on the other hand, had retained a sharper and livelier awareness of the organic bonds between them and their people... But their whole conceptual apparatus showed how far they had been influenced by Western thought.[8]

The new ideological currents, which were the contradictory echo of Hasidic popular messianism, all, in their way, reflected the influence of ideas that were sweeping European society, either in Hebrew, in the tradition of the *Haskalah,* or in Yiddish, in a populist approach marked by the spread of socialist ideas in eastern Europe. The difficulty of capturing this effervescence of ideas derives from the complexity and scale of the migratory movement westward: towards Prague and Vienna (in fact, from Galicia, a southward movement), towards Berlin and Paris, towards New York and Buenos Aires, towards Sydney and Johannesburg. In the course of the second half of the 19th century, the problematic of the emancipation of the Jews by Western democracy was nationalized by the new bourgeoisies of central and eastern Europe struggling against absolutism. The modern strata that emerged from the decaying *Shtetl* and took shape in the emigration movement, took part, here and there, in the elaboration of these new national cultures, creating a previously unknown type of assimilated Jew: a lover of the Polish, Czech or Russian language, a patriot, with no attachment to Judaism. As socialist ideas spread through eastern Europe, coinciding with the formation of an intelligentsia traumatized by the effects of a brutal proletarianization, the messianism of the proletarian revolution, internationalist and universal, secular and fraternal, added a new dimension to this assimilation. Unlike formal conversion (that of Marx's father, for example) to Christianity, which implied a self-denial of the Jew as Jew, acceptance of the universalist ideal of socialism supposed going beyond, at the same time as fulfilling, the social mission of the prophets. In 1913, Lenin wrote that the Jew made "his own contribution, as a Jew, to the international culture of the workers' movement";[9] but in 1865, Moses Hess, born in Bonn into a family of Yiddish-speaking immigrants, and a childhood companion of Marx, wrote: "the principles of Judaism, that is, the principles of socialism". And while it is true that by the end of the last century socialism had become an integral part, not only of the culture of the youthful proletariat of eastern Europe, but also of the frustrated nationalist bourgeoisie and of all the intelligentsia of the middle strata ruined by large-scale industry, it had, in the eyes of young Jews yearning for emancipation, the added advantage of providing a reply of a clearly messianic type to the traditional problematic of Jewish identity and the concrete problematic of anti-Semitism.

Emigration to more clement climes became the dominant dynamic perspective of Jewish society in the east throughout the 19th century. Departure for America or Australia represented the sharpest break with the *Shtetl*, even if it was in the United States that the most intense Jewish community life was later reconstituted. Nevertheless, Austria and Germany constituted (until the rise of Nazism) a mental, sociological and cultural screen to emigration to far-off places: why go and seek prosperity and emancipation in some far-off country if the *Haskalah*, Reform and democracy could assure them in this Ashkenazi world which the Jews of Russia themselves recognized as their cultural cradle, and where Judaism, flourishing in mediaeval times, then obscure and persecuted (whereas it prospered in Poland), was not participating fully in the common Judaeo-Christian civilization?

It was thus natural that the first modern Hebrew periodical (Mendelssohn's friends' "Gatherer", in 1783, had not survived), symbolically entitled *Ha-Magid* ("The Preacher", the nickname of the *Besht's* successor) was published in 1856 on the Russo-Prussian border, i.e., in Poland, which did not then exist as such. It was at this precise point where the German *Haskalah* (Hebraist by rejection of Yiddish and the post-mediaeval rabbinical heritage; *pilpul*, Hasidism) and the problematic of the *Shtetl* met, that is, alongside the millions who were emigrating and the millions who stayed, that the synthesis occurred in which the Enlightenment engendered Jewish nationalism.

It was at first a literary movement which inherited the cultural achievements of the *Haskalah:* modernist, Westernizing, and struggling openly against primitive and Yiddish-speaking orthodoxy and traditionalism. However, the Hebrew literary and journalistic output thus inspired was addressed first and foremost to Jews. It thus became a "national" literature, a tool for the social transformation of the *Shtetl,* while the poets of the renaissance became the new pastors of the tribe in distress.

In a manner similar to that by which French philosophy was appropriated by the German romantics and these latter by the Russian Karamzins and Kireëvskys in the 1820s, but later, the new Hebrew writers and publicists of the 1860s laid the bases for Hebrew nationalism by asserting their militant neo-paganism, like Saul Tschernichowsky who published in Hebrew the following poem:

> And I come to you
> I come to you, before your statue kneeling,
> Your image – symbol of life's brightness;
> I kneel, I bow to the good and the sublime,
> to that which is exalted throughout the world,
> to all things splendid throughout creation,
> and elevated among secret – mysteries of the Cosmos.
> I bow to life, to valour and to beauty.[10]

At the other end of the *Shtetl,* but at the same time, where pietism no longer sufficed to absorb despair, powerlessness and revolt, messianism and the Hebrew *Haskalah* cross-fertilized one another and inspired new modes of semi-clandestine self-organization in open revolt against the traditional order. From these clubs, associations and circles of friends would emerge simultaneously both the first organized self-defence groups and the first groups advocating settlement in Palestine, one current of which had become organized in the mid-1860s with the name *Bilu* (the Hebrew initials of *Beit Ya'akov Lekhu ve-nelkha,* "O house of Jacob come ye and let us walk", an injunction taken from the prophecy of Isaiah). A small fraction of the rabbinate, including some talmudists of great authority, rallied to the messianic watchword of the Return (Kalischer, Kook) and some rabbis, such as Shemuel Mohilever, themselves went and settled in Palestine, not to teach and die there awaiting the Messiah, but to work the land with their own hands: to make for themselves there, as the Marrano Usqves had said three hundred years earlier, "a new life". This as yet unsecularized messianism, as far from the Reform and assimilation as from secularism and statism, nevertheless rested on the *Haskalah* to the extent that it made of the renaissance of Hebrew as a living language the sign of its return and the ending of exile.

After the Odessa pogrom of 1871 and the Kishinev ones in 1881, all these groups federated in a heterogeneous movement called "The Lovers of Zion". No one was yet speaking, among Jews, of "Zionism"; the term only appeared after 1896, with the about-turn of Herzl, a Viennese advocate of assimilation and himself totally integrated into high society, traumatized by the Dreyfus affair and converted to Jewish nationalism. But before political Zionism was founded in western Europe in 1897, at the Basel congress, Hebrew cultural nationalism and "Palestinophile" migratory messianism had already come together at the conference held at Kattowice – in the Russian empire – by the Lovers of Zion. It was then that Leo Pinsker, a Jewish doctor in Odessa and author, in 1881, of *Auto-Emancipation,* formulated for the first time the so-called "territorialist" thesis: the Jews, persecuted everywhere, needed a state of their own where they would be able to live like others. And he said:

We must, above all, not dream of restoring ancient Judaea. We must not attach ourselves to the place where our political life was once violently interrupted and destroyed. The goal of our present endeavours must not be the "Holy Land", but a land of our own. We need nothing but a large piece of land for our poor brothers, a piece of land which shall remain our property, from which no foreign master can expel us.

But the Lovers of Zion still preferred Zion without a state, as they were promised by Ahad Ha'am, the greatest moral and literary figure in the movement, to a state elsewhere than in Zion. It was only in the following century that the synthesis – the Jewish state in Palestine – came to be seen as possible and became a reality.

Of the some five million Jews enumerated in the Russian empire at the beginning of this century, some 200,000 enjoyed privileges assimilating them to citizens. As in neighbouring countries, this sprinkling of emancipated Jews became an integral part of the democratic intelligentsia. Their proportions in the revolutionary movement, particularly in the socialist movement, far exceeded their numerical importance. But the ups and downs of the democratic revolution, like their position of objective hostages in the Russian empire, led many of these assimilated Jews, often without previous attachment or links to the life of the *Shtetl,* to turn to Jewish nationalism. They introduced into it the ideas that they had absorbed in the revolutionary movement: agrarian naturalism *à la* Tolstoy, labourism and Marxism. This return forced on the assimilated petty and middle bourgeoisie by anti-Semitism, introduced into the mental world of the *Shtetl* the body of ideas that were circulating in Europe: the Enlightenment and socialism, but also the colonialist re-organization of the planet, of which Jewish emigration to America gave an example.

The literary and journalistic, and later trade union and political, Yiddishist movement that developed after 1881 and soon came to be at odds with the Hebraist Lovers of Zion was also born of the *Haskalah.* But it was articulated on the diffusion of socialist populism that accompanied the proletarianization of the *Shtetl.* The end of the century Yiddish writers, just as much as their Hebraist elders, had no sympathy for the traditional organization. Scholem Aleichem, the best known of them, makes the hero of his *The Bewitched Tailor* say

> Shimon-Eli did not fail to drag through the mud the petty officials who collected the tax on kosher meat; he called them thieves, blood-suckers, even cannibals, telling anyone who cared to listen that the ritual slaughterers, as well as the rabbis themselves had – for a long time – been making common cause with the *baale-takse,* in other words that they were all in the same clique, a club of evil-doers, crooks and brigands, devil take them.... [11]

Simplifying, it could be said that the Hebrew press and literature that developed after 1860 were nationalist in inspiration, whereas the Yiddish output which began in the 1880s was altogether oriented towards socialism.

Such a dichotomy, however, overlooks the complexities of the interaction between the two literatures. In the first place, because the Hebrew literary renaissance preceded the emergence of Yiddish as a language of written culture (with the "Hebrew", that is, Aramaic, alphabet): "Hebrew, a scholarly language ill-equipped for modern literary writing, was almost invariably the first choice of the 19th-century Jewish writers – including those who would later become famous as Yiddish writers."[12] Second, because the religious world, that is, the *Shtetl* such as it used to be, absolutely hostile to any profane literature, was even more vigorously opposed to the profane use of the language of the sacred *(Leshon ha-Qodesh)*, Hebrew: the *Shtetl* was thus an objective ally of considerable strength against modern Hebrew. But, even more, because the emergence of Yiddish in revolt against Hebrew was one element of a discussion as to the character of Jewish identity.

Behind the accusations of the Hebraists, who saw Yiddish as the language of the ghetto, exile and servitude, there was modern nationalism – on the German model – based on the absolute identification of the nation (the "race") and the language "of the ancestors": a supremely Western source of the historicist archaism that made the ancient Hebrew nation the essence of the contemporary Jewish social formation. But there was also the secular expression of the tribal fiction on which Judaism had rested since Ezra and Nehemiah: a modern expression, in the ancient language, of the historical concepts inherited from rabbinism.

In the accusations of the Yiddishists, who saw Hebrew as the language of the rabbis and their class culture, there was certainly an existential and popular bias, which calls to mind the problematic of modern languages faced with Latin in mediaeval Europe, or that of Arabic dialect in the Maghrib, without being exactly like either of them. But while the Yiddishists, and following them the Bundists who were to make Yiddish a political and social war-horse, rejected the Zionist idea of an organic Jewish nation which would supposedly have maintained its Hebrew identity from the Egyptian exodus through to emancipation, they were passionately attached to the idea of a separate Yiddish-speaking Jewish people, jealous of its identity, for which the Bund would claim, in the framework of the common victory of socialists of all the nationalities of the Russian empire, "national-cultural-autonomy".

The social and historical base of the Bund, the Jewish proletariat in eastern Europe, was to be broken up by objective factors: emigration westward, followed – as in the United States where the Bund long continued to dominate unions in the clothing trade – by the embourgeoisement of the second generation; and the Bolshevik revolution in the east, which dismantled the *Shtetl* and absorbed the Bundist heritage, rejecting those who could not be won over into the camp of emigration and Zionism. Only the Bund in the Polish republic restored after the First World War was to survive as a Jewish labour movement until the Nazi occupation.

The Bund had been one of the first components of the Russian social-democratic party, and Lenin, several years before disputing sharply with its leaders, had hailed it as "the revolutionary vanguard of the Russian proletariat". The scriptural and communal cultural background of the Jewish workers of Poland in the 1890s certainly prepared them better to take on the intellectual and organizational tasks assigned by theory to the proletariat than the illiterate peasantry who served as the hinterland to the Russian proletariat. But despite the virulence of the movement's divergences with the Lovers of Zion and the Hebraists, it was nevertheless, by virtue of its own dynamic, oriented towards cultural nationalism. Expressing itself at first in Russian, as a component of social-democracy, it went over to Yiddish after a few years, given the impossibility of disseminating the ideas of socialism among the masses of Jewish workers in a language that they did not understand, that is, literally, in a foreign language. (Lenin would later experience the same problem, and would create the *Yevsektia* for this purpose, relying essentially on former Bundists.) But this shift to Yiddish displaced the movement: the Russian empire was no longer its only setting, since Yiddish-speaking workers formed a diaspora that straddled empires, states, and even continents. Henceforth, Jewish popular culture became the subject: cultural nationalism came to express in secular terms the old challenge of existence as a diaspora, and naturally led to the Bundist programme of separate education for Jews, outside any territorial logic, i.e., on the basis of ethno-linguistic criteria.

Zionism

Political Zionism which finally formulated the state objectives of Jewish nationalism came from the west, with Herzl, in 1896 – from Austria, where, in one generation people moved from rabbinism to emancipation, from Hasidism to the *Haskalah*. A territorialist like his predecessor Pinsker, Herzl was tempted, in 1903-4, to accept the British proposal of building the Jewish National Home in Uganda. The mass of the Lovers of Zion – children of the *Shtetl* – categorically rejected any "Zionism without Zion". For already, over forty years, Hebrew nationalist messianism had begun to feed a thin but continuous trickle of emigration to Ottoman Palestine. Less than the flow to western Europe, less than the one to the Americas or other European colonies, but important because of the place it would later come to occupy.

It is true that, without the organized intervention of political Zionism which saw the light of day at the Basel congress and wove new alliances with the great powers, this Jewish emigration to Palestine would have had no great political consequences. Of very modest dimensions (a few tens of thousands of Jews left Europe in this way), and with no clear political and territorial demand, this emigration aspired to build in Palestine a spiritual centre, to use Ahad Ha'am's expression, in which the Jewish people would be able to regenerate itself morally and socially, by abandoning its commercial practices and returning to working the land. Here it can be seen that it was not only Marxists who were critical of the economic function of the people-class, responding to the concerns of the tsars who at the same time were drawing up various plans to "productivize the Jews". We can also see that the cult of working the land was a theme of "spiritual Zionism", with no reference to socialism or class struggle.

Here, again, the relationship of the *Shtetl* to the emancipated Jews of the great Western nations – England, France, Germany – comes in. Denouncing the anarchy, corruption and incompetence of the Lovers of Zion in the Palestine of 1893, Ahad Ha'am, who watched with anguish as speculation and private interests dominated the *Yishuv,* launched an appeal to his "brothers" in the West: they alone, being civilized, could save the Lovers of Zion movement from ruin. In this new construction, the geography of Europe had replaced the mediaeval social ladder, and the Jewish bourgeoisie in the West played the role of the *chtadlanim* of yesteryear: notables external to the communal order, but indispensable to the functioning of the protection of the prince and to the financing of Jewish "charities". The assimilated Jewry of the West was to assume this role that Ahad Ha'am assigned to it, in two stages. But, in doing so, it was to transform the nature of the project.

In a first stage, it was the assimilated bourgeoisie of France, and to a lesser extent of Germany and England, that embarked in Palestine, both among the Lovers of Zion immigrants and among the local Jews, on concerted philanthropic efforts designed to ensure the profitability of very classic colonial investments; the Rothschild family (French branch) invested in communion wine on the slopes of mount Carmel as it had invested in Algerian wine in the shadow of Bugeaud. But here that bourgeoisie had an extra motive; although couched in the language of a notable assuming communal responsibility, its aims proceeded from a desire to channel – elsewhere than to its own social environment – the flood of Jewish emigrants from eastern Europe. The Jews of Williamsburg in the United States at the beginning of the century signed a petition to prohibit the settlement of "folkloric" Jews coming from Russia. Whence the classic "definition" of Zionism: an American Jew giving money to a French Jew for a Polish Jew to settle in Palestine.

In a second stage, the recently assimilated Jewish bourgeoisie of Austria and Germany took over the leadership of the movement, with Herzl and the institutions that emerged from the first Zionist congress. As for the third stage, with which we shall deal below, it was one where the immigrant workers from the decayed *Shtetl* took power in the colony.

Between the political spiritualism of the Lovers of Zion and the French patriotism of the "benefactors of the *Yishuv*", there was scarcely any place for a project for a Jewish state. Rothschild, like Lord Montagu in England,

clearly saw the contradiction that existed between the national development of the Jews, in Palestine or elsewhere, and their "acquired rights" in
countries such as France and England. Under the auspices of Herzl and the
Zionist congress, on the contrary, there emerged a synthesis and
articulation between the various ideological and practical components of
Jewish nationalism and the strategies of those great powers that Herzl
called, "the governments".

Like Nordau and Zangwill, Herzl was a "territorialist" and favoured
first Argentina before dreaming of Uganda. As modern Europeans they
knew that Utopia was the twin sister of the discovery of worlds unknown.
And it was some time before they became used to calling *Palastina* "Land of
Israel". Moreover, for a long time, they wanted to make German the
language of the *Yishuv*.

The fact was that the sole starting-point of their Jewish national utopia
was European anti-Semitism, which blocked the escape route for the
inhabitants of the *Shtetl*. Fifteen years after Pinsker, in Odessa, had drawn
his territorialist conclusions from the Kishinev pogrom, Herzl, a minor
Viennese journalist, saw the light in Paris, where he was covering the
Dreyfus trial. If a Jew as assimilated as Dreyfus, conservative and
chauvinist, a military man and a militarist, a conformist and at least as
ordinary as Herzl himself – if such a man could become the victim of an
anti-Semitic plot in France, the cradle of emancipation and the rights of
man, then there was no security anywhere for the Jews so long as they had
no state of their own. The territory, as we have seen, was not defined. Nor
were the people: Herzl had no experience of Judaism, and he felt a definite
antipathy for the world of the *Shtetl*. The customs and way of life or
thought of the people, then, were to be swept away and replaced by the
futuristic abstraction of Utopia. In *Altneuland* (Old-New Land), published
in 1902, Herzl described in detail the liberal-model society of the future
state. And Ahad Ha'am wondered "what there was that was specifically
Jewish in the new state: the language is not Hebrew, Jewish culture is
scarcely touched on, even the name of Zion is not mentioned!"[13] This was
because

> the dispute between the territorialists... and the others was, broadly speaking,
> one that separated the Jews of western Europe from those in eastern Europe, the
> Judaism close to assimilation from the Judaism of the ghetto, such as it still
> existed in Poland and, above all, in Russia.[14]

This Europeanness of Herzl and political Zionism was necessary for it to
be effective: Herzl, Jewish by sole virtue of anti-Semitism, opted for a
Utopia which was to make him, through an enterprise that was inseparable
from the geography of colonialism, into a fully fledged Westerner. He
therefore undertook to knock on doors where he had the most chances of
being listened to. To Kaiser Wilhelm he explained that the establishment of
Yiddish-speaking settlers in Palestine would enlarge the sphere of influence

of German culture. To Chamberlain, he would demonstrate the strategic advantages of an Anglo-Zionist alliance. To the Sultan, he would dangle the prospect of Jewish money to replenish the finances of the Porte. To von Plehve, the tsarist Minister of Police responsible for the provocations, pogroms and massacres of Jews, he would explain that the strengthening of Zionism would weaken the revolutionary movement in Russia, and vice-versa. This was because he was convinced, says Hagani, "that it is possible to come to an understanding with one's fiercest adversaries when their interests coincide with yours".[15] For Herzl, precisely because he reasoned like a European petty bourgeois, understood anti-Semitism, and, like many Zionists after him, considered it to be well founded: the Jewish state would normalize the Jews. "Let sovereignty be granted us over a portion of the globe adequate to meet our rightful national requirements; we will attend to the rest", he wrote in the *Der Judenstaat* (The State of the Jews), paraphrasing Pinsker. But he added at once: "The governments of the countries where anti-Semitism flourishes have the most interest in granting us this sovereignty."

When the Zionism of the Jews of Europe disembarked in Ottoman Palestine in the 1860s, it became entwined with the Zionism of Bonaparte and Napoleon III, of Bicheno and Byron: Western imperialism enveloped in mysticism and archaeology, assuring for itself markets and strategic positions by brandishing the most varied of banners. Post-Herzlian political Zionism would transform this meeting into an alliance.

Thirty years earlier, an authentic precursor of Zionism had already conceived the synthesis of the still scattered threads of practical Zionism. Hess, a repented assimilationist, no doubt influenced by Laharanne's famous pamphlet on *The New Eastern Question,* wrote *Rome and Jerusalem* in 1862 and, in 1865, a *Proposal for the Colonization of the Holy Land.* In it he already foresaw the "need to be armed against the Bedouins", and endeavoured to have the proposal patronized by France, which he saw as the best placed to do so. In a letter dated 1 December 1865 to the grand rabbi of Amsterdam, Dünner, Hess set out the support he claimed to have found among French high political and financial figures involved in the agricultural colonization of Algeria, who had led him to believe that they would give "very favourable consideration" (these are almost the exact words of the Balfour Declaration fifty-two years later) to "the establishment of Jewish colonies in Palestine and the surrounding areas, more particularly in the proximity of the Suez Canal".[16]

If Hess sought an alliance with imperialism, it was because he, like Ahad Ha'am, was conscious of the cultural chasm that separated the west from the east of European Jewry. "The Western Jews", he wrote, "feel settled in the countries in which they have lived for hundreds of years." They would not emigrate, he predicted, "even if the country is restored to the Jewish people". And he added, after mentioning the "parasitic structure" of the Jewish economy of eastern Europe:

The acquisition of a common national territory, the active aspiration to legal conditions in which, and thanks to which, the foundation work of Jewish agricultural, industrial and commercial communities will operate in accordance with the principles of Judaism, that is to say along socialist lines – such is the basis on which Eastern Jewry will be able to climb out of the dustbins, the bright flame of Jewish patriotism will revive, and the whole of Judaism will come to life again.

It is necessary, says the Arab proverb, to follow the liar to his door. It is necessary to follow Zionism to Palestine and to see it at work. But it is also necessary to follow the Zionist approach all through this conviction that "the governments of the countries where anti-Semitism flourishes have the most interest in granting us this sovereignty", and reflect on the implications of this faith in the light of the persistence of anti-Semitism.

The multiplicity of currents that claim allegiance to Zionism, the sometimes violent contradictions that set them against one another without however precipitating actual splits, may be somewhat disquieting: the observer oscillates between feeling that the diversity is so great that generalization seems misleading, and observing a practical unity that makes one suspect the polemics of being artificial, and gives divisions the appearance of a division of labour. This is because Zionism, as an ideological movement, as a Church, aspires to a united discourse, and consequently fuels a multitude of rival factions. But, as a social movement with a nationalist vocation, in which a mass colonizing action led to the building of a very real state, it implies a class alliance: coexistence and complementarity between the conceptions and practices of the various components of the movement.

How, in these conditions, can one grasp the peculiar character of Zionist ideology? It is neither secular nor religious, since there are atheist Zionists as well as believing Zionists: it is neither capitalist nor socialist, since both languages coexist in it... The core of the Zionist consensus concerns the Jewish fate, the nature of the State of Israel and the essence of the Arab rejection: fundamentally, Zionism is an optic on anti-Semitism.

Historically, Zionism was the product of anti-Semitism. It is true that, when it first emerged, Zionism was articulated on a plural and very real religious or socialist Ashkenazi Jewish nationalism, the child of the *Haskalah* and the *Shtetl*. But it was anti-Semitism that caused assimilated Jews like Hess, Pinsker, Herzl or Borokhov (the theoretician of socialist Zionism) to turn to abstract, Westernized and ahistorical Jewish nationalism; it was anti-Semitism that transformed the ideological and cultural currents sweeping the *Shtetl* into a political movement, a colonizing organization and finally a state.

Pinsker was a doctor. "Anti-Semitism", he wrote, "is a disease; and, as a congenital disease, it is incurable." In Zionist ideology, anti-Semitism is a structural disposition of non-Jewish societies. Two contradictory and complementary lines of argument are used to demonstrate this essential incompatibility.

For some, the hatred of Jews has its origin in the superiority of Jews themselves (in a toned down version: their singularity), so obvious that non-Jews are incapable of facing the comparison, and therefore hate these supermen out of jealousy. But the imagery was not always so gross. While the idea that the Jews are racially superior, a secular reformulation of the theme of a chosen people, finds its adepts above all among religious Zionists, the idea of a moral, cultural and intellectual superiority is, on the contrary, extremely widespread. Christianity and Islam had, moreover, each in its own way, endorsed this claim, decreeing the Jews to be the inventors of monotheism – a category that Judaism, for its part, in no way recognizes. Nineteenth-century evolutionism, which saw the well-known stages of savagery, barbarism and civilization as parallel with the no less famous stages of fetishism, polytheism and monotheism, made the Jews the inventors of civilization, the Law, morality, etc. Such is the pseudo-rationality with which the Zionists apprehend anti-Jewish persecution.

Another line of argument strengthens similar illusions. This consists, on the contrary, in seeing anti-Semitism as a normal reaction, of self-defence in a way, of societies confronted with the anomaly of Judaism. This classically anti-Semitic way of seeing things constituted the starting point of the approach pursued by Herzl, Borokhov (obsessed by the need to "normalize" the Jews) or Ben-Gurion. In this perspective, it is all the more pointless to struggle against anti-Semitism because it flows inevitably from the abnormal situation represented by the existence of a diaspora: here, and especially among the socialist Zionists, the people-class theory came to the rescue of territorialism.

A macabre illustration of this problematic of normality is to be found in the ravings of Alfred Rosenberg, co-founder of the Nazi party who, in 1935, wrote a book with the shock title, *The Myth of the 20th Century,* devoted to a combined denunciation of Judaism and Zionism. Rosenberg was particularly virulent against two diabolical Jews: Ahad Ha'am, an opponent of the political Zionism of Herzl and Westernized territorialist statism, and Martin Buber, then the moving force in the Peace Alliance which advocated Jewish-Arab bi-nationalism in Palestine. It was in these two, precisely, that the Nazi identified the object of his death wish: multinationalism, in which he saw the Jewish will to rule the world. Yet, he added:

> In some leaders no doubt one can also find, living and upright, the desire that a non-Jew might have: to build on his own patch the pyramid of life which would be peculiar to the "Jewish nation", that is a vertical figure, in contrast to the horizontal mode of its former existence.[17]

But he considered this "ideal" as "opposed to the instincts of this anti-race" that the Jews are. That is why Zionism's determination to normalize worried and intrigued him, and he preferred in any case to see it as a sham. He consoled himself by looking to the opposition of the Orthodox rabbinate to political Zionism:

> The orthodox Jews thus altogether represent the Jewish essence when they absolutely refuse this aspect of Zionism as a conception of life peculiar to the west, and lay claim to "the world mission" of consciously fighting, as a lapse, the attempt to make "Israel" a nation like others.[18]

Of course, the Nazi theoretician only saw this "uprightness" in "some leaders", whom it is to be regretted he failed to name, and thought that Herzl and his ilk were not the Zionists they claimed to be: they "claimed" to want "to create a Jewish state", but the reality was completely different, since they wanted in reality to make Jerusalem into "the best place for the world money market".

Decidedly, anti-Semites are never happy! Yet, the political Zionists who took practical and ideological control of the European Jewish emigration to Palestine at the beginning of the century were well and truly inspired by an ideal of normality which, in some ways, calls to mind the nationalist-racist conception of world space that Nazism would carry to its paroxysm, and which can be summed up in a formula "Each to his own!" Or, again, in "the song sung by the Polish Jewish *jeunesse dorée* parading in brown shirts, throwing stones at the windows of left-wing Jewish papers. 'Germany for Hitler, Italy for Mussolini, Palestine for us!' "[19] And it is indeed true that this conception represented, as Rosenberg stressed, "a contamination by the national feeling and state conception of the peoples of Europe".

In practice, as always, ideas and images circulated, were exchanged, contaminated one another: positive Jewish nationalism and normalizing Zionism fed on and impregnated each other for several decades, distilling the elements of the normative synthesis of contemporary Zionism.

The first political Zionists were assimilated men who fell back on a Jewishness of which they knew nothing. They confessed without shame their philosophical and practical agreement with the anti-Semites, as much as their aversion and scorn for the traditional Jewish world. "The persecuting governments will help us", wrote Pinsker, since they "will doubtless feel as much pleasure at seeing us leave as we will to leave them." Herzl, who wrote, in 1896: "At present, my strongest supporter is the anti-Semite from Pressberg, Ivan von Simonyi", made an agreement with von Plehve, whose police had forged the *Protocols of the Elders of Zion*, and dreamed of the time when, liberated at last, the Jews would be able to say "The anti-Semites were right. But we should not be jealous, as we too will be happy."[20]

The first religious Zionists (rabbis Alkalay and Kalischer in the 19th century, Kook in the 20th), at the other extreme, loved the Jews. But their eschatology of Return and their metaphysical tribalism absolutely prevented them from choosing between one *goy* and another, between emancipation and anti-Semitism, between dissolution through assimilation, and extermination. So that, in the interplay of Zionist syntheses, anti-Semitism was never the principal enemy. Quite the contrary, it might sometimes be said: in a fit of depression, Herzl wrote: "We shall have to sink even lower, we shall have to be even more insulted, spat upon, mocked, whipped, plundered, and slain before we are ripe for the idea."[21]

This convergence of anti-Semitism and Zionism is a fact. That some anti-Semites refused to accept this and wished at all costs to be anti-Zionists, is a good illustration of the passion to which they are a prey: for, on what they consider the essential, that is, that the Jews must get out, there was agreement. The conversations between Herzl and the Russian anti-Semites is evidence of this. Since we cannot kill all the Jews, von Plehve said to him, we must let them leave. And he added: "But this doesn't mean that we want to lose all our Jews. Those of superior intelligence – and you yourself are the best example – we would like to help." Quoting L. Hirszowicz[22] and the secret archives of the Wilhelmstrasse,[23] Maxime Rodinson mentions the agreement on the "Transfer" between the Jewish Agency and the Reich, in order "to faciliate the emigration to Palestine of German Jews". Dr. Fraenkel of the Hebrew University of Jerusalem's thesis on the relations between the Third Reich and the Zionist movement in Germany, reproduces a Nazi police circular, dating from the summer of 1938. It says that: "despite the ordinance dissolving Jewish organizations, the members of the Betar[24] must be permitted to meet behind closed doors and to wear the uniforms of their movement", since it "disseminates the spirit of national socialism among the Jewish youth of Germany."

The list of points of contact could be lengthened. At times it culminated in moments of short-lived cooperation; but the anti-Semitic logic itself, once it moved from proposals for transfer to plans for extermination – as was the case with the Nazis by the end of 1941 – made collaboration impossible. That did not prevent the ultra-Zionists of the Stern Gang from still seeking an alliance with the Nazis against "British imperialism" in 1942.[25] Nor the strange negotiations between the Germans and the Zionists in Hungary on the principle: Jews in exchange for lorries.[26]

But these were only episodes: from the time when the Nazis began to put into effect the "final solution", any alliance with the Zionists became void, or marginal. Moreover, while such an alliance corresponded to an anti-Semitic logic within Germany, it conflicted with the main alliances of Zionism internationally: the pro-British turn-around of the Zionist leadership after the First World War, the weight of American Jewry, and even the pro-Soviet orientation of part of the *Yishuv* between the wars were so many factors that ruled out a strategic alliance.

However that may be, Zionists did in fact fight, armed, as Zionists, against the Nazis in occupied Europe. Collaboration of Jews with the Nazis – whether it was naïve as in the case of the French Jewish notables in the U.G.I.F.,[27] or shameless like that of the "Jewish councils" (*Judenratten*) in the ghettos of occupied Poland – was not specifically the work of Zionists, who were in general hostile to these institutions. But we must nevertheless consider the passivity, and even the theoretical satisfaction ("We told you so!") of the Zionists, all through the 1930s, as anti-Semitic fascism rose to power in Europe: it was proof of the need to abandon the farce of assimilation. We must meditate on the attitude of Ben-Gurion in 1938, when he asked that everything should be done to abort plans to evacuate the Jews of central Europe to the United States or South America. "If our brothers in America", he wrote, "have to choose between the physical rescuing of the Jews of Europe and Zionism, they will choose the former, and that will be the end of our movement."

In a work recently published in Hebrew,[28] S.E. Beit-Zvi, from a Zionist viewpoint, accuses the labour-Zionist leadership of the time of having discouraged the Allies from putting into effect rescue solutions involving the massive transfer of the Jews of occupied Europe elsewhere than to Palestine. Significantly, Beit-Zvi entitles his work: *Post-Ugandan Zionism in the Crisis of the Holocaust.* The shadow of Uganda, which had almost divided the Zionist movement in 1903–4 – the spectre of territorialism and a capitalist Byrobaijan somewhere in America – had still not dissipated, suggests Beit-Zvi. Although the territory had started out indeterminate, the very fact that it was finally chosen in Palestine, under pressure from the *Shtetl*, made it unique, irreplaceable and indivisible. Any other solution could only be a distraction. In Ben-Gurion's socialist Zionism, territorial concentration constituted a revolutionary solution to the Jewish problem. Rescuing Jews was thus rather like those reforms that slightly alleviated the lot of the oppressed with the sole aim of distancing them from the sole solution, the Return to Zion. Beit-Zvi accuses Ben-Gurion and Moshe Sharett[29] by name of having blocked the publication of information that was reaching Palestine by 1942 concerning the massacres of Jews in occupied Poland and Russia, for fear that this "allied propaganda" would distract energies towards "physical rescue". "For a while, which was decisive and fatal, Zionist newspapers expressed open and vigorous support for the versions and denials of the Nazi propaganda minister, Goebbels, faced with the 'exaggerations' and 'inventions' of his free world enemies." And Beit-Zvi adds that "these atrocious acts were committed by their authors in all good faith", and with the support "of the Zionist public at all levels".

This wait-and-see attitude of Zionism confronted with Nazism flowed from the conception of anti-Semitism as a permanent structure of society. It was for the same reason that the extermination of the Jews of Europe, particularly of Poland, where Nazi barbarism annihilated even the memory of the centuries-old Jewish community culture, was transformed after the war, into the key argument in Zionist language. For the Nazi attempt to empty Europe of its Jews, first by allowing them to leave, then by exterminating them, had "readied" the survivors "for the [Zionist] Idea", as Herzl wanted. If the Odessa and Kishinev massacres, the pogroms and riots, the trials and forgeries, the incitements and caricatures, the discrimination and persecution of the pre-war period had not been enough, perhaps this enormous crime would serve for the edification of the Jews in exile, naïve and carefree, who persisted in believing in democracy and the brotherhood of peoples!

The "Holocaust" became, in the Zionist mental world, the time when the clock of history stopped and when the world revealed its anti-Jewish obsession. The Zionist representation of this "Catastrophe" touches on the meaning and context of the genocide, not how it actually happened. Certain areas are highlighted in a way that leaves related facts in the shadow, so that the Zionist predicate stands out, isolated from distracting issues, such as the existence of a Nazi policy of extermination aimed at other "useless" ethnic groups, like the Gypsies, or the policy of slave exploitation and massacres with regard to other "inferior races", in particular the Slav ones. In the Zionist account, the racist system of the Nazis seems to have concerned only the Jews. But the feature that is most obscured is the struggle waged by non-Zionist Jewish partisans against the Nazi war machine, either in the communist movement or in the nationalist resistance in the various occupied countries. The Zionist attempt to present the Zionist partisans as the only fighters in the Warsaw ghetto uprising, for example, leaves out the communist and Bundist defenders of the ghetto. This representation obscures the powerlessness of Zionism as such to halt the Hitlerite war machine: for it was the British army that stopped Rommel at the gates of Alexandria. What would have happened to Palestine if the Reich had "liberated" it from "Jewish-British imperialism"? Was not the idea of a refuge ridiculous from the time when the conflict became worldwide?

It would be wrong to see in this reconstruction no more than a propaganda device to blame non-Jews in general, and Europeans in particular. It also reflects an internal ideological need of Zionism itself: this vision – and the cult of the "memory" thus rearranged – are now offered by Zionism to the Jews themselves, as the moral foundation of the Return. And it cannot be denied that the universal condemnation of Nazi crimes after the Second World War allowed the Zionist leaders, not only to make their territorial demands in Palestine triumph, but also to promote, above all among the Jews themselves, a vision of history in which anti-Semitism is the centre, the Alpha and the Omega, the beginning, the base and the end.

"We hold", wrote Luc Rosenzweig in *Libération,* "the number one position in the hit-parade of horror." If one agreed to stop treating the frontiers of the European diaspora as those of humanity, one could count and recount the tens of millions of Africans murdered by the slave traders in two centuries of the slave trade. The Indians in the Americas – both north and south, in varying degrees – belong to civilizations that have been decimated, and, for some, annihilated. Whole ethnic groups have disappeared. In North America, by the 18th century, it was no longer a matter of exploiting these men or enslaving them, but of seizing their land so as to forbid it to them, and establish there a new society, which even imported its own proletarians and its own slaves. The Indian tribes were starved, deported thousands of kilometres from their lands; they were poisoned, their economy was destroyed. At certain times, in some American states, there was a bounty of one dollar on Indian heads, any Indian head: Indians were hunted like wolves. But while animal fur had a use and exchange value, only the government bought Indian scalps, with which it did absolutely nothing: the costly gratuity of extermination!

The Jewish martyrdom in the Second World War is perceived as unique in history, quantitatively and qualitatively, and the destruction of the Jews as the unique purpose of Nazism. Thus, the peculiar nature of the crime must have something to do with the mystery of Jewish history, as one aspect of being a chosen people. Thus, the refusal to contextualize the tragedy becomes the consecration of Jewish otherness in history, while at the same time granting immunity from criticism to the Jews in general, and the Zionists in particular.

At the end of the war, with the discovery of the scale of the massacres, murderous anti-Semitism became for the Zionists the major justification. As though the Nazi camps were the reason, prophetically foreseen, for the Basel congress in 1897, or the declaration by which Balfour, in 1917, promised in the name of Great Britain to hand Palestine over to the Zionists. This fixation arises from multiple reflexes, among which we must not exclude shock: after all, it is accepted that individuals can become mad, or "as if mad", under the pressure of external events – bombardments, torture, death of loved ones or captivity – and it is difficult to see why, in this fixation, there might not also be a degree of collective madness. What is ideology, if not precisely the "alienated consciousness" of which Marx writes?

The point is that Zionism and anti-Semitism cannot be treated as simple opposites; on the contrary, it is important to show how Zionism, a product of anti-Semitism and a reaction to anti-Semitism, is built upon and consolidated by anti-Semitism. And to show that having abandoned the messianism that made the end of nations the purpose of their history, or the withering away of the state the future of societies, it could only conceive of a Jewishness eternally based on an eternal anti-Semitism. If one makes anti-Semitism the sole evil principle in societies, the Jews are by definition innocent: not only of any responsibility for their own misfortunes, but also of what – in other places, at other times – they make others suffer.

The anti-Semite saw in the Jews a malevolent essence: banking and democracy, Freud, Marx, terrorism, inflation, military defeats, economic crises, literary failures or colonial expenditures were all so many manifestations of it, linked by a diabolical thread. This anti-Semitic demonology has often been described, but its pathological character does not make it any less dangerous. What has been less described is the place that anti-Semitism came to occupy in the mental universe of the Zionists, as a metaphysical principle that reduces human history to a universal and permanent anti-Jewish conspiracy.

It may, at first sight, seem paradoxical that the Zionist movement, which had invoked nationalism and the eternal Jewish nation at the time when it was anti-Semitism that was giving it birth, today invokes the Catastrophe instead of relying on the concrete existence of the Israeli nation-state. But this paradox is part of the reversal of values provoked after the war, by the move from Zionism to state. For, in the subjective geography of the Zionists, the state that was born three years after the gates of the death camps opened for the survivors replaced and compensated, perpetuated and eternalized the destroyed *Shtetl*. And Israel at once proclaimed itself the sole heir of the dead.

In the real history of the Zionist movement, Herzl's determination to come to an arrangement with anti-Semitism, to find common interests with "the enemies of the Jews", met the ethnocentrism of the *Shtetl*: what Kafka in his Yiddish period called "the lack of curiosity for what is not Jewish". From this meeting arises the everyday renewal of the Zionist perception of hatred of Jews as a normal and inevitable natural phenomenon, and also of the natural order as the enemy of the City, that is, of the Law.

Zionism was not only to settle its spiritual debt to European anti-Semitism in a dialogue with the Jews, but in the building of its state. There, as Herzl had promised, the liberated Jews would no longer have any need to be "jealous": they too – like the anti-Semites – would be "happy"! The colonization of Palestine, the creation of the State of Israel and its consolidation, its expansion and the colonization of new areas: in short, the "happiness" of being, at last, the sovereign proprietor of one's own domain, the legislator of prohibitions and the armed majority.

Such is the spectacular apprenticeship, the exchange of masks, that Zionism accomplished in Palestine, and that constitutes its history. Herzl's Utopia began to crystallize around the concrete circumstances of its achievement, and learned, day by day, to discover its own face altered in the process. Day by day, the Arabs of Palestine, who knew nothing of the terms of the European Jewish question, held up to it, like a reflection, the face of its practice.

Notes

1. This is the subject of Martin Buber's novel, *For the Sake of Heaven: A Chronicle,* in which the political upheavals in Napoleonic Europe are translated into the terms of Hasidic messianism.

2. "Antisémitisme éternel ou judéophobies multiples?" in M. Rodinson, *Peuple juif où problème juif?* (Paris, Maspéro, 1981).

3. Israel Shahak, "The Jewish religion and its attitudes to non-Jews", *Khasmin* (London, 1981) pp. 8–9.

4. Arthur Ruppin, *Die Juden den Gegenwart* (Berlin, 1911); Eng. translation by M. Bentwich, *The Jews of To-day* (London, G. Bell and Sons, 1913) pp. 5–6.

5. Théophile Grol, *Grands moments*, pp. 164–72.

6. Ibid., p. 170.

7. Albert Memmi, *La Libération du juif,* p. 19.

8. Alexandre Koyré, *La philosphie et le problème national en Russia au début du XIXe siècle,* lectures given in 1924–25 at the Institut des Etudes Slaves, at the University of Paris (Paris, Gallimard, 1976).

9. V.I. Lenin, "Right of Nations to Self-determination", in V.I. Lenin, *Collected Works,* vol. 20 (London, Lawrence and Wishart, 1964).

10. Eng. tr. in E. Silberschlag, *Saul Tschernichowsky, Poet of Revolt* (London, East and West Library, 1968).

11. Scholem Aleichem, *The Bewitched Tailor,* tr. B.Isaacs (Moscow, Foreign Languages Publishing House, 196-?).

12. Ouri Eisenzweig, *Territoires occupés de l'imaginaire juif* (Paris, Christian Bourgois, 1980) p. 102.

13. Ibid., p. 30.

14. Ibid., p. 31.

15. Baroukh Hagani, *Le sionisme politique et son fondateur* (Paris, 1918) p. 245.

16. Letter from Moses Hess to chief rabbi Dünner, quoted by Nathan Weinstock, *Zionism: False Messiah,* tr. A. Adler (London, Ink Links, 1979) p. 36–7.

17. Quoted by Jean-Pierre Faye in his anthology of anti-Jewish writings, *Migrations du récit sur le peuple juif* (Paris, Pierre Belfond, 1974).

18. Ibid., pp. 124–5.

19. Maxime Rodinson, "Israël, fait colonial?", *Les Temps modernes* (June 1967); also in his *Peuple juif ou problème juif?.*

20. André Chouraqui, *Theodore Herzl, A Man Alone,* tr. Y. Guiladi (Jerusalem, Keter Books, 1970) p. 175. Also M. Rodinson *Peuple juif,* pp. 174–5.

21. André Chouraqui, Theodore Herzl and Eli Lobel, "Les Juifs et la Palestine", introduction to the book by Sabri Giries (Jiryis in the English-speaking world), *Les Arabes en Israël* (Paris, Maspéro, 1969); (a revised version tr. by B. Pearce and A. Ehrenfeld is in *The Arab World and Israel,* two essays by Ahmad El Kodsy and Eli Lobel (New York, Monthly Review Press, 1960).

22. L. Hirszowicz, "Nazi Germany and the Palestine Partition Plan", *Middle Eastern Studies,* vol. 1, no. 1 (October 1964) pp. 45 *et seq.*

23. *Les Archives secrètes de la Wilhelmstrasse,* vol. V, 2 (Paris, Plon, 1954).

24. A so-called "revisionist" right-wing youth movement of Zionism, today affiliated to the Herut party of Menachem Begin.

25. See *Israël Israël... Histoire du groupe Stern (1940–1948),* by Nathan Yellin-Mor, himself directly involved in the search for contacts with the Germans on behalf of the *Lehi (Lohamei Herut Isra'el),* known in the West by the name of its leader Yaïr Stern, executed by the British before the creation of the State of Israel.

26. The ultra-Zionist American writer Ben Hecht brought together in *Perfidy* (New York, Julian Messner, 1951) all the known facts about this collaboration. Many facts were revealed during the notorious Kastner trial in Israel, in the early 1950s, about contacts between certain Zionist leaders in occupied Hungary, including the Israeli deputy minister Kastner, and the Germans.

27. See the survey by Maurice Rasijfus, *Des juifs dans la collaboration, l'U.G.I.F. (1941–1944)* (Paris, E.D.I., 1980).

28. S.E. Beit-Zvi, *Ha Tsionuth ha-post-Ugandith be-mashber ha-cho'ah, mehquar 'al gormei mishgueiha shel ha-tnu'ah ha-tsionith ba-shanim (1938–1945)* (Tel-Aviv, Bronfman Publishing House, 1977).

29. Sharett (1894–1965), a labour leader, and co-founder of the Mapai (Israeli Labour Party) became the head of the Political Department of the Jewish Agency in

1933, at the same time as being the editor-in-chief of the *Histadrut* daily, *Davar*. He was minister of foreign affairs, and later prime minister of the Israeli government between 1951 and 1953. His personal diary has recently been published by his son: eight volumes cover the years 1953–57 alone. The most interesting parts have been decoded by Livia Rokach in *Israel's Sacred Terrorism, a Study Based on Mosche Sharett's Personal Diary and other Documents,* published by the Association of Arab-American University Graduates Inc., Belmont, Mass., 1980.

6　Palestine

And so we return to where we began: Ottoman Palestine at the time when the crisis of European Judaism was beginning to break over it, as well as over the Jews who were living in the Arab East. And we begin to grasp that what was at work here was history, not a mere plot.

Like any history, it was both specific and universal, unique, and in that similar to all histories. Here the notion that only classes, or duly constituted nation-states are the subjects of history reveals itself to be erroneous. Yet this notion, which dismisses two-thirds of humanity from history, is very widespread. Not only in France, where Jacobinism is the common heritage of both right and left, but in Europe, especially central and eastern Europe, where the French model of the nation-state had inspired the democratic revolutionary battles, from 1848 to February 1917. And this notion, systematized by Stalin in 1913 in his famous article on the national question, has long been part of all forms of modernist thinking about the state in the Third World itself: sometimes in the name of nationalism, sometimes under the banner of socialism, and in most cases in various "national-socialist" syntheses. In my opinion, these must be understood as "a contamination by the national feeling and state conception of the peoples of Europe".

The criteria of a nation according to Stalin do not, he wrote, concern "tribes". But it is clear that the homogeneous bourgeois nation-state, based on a common origin, history, language, economic structure and territory, represents an occurrence which, while it may be decisive, is relatively rare compared to the multiplicity of transitional social formations between the tribe (the clan) and the multinational empires.

The social and political organization of mediaeval society, like that of the ancient empires and kingdoms, rested on mechanisms of communal solidarity that varied enormously depending on place and time, history and special circumstances. These networks of practical and ideological loyalties integrated the clan, without dissolving it, in the system of power born of their interaction. The oldest forms co-existed with the new ones in a relationship of rivalry subject to all sorts of fluctuations and determinisms, grafts and re-arrangements. Invasions and dispersions; migrations, sometimes as conquerors, sometimes forced; the acculturation of groups and the redefinition of the frontiers of their identity – sometimes in the enthusiasm of ideological movements or the spontaneity of economic relations, at others in violence and domination – are the statistical rule of human history, not the exception.

The norm is surely the unstable, incomplete and fluctuating character of the discordant circles of collective identity and the boundaries of the "we": one has only to think of the Gypsies, the Afro-Americans, the Indians of North America, the Armenians. One has only to think of the process by which the Brazilian or Nicaraguan "nation" is being formed: of the Creole-speaking Indians and Pakistanis in the West Indies; of the Chinese diaspora in south-east Asia; of the Fulani diaspora from Mauritania to Cameroon. One could compile a whole list of ethnic groups and tribes, peoples and societies, whose history is one of comings and goings and wanderings, which it may strengthen or dissolve, some of which survive and some perish: when they are dominant for a while, they may inspire lasting processes of fusion, or, on the contrary, reduce others to slavery. Every combination and permutation is possible.

A radical reconsideration of the concept of nation implied by prevailing Eurocentric views seems essential if we are to improve our understanding: better still, if we want to act. Every day we see the totalitarian and repressive effects of numerous nationalisms that deny particular identities, in their determination to persecute real and operative social formations in order to force them to enter the unitary straitjacket of happenstance boundaries. The modern states that have come into existence in Africa and Asia since the end of the Second World War, all inspired by related concepts of the nation-state, sometimes corresponded to former ethnic groups, sometimes to former kingdoms, sometimes to former empires, and sometimes, too, to administrative divisions imposed by the foreign occupying power bearing no relation to pre-colonial cultural boundaries. China and Egypt, each in its own way, have been nations for thousands of years. However, the fact that a nation has existed for millennia is not proof of ethnic continuity: the contemporary Arabs are not only descendants of the pre-Islamic Arabs, but also of Aramaeans and Babylonians, Sumerians, Akkadians, Elamites, Phoenicians, Canaanites, Philistines, Arabized Hebrews and Egyptians. In this sense, the Judaization of populations of diverse ethnic origins, the reality of which is not in doubt, says nothing about the existence or otherwise of a Jewish entity. Nations are not races, even when they claim the opposite. Two basic criteria, less restrictive than the signs of recognition of the nation-state built *à la française*, emerge from the features that make up these entities: language, and group consciousness – frames of reference of the group's self-image and experience, as institutionalized through internal power arrangements.

It is not at all surprising to see the Zionists, who assert the existence of an eternal and organic Jewish nation, refer precisely to the dogmatic and mechanistic definition of the nation mentioned above. The attempt to consider, as Ben-Gurion did, the Jewish nation as a single entity all through history, from the exodus from Egypt to modern Israel, with the same identity, was bound to lead Zionist theoreticians to an apologetic and essentialist falsification of the history of the Jews, with which the whole Israeli educational system is deeply impregnated: the mass production of false consciousness. The determination to secure entry for the Jews into the exclusive club of established nation-states, and to attribute to Jews across time and space the characters of nationality as defined by Europe, identified purely and simply with normality, led to a practical syllogism: "The Jews are a nation: a nation cannot exist without a common territory, but the Jews have no territory; so they need one, without which a nation cannot exist." In the desperate desire of political Zionism, that is of territorialism, for normalization, the Jacobin-imperial-reformed-enlightened view of the Jews ("Not a people but a religion"), the Stalinist view ("Not a nation but a language"), and the Nazi view ("an anti-race") were all treated in the same way: they were used as the basis of the counter-myth into which the myth-maker himself fell, taking on the role assigned by his fantasy. Lenin, it is true, had recognized the Jewish nationality in Russia, which he saw as Yiddish-speaking, like the Bundists whom he was fighting. He had never shared the Zionist notion of a worldwide, three-thousand-year-old "Jewish nation"; he recognized a Yiddish nationality that came into being in Poland in about the 14th century as a linguistic and religious minority. Moreover, Lenin was ready to grant national self-determination to the Cossacks, who quite obviously were not a nation ... For Nietzsche, the Jews were not only a people but "the only true people in Europe". But then Nietzsche, a Germanophobic German, delighted in asserting that the north shore of the Mediterranean marked the beginning of northern barbarism ... Each claim expressed to reduce the Jews to less than what they were in a given time and place fuelled the Zionist claim to restore the fullness of the nation by providing it with its missing dimensions. Behind the metaphysical debate on nationality, there was the obsession with Western normalization, which resolved itself in the affirmation of the inherent otherness of the Jews and history. As if groups could only be typical nations or nothing, either nations or fictions.

In the case of the Jews, as in many others, there was no essence at work in the trajectory by which an ancient formation progressively changed its appearance and configuration under the effects of the social transformations to which it was subjected. A series of groups, tracing their social origin to a common stock, have been shaped by history into various different sorts of entities: in one place articulated on a whole, in another fusing with others, or in others again separated by history and economics. The Jews of western Europe were transformed into Frenchmen, Englishmen, or Germans of Hebrew faith or Jewish origin, while the Jews of eastern Europe were formed into a distinct nationality and those of the Arab world into a confessional community. While the proportions and combinations of the factors at work in these situations were unique to each, the dynamic at work in these diverse destinies proceeded from the normal, ordinary functioning of human societies. One can neither treat this history as a special one and make it an exception to history, nor reduce it to some metaphysical will-to-exist, nor simplify it in order to force it into some fixed norm.

Everywhere, throughout history, people have described as Jews men defined by their membership of a religious community which conceived of itself as a people from the representation of its ancient history and its mythified tribal prehistory. Until the 18th century, the cultural disparities that existed between the various Jewish communities, as well as the affinities arising from prolonged contact with non-Jews, were considered as inessential, and adherence to Judaism as decisive. This assumption, which was as much part of Christian and Muslim conceptions of the world as it was of Jewish ideology itself, denied the movement and the metamorphoses of a Judaism that had ramified into complex regional sub-problematics. Emancipation, which effected at the level of law what the industrial revolution had accomplished in social relations, by exporting itself as part of an imperialism which liberated peoples, made this assumption untenable.

In the proliferation of situations and transitions which ensued, the essentialism of language continued to suggest for the Jews, and even for the Jew, the existence of a single identity, a unique entity, whereas in fact this name now described realities that were both distinct and different. Hence, there was a great temptation faced with this ahistorical abstraction, to replace the ideological myth of the eternal Jewish nation by the symmetrical myth of the non-existence of any Jewish entity, community or culture anywhere at all. Judaism was then perceived as a religion, in the modern sense of a voluntary philosophical choice, which it quite obviously is not in the eyes of the majority of Jews.

What is common to both, to the partisans of the "Jewish people" and to those who deny it most ardently, is the false idea that all Jews, wherever they are and over and beyond the diversity of their concrete situations, share a single unequivocal character, a common and unchanging essence: either national, or religious. The dogmatic assertions made in the very debates among nationalist Jews, religious Jews and assimilationist Jews encourage this essentialism, refusing as they do to take into account the variety of places, times and conditions.

Zionism, born of the blocked emancipation and incomplete assimilation of the Jews of central Europe at the time when the majority of Ashkenazi Jews were living in the twin grip of Russian absolutism and its own separate culture, was born precisely where all this confusion met: it made it its theoretical and practical point of departure.

While the "Jewish nation" in whose name the Zionists laid claim to Palestine was by definition mythical, ignoring as it did the denationaliza-tion of the assimilated Jews of the West and the transformation of the Jews of the Muslim world into tribal-confessional communities, the Ashkenazi socio-cultural entity, whose masses were to provide colonization with its shock troops, was indeed real. The Zionists themselves, of course, caught up in their own pan-Judaist rhetoric, neither wanted nor want at any price to recognize that nationality, whose fate was to fade away and be transcended ín the vision of the ingathering of the exiles and to impress only clandestinely its own character on the culture of Zionist colonization, the *Yishuv* and the State of Israel.

The Zionist movement, whose establishment in Palestine was accomplished in the framework of alliances with various imperialisms (French and German until the First World War, British until the Second World War, American down to the present day) acted as a self-motivated subject, and not merely as the hypocritical mask of Western economic or strategic interests. Its alliance with these interests proceeded from both convergence and expediency, but it was always short-lived, and often conflict-laden. What concerns us here is its area of freedom of decision-making, the determination on the part of the Zionists to play an autonomous role in the Western world's onslaught on the Arab world.

Western efforts to penetrate Palestine in the 19th century had the same goal as the rest of their undertakings in the Ottoman East. They were aimed at exporting bourgeois economic relations by war and conquest, or by diplomacy and trade, and usually using a combination of these methods. The aim was to free the productive forces of the old system of reproduction, to enable the labour of the peasants of the Middle East to contribute to an accumulation of capital, and not simply to the stability of the social and communal order.

Such a project obviously needed to make use of every available local agent, be it privileged classes ready to take on the role of "compradors", or religious or tribal minorities ready to rely on the foreigner to tilt the inter-communal balance in their favour. It could, as in Algeria, rely on a systematic colonization by settlement: even in this case, capitalist exploitation of indigenous labour remained at the heart of the colonial endeavour. It is clear that, at the turn of the century, the Zionists constantly dangled before their European interlocutors this possibility of using Jewish colonization. But this function, essential for winning the support of the Western powers for the Zionist project, was only the instrument, not the goal. For the Zionists, as history was to show, it was not a matter of transforming Palestinian society but of taking over its domain, its territory, by "sending it back to the desert". This determination to lay exclusive hold of the domain, which is comparable to the European colonization of North America, constitutes the specificity of Zionist colonialism, and the core of why it cannot be reduced to the economic logic of modern imperialism.

At the root of this demand for the domain was Zionist nationalism: the determination to create a complete society in which the Jews would occupy every level of economic organization. This determination did not derive from the spontaneity of the *Shtetl,* but from the state-territorialist logic of political Zionism. And yet, it rested on the spontaneous "separatism" of the immigrants, directly inherited, not only from rabbinical-Judaic theory but also from the theory and practice of the *Shtetl.*

As the concrete process of colonization unfolded, the various conceptions that ran through the Zionist movement at its beginnings were proved wrong and modified, mutually influencing one another. The earliest colonists did not ask themselves questions about sovereignty or the state of the Jews: absorbed as they were in their spiritual vision, and considering the self-separation of Jews from among the Nations as self-evident and automatic, *a priori* they no more asked themselves questions about the problem of the Arabs in Palestine than they had about the Ukrainians under Polish or Russian rule. But they were to become aware of the question – even without recourse to a state – they affirmed by migrating, by "ascending" to Zion, the continued survival of a special bond, of an ontological possession of the land of Palestine, *Eretz Israel.*

As Maxime Rodinson writes:

> There was not necessarily any colonialist or imperialist orientation *per se* in the motivations underlying this choice. The element that made it possible to connect these aspirations of Jewish shopkeepers, peddlers, craftsmen, and intellectuals in Russia and elsewhere to the conceptual orbit of imperialism was one small detail that seemed to be of no importance: Palestine was inhabited by another people. It would be very interesting to go through newspapers and books to see what kind of ideas the Jewish masses of Eastern Europe had about the indigenous population of Palestine.[1]

Ahad Ha'am's article, written in 1893, "Truth about the Land of Israel"[2] responds specifically to this question. It sets out to be precisely a refutation of "received ideas" about Palestine among the "Jewish masses of Eastern Europe": "We are accustomed to believe, outside Israel, that the land of Israel is today almost entirely desert, bare and uncultivated, and that anyone who wants to buy land there can do so without hindrance. But the truth is quite different."

The "we" to which Ahad Ha'am refers may be defined quite precisely. For the very pseudonym Ahad Ha'am, "one of the people", chosen by Asher Ginsberg, a Lover of Zion from the Polish-Ukrainian *Shtetl* that had become the compulsory Zone of residence of the Jews in the Russian empire, proclaimed the intention of one of the greatest Hebrew writers of his time: the "people" (in Hebrew, *'Am*) understood here as everywhere in 19th century Europe in its double meaning, both social and ethnic. In Ahad Ha'am, the espousal of the popular cause even inspired, as it did here, the most unpopular of his campaigns. The plural here is thus not the royal "we"; it denotes the "ordinary people" of the *Shtetl,* the implicit ideology of the "street" in the ghetto and its autonomy, transformed by powerlessness into idle gesticulating.

It indeed seems here that the Lovers of Zion (unlike the Zangwills and Nordaus in England and France) whose nucleus was in the Ukraine, on the borders of the Sublime Porte, did not really think that Palestine was uninhabited: "We are accustomed to believing, outside Israel, that the Arabs are all desert savages, a people like donkeys, and that they neither see nor understand what is happening around them. But that is a great mistake."

Thus the feature that "connected the choice of Palestine" to "the conceptual sphere of imperialism" was not only that Palestine was inhabited. Ahad Ha'am is quite clear: the human desert derives from the inhumanity, the animality ("a people like donkeys") of its inhabitants, whose existence was indeed known. This view of the native as "human dust"[3] does not flow simply from his "non-Jewishness", but precisely from his "Arabness": "The Arabs are all desert savages." This is the colonial stereotype, there is nothing peculiarly Jewish about it; it is "modern" racism, based on a hierarchy of nations starting from Western supremacy, "connected to the conceptual sphere of imperialism".

For his part, Ahad Ha'am sees in it "a great mistake". Faithful to a spiritual vision nurtured on Judaism, he sets his own "philo-Semitism" against this racist contempt for the Arabs: "The Arab, like all the sons of Shem, has a sharp and cunning intelligence. Every town in Syria and the Land of Israel is full of Arab traders who also know how to exploit the populace and relentlessly promote their own interests, all exactly as in Europe."

Here we have a glimpse of the gap between the coherent ideological language of the Lovers of Zion, rooted in the intellectualism of the *Haskalah* and the Hebrew renaissance, and the implicit language of the street, that is, of the "base". The competition between rival ideological languages engendered all sorts of incoherent and syllogical grafts and syntheses: "We are accustomed to believe ... that the Turkish government is so weak and so savage ... that for a little money we could do what we like there, and that in addition we will be protected by the representatives of the European kingdoms. But that too is a great mistake."

Right at the beginning of this century, Izhar Smilansky wrote, in Hebrew, numerous stories about this first *aliyah* of the Lovers of Zion in Palestine at the end of the last century. They contain eloquent testimonies to the mode of thinking of the settlers of this wave, considered by some as pre-Zionist since it occurred before the birth of Herzl's political Zionism. In *Rehovoth 1891*[4] he reproduces a dialogue between colonists which is a good illustration of this change of languages and perceptions precipitated by effective settlement on the soil of Palestine: "The Zionists have lied to us. The country is inhabited by the Arabs. And as the same country cannot be the homeland of two different peoples, the Lovers of Zion must leave, and seek another homeland." The idea that the Lovers of Zion should go and seek Zion elsewhere than in Zion (one of the biblical names of Jerusalem), in every way in conformity with Pinsker's territorialist approach, shows how far the theoretical distinction between spiritual and political Zionists was blurred in colonization. And the reply is even more significant: "We only need to chase the Arabs across the Jordan... How? A *revolutionary* [my italics] doesn't ask questions".

Here, the broad outlines of the practical synthesis of Zionism-in-action are prefigured: in it Jewish subjectivism and Western racism are articulated on the language of revolution in order to legitimize the exclusive taking over of an already inhabited territory.

Perhaps the most Westernized among the Zionists, befuddled by their indeterminate territorialism, had at one point so little curiosity about Palestine as to believe it was uninhabited. We know that when the French Zionist Max Nordau discovered with horror that there were Arabs in the country he had dreamed of as empty, he burst out in front of Herzl: "But then, we are committing a grave injustice!" Israel Zangwill is generally credited with inventing the famous slogan: "A land without people for a people without land";[5] he is said to have thought of it in England. But, as early as 1855, Moses Hess was already thinking of the need for the armed defence of the "colonists of the Holy Land" against the "Bedouins", while Borokhov, an assimilated Russian Jew who knew neither Yiddish nor Judaism, naïvely thought that the Arabs of Palestine would be assimilated to the new entity and become "Hebrews".

On the spot, Ahad Ha'am wrote

what are our brothers doing?... They were slaves in the land of their exile. Suddenly they found themselves faced with boundless freedom... This sudden change engendered in them a tendency to despotism, as always happens when a former slave becomes king, and they behave in a hostile and cruel manner towards the Arabs, trampling on their rights without the least justification, hit them shamelessly without adequate reason, even bragging about this behaviour, and no one stands in their way to put an end to this despicable and dangerous tendency.

In a lecture given in Paris in 1914, Chaim Weizmann declared:

In its initial stages, Zionism was conveived by the pioneers as a movement completely dependent on mechanical factors: there is a country which happens to be called Palestine, a country without a people, and, on the other hand, there exists the Jewish people who have no country...

Ouri Eisenzweig notes the difference

between the perception of the indigenous inhabitants by Herzl, and the impression made on him, on his journey to Cairo, in 1902, by young Egyptians. These, then under English rule, seemed to him to be the "coming masters". And he adds in his diary "It is a wonder the English don't see this. They think they are going to deal with fellahin forever." On the other hand, nothing similar about the Palestine... To Prince Hohenlohe, the Prussian imperial chancellor, who had asked him who the owners of the lands that Herzl intended to purchase in Palestine were, he replied: "Arabs, Greeks, the whole mixed multitude of the Orient."[6]

What is at issue here is not the perception of the human landscape, but the nature of the observation. In Egypt, indeed, as Ouri Eisenzweig stresses, Herzl was subject to "the good will of the real master, the British colonial governor". Whereas in Palestine, where he intended to be master, "Herzl's vision is colonial even if his motivations are not. Palestine, the necessary domain, will thus be virgin and natural. Individuals, or rather natives, may live there (just as there are stones and trees there), but there is no determinate social group."

This is what Golda Meir, then prime minister of the government of Israel, expressed with a mixture of candour and spite when, outraged by the moral accusation levelled against Zionism by public opinion, she declared: "It wasn't as if there had been in Palestine a Palestinian people that felt itself such, and that we drove out to take its place. They didn't exist!"[7]

In the practice and implicit ideology of the pioneers of Jewish colonization in Palestine, if not in the discourse of their leaders, the ways in which the various forms of the negation of the Palestinians were mixed make any dogmatic distinction between Zionism and pre-Zionism altogether equivocal, and, generally, apologetic. For the removal of the Palestinians outside the dreamed of domain was not simply accomplished on the basis of the alliance with imperialism made by political Zionism: it also derived from the way the pioneers themselves saw the world.

At the place where discourse and the act of colonization met, it can be seen how pointless it is to claim to reduce Zionism to just one of its many systems, declare this one essential and then give it a single social nature. Each of the social strata successively and simultaneously affected by Zionism among the Jews of Europe contributed its own sensitivity to the nationalist structure: each reacted, both in terms of these representations and in terms of its own aspirations and interests, to the unforeseen problems posed by the actual Arabness of Palestine. While it is clear that the ideas of the Jews of the Polish-Ukrainian *Shtetl* at the turn of the century about Palestine and its inhabitants were, as Rodinson stresses, "very vague" and had only "a remote relationship with reality", this ignorance in itself proves nothing. The same could no doubt be said of the poor Whites in every colonial undertaking: candidates for settlement on lands taken from indigenes are rarely students of the civilization they are crushing. As a nationalist movement, Zionism was part of the modern re-ordering of Jewish identity, which was both a social restructuring and a redefinition of "we". The big assimilated Jewish bourgeoisie in the West (Rothschild), the middle bourgeoisie in central Europe (Herzl), the petty bourgeoisie, whether assimilated (Borokhov) or Hebraist (Ahad Ha'am), the rabbis (Kalischer, Mohilever, Kook), and the workers (including the young Ben-Gurion) all found what they were looking for in it, while imprinting something of their personality on the movement as a whole.

Thus, behind the fog of the metaphysical categories of nation, religion and imperialism one can discern the active agent of this colonization that brought forth its nation-state. It is no doubt too easy to say "the Zionist movement". For the subject is not a party, nor even a single ideological-political movement. Parties and factions, discourses and polemics do not fully define the Zionist movement. In the movement of the Jewish society of the Russian empire to Palestine, what relationship existed with the double movement of European Jewry to Western bourgeois civilization and of this latter towards the Ottoman empire? It was a movement too within the *Shtetl* which was gradually disintegrating and moving elsewhere; it was a social movement within the *Yishuv* itself. The colonizing subject was an alliance of classes being continually reconstructed. The classes in question were pieces of the *Shtetl* that landed up in Palestine: a minority compared to the mass of those who remained in Europe or emigrated to other colonies, but the overwhelming and, before long, hegemonic majority in the *Yishuv;* the ten thousand Palestinian Jews were soon swamped: in 1914, there were more than 80,000 Jews (out of 700,000 inhabitants, according to Balfour) in Palestine.

The overwhelming majority of the newcomers were Yiddish-speaking Ashkenazim, and were participating in moulding the separate Jewish society in Palestine into a nation. In Palestine, through a many-sided and continuous struggle, they established a state and a social order that consecrated the emergence, from the popular strata of colonization, of a new bureaucratic-military ruling stratum. It was a considerable change, itself the prelude to the formation of new bourgeois strata, and, mainly after the creation of the State of Israel, in 1948, of the massive proletarianization of the new immigrants from the Arab countries of the Maghrib or the Middle East. In the final synthesis of Zionism – that is, with hindsight – it is possible to retrace, historically, the threads that go back to the great social originators of this or that conception, this or that slogan, this or that Zionist practice and its genealogy. It would be possible, when drawing up this list, to consider the relationship of each of these distinct milieux to the "conceptual sphere of imperialism", the replies that each would provide to a questionnaire on their opinions with regard to 1) the domination of the world in general, and of Asia in particular, by the great Western powers; 2) the Arabs in general, and the Arabs of Palestine in particular. The inferiority of non-Western peoples, the non-existence of their cultures, the historical legitimacy and the morality of their subservience to the West were all themes which underpinned the discourse about the Jewish nation. In fact, the idea, put forward by Herzl in *The State of the Jews*, that the Jews and their state constitute "a rampart of Europe against Asia, of civilization against barbarism", reflects at least as much the ethnic problematic of the central empires, and of Russia in particular, as it does that of the industrial rush to colonial markets. Had Askhenazi Jewish society, in historical Poland and in Russia, ever been other than a human rampart, the fragment of an imperial social order?

The link with classical colonialism is quite clear in the cases of the Rothschilds and other Western benefactors of the *Yishuv:* as pioneers of the imperial expansion of their governments, the Jewish notables of France,

England and Germany – while adding a touch of sentimentalism and brotherhood with their co-religionists to their Syrian and Palestinian business affairs – had involved themselves in the political and philanthropic support of Jewish colonization in Palestine, moved by the same ideal as the one that inspired the vine-growing and philanthropic enterprises in Algeria. In a first stage, this colonialism saw itself as a civilizing one: it did not despair of integrating the indigenes in the movement of "progress". The fact was that it was part of the global project of imperialism, the export of the bourgeois revolution: so that these very classic colonialists who still dominated the *Yishuv* at the beginning of the century were not truly Zionists. They did not base their practice on the absolute negation of the indigenous presence: on the contrary, the logic of their social position led them to exploit Arab labour, which amounted to ensuring, even strengthening, the permanent presence of non-Jews as part of the social scene.

The formerly assimilated intelligentsia, for its part, continued to cling to the abstract territorialism of its Utopia. Palestine must be empty, therefore it is, and that's all there is to it. What prevailed here was the myopia that we have observed in Herzl, and also the terrible bad conscience in Nordau, Max Brod or Ruppin.[8] For ignorant innocent could not last: it ended with disembarkation at Jaffa or Haifa, where the Arab presence hit the immigrant in the eye. From that point, another history began: how to integrate this presence into the Zionist discourse and project without imperilling it? Colonial racism in its various formulations (the conquest of the American West, the South African Great Trek, the Russification of the Bashkir lands along the Volga) legitimized despoliation by asserting the non-humanity of the Arabs. Palestine would henceforth be perceived as inhabited: but the inhabitants would be "desert savages"; even inhabited, the country thus remained a desert. In 1899, Herzl spoke of the Jewish colonies as "oases", which lumped the Palestinian population, a hundred times more numerous, with sand, palm trees or camels.

In some cases, such a denial of the humanity of the Palestinians conflicted with general philosophical opinions cherished by the colonists: this was the case with the socialist-Zionists. It then became necessary to prepare complicated theories to remove – on paper – the Arab presence out of Palestine. In the one case, theorization preceded the act; in the other, it legitimized it after the event. Statistics were doctored, history and archaeology were falsified, a vacuum was invented where there was plenty, a desert was conjured up where crops flourished and established settlement was described as nomadism. Even the contemporary argument of "Arab unity" has been mobilized to deny the Arab evidence of Palestine in the name of the pan-Arabness of the Palestinians: it all reflects the universal need of colonizers to erase the traces of pre-colonial history and transform exterminations into natural wastage, as in South Africa or the United States. This propagandistic and mystifying Zionism is obviously the one that is best for export, but it is not necessarily the one that succeeded best among the pioneers.

Applied Zionism emerged from the utopian stage of colonization when its centre of gravity moved from exile in the West to the Palestinian *Yishuv*. From this displacement a new political leadership emerged, which engendered the Israeli state bureaucratic bourgeoisie, with one foot in the crisis-torn *Shtetl*, and the other in the concrete conditions of colonization. This rising stratum which provided the cadres of the Zionist movement in Palestine for several decades was drawn wholly from people of east European, Yiddish-speaking, origin, torn between nationalist mysticism and social messianism, between the Jewish heritage and the twin influence of the Russian revolution: the influence of Russian revolutionary ideas and conceptions, and the influence of Russian counter-revolutionary ideas and conceptions; the influence of Russian Westernizing servility with regard to European civilization and the influence of Slavophile nationalist messianism. The social-nationalist synthesis which resulted, of which Ben-Gurion was surely the most representative spokesman, took root in the *Yishuv,* and imposed itself by occupying the domain of colonization on the ground.

It was in the labour base of colonization, among immigrants making a messianic or revolutionary break with the *Shtetl*, that the mental removal of the Palestinians outside the projected domain occurred. In official Zionist photos at the beginning of the century, one can see Jewish colonists in European dress, on a deserted beach, holding a few spades, "founding Tel Aviv". These pictures had to be carefully touched up before they could become part of the official album, in order to remove the Arabs who are visible on the original photos, to the right and left of the group of pioneers in ties: those who built Tel Aviv, and whose houses and tents, simply by being there, turned this "desert" into a building site. This presence everywhere of the Arabs traumatized the territorialists: but, conversely, it seemed natural to the offspring of the *Shtetl*. Their cultural narcissism constituted a mental rampart around the ethnic frontiers of the community and the group. It also constituted a better preparation for the physical expulsion of the Arabs and its legitimation.

This feature is vital if one is to avoid the idealized representations of innocent and generous pioneers caught against their will in a colonial mechanism that they did not understand. Such a naïve view is very widespread, even among some virulent critics of present Israeli policy. Everything had begun so well, and things then went sour: innocent colonists moved by noble ideals found themselves unknowingly caught up in a racist and warlike mess, driven to imperialist alliances, cynically used by the West, repelled by Arab hostility.

Behind this idyllic interpretation, there is not simply the effect of propaganda, there is the refusal to identify the real agent of the expulsion: a whole social movement, and not only a few conspirators. Certainly this movement was articulated on a strategic alliance with Europe in its struggle against Ottoman Turkey and against the Arab threat half-seen in Muhammad Ali. But it was an alliance, not mere vassalage.

Well before there was any question of political Zionism, outside any alliance organized and negotiated with imperialism, Lovers of Zion pioneers had perceived, in their way, what Ben-Gurion was to call the "Arab problem". At the root of this perception there was neither identification with the West, nor the desire to serve it, nor a determination to exploit the indigenes. The source of the dilemma that the Palestinian Arabs posed to the pioneers was the determination to create in Palestine an exclusively Jewish society. From the very time of the establishment of the first waves of colonists, the Arab problem was: how to get rid of them? This colonialism bent on expulsion, which claimed exclusive possession of the domain, flowed naturally from the idea that the colonists held, not of the Arabs, but of themselves: from the character of their own society. It was the least Western cultural element of the *Yishuv*, the most "traditional" but also the most "revolutionary" one (in a word, the heritage of the *Shtetl*), which fuelled the most categorical negation of the Arab presence. It was this that ensured, concretely, through all its transformations, the existence of a separate society, and the imperviousness of the Ashkenazi *Yishuv* to Palestinian society.

The second wave of pioneers, on the eve of the First World War, expressed this continuity of the closed identity of the transplanted *Shtetl*, no longer in messianic-religious terms like the Lovers of Zion, nor in enlightened-liberal ones like Herzl, but in the language of socialism, the proletariat and the revolution. It was a language which saw itself as diametrically opposed to the "conceptual sphere of imperialism", and which yet inspired, in practice, the most intransigent removal of the non-Jew, the Arab, the Palestinian, the other, from the domain first dreamed of, and then conquered.

Labour Zionism

Ahad Ha'am, continuing, in the article quoted above, his work of setting out the truth, wrote in 1893: "In recent years a party of the new immigrants has emerged, the labour party, that is, of people who have come to the land of Israel to be paid day-labourers." It was, he wrote disapprovingly, the fact that

> some in Israel are endeavouring to increase the number of workers among our brothers artificially, not with natives of the country – something that would doubtless be good and useful – but from outside. So much so that at the end of the day we risk witnessing an unprecedented spectacle: seeing the question of labour and property posed even before property has had the time to enjoy the fruits of labour.[9]

Among the many ideological and politico-literary syntheses of the dying days of the dispersed Ukrainian *Shtetl,* somewhere between the Lovers of Zion and the Bund, Hebraist and Palestine-centred like the former and "socialist" like the latter, had emerged the "Workers of Zion" (*Paole Zion*). Like the Bund, this Labour-Zionism was born of the proleterianization and sub-proletarianization of the sons of artisans and shopkeepers. But it was strengthened, above all, in the forced proletarianization of the Jewish immigrants in Palestine. Like the Bund, it claimed to be a national component of the international socialist revolution, and even applied to join the Third International at its foundation.[10] But, whereas the Bund and its social base went westward, to western Europe and the United States, the workers of Zion emigrated to Palestine where they soon appeared as the dominant force in the *Yishuv.*

An unbreakable faith in the intrinsic virtues of the proletariat can heroically resist all the lessons of historical experience and refuse to admit that workers can ever be racist on their own account. The chauvinism and segregationism of workers' groups in given situations are always imputed to their ideological submission to the bourgeoisie. The history of the rise, within the *Yishuv,* of "Labour" Zionism and its organizations is a good illustration of the naïveté of such a picture. The history of the European labour movement, and even more of the labour movement among workers in European colonies, should be studied so as to re-establish the context of this social-colonialism, which is epitomized by the slogan of the White miners of South Africa at the beginning of the century: "White workers of the world, unite!" It is an exemplary story in more ways than one, since in it we can see the graft of ideology onto the real world, and their common transformation.

With the worsening of anti-Jewish persecutions in Russia, the number of Jewish workers who emigrated to Palestine grew, and with it the number of young *déclassés* of the *Shtetl* who "came to the Land of Israel in order to be day-labourers there". These immigrants, who "raised the question of property" even before being employed, went first to swell the ranks of the agricultural proletariat which was forming in the settlements. These took varying legal forms and were of varying sizes. There was first of all the agricultural empire of the Rothschilds: as in Algeria', wine was their business, and they drew in a mobile and vulnerable seasonal labour force. In 1870, with the opening just outside Jaffa of the Mikveh-Israel agricultural school, the "Barons" – as the Workers of Zion contemptuous-ly called them – became the philanthropic benefactors of the *Yishuv.* As model patrons they were not content with providing work for the penniless masses of Lovers of Zion and worker-immigrants: they also ran, in their paternalist and Francophile way, modern community institutions: schools and training schools, social housing for workers. In a manner altogether similar to the functioning of the Western Christian missions at the same time, this Jewish mission was both a politico-cultural enterprise and an economic monopoly with numerous banking, land and property ramifications. A bureaucracy in which French and Ottoman ("Arab" or

"Spanish") Jews predominated managed all these enterprises on the spot.

Alongside this sector, whose dominant and impersonal character prefigured state ownership, there were all the intermediate forms of medium and small private property, of tenant farming and share-cropping that arose from the purchase of land by private individuals, associations, speculators and big companies. Among the latter were the various European and American organizations devoted, like the PJCA (Palestine Jewish Colonization Association), to the establishment of Jews from eastern Europe in agricultural colonies in North America, South America and Palestine – and, of course, the Zionist organizations.

The sale of agricultural lands to foreigners had been facilitated, since 1858, by the land reform introduced by the new Ottoman Code, which involved confiscation, followed by the sale of communal lands, thereby creating from among the urban owning classes a class of absentee land-owners particularly given to property speculation. It is true that, in 1908, with the "Young Turk" revolution, the government, in order to pacify Arab opinion in Palestine, adopted a number of measures to limit the unforeseen effects of this "kulakization": notably a ban on the sale to foreigners of land situated thirty kilometres on either side of the Hejaz railway, which took pilgrims to Mecca. The Zionists got round the ban by having land registered in the name of Oriental Jews who were Ottoman citizens.

While these limited measures demonstrated Herzl's axiom that "Infiltration is bound to end badly. For there comes the inevitable moment when the government in question, under pressure of the native populace – which feels itself threatened – puts a stop to the further influx of Jews", and encouraged the Zionist leaders to look for a charter by which the "national sovereignty" of the Jews in Palestine would be guaranteed, they were not enough to halt the process of "conquering the land" in which the central institutions of the Zionist organization (Jewish Agency, Jewish National Fund, etc.) played a decisive role.

The extreme subdivision of this pattern of ownership, however, and its essentially private character – its role as producer of saleable goods and a surplus – gave rise to simple considerations of profitability and productivity. But – and this was the core of the contradiction – the Arab workers, whose numbers grew with the expropriations, were infinitely more productive than the new immigrants: they worked harder and better for less than the Jews, and unlike the latter, were not organized.

It was thus against "Arab labour" and for the "conquest of Jewish labour" that the Workers of Zion waged their first great class struggles: they attempted to make employers impose racial segregation in the hiring of labour. It was a bitter, often violent, struggle on two fronts: the Jewish bourgeoisie which preferred "the Arab to the Jew", and the Arab workers who were its tools and its "allies". In 1908 Doctor Thon, who was soon to organize the first "importation" of Yemenite Jews into the agricultural colonies, stated in a memorandum presented to the Jewish Agency: "It is easy to show that the employment of Jewish workers in place of Arab agricultural workers is one of the most important problems of the colonization of the Land of Israel." It was during anti-Arab skirmishes at Sejera, in Galilee – an episode in the "conquest of Jewish labour" – that a young worker of Zion recently arrived from Russia made his mark, and was first noted for his decisiveness and authority: he did not yet call himself Ben-Gurion, but he was to make the Jewish labour movement in Palestine the springboard for his rise to power and the essential instrument of the creation of the Zionist state.

The systematic expulsion of the Arabs from the new labour market not only reflected an ideological and political necessity of Zionism; it was also an economic and social imperative for the masses of new immigrants from central and eastern Europe, who had no other capital than their hands, but who were not competitive compared to Arab workers. From this meeting of theory and practical need was born the dynamic which was to make a reality of the empty domain dreamed of in Palestine: and it was precisely the Workers of Zion who were to forge the tools for the expulsion of the Arabs. First socio-economic expulsion, then physical expulsion; the conquest of Jewish labour, which could only have been carried on by workers, in their struggle against the Jewish capitalists in Palestine, formed a first link in the chain.

The Zionist institutions elaborated two types of response to the problematic of "Arab labour": one consisted in subsidizing the employment of Jewish workers, that is, paying employers the difference between Arab and Jewish wages (1:3 at the time of the Mandate). The other consisted in importing Arab Jews (essentially Yemenites until 1948), who worked like Arabs, for lower wages than Arabs, while fulfilling their function of occupying the socio-economic domain with Jews, that is, removing the Palestinians.

Of course, the conquest of Jewish labour was only one link; since the work was initially agricultural work, it pre-supposed that lands had been bought, on which these determined and demanding European workers were to be employed. Foreign private capital provided by the Rothschilds and other barons, better established than the small colonists, the vine and then citrus fruit estates in the settlements dating from the first *aliyah,* the tenanting of lands by credit companies, whether profit-making or philanthropic, then by the central institutions of the Zionist movement, and even the renting out of land leased by the Jewish National Fund, whose statutes laid down that the land could not be granted or sold back to a non-Jew – all these were essential to the functioning, and even to the existence, of the whole enterprise. Nevertheless, if the proletarianized Palestinian peasants had worked the lands thus acquired alone, if the colonists had had in the new agrarian social relations the same role that they played in Algeria, or in Rhodesia, history would have taken a quite different turn. The presence, in large numbers among the immigrants, of young wage workers was to provide Herzl's political project with resources that the founders had not foreseen.

The social and political vision of the founders of Zionism oscillated between philanthropic paternalistic liberalism and the most extreme conservatism: Ussishkin, who was the first head of the Jewish National Fund, supported restoring a monarchy in Israel, which he conceded might be a constitutional one, on condition that it was legitimist – that is, attached to the dynastic principle of the line of King David! For Westernized bourgeois Zionists, capitalism meant progress and emancipation, technological revolution and the discovery of new frontiers. Defending the Suez Canal, constituting, as Herzl promised, "a rampart of Europe against Asia, of civilization against barbarism", all that appeared very honourable to them, and even glorious. Nothing, in any event, was possible in their eyes, without "the agreement of governments".

The penniless immigrants who flooded in from Russia could only sell their labour power. However much schooling they had had, it had been in Yiddish, Hebrew or Russian ... not in Turkish, or Arabic, or English: so they could not enter the administration. A proportion of them, which is difficult to estimate, had already fallen into proletarian poverty before they emigrated. For the majority, however, it was emigration that consummated the fall into wage slavery.[11] Thus, immigration was settlement: proletarianization was accepted, if not voluntary. "To be a café waiter in Tel-Aviv", Kafka would later exclaim, although he would never have dreamed of being one in Prague.

However, while this settlement proletarianized, it did not thereby make wage labour desirable. It was the status of small peasant proprietor – the return to work on the land – that was sought.

The emigration to Palestine at the beginning of this century, which produced the bulk of the working class of the *Yishuv* under the Mandate, and the bulk of the cadres of labour colonization was impregnated with the Russian intellectual climate, the climate of the uprising of Russian society against tsarism. The Workers of Zion, like the Bundists, were influenced by the ideas and language of socialism. In 1904, Ber Borokhov, a former social-democrat turned Jewish nationalist, prepared the Workers of Zion's political programme, "Our Platform", for the Zionist congress at which Uganda was to be discussed. This was the first synthesis of Marxism and Zionist territorialism: it was moreover no doubt the first synthesis of socialism and nationalism. Borokhov, obsessed with normality, the man of the inverted pyramid, considered the Palestinians as "not forming a nation and not being destined to form one for a long time". He concluded: "The Jewish immigrants will take in hand the development of the factors of production and the indigenous population will end up being economically and culturally assimilated to the Jews."[12]

Another school of thought, more important even than the influence of Borokhov, and older, had introduced into the culture of the Lovers of Zion ideas drawn from Russian society: A.D. Gordon, the founder of Degania in 1905, and thus, in a way, "the inventor of the kibbutz", was Ben-Gurion's mentor and certainly represented the strongest ideological influence on the new *Yishuv*. While Borokhov was a Marxian labourite, Gordon, a poet, a visionary and a practical man, was a Tolstoyan: like his model, he was both mystical and secular, a naturalist and an agrarian. He brought to the Lovers of Zion populist messianism based on the idealization of the *mujik* and the cult of the land.

Among the Russian intellectuals at the end of the 19th century, this "narodnikism" bore the imprint of the Russian social formation: the weight of the peasantry and its dispersal eastward and the first attempts at the modernization of agrarian relations, the abolition of serfdom and kulakization. Contrary to socialism, which advocated the inevitability of capitalist domination, this populism kept up the idea that the agricultural commune (*mir*), which continued to survive on the fringes of serfdom, constituted the core and the basis of the just society . . . In Russia, populism was Slavophile: against the aggressive pan-Slavism of the tsars. It was also practical and anti-intellectual, the obscurantism of the popes being transformed here into a cult of peasant common sense against a background of pantheism. Finally, this Russian populism was patriotic Great Russian of the most chauvinistic kind. From affirming the ancestral values of the Russian peasantry, the ultimate European repository of "primitive communism", to affirming its unique national essence (implying the necessary political unity of peoples speaking Slavic languages), was only a short step, one often taken by various components of Russian and especially Ukrainian peasant populism. In the Ukraine, populism was engulfed in peasant nationalism – aggressive pan-Slavism and social anti-Semitism. But, in Russia itself, that is, in Muscovy, where the Jews were Russified and few in number, this humanist populism – whose poet Tolstoy had made himself – had attracted the eager minds of the Russified young Jewish intelligentsia: the influence of Russian agrarian populism on the Zionist mystique of a return to the land and on the final formation of Socialist-Zionism was considerable and, in an initial stage, more determining in terms of its practical effects than the influence of the European labour movement.

Tolstoy's universalism and secularized mysticism no doubt corresponded to the felt experience of the crises affecting the whole of Russian society within which the *Shtetl* was disintegrating. But the discourse about the land, physical labour, calloused hands, dirty clothes and nature took on a special meaning for the Jews: was not the absence of any involvement with the land the fundamental characteristic of Jewish society in Europe? The practical return to the land introduced an absolute sociological and philosophical break with the discourse of the *Shtetl,* in the line of the declared paganism of the poets of the 19th century. But above all, this return was physical: it was an act. Tolstoy returned to live in his village, while the young agrarian Zionists prepared for migration by working, in Russia itself, or in Hungary, in small and medium agricultural enterprises that were more or less cooperatives. Once they had decided to emigrate, they organized themselves into communes, into "groups" (*kevut-soth*). Unlike the other colonists, but also unlike the wage-workers, they aspired to a colonization whose subject would be an egalitarian, agricultural and fraternal community.

This communal practice engendered the institutional and legal form of the kibbutz, as the core of the new Jewish society, while the ideology of personal redemption through return to the land and the community experience mobilized the colonizing vanguard that it needed for the conquest of the land in the service of the Zionist movement. For, without colonists ready to live there in poverty and danger, in the pioneering exaltation of their own heroism, the Jewish Agency's efforts to buy lands from absentee proprietors or from property speculation companies would have been futile; the lands would have remained unoccupied, like those in the Jezreel valley, about which Chaim Weizmann noted, in his diary in 1924, that arrangements had to be made to have them watched by the British army to prevent the *fellahin* who had been driven out of them (by virtue of lawful sales) from coming back. Or else these lands would have been worked by the dispossessed peasants who had become proletarians. For, as Eisenzweig recalls, "Gordon's socialistic and pacifist philosophy could only link up with his 'naturism' at the price of a pronounced blindness about the non-Jewish inhabitants of Palestine". And, as an example of this blindness, he gives Gordon's definition of national identity: "There is a cosmic element in national identity that forms its basic content. The best way of describing this cosmic element is to consider it as a mixture of the natural landscape of the homeland with the spirit of the people who live there."[13]

The removal of the Palestinians from the domain coveted by the colonists, in order to establish their sublimated *Shtetl* in the utopia there was only really accomplished in 1948 "in blood and fire".[14] In 1947, the Jews owned 6 per cent of the land, whereas they represented one-third of the population. It was military conquest that made the appropriation/expropriation of the land of Palestine a sweeping reality. A large part of this 6 per cent of the land had been acquired before the 1930s, that is, before the attitude of the British government had begun to swing in the direction of imposing severe restrictions, both on immigration and on land sales; the rhythm of land acquisitions slowed during the 1930s, after reaching a peak in 1924, with the end of the big scandal of the lands of Marj Ibn 'Amr, bought from the Beirut Greek Sursok family by the Jewish National Fund: 24 hamlets and villages sold as a single lot, and the whole population evacuated by the British police. And already there was a shortage of peasant-colonists for these lands. Only the pioneer movements – the Gordonians and the Borokhovists – supplied colonization with the manpower that it required. Ussishkin, Ben-Gurion used to say, wanted land, land and yet more land. And Ben-Gurion used to say to him: it's not land we need most, but Jews. Ben-Gurion was obsessed by demography and immigration. After 1948, when the JNF inherited at one go the lands of 800,000 "absentees" driven out during the war, it was the already existing settlements that spread, and sent out groups that went off to found the new kibbutzim: a few old people, the children of the second generation and small numbers of new immigrants. It is indeed true that this form of colonization appeared at a crucial moment to play an irreplaceable role, and one that has still not been replaced.

The British Mandate regime created an entirely novel framework for the Zionist enterprise: at first – until Churchill's White Paper in 1931 – this framework was favourable to colonization, then increasingly became obstructive. During the first ten years of the Mandate, the Crown was engaged in a basically pro-Zionist policy, of which Lord Balfour set out the broad outlines at the Paris Conference in 1919:

> In Palestine, we do not even propose to consult the inhabitants of the country... The Four Great Powers have made commitments to Zionism, and Zionism (whether it is good or bad, right or wrong) has its roots in an ancient tradition, in immediate needs and in hopes for the future that are much more important than the desires and prejudices of the 700,000 Arabs who presently inhabit Palestine.

There was no unanimity in British imperialist circles about this bias: neither in pro-Arab military circles (such as Lawrence), nor in the assimilated British Jewish bourgeoisie, which feared the side-effects of Zionism on its own status. On the spot, however, the sympathies of the Mandatory administration towards the Jews increased as the Foreign Office began to move away from Zionism. The peasant revolution of 1936–39, and then the Anglo-Zionist alliance against the Axis during the war, wove new links of political and military cooperation between the occupying power and the Zionist movement. These links would only be broken at the end of the war, when the Zionist organizations launched a "struggle for independence", essentially terrorist in nature, both against the Arab civilian population and against the British occupying forces.[15]

Through the meanders and contradictions, the hesitations and reversals of British policy can be glimpsed what was an ambiguous role, and a certain failure. The Palestinian imbroglio was undoubtedly quite beyond the British, who were only formally in control. Their many and contradictory undertakings – hypocritical to the extent that they knew they were incompatible when they made them; but sincere to the extent that each one reflected the demands of a particular lobby – virtually ruled out any active policy in practice, and condemned them to waiting and defending an unstable equilibrium that they did not control. Of course, the military occupation of Palestine by Great Britain, which had let it be known, in the middle of the war, that they "would look favourably" on the establishment of a "national home" for the Jews in the country, had had immediate consequences for the Zionist colonizing enterprise: a risky enterprise, ill-viewed by the distant power of the Ottomans, became overnight the official spokesman and autonomous administration of the Jewish community of Palestine daily swollen by immigration, a government-in-waiting recognized by the Mandate. The "basic laws" (the Land Transfer Ordinance and the Mahlul Land Law) adopted by the British occupying power in 1920, that is, even before the promulgation of the League of Nations Mandate in 1922, completed the timid tendencies contained in the Ottoman Code of 1858, breaking up communal and corporate property, and allowing sales like that of Marj Ibn 'Amr. But, by 1929–30, years marked by violent anti-Jewish riots in Jerusalem and Hebron, the British government was attempting to play a moderating role, which was often translated in the apparently cynical balance maintained between the extremists on both sides. By 1942 in any case, Britain was committed to leading the whole of its colonial empire to independence. Her manoeuvres, by then, were no longer aimed at securing a lasting domination, but only at slowing down and controlling the process of self-determination.

A careful weighing and examination of all the factors shows that one cannot hold the British government solely responsible for the dispossession of the Arabs in Palestine accomplished under its rule. While the creation of a buffer state (Christian or Jewish) separating the Arab East from Egypt had been a strategic British concern throughout the 19th century, the expulsion of the indigenes by the Jewish immigrants at the very moment of the decolonization of the rest of the region had never been part of the British programme. The Balfour Declaration itself, significantly addressed to Lord Rothschild, apart from the fact that its initial formulation, which was rather vague, was soon hedged about with reservations, of both a territorial and a political kind, did not mean, as Chaim Weizmann said, that "Palestine would be Jewish, as England is English".

However, the British Mandate had one important consequence: it "Palestinized" the Zionist movement. For it conferred on the institutions and internal political debate of the *Yishuv* the dimension of a representative game. It thus contributed to displacing the political centre of gravity of Zionism and fixing it in Palestine, while institutionalizing the structures of Jewish self-government.

It was in this framework that the pioneers, who had already, with the kibbutz, invented the colonizing phalanstery, were to create the Histadrut, the "General Confederation of Hebrew Workers in the Land of Israel", restricted, from its foundation, in 1920, until 1966, to "Hebrews" alone, and pledged by its statutes to Jewish colonization and "the building of the Jewish society of labour". The Histadrut was created in the midst of "the struggle for Jewish labour", and was to become the popular expression of colonization: against the competition of Arab labour and against the private interests that did not mind using it. This taking of power by the Workers of the *Yishuv* precipitated the split of the "general Zionists", the liberal European heirs of Herzl: the most determined wing of the "general" Zionist petty bourgeoisie under the leadership of Jabotinsky challenged the labour hegemony over the *Yishuv* and denounced Ben-Gurion's policy. These "revisionists" refused to accept the "gradualism" of the labourites towards the Mandate, the temporary and tactical self-restraint *(Havlaga)* of the nation-state ambitions of Zionism: they continued to demand Transjordan – originally included in the "Palestine" of the Balfour declaration, but physically detached and transformed into an emirate at the end of the First World War. They preached the inevitability of armed confrontation with the Arab population. In the 1930s, many of them advocated an alliance with Mussolini's Italy.[16] At the head of the "labour movement" whose operations dominated the Zionist institutions, Ben-Gurion waged a merciless fight against the "splitters": Menachem Begin, the leader of the revisionists after 1942, was described in Socialist-Zionist propaganda as a fascist, and in 1948 Ben-Gurion did not hesitate to fire on Begin's men who were breaking the truce declared by the UN in agreement with the Zionist leadership, and to hand them over to the British. On several fronts, the Workers of Zion who now dominated the institutional apparatuses of the Zionist movement, waged a triple struggle, diplomatic, political and – after the 1939–45 war – military, to establish their sovereignty over the territory of Palestine.

Just as the preceding generation of Lovers of Zion had imposed Palestine on Herzl and the territorialists, so the unionized and mobilized Jewish Workers of Palestine, organized in powerful networks based on the cooperative and bureaucratic management of a separate and pre-state economy, imposed on the Zionist leaders the language of socialism and revolution within the Zionist national and colonial discourse.

The socialism of this colonization was important: the Bolshevik organizational model in particular – democratic centralism – effectively served in the structuring and control of a true mass energy among the settlers and immigrants. There is, moreover, no doubt that while the labour institutions, of which the Histadrut became the backbone, continued to pursue a goal of root and branch expulsion of the Palestinians, they did considerably democratize the life of the *Yishuv.*

Over the years, the conquest of the land initiated at the beginning of the century tapered off; it ran up against the resistance of Arab owners, British restrictions, etc. By the beginning of the 1930s, it had become difficult to find a plot for sale. Yet these were the very years when the rise of fascism in Europe was sending new waves of refugees to Palestine every year, pioneers of a new sort. Some brought private capital along with an industrial mentality from Germany, others brought their pioneering determination and their socialism from central Europe, and especially from Poland, restored in 1918. The conquest of the land – "a *dunum* here, a goat there" – went on uninterrupted. Like the conquest of Jewish labour, the first anti-Palestinian labour slogan, it was extended into the struggle of the new Jewish bourgeoisie of Palestine – the "state sector" prefigured by the Histadrut and its enterprises, as well as by the institutions of the Zionist movement – against indigenous production. A new slogan was launched: *Totzeret Haaretz,* literally, "produce of the country". Decoded it meant: produce Jewish, buy Jewish; boycott – and sometimes destroy – indigenous production. "It was not easy in the 1930s", confessed David Ha-Cohen, the Labour Zionist member of the Knesset, in 1968, "to explain to our comrades in the British Labour Party why we had to pour petrol over the tomatoes of Arab women..." This was the Zionist science of doublespeak and muffled reality: the silent removal of the Palestinians from the country. Only the stranger, the immigrant, the newcomer was "of the country". The indigene, the inhabitant, was the foreigner.

The new waves of immigration brought proletarian colonists who came from the whole semi-assimilated petty bourgeoisie of Poland and Galicia, Hungary and Czechoslovakia: less imbued with Judaism, more traumatized by anti-Semitism, very marked, often negatively, by the influence of the labour movement in these countries, and of the Russian revolution. When the rise of anti-Jewish restrictions and laws in these countries slammed the doors of society against them, they went off to dream of revolution in Palestine: there they became, in colonization, workers and peasants, cooperators and bureaucrats, political leaders and armed fighters.

In the appropriation of the Palestinian domain by the Zionist movement, the language and institutional forms of socialism and revolution were not principally masks for external consumption: they were first and foremost the formal and semantic wellsprings of a certain type of commitment. This mode of identification is neither mysterious nor peculiar to Zionism: it is found, in various forms, in all ideological movements, whether laudable or repugnant. It can be seen alternatively, depending on whether one is well- or ill-disposed to the ultimate aims of such massive commitment, as the effect of the most sublime patriotism or the most bestial fanaticism, of the highest revolutionary consciousness or the most alienated and despotic depravity. It does not alter the fact that this ideological character is what has assured for the Zionist movement, throughout its history, an essential element of its cohesion and effectiveness: the collective determination in which the language of socialism sees the transformation of the mob into the mass, whose quality is decisive in a violent and prolonged confrontation. But it would be dishonest to argue from this revolutionary character to deny its concrete function and effects: the many-sided expulsion of the Palestinians from the domain. Land expropriation, exclusion from the labour market, boycotting of Arab produce, military repression and intimidation, and, at the end of this progress towards the state, in the heat of 1947–48, physical expulsion from the territory and the establishment of what Elias Sanbar calls "the empty state". All through this process, the language of emptiness and the language of revolution were mixed up together; and, in 1953, justifying the dynamiting of houses in the village of Bir'im, in Galilee, whose population had been evacuated "for a few weeks", in 1949, by the Israeli army, the Labour minister of defence, Pinhas Lavon, said: "A revolutionary movement like Zionism cannot consider as sacred all the accomplished facts inherited from the past".[17]

The Arabs

The transfer of the Arab population ("Let them go to Transjordan"), spontaneously conceived by the settlers from their first confrontation with the reality of the Arab presence and establishment in Palestine, was on the agenda of Zionist aspirations from the beginning of the century. In 1897, Herzl had written:

We shall endeavour to encourage the poverty-stricken population to cross the border by securing work for it in the countries it passes through, while denying it any work in our own country. The twin process of expropriation and displacement of the poor must be carried out prudently and discreetly. Let the landowners imagine that they are cheating us, and sell us their land at exorbitant prices. We shall sell nothing back to them.[18]

Later, in 1915, Shmuel Hugo Bergmann wrote to Max Brod:

It is true that the first phase of the conquest took place under the sign of the money given to the effendi more than under that of the sword. The effendi was the legal owner. But the result of this was the expulsion of those who were working the land. That land which we are cultivating today, was indeed previously cultivated by Arab peasants!... And even the alternative already offered to the Arabs (resettlement outside Palestine) constitutes an unjustice, if we consider it from a strictly private point of view, and not a national one. Why should the Arab have to go and look for a plot of land in Mesopotamia if his ancestors have, for generations, always lived on the land of Merhavia, Kinnereth, etc.?[19]

In 1937, with the debates of the Zurich Congress (World Congress of the Workers of Zion, 29 July to 7 August), transfer became a political demand made by the revolutionaries of colonization. The British commission of enquiry, known as the Peel Commission, appointed by the government of His Majesty to investigate the causes of the violence and armed incidents that had been disturbing public order in Palestine since 1921,[20] proposed, for the first time, the partition of Palestine and the creation of an independent Jewish state in part of the Mandatory territory. The majority of socialists present in Zurich rejected the idea of partition in the name of the "unity of the country", and their "historic rights" over the whole of the territory. Only Ben-Gurion pleaded for a partition that he was sure would be temporary, for, he said, "despite the smallness of the territory offered to the Jewish state, there exists in the commission's proposals the possibility of transferring the Arab populations, with their consent, if not by force, and thus of extending Jewish colonization". And he spelled out "the profound, fundamental difference between transfer and expulsion: until now, we have only been able to settle by transferring populations ... There are only very few places where we have been able to colonize without being forced to transfer the inhabitants."[21]

The Zurich congress did not bring together all the tendencies in the Zionist movement, but only the various factions of the labour movement. This congress was the first to pose clearly the question of transfer, which had previously never been mentioned in the official discourse of the bourgeois Zionists, which was conservative and law-abiding. In order to demolish further the imagery of Degania and Zionist socialism, which blames the revisionist right for all the sins of Israel, while protesting the idealistic internationalism and humanism of the pioneers, we need to follow the stages of this morality of labour colonization: from the exclusion of the Arabs from the labour market to the constitution of a Jewish society closed to intercourse with the indigenous society.

In 1865, Hess had spoken of the "Bedouins". As a "progressive" colonialist, he accepted the imperialist violence of his time. Herzl was wholly absorbed by his territorialist logic, and translated his diplomatic conception of nationalism into endless badgering of established governments. This badgering was quite indiscriminate: Herzl offered his services, and those of the Zionist movement and the whole Jewish people, successively and simultaneously to the Germans, the Russians, the British and the Turks, until the effective conquest of Palestine by Allenby's troops sealed for the time being the Anglo-Zionist alliance. But, even after his forced conversion after the "Ugandan crisis", to the Palestine-centredness of the Lovers of Zion and the religious Zionists, Herzl continued, as an ex-assimilated petty bourgeois, to work to obtain "the agreement of governments" and their guarantee of Zionist "sovereignty" over the territory.

The revisionists, who, following Jabotinsky, stressed the problem of the autonomous armed strength of the *Yishuv* as much as the demand for sovereignty over both banks of the Jordan, absolutely avoided the question of the displacement of the population, as indeed, contrary to their own imagery, they avoided the question of British imperialism, for which Jabotinsky had the greatest admiration. Backed by the private petty and middle bourgeoisie of the *Yishuv,* they raised the twin problems of the programme and self-armament, arguing precisely from the existence of an Arab population imbued with a national feeling. The determination to organize to use force to repel Arab demands, which Jabotinsky, alone in the Zionist camp, saw would inevitably emerge, thus proceeded from what was surely a less negative vision of the *fellahin* than Herzl's, and one less negative too than the socialist phraseology that portrayed Zionism as conferring objective benefits upon the Arabs themselves.

Herzl himself touched on the "displacement of the poor" "discreetly": this was because the bourgeois right of peoples still had not lost all its appeal; Herzl, like Sharett later, proposed purchasing the land, not nationalizing it by revolutionary decree. It was the labour current, and above all Ben-Gurion, which was to make transfer – a moral dilemma for the bourgeois and pro-imperialist Zionists – a clearly expressed demand of revolutionary morality.

A reading of the debates of the Zurich Congress illustrates this unanimity: while Ben-Gurion was placed in a minority on the acceptance of British proposals for partition and transfer, the disagreement was not on the morality of the latter term. "I see nothing wrong," said Golda Meyerson (later Meir), a participant in the Congress, "in the Arabs leaving the country, and my conscience would be quite clear if they did so. But is it possible?" In fact, what the majority of these socialists rejected was being satisfied with sovereignty over too small a territory. The woman who, in

1969, would become prime minister of the government of Israel said as much herself: "War alone can change borders. Perhaps there will be a war in the near future. But how can we be certain that this war will change them in our favour?"

On the morality of transfer, there was unanimity. "I do not deny", said Cizzling, the leader of the Mapam faction, "our moral right to call for an exchange of populations. On the contrary. That could be – probably will be – in a different world order, a great humane vision." Berl Katznelson was indignant that Ben-Gurion could speak of transfer within Palestine, when it "was a matter of transferring them to Iraq and Syria", he said, using the biblical term to describe Mesopotamia – Aram of the two rivers. But he spelled out his position on the morality of transfer: "My conscience is clear, it is absolutely permissible." The fact is that for all these "revolutionaries", the demand for the removal of the Palestinian population was, as Abraham Lulu said, "a logical and just programme, moral and humane in every sense". And he concluded: "If we deny ourselves this right to transfer, we condemn all that we have so far accomplished."[22]

Yossef Weitz, appointed head of the colonization department of the JNF in 1932, bought Arab Palestine plot by plot. He knew from professional experience that at this rate and those prices Palestine would remain an Arab country. He was obsessed by what he, like his model Ben-Gurion, called "the Arab question", and he was of course a strong supporter of the transfer solution. On 19 December 1940, he wrote in his diary:

> Between us, it must be clear that there is no room for two peoples in this country... If the Arabs leave the country, it will be enough for us... There is no other means but to remove the Arabs to the neighbouring countries, all the Arabs.[23]

And Yossef Weitz spent the following years, during which the Nazis were endeavouring to create a Europe that was *Judenrein,* empty of Jews, sounding out the possibilities of resettling the Palestinians outside Palestine: in Syria, Iraq, Libya, and even in Argentina, with the hope of seeing the Land of Israel at last *Araber-rein,* empty of Arabs.

War made it possible to modify the frontiers in favour of the Jewish state. After three rounds, this would embrace the whole of Mandatory Palestine and even a little more. As for the transfer, this was largely achieved in the expulsion, between November 1947 and December 1948, of some 800,000 Palestinians.[24] While the expulsion of the Arabs under cover of war did indeed constitute, as Chaim Weizmann said, "a miraculous simplification of the tasks of Israel", it was not really a miracle, but the result of a sustained and concerted action.[25] In his diary, Weitz traces the activities of a secret commission of which he was a member, which worked in direct liaison with Ben-Gurion, Sharett and a few others, including the future mayor of Jerusalem, Teddy Kollek. The purpose of this commission was poetically described by the term "retroactive transfer": it was a matter of "transforming the Arab exodus into an accomplished fact". To this end, it was necessary to raze abandoned villages so that the refugees "know that we have no intention of letting them return". These large-scale destructive operations were code-named "improvement" and "restoration" of the villages.

However cruel, cynical and inhuman the means used to effect this expulsion may have been, it cannot be claimed, without being wilfully blind, that Zionism had a monopoly of them. The atrocities committed on both sides in war do not define its real issues and do not obliterate the nature of the purpose. Thus Pierre Vidal-Naquet, who rightly waxes indignant about ahistorical and disproportionate comparisons, writes that the Deir Yassin massacre, in which Zionist partisans of the Irgun, which was led by Begin, massacred the population of an Arab village, cannot be compared to the massacre of the internees in Auschwitz by the Nazis. But, by immediately after comparing Deir Yassin with Oradour-sur-Glane, does he not commit another sort of simplification? For, ultimately, while both cases involved the massacre of peaceful and unarmed villagers, perpetrated on the pretext of reprisals against "terrorists", the justifications invoked after the event by the authors of these crimes illustrate the difference in nature between the actions: not in terms of technique or numbers, but in terms of purpose. The Germans would claim that Oradour was a mistake: the village was said to have been confused with another one which was a "nest of terrorists". Whereas the authors of the massacre at Deir Yassin would boast that, by sowing panic among the Arabs, they had precipitated the flight of "over 100,000 Arabs from the Jerusalem region". Moreover, the leaders of the Irgun would add, after the independence of Israel, that the socialists in the Haganah had themselves committed more than a dozen massacres of this type.[26] The Nazi crime at Oradour proceeded from the terrorist logic of occupation, the Irgun crime at Deir Yassin from that of expulsion and transfer.

It is Yossef Weitz, once again, who expresses in his own way, at once candid and cynical, the profound meaning of this transfer, which was not only an exchange of populations, but also an exchange of roles. On 18 December 1948, he wrote in his diary:

> The village of Ziv (formerly Akhziv) has been razed, and now I wonder whether this destruction is good, and if the *revenge* [my italics] would not have been more striking if we had settled a colony of Jews in the houses in the village. The village of Bassa too is deserted, empty and mined. At this moment, a profound emotion has welled up in me, rising from the ancient days of Genesis: a feeling of victory, of domination, of vengeance. The feeling of being freed of a suffering.

Thus, in 1948, Palestine was emptied of the bulk of its non-Jewish population, and the Zionist organizations were transformed into state apparatuses. The reversal of positions was at last accomplished: the Jews had become, as Utopia had promised, the sole masters of the Palestinian domain, while the Arabs had become their "Jews": without land, and without a nationality, a universally rejected diaspora. Within the territories directly ruled by the new state, what remained of their land was confiscated, and they were forbidden to bear arms, and confined in a "zone of residence". In the territories occupied since 1967, Begin even went so far as to offer them an autonomy very comparable to the one the Jews had enjoyed in Russia under tsarist rule.

In fact, the whole colonizing process had been accomplished in the complementarity and synthesis of the various social and ideological components of the Zionist movement. Practical complementarity between the bourgeois line of alignment with imperialism (and, on the spot, of "Arab labour"); and the "Labour" line of the manipulation of international contradictions (and, on the spot, "Jewish labour"). This complementarity did not exclude conflict, but it did favour compromise solutions. Thus, South African apartheid constitutes a compromise between the Boer settlers, supporters of "White labour", and the English capitalists, anxious for "Black labour": economic integration, but social separation. It is towards this type of compromise that the whole of Israel society has been moving since the occupation raised the number of Palestinians under Israeli rule to over a million. The relationships of force between the two "lines", however, are all the time being modified. The occupation and *de facto* annexation of the territories conquered in 1967 gave a new impetus to the forces that fed on the exploitation of Arab labour. Yitzhak Ben Aharon, an old Worker of Zion, a pioneer of the struggle for Jewish labour and, until 1971, secretary-general of the Histadrut, had understood it at once: from right after the June 1967 war, he advocated restoring the territories to the Arabs, "even without a peace agreement", because they constituted "a bomb under the Jewish character of the state". And it is significant that such was, at the end of his life, the opinion of Ben-Gurion himself.

Again, while it is true that the so-called Zionist left, strong in its clear revolutionary consciousness, was often more brutal in practice, while being more hypocritical in language, than the openly right-wing tendencies, it is also undeniable that fidelity to abstract proclaimed ideals could in some cases lead to a breach. The dilemma had been brought out by Arthur Ruppin in the late 1920s: it was not possible, he said at that time, to reconcile Zionism and universal morality. When he first became aware of this, he had chosen universal morality, joining the Peace Alliance led by Martin Buber, Magnes and others. Later, he returned to Zionism, this time knowing clearly what he was doing. Ben-Gurion used to mock Mapam, the "extreme-left" of Labour Zionism, whose slogan remains: "For Zionism, socialism and the brotherhood of peoples." "It must be said to its credit", the leader would say ironically, "that Mapam has only ever worked concretely for the first of these terms." It is true that Mapam, and its youth movement, *Hashomer Hatsair* (the Young Guardians), represented an extreme example of social-nationalist schizophrenia; until 1952 and the Prague trials that consummated the break between the Zionists and the Soviet Union, on 1 May the portrait of Comrade Stalin was displayed in the canteens of kibbutzim affiliated to this movement! In some cases, the tension was resolved in favour of values and language, in favour of socialism and at the expense of Zionism. Thus, at the time when the Histadrut was founded, the minority of Left Workers of Zion split: they created first the Socialist Workers' Party (MPS), and then after a few avatars, the Palestinian Communist Party. Thus, a considerable part of the present extreme left in Israel is directly descended from these dilemmas posed to the socialist-Zionists by the desire to reconcile mutually exclusive terms.

The emptying of Palestine realized a century-old project. At the centre of it, was the transfer. If the society that established itself in the still warm place of the expellees was formed and transformed in the process, it nevertheless existed, and not only as an organ of imperialist domination over the region. Certainly, the colonial context and relationships of force had enabled the Zionists to lay the bases of their enterprise. The sad dynamic of anti-Semitic exclusion in central Europe, ensuring a growing flow of immigrants, had strengthened the grip of Zionism on the Jews of Europe and the United States. But it was labour colonization, in which were combined the most archaic features of pre-industrial settler colonization and the most modern features of bureaucratic organization, which, in agreement with the abstract and utopian logic of Zionism, but using unforeseen modes and contents, provided the impetus for the constitution in Palestine of a separate Jewish society independent of indigenous social forces.

It was the Zionist ambition to build, in Palestine, an "inverted pyramid", to alter radically the social structure of the transplanted former *Shtetl,* which gave the colonizing enterprise its cohesion and its autonomy. It was this that made the Palestinian and Arab reaction at the time of the Mandate ineffective and condemned them to failure. Palestinian society, different strata of which perceived at various rates the reality of a Zionist threat, did not understand the internal well-springs: the notables and the great landed proprietors denounced "the Jews", which led to confessionalization and pushed the Palestinian Jews into the arms of the Zionists; the revolutionaries of 1936–39 and the Palestinian communists, Jews and Arabs alike, globally denounced British imperialism, evading any analysis of the Zionist movement's own dynamic. The inadequacy of these responses found a tragic illustration with the general strike of the Arab population of Palestine in 1936. Whereas a similar strike in Syria, in the same year, had forced the French Mandatory government to retreat and grant the national movement the promise of a process leading to independence, the strike in Palestine had only one practical effect: the definitive taking over of the Mandatory economy by organized Jewish labour, and the self-exclusion of Arab workers from the labour market, onto which the new immigrants flocked.

The stress placed on the role of the masses in the Zionist movement shows the inadequacy of the anti-Zionist imagery that sees the settlers as mere instruments of international finance capital in its system of domination of the Arab peoples. It also suggests another geopolitics of the displacement and transplantation in which the move from the *Shtetl* to Turkey, from the empire of the tsars, the protector of the Armenians, to the Porte, which massacred them as a sideshow in its war with Moscow, does not detour via Britain and the West, except by way of that imaginary West which haunted the provincial élites of the two neighbouring empires.

The transplantation was also a social reordering: what the Histadrut built under the name of "Jewish society of labour" was a new socio-economic formation, in which cooperation constituted, alongside the community phalansteries, the basis of a monopolistic and corporative capitalism inspired by the state socialist model, of the mixed economy variety. From this reordering there emerged a new stratum of popular leaders, which was transformed into a state bourgeoisie.

But the stubborn material and human facts of Mandatory Palestine limited the scope of the transformation: when, in 1947, war broke out, the Jews, one-third of the population, still owned only 6 per cent of the land. In December 1940, Yossef Weitz had written in his diary:

> By preparing the ground, by paving the way for the creation of the Jewish state in the Land of Israel, the Zionist enterprise has done its work well. It must continue by buying land. But all that does not give us a state. The state must be given to us, at one stroke, like salvation (is that not the secret of the messianic idea?)

Even after the 1936 strike, most of the public services and agriculture in Palestine remained in the hands of the Arabs. Only war gave the Zionists a state. And Weitz records in his diary, on 18 December 1948, his visit to Galilee, emptied by the wind of expulsion of most of its Arab population:

> The whole day we rolled over Galilee and we saw all the agricultural wealth that they have left behind them. And the heart is heavy. Shall we have enough strength to continue all these crops, to improve them and extend them? Shall we be capable of settling here thousands of Jews to repeople the human desert, and make Galilee flower again?

In the socio-economic domain of Palestine now occupied by the State of Israel, the 800,000 Palestinians driven out of their homes and their fields left a great emptiness. It was the Oriental Jews who were to fill it.

Notes

1. Maxime Rodinson, *Israel, A Colonial-Settler State?* tr. D. Thorstad (New York, Monad Press, 1973),
2. Ahad Ha'am, 'Emeth me-erets Isra'el", in *Kol kitvei Ahad Ha'am* (Complete Works) (Tel-Aviv, Dvir-Hotsa'ah 'ivrith Publishing House, 1947). The article is almost wholly translated into French in *Sous Israël, la Palestine* (Editions du Sycomore, 1978).
3. The expression *'avaq adam,* human dust, seems to have been common among the Zionist colonists at the beginning of the century. See the concordant testimony of Moshe Menuhin, the father of the violinist, a disillusioned Lover of Zion, and Nathan Hofshi in M. Buber, J.-L. Magnes and E. Simon (eds.) *Towards Union in Palestine: Essays on Zionism and Jewish-Arab Cooperation.* (Jerusalem, Ihud Association, 1947).
4. Quoted by Eli Lobel in "Les Juifs et la Palestine".
5. Zangwill's daughter and heiress, who lives in Israel, strongly denies that her father was the author of it.
6. Ouri Eisenzweig, *Territoires occupés,* p. 83.
7. Interview on Israeli television, August 1973.
8. For Nordau, a Parisian born in Budapest, see above, p.170. For Max Brod, see p. 186, and for Arthur Ruppin, p. 190.
9. Ahad Ha'am, *Truth...,* op. cit.
10. Letters on this subject were exchanged during 1920 between the Lovers of Zion movement and the Secretariat of the 3rd International. The minority of *Paole Zion* members who advocated accepting the conditions of affiliation – in particular the creation of Jewish-Arab trade union organizations in Palestine – then founded the communist movement, which in 1924 became the P.C.P.
11. A Yiddish proverb of the time says: "Better a penny from trade than a shilling from wage-labour."
12. Quoted by S. El Hajawi, at the Brussels Colloquium on *Les Arabes dans les territoires occupés,* February 1981.
13. From an article written in 1920, in the collection edited by Arthur Hertzberg, *The Zionist Idea* (New York, Atheneum, 1959).
14. *Be-dam va-esh* a biblical expression which had served during the period of the British Mandate to provide the slogan of the "revisionists" who supported Jabotinsky: "In blood and fire Judah fell, in blood and fire Judah will arise again."
15. Israel Shahak, president of the Israeli Association for Human and Civil Rights (independent) has assembled, under the title *Begin & Co.,* a collection of documents on Irgun terrorism, including a series of terse "victory communiqués" on the theme: "Our forces have wounded an Arab", "Our forces have killed two Arabs", etc.
16. In 1936, Zvi Kolitz, a "revisionist" militant, published in Hebrew, in Tel-Aviv, an anthology of selected texts by the Duce. In his preface, Kolitz praised the Italian example, "from which the Jewish people could learn much", and denounced the Labourite "columnists" of fascism "which they wrongly assimilate to Nazi anti-Semitism".
17. Reported by S. Giries, *Les Arabes en Israël.*
18. Theodore Herzl, *Zionist Writings* (New York, Herzl Press, 1975).
19. S.H. Bergman, "Correspondence with Max Brod in 1914-15", translated by Moshe Mikam in *Molad,* the literary review of Mapai, 1970 pp. 224-5.

20. The first violent incidents broke out in Jaffa on 1 May 1921; the Zionists had attacked a procession of Jewish communists, and the resulting riot turned into an Arab uprising.

21. David Ben-Gurion, "Les voies de notre politique", *Compte rendu intégral du conseil mondial de l'union des Ouvriers de Sion* (Tel-Aviv, Paolei Tsiyon Publishing House, 1938).

22. Ibid.; Abraham Lulu, at the same Zurich Congress.

23. Yossef Weitz, *Yomanai ou-mikhtavim la-yeladim* (My diaries, and letters to my children) (Tel-Aviv, Massada Publishing House, 1965). Extracts in *Sous Israël, la Palestine.*

24. On the expulsion, and the myth of Arab broadcast incitement, see Erskine Childers, "The Other Exodus", *The Spectator* (London), 1952, and, by the same author, "The Wordless Wish", in *The Transformation of Palestine,* edited by Ibrahim Abu-Lughod (Evanston, Northwestern University Press, 1971).

25. A plan did indeed exist in the unified Zionist headquarters of the *Haganah,* led by Ben-Gurion, the famous "Daleth plan", or "D-plan", which envisaged "the evacuation of the population" outside the combat zones, that is, outside the areas allocated by the UN to the still-born Arab state. The details of this plan, which dates from 10 March 1948, 2 months before the creation of the State of Israel, and one month before the Deir Yassin massacre, were published *inter alia,* by Rami Livneh in *Ha-meth 'al parshat Khirbet Hizeh* (The truth about the Khirbet Hizeh affair) (Tel-Aviv, Ketem Publishing House, 1977).

26. For example, at Illabun, in Galilee, where soldiers of the Haganah burnt dozens of young Palestinian Christians alive in their village church. It is true that at Deir Yassin, 254 men, women and children were murdered in cold blood. But, while Begin's men had "cleared" Jaffa of its Arab population, it was the Labourites who had perpetrated the killings in Haifa. On these events see Uri Milstein, "The First Reprisal Operations", in the weekly edition of *Ha-aretz,* 7 April 1978, and R. Barkan, "The Strange Case of Shmuel Lahis", *Al Ha-Mishmar,* 3 March 1978 (both in Hebrew). French translation in *Nouvelles de l'intérieur,* no. 6, June 1978.

7 Israel

The Oriental Jews

The state was born amid blood and fire in 1948: one-third of the population took over exclusive control of two-thirds of the domain. The *Yishuv*, where the European immigrants were the majority and sovereign, was transformed into a nation-state, while a people was driven out, defeated, denied and dispersed. There then began, in its exile, the history of another Return, which it is not my purpose to tell here. But this Palestinian return born in exile – from the infiltrators of 1949 to the Gaza commandos of 1955; from the prehistory of modern Palestinian nationalism in Kuwait and Cairo to the taking of power by *Fatah* in the refugee camps in Jordan and Lebanon in 1965 – repeatedly ran up against the resistance of the Palestinian domain and society to this change. So-called "Israeli" Arabs who remained, as their poets said, "clinging to your chests, attached to the rocks"; Palestinians of the West Bank and Jordan, who had had the "good fortune" to live in areas annexed by the Hashemite kingdom; so many concrete roots on which the denied Arabness of Palestine could grow again. Even dispersed, the Palestinians have never ceased to be linked to this part of the people that experiences not exile but occupation and continued oppression. Since their exile scattered them all over the Arab world of which they were part, they have never ceased to struggle and to invoke it in the idea of return.

In 1947, the UN Partition Plan allocated 55 per cent of the territory to 30 per cent of the population. The Arabs would constitute 95 per cent of the population in the Arab state and 45 per cent of the population in the "Jewish" state. This Plan was never implemented. What was accomplished conformed to the project set out by Ben-Gurion in 1937, as we have seen: war, and under cover of war, the expulsion of most of the Palestinians from most of the domain.

In 1948, however, there were only 650,000 Jews in Palestine: fewer than the Arabs driven out. Almost 180,000 Arabs, mostly in Galilee, had clung to the land, to the great discomfiture of the socialist-Zionist leaders. "An Arab minority, small or large, in time of war as in time of peace, is a danger for Israel", Yigal Yadin, archaeologist and general, then Chief of Staff and future minister, had declared in 1949. In order to hold the country, as Weitz and Ben-Gurion had clearly seen, large-scale Jewish immigration had to be organized. This was not simply an ideological necessity, it was also a military imperative. Only the settlement of a large Jewish population could enable the newborn state to occupy the ground without military action, and transform the annexation of land situated outside the frontiers set out in the 1947 Partition Plan into an irreversible *fait accompli*.

From the time of the publication of the White Paper in 1931, the Mandatory government had placed serious restrictions on Jewish immigration into Palestine, which had been tightened as the Jews fled Europe, and had become a virtually total blockade during the years of the great killings. These restrictions, which were continued after the war, precipitated, on a much larger scale than before, the political struggle by the Zionists for the right to immigration, and their struggle on the ground to organize clandestine immigration. With the creation of the state, constitutionally bound to the Ingathering of the Exiles, the barriers to immigration fell, and it was possible to believe that the Zionist slogan of territorial concentration was at last to be realized.

Nothing of the sort happened. Those among the survivors of the genocide of their communities in Europe who had preferred Palestine to western Europe or America were already in Israel: it was they who had infiltrated under the noses of the British coastguards during the years of the *Haapalah* – illegal immigration. The Jews who had already reached the United States and western Europe, for their part, seemed more than ever committed to the social integration that the Nazis had called into question. Few of them were to move to the new state.

With the help of the actively pro-Israeli Soviet policy in 1947–48, and under cover of "reuniting families", the Jews of the USSR and the new "people's democracies" were allowed, between 1948 and 1950, to choose between Israel and the land of their birth. They massively chose the latter.

After all those years during which the Zionists had finished up convincing themselves that it was the British who were preventing the Jews from "ascending" to Palestine, the opening of the doors to the millions of Ashkenazim of America and Europe revealed that the king was naked: however much sympathy, and even enthusiasm, the Zionist cause and Israel aroused among the Ashkenazi diaspora, the Jews did not want to leave the societies that had absorbed them and protected them. They did not even leave the countries of Europe where their loved ones had just been murdered, once democracy, bourgeois in some areas, "popular" in others, assured them the rights previously denied them. The ten or fifteen million Jews in the diaspora, free to join the colony that had become a state if they wished, did not, on the whole, do so. Quite the contrary, it might be said: the very existence of a Jewish state somewhere, by normalizing the image of Jewishness, made the diaspora more liveable, and confirmed Jews in their preference for Europe or America.

This lack of European Jewish immigration reflected the objective weakness of the Zionist movement among the Jews of the West: of the massive flow of Ashkenazim from old Poland to the West (western Europe, the Americas and other European settler colonies), Zionism had been able to draw off only a thin trickle, fed essentially from the geographical and social sources of the modern Jewish question: the remains of the *Shtetl*. When the State of Israel was created, this world no longer existed: the Nazis had wiped it out. The survivors had migrated westward; others, retreating before the Nazi advance, had settled further east. Some 300,000 Jews, survivors of the camps and occupied Europe, had indeed come, at the Liberation, to the *Yishuv* armed and ready to become a state; but the majority did not come. The USSR illustrates the dilemma: in periods of liberalism the Jews there did well, and did not want to leave. In periods of repression, when criticism of Zionism lapsed into the classic language of anti-Semitism and police practice, Jews who would have liked to leave could not do so, and it even became dangerous to think of it out loud.

When the state came into being, its leaders, and particularly Ben-Gurion, were very much aware that, for all these reasons, the ten or fifteen million Ashkenazim of Europe and the Americas, the USSR and South Africa, Australia and New Zealand, were not about to rush to the immigration desks. Certainly, the leadership offered to Jewish youth in the West by the Zionist movements might be able to ensure a continued flow of immigrants of quality – technical and scientific cadres, liberal professions – which the small state needed. But, as for the numbers needed to fill the evacuated domain, and create a social, demographic and military power, so long as the conditions remained so favourable for Jews in the West, Ashkenazi immigration would remain tragically inadequate.

It was against this background that the Labour-Zionist leaders of the *Yishuv* decided to use every means to make the Jews of the Muslim countries of North Africa and the Middle East come to Israel. From non-Arab countries, like Turkey and Iran, there was less immigration but it was more spontaneous. From countries like India and Ethiopia, whose Jews were not recognized as such by the rabbis, Jews hardly came at all: political and religious forces within the Israeli Establishment were opposed to their coming. But, between 1948 and 1967, one million "Arab Jews" came from Morocco, Algeria, Tunisia, Libya, Egypt, Yemen, Iraq, Syria and Lebanon to Palestine, where they were to become the workers and soldiers of the new Jewish state, thus peopling the evacuated Arab domain. The Jews "from Africa and Asia", as they are called in official Israeli terminology, were a minority among the Jews throughout the world, but they became the majority in the State of Israel: their numbers, behaviour and customs and the new situations resulting from the transplantation, all radically altered the face of the society being formed.

It was, in fact, a second transfer, following on the first one, articulated on the expulsion of the Palestinians, but equally significant in its scale and implications: and it was from this second transfer that there emerged Israeli society as we know it.

197

The idea of transplantation was not new. It predated the great projects for massive transfers, that emerged, at the end of the Ottoman period, from the problematic of "Jewish labour". Dr. Thon had set out its principles in 1911. It only remained to apply its logic, not to a few tens of thousands of volunteers, but to a million people and whole communities. The advent of the state, which made this displacement necessary, also made it possible: the Arab–Israeli war transformed the Jews of the Arab countries into hostages of the conflict, while the restoration of the "kingdom" promised them salvation, "redemption". "The most realistic and reasonable thing", A. Cizzling, one of the leaders of Mapam at the Zurich Congress in 1937, explained, "is an exchange of populations between the territory of Israel and Iraq, or any other Arab country, by bringing their Jews to the Land of Israel . . ." But the Zionist idea of an exchange of populations dear to Ben-Gurion and his disciples does not stand up to an examination of the facts: the largest number of Jews came from countries which the Palestinian refugees could never reach. (Morocco, Yemen, Iraq); in addition, the Palestinians were driven out of a country where they wanted to stay, whereas the Arab Jews were attracted to Israel: they thought they were voluntarily leaving the countries that they were abandoning. At the end of the forced exodus of the former, there was exile; at the end of the long march of the latter, the kingdom.

One must be careful not to reduce this movement to a single pattern, or this problematic to a simple and contingent event. The Jews of the Arab countries did not spontaneously uproot themselves from the world where they had lived for centuries moved solely by their own will, and without heartbreaks: the double pressure, both repulsion and attraction, of the changing Arab society within which they were living, and the alluring devices used by the Zionists already established in Palestine, played a decisive role in this self-extraction. But neither can one assert that these million men passively experienced the event of their own departure from among the "Nations", simple victims and playthings of Zionist manipulations. The fact is that the Judaeo-Arab world, whatever the particular regional variations, was shot through and swept by contradictory messianic and Westernizing impulses which led them to demand this departure, this exodus from Egypt.

We may look at extreme cases: that of Yemen, where the Jews were attracted by Zionism and its establishment in Palestine, in two main waves, even before the British occupation; that of Iraq, where the Jews assimilated into Arab society only left when driven out by bombs; that of Algeria, where the Jews did indeed leave, but for France. We may meditate on complex cases such as that of Egypt, where any unilinear representation of "the Jewish community" overlooks the extreme diversity of social and cultural situations, as well as of attitudes and behaviour towards Zionism. Here and there, in a Zafrani, an Eskandarany or a Daniel Cohen,[1] one can see glimpses of a real understanding, at the other extreme from the pseudo "global histories"[2] in which Judaeo-centric apologetics vies with neo-messianic obscurantism.

Two opposed representations – two myths – confront one another on the subject of the Jews in the Arab countries. The first, Zionist and Western, describes the constant oppression and debasement of the Jews under Islam. The second, anti-Zionist and Arab, boasts of the tolerance of Islam and marvels at the unbroken happiness of the Jews in an Arab society in which there is supposed never to have been any problem. It is true that the Arab world was much more tolerant than the Christian West towards the Jews living within it, and that, in the lands of Islam, and especially in the Arab world, the concept of anti-Semitism such as it developed in Europe in the 19th century lacks the roots and encrustation that it has in Germany or Russia. But this generally positive assessment of the fate of Jewish communities within Arab Islam cannot obscure the reality of dark periods: persecutions, expulsions, massacres, certainly in proportions in no way comparable to the scale of the European ones, were nevertheless part of the history of these communities. These explosions, which some like to see as quite unforeseen and hence without any reason, can be understood in the light of the social, economic and political contradictions that rent these societies: it is the structural vulnerability of minority communities that makes them the favoured victims of social crises.

Discussion of the fate of the Jews in the land of Islam is not only dogmatic and generalizing: it is also beside the point, in that most of the Arab world in which Jewish communities lived had been subjected for a century to various forms of European penetration, influence or conquest, which profoundly altered the modes of coexistence and re-arranged their problematic. The most extreme example of this re-arrangement is provided by Algeria: by a decree named after the Jewish minister Crémieux, the local Jews became Frenchmen in the eyes of the law, enjoying civil rights not enjoyed by 90 per cent of Algerians. This was at the end of the last century, and France offered the same rights to any European, Christian or Jew, who was willing to settle in Algeria. Thus the Algerian Jews, under the shelter of colonization, not only changed their legal status: they became integrated into the "Pied-Noir" society that was being formed, although they had some problems, as evidenced by the "anti-Semitic" (anti-Jewish) demonstrations by French settlers in Algeria before the First World War, and the hesitant pro-Vichyism of the Pieds-Noirs at the beginning of the Second World War. There were hesitations among the Jews too, as evidenced by the attachment of a minority of Jews to their Algerian nationality, all through the liberation war and up to independence. But the dominant tendency remained: Jewish community life in Algeria – a confessional component of Algerian society until French colonization – gradually detached itself from its cultural and social immersion and became integrated into the colony: the virtually obligatory linguistic switch from Arabic to French, and even more to French culture, expressed this change.

The Algerian situation concentrated within it the main ingredients of the "Jewish question" of the Arab world at the moment of its subjection to

European colonial rule. A new hierarchy began to emerge, at the top of which were the French Jews, powerful and assimilated, and at the bottom of which were the still not de-Arabized Jews of Constantine or the Mzab, or of Djerba in Tunisia. In Morocco, the proportions were reversed, and the numerous Jewish masses were both indigenous by legal status and Arabic-speaking. The small Pied-Noir society, with its French (often Algerian) and even Ashkenazi Jews, competed with the old Moroccan Jewish bourgeoisie that had remained close to the throne even in times of retreat. It stood apart from the diffuse Moroccan patriotism prevalent in the Jewish petty bourgeoisie and among wage-earners. In Tunisia, some towns, like Bizerta, made the Jews French as in Algeria, while elsewhere the presence of the Frenchified Jews of Algeria created the new social space, with its rising hierarchy from the indigenous Jew to the foreign Jew and through him to France. The network of schools and charitable and vocational institutions set up by the Alliance Israélite Universelle, and integration into new economic and administrative circuits tended to recreate around the Mediterranean basin, in varying proportions, and thus with dissimilar consequences from country to country, the same challenge, the same image of the world, the same hierarchy.

With all the specific features of local situations, some aspects of this problematic were to be found in Egypt, where, like some factions of the Muslim bourgeoisie, Jews became French-speaking under British rule, without ceasing to be Egyptians in the eyes of the law and in their own eyes. At the end of the last century, the adoption by the Jews of the Mediterranean of Western, especially French, social behaviour and values constituted a dominant characteristic in the fate of the urban élites of these communities. Even in Ottoman Turkey, the "Spaniards" became Frenchified, protected as they were by the foreign consuls.

In the Maghrib, there were no Christians, nor indeed any great confessional cleaves within Islam which coincided with the structure of the tribe or ethnic-cultural identity: the least "Arabized" Berbers, the Chleuhs of Morocco or the Kabyles of Algeria, were not Islamic dissident movements, while the old sectarian dissident movements and the brotherhoods remained faithful to the supra-tribalism of Islamic theory.

In the Mashrek, on the contrary, the Islamic community was divided into confessional blocs which had acquired over the centuries the closed character and solidarity of super-tribes: Sunnis, Shi'ites, Druzes, Alawites – theological and political parties that had become states and phalansteries, and been transformed into hereditary social roles. Then came the Peoples of the Book: Christians and Jews. But first Christians. The Christians were numerous, often prosperous and powerful, and divided into a dozen rival churches-cum-clans: so many communities jealous of their social boundaries, barricaded in by the strictest endogamy and parish pump concerns. The Jews, who, until the 19th century, constituted a single community without any internal schism throughout the Muslim world, often few in number and far less prosperous than their

transmuted into nationalism made the homeland a so-called place of exile and of Palestine fallen from Arab hands into those of the Ashkenazim the seat of a new memory. Some would reject this meaning: some would remain, others would go elsewhere than Palestine, others again, reticent immigrants, would spend the rest of their days cursing the day of their arrival in Israel. For the most part, the Arab Jews experienced their transfer as destiny, congenital and irreversible, which contained within it a promise. That the hope was in the end disappointed is another story, which does not alter the reality of this participation in the Expectation. Whatever the case, the result is there: virtually all Arab Jews are now in Israel, leaving behind them only a few isolated families, abandoned synagogues and empty quarters.

In January 1974, I interviewed in Jerusalem, for the daily *Libération*, my friend Naïm Giladi, an Iraqi Jew who was then the representative of the "Black Panthers of Israel" on the council of the Histadrut. Naïm described his move in these words:

I was born in Iraq into a feudal family: my father had land, plantations and share-croppers. From my earliest childhood I was brought up to love the Arab language and culture, and even when my family later settled in Iran, my father insisted that I continue, alongside my Iranian studies, to prepare the *baccalaureat* in Arabic.

During the war, there was a national, anti-imperialist uprising in Iraq, which was accompanied by anti-Jewish violence. I know today that these incidents were the work of *agents provocateurs* in the service of the British, but we did not know that at the time.[4] Like many young Jews, I was attracted by the underground Zionist movement and that led to me going to prison. There, I met Jewish communists who convinced me of my error, and I decided that when I got out I would fight for the cause of socialism. My family decided to settle in Iran. I was active there in various democratic movements, which again led to me having trouble with the authorities. To save me from prison, my family sent me to Israel where the state had just been founded.

Along with other new Iraqi immigrants we were put in a *maabara*, a transit camp, near Askallan which is now Ashkelon. We slept in tents, we had nothing, and we were supposed to wait until we were sent to places where we would get jobs. Later, a group of Romanian immigrants was put in the same camp: but for them wooden huts were built, with windows and doors. The group of young Iraqis to which I belonged sent a delegation to the authorities, that is, to the official of the Jewish Agency who ran the camp, to complain about this discriminatory treatment. We were told that the Romanians came from a country where it was very cold, and that they could not bear the climate like us who were used to the great heat of Mesopotamia. We agreed. Nevertheless, when our first winter in this country came, thinking we were going to die of cold, we went back to see the official, who sent us away.

Then the Iraqis in the camp threw stones at the Romanians' windows, and several important figures in the Jewish Agency came to calm us down. They said to us in substance: "Be patient: soon we shall drive the Arabs out of Majdal and you will be able to have their houses."

For us this was a shock. Majdal was a nearby little town, and we knew nothing of its inhabitants. One night, five or six of us crossed the barbed wire that surrounded Majdal to go and speak to the inhabitants, to see who they were, and why they wanted to drive them out. Talking to them, we discovered that they were very peaceful people, very hospitably disposed towards us, and ready to behave as loyal citizens of the state that had just been founded. And it was those people they wanted to drive out to settle us in their houses!

Among the officials of the Jewish Agency who came to visit the inhabitants of the camp from time to time there was one who belonged to Mapam, and who was always talking about socialism, internationalism and the brotherhood of peoples. As he had left us his address at the headquarters of Mapam in Tel Aviv, we decided that I should go to Tel Aviv by bus to speak to him about this business of the Arabs in Majdal whom the Jewish Agency wanted to expel. And, to be sure of finding him, I wrote him a letter announcing the date of my visit.

When I arrived at the headquarters of Mapam that day, I was pleasantly surprised to be at once reassured: I was expected. I had scarcely opened my mouth to ask my way of an employee who was passing in the entrance hall than he had already replied, even before hearing my question: "Room 41!" As I wanted to be certain that there had not been some mistake, I again asked a woman, and even before I had finished, she said to me with a smile: "Room 41!" When I reached Room 41, I read on the door: "Department of Oriental Communities and Yemenites." I put my speech back in my pocket and turned right round without looking any more for the man I had come to see. I had understood: my brown skin and my accent obviously assigned me to Room 41, and only there. And we wanted to talk to them about the Arabs?

This story is rather too pat, and too well told, not to contain some apocryphal and vaguely apologetic rewriting: Naïm is a very talented story-teller, and the written account does not properly record his fluency, mimicry and dramatic way of telling the story. But this tale throws light on the broad outline of the trajectory. Time and again, I have heard Iraqi Jews living in Israel lament bitterly over the humiliations that the Ashkenazim made them suffer. The story that I was told with the most bitterness years after the events, concerns Iraqi doctors, lawyers or feudalists, traumatized by the symbolic meeting with the Zionist state: on the soil of the Holy Land, as they got off the plane, they were met by medical teams made up of silent Ashkenazim who sprayed these primitive Asiatics with DDT to make sure that they did not come in with their fleas.

There were the Moroccans dumped from buses at Dimona, in the middle of the Negev desert, and left to build for themselves the houses in which they would live and the factories where they would work. There was the sub-proletarianization in the transit camps which lasted forever and the transformation of a whole population into a mass of needy dependants on state charity; the forced direction to agricultural colonization, which ended in a resounding failure; as soon as they could, the new immigrants settled in Galilee or the hills around Jerusalem, abandoned their *moshavim* for the towns and their mercantile social relations. There was the massive proletarianization of the immigrants which was to transform the *Yishuv* that had become a state into a capitalist society.

The state and its leaders faced the contradiction between the strategic need to disperse the population – particularly along the provisional borders – and the determination to blend it in a unifying melting-pot. The imperatives of social control obliged them to rely on the family, community and religious structures of the Arab Jews: so agricultural colonies were established on the basis of particular waves of immigration, often homogeneous in origin – Moroccan, Kurdish, Yemenite – and the community notables were "grand electors" for the Zionist parties that shared their votes. However, this clientelism contradicted Ben-Gurion's fixed idea after 1949: to mix, crush, unite and blend the Oriental majority into the dominant Ashkenazi minority. Military service and schooling in Hebrew were to accomplish part of this fusion: the development of industry and trade in the three cities (Tel Aviv, Haifa and Jerusalem) where, for over ten years, two-thirds of the Israeli population have lived contributed to it in another way.

There was a contradiction between the abstract declared will to form only one people and the existential certainty that such a fusion was only conceived of in the form of dissolving the culture of the one in the other – meaning: in the mould of the culture of the Ashkenazi Zionists. It was a contradiction between the fraternal fiction and spontaneous, concrete discrimination.

In 1971, following the appearance of the "Black Panthers of Israel", Yehuda Nini, a Palestinian Jew of Yemenite origin, and a Zionist militant since his youth, published a testimony entitled "Reflections on the Destruction of the Third Temple" (*Ir'ourim 'al Hourban ha-Beit ha-shlishi*) in *Shdemoth*, a literary review of the kibbutz movement. This socialist who accuses the Israeli leaders of having made "the Hebrew society of labour" into an "ordinary colonial country", begins his essay with a story: he tells the story of the vigil of arms of the Black Squadron (*Plugath-ha-schekhorim*), a special Yemenite unit of the Haganah, in 1948, before a battle from which most of them would not return.

Ben-Gurion was to come in person that night to encourage those who were to sacrifice themselves the next day by his charismatic presence, and they had organized a party to welcome him: coffee, singing, speeches, everything was ready. He arrived very late, visibly absorbed in the discussion he was having with the people accompanying him, paid no attention to anything, did not drink the coffee, muttered a few words, and left. "I shall not repeat", Nini writes,

> the wild and bitter words that were spoken around the fire that night. Let the wind carry them away, since those who spoke them were to die the next day...

> But I, who have lived to today, I say: so much the better! They are lucky to be dead, and they are lucky they never knew that they had died to hand this country over to the Avramovitches!

Speaking of the Yemenites in 1912, Ahad Ha'am wondered whether "an increase in their numbers will not change the whole character of the settlement". The second transfer, which made the Oriental and Arab Jews the majority of Israelis, altered the character of the Zionist enterprise without those who had conceived the transfer even knowing it. Initially, the alteration was socio-economic: the presence of a mass that could be proletarianized was to engender – despite the structural dependence of the state on the inflow of foreign capital – an Israeli bourgeoisie, first state-corporative, then private. When this million landless, penniless Arab Jews, without administrative skills in Hebrew, entered the cycle of production and consumption, they paradoxically gave Israel the features of a capitalist national social formation. The state became the site of a "modern" class struggle.

Thus, Herzl's and Borokhov's dream of a Jewish capitalism and a Jewish proletariat seemed to be coming to pass; but it was taking concrete shape only in a crystallization in which Arab Judaism imprinted on the whole state, and on the society being formed within it, its own character and its problematic. Such a covert shift seems at first sight incapable of counterbalancing the opposite mechanism, whereby the educational matrix of the state, the Zionist institutions and the army, shaped and operated by the Ashkenazim, reorients the identity and behaviour of Arab Jews to make them, in the candidly racist words of a typical Israeli Ashkenazi, "men". But history is cunning, and the force of inertia of the intermediate networks of social organization, with the ideological loyalties attached to it, is more potent than the utopias and dreams of planners. For twenty years, the deculturation of Arab Jews in Israel, the disruption of community ways of life and the acceptance by the victims of the hierarchy of values that inferiorized them constituted the web of everyday life for those whom official Israeli society called, in the late 1950s, "the second Israel". But this terminology has long since been abandoned in Israel, where the Orientals no longer want to hear it said that they are second, and where the language of ethnic-communal cleavage between Jews is today far more subtle. For, over the last twenty years, the "weight of numbers", as Braudel says, and also the renewed importance of the facts of geography after the conquests of 1967, have begun to reverse this movement.

The end of the 1950s marked a turning-point: it marked the beginning of the revolt of Moroccan Jews in the poor quarters of Haifa, which led to the riots at Wadi Salib in 1959. It was the time when, with the displacement completed, relations between the old and the new newcomers became structured. In 1964, there was a scandal: an official in the ministry of the interior, Kalman Katznelson, published a book entitled *The Ashkenazi Revolution*, in which he wrote, he said, "plainly what everyone thinks quietly". In it he expounded a simple thesis: the Oriental Jews are more numerous and more prolific than the Ashkenazim. They are, moreover, like the Arabs, not only in their appearance, but in their mentality. They must, therefore, be prevented from uniting against the European minority and appropriate measures must immediately be taken to prevent Orientals obtaining posts of power. There followed a series of discriminatory proposals aimed at excluding the Oriental Jews from the administration, etc.

The book was banned and seized. Ben-Gurion, who at about the same time used to say "We shall have succeeded when we have a Yemenite pilot", was furious, and recalled that racism between Jews was strictly forbidden since it threatened national unity. It was not until 1971, and the emergence of the Black Panthers, that people dared to speak openly of discrimination. And even then it was only the Orientals who spoke of it: the Ashkenazi bourgeoisie and the Zionist parties, while recognizing the existence of social and cultural problems, denied that there was any ethnic-communal discrimination, and preferred to speak, like Arieh (Liuba) Eliav,[5] of the progress still required to close the "gap between the communities" (*Ha-pa'ar ha-adati*). For several years, what Israeli political discourse now delicately calls "the gap" has been measured. Official Israeli sociologists, such as Eisenstadt or Weingrod, have observed it. Others, such as Yonah Rosenfeld and Avraham Zlatchower, showed, as early as 1965–67, that the socio-economic inequality between Ashkenazim and Orientals, not only was persisting, but was tending to grow in the second generation of children born in Israel. The Israeli extreme left[6] and the Black Panthers[7] have provided statistics, and even the beginnings of an analysis, a few figures from which are suggestive: 65 per cent of Orientals in the Israeli Jewish population, 4 per cent of those leaving university, 0 per cent at the head of the Histadrut and the big nationalized companies, 0 per cent among senior officers of the army. There are, of course, a few exceptions, the most notable being the permanence, for years, of a token Oriental service ministry (usually the police). After 1977, Begin's former Moroccan representative in the Histadrut, David Levy, became minister of labour, while Aharon Abu Hatzera, heir of the Moroccan grand rabbinate and the Israeli municipality of Ramleh (an Arab town before 1948, emptied and repopulated with Jews, mostly Orientals: Moroccans and Iraqis), became minister of religious affairs.[8]

The fluctuations in the language of everyday life demonstrate the ambivalence of these relations. While the Yiddish words *Frenk* and *Schwartze* (Black) are openly and clearly contemptuous, and thus excluded from the official vocabulary, although widely used by Ashkenazim among themselves, official terminology, which quite calmly lumps together "people of European and American origin" as opposed to "people of African and Asian origin", scarcely masks its lack of coherence: the Ashkenazim of South Africa, by some unknown miracle, belonging to the first category. The term Sephardic, currently used in Israeli usage as a synonym for Oriental, is understood quite wrongly: while it is true that some of the Jews of North Africa and the Levant still until recently spoke Spanish Jewish and for this reason claimed to be *Sefaradim Tehori*, like the Spanish-speaking Jews of Turkey and the Balkans, the majority of them, particularly in the Middle East, were in no way Spanish: the Iraqis, the Yemenites, even more the Iranians, are only "Sephardic" by a misuse of language. The expression "Oriental communities" (*'Edoth ha-mizrah*) has the advantage of describing all the communities of Muslim countries, but the Western usage of the concept of Orient (the "Orientalist" usage in Edward Saïd's sense) suggests a mistaken geography, which makes the Maghribis – that is, literally, "Westerners" – "Orientals", "Easterners", and puts half the East to the west of Palestine.

The Israeli rabbinate, which holds the whip hand over the registration and status of Jews, continues for its part to classify citizens according to whether they belong to the Ashkenazi, Sephardic, Yemenite, Babylonian, Italian, etc., communities (*'edah*), while the grand-rabbinate is bicephalous: an Ashkenazi and a "Sephardi", the latter representing all the "Orientals". So far as the Israeli police are concerned, they also list the citizens who find their way into their files in two categories – Ashkenazim and Sephardim – plus the "mixed".

The term "Arab Jew", which ought to be able to apply to Arabic-speakers (and, of course, not to the Sephardim of Turkey and the Jews of Iran and India) is never used by anyone in Israel. As Amnon Kapeliouk wrote, about a film entitled "We are Arab Jews in Israel":[9] "the term Arab Jew is a contradiction. Either one is a Jew or one is an Arab."[10] Here we are touching on a taboo: one can be a German Jew, or a Polish Jew or a French Jew but not an Arab Jew. One can be a Moroccan Jew, an Egyptian Jew, an Aleppo Jew: the description proceeds from the place, or from the state. Whereas a Jew who called himself Arab would be belonging not to a territory but to a "nation", that is, to another tribe. And it is true that the term Arab Jew, unknown to the Arab Jews in the Middle Ages, refers to the idea of a single Arab entity, and, what is more, to a non-confessional, secular and pluralist conception of that entity: that is enough to explain the persistent obfuscation, the "blockage", to use Abraham Sarfaty's word, of the concept of Arab Jewry.

These vaguenesses of vocabulary, reservations and obstructions reflect in reality the shifting character of the barriers themselves, and the fact that the language is not ready for the social reordering that is underway. That indeed is why the contemptuous Hebrew word for "Black" (*Shakhor*) was ultimately the one that the youthful rebels of 1970–71 spontaneously chose to pick up and turn against those who used it: for the cleavage that lay behind their protest was not the one that separated the old communities from one another, but the one that was growing, in the new Israeli society, from the division of labour and class stratification. The almost mechanical overlapping of this stratification and community membership might create the illusion that it was the communities as such that were defending themselves, or were engendering the revolt and the struggle. But this was not the case at all. Unlike the Moroccans of Wadi Salib, in 1959, who had dug old Moroccan flags and pictures of Mohammed V out of their trunks, the Black Panthers of Jerusalem, Acre or Beersheba emerged from the very conditions of their birth, childhood and life in a state where they knew no alternative. Hebraized from their earliest childhood, caught up in the delinquency and petty criminality that flourished in the pores of the new urban social organization and under-employment, then engaged in a process of politicization through a series of alliances with the extreme left and the left (both Zionist and non-Zionist); profoundly, and no doubt irreversibly, "detraditionalized", confronted with the implacable laws of the labour market: in quest, not of an autonomy, but a unity.

This demolition of the old forms of community socialization, and the integration of the Orientals into an economic system based on the omnipotence of the state, certainly constituted the essential transformation. The rise of private capitalism in the interstices of this order is both a planned development and an unforeseen contradiction. The system of social control – from the compulsory nursery school to the three years of military service, extended by annual periods of a month or more in the reserves, up to the age of 56 – which provides the basis for the subjection of the citizens to the institutions and laws of the state replaces the community organization of the *Yishuv* at the time of the Mandate with the social relations of a peripheral capitalist state, and, in the long run, is turning the Jews of Palestine into a new Israeli nation.

Thus, a fundamental displacement is at work, attaching the sources of collective identity to the territory where this system of production and consumption is established. Thus, the power of the Israeli bourgeoisie is constituted, both state and private. In the process of normalization thus embarked on, and for the first time for centuries, the pattern of imperial protection through the intermediary of rabbinical control has been eliminated. Certainly, it is still there, and remains essential to the very existence of a "*de facto* state" which its neighbours refuse to recognize. But the internal structure of its subordination is henceforth that of capitalism and militarization.

The dialectic of unequal integration expresses the history of the social formation: the bourgeoisie is essentially Ashkenazi, whereas the new proletariat is essentially Oriental. So that the social struggle is also a cultural struggle, and the struggle against ethnic discrimination equally a class struggle. It is this overlapping that prevents the revolt of the Orientals from being separatist and causes it to swing constantly between integration and social reform. For the whole socio-economic system is rooted in a territory whose original population was removed by force: the new society as a whole is threatened by the Palestinians' demands on this domain. And internal upheavals break on this insuperable reality.

After June 1967, the military occupation of vast new territories, where over a million Palestinians remained, again altered the shape of these contradictions. While the economic normalization imposed by the tapering off of grants (American public aid, German governmental reparations) which had served to finance the absorption of immigrants and the infrastructure of their employment continued, reducing all the time the purchasing power of Israeli wage-earners, the sudden appearance of hundreds of thousands of unorganized Arab workers on the employment market led to a booming of petty private capital, part of which became large-scale. And, unlike the previous waves of embourgeoisement, this one also affected the Orientals, among whom a new owning stratum emerged, the sociological prototype of whom was the private and public works contractor, with a labour force that was mainly, if not exclusively, Arab.

The occupation broke the geo-cultural isolation of Israel in the Arab world. It accentuated the bi-national character of civil society. Retaining a large population under Israeli military administration, together with the policy of "open bridges" with the kingdom of Jordan – one-way trade and the movement of people – and, beyond, with the whole Arab world, led to a pooling of experiences, and thus broke the cultural wall of China that had isolated Israel from the region between 1948 and 1967. The "Israeli" Arabs, long looked upon with suspicion by their "free" brothers in exile, were transformed by this contact: their sometimes complex reunions with their relatives in Gaza or the West Bank once again put them in touch – and not only by radio – with the Arab world and the contradictions running through it.

This transformation, which marked the movement from self-contained settlement colonization to expansionism, also affected the Arab Jews. They who had attempted to forget the language of their parents could now, thanks to their knowledge of Arabic, do good lucrative business with the Arabs in the occupied territories, speculate and trade, and even move up a military and police hierarchy in which knowledge of Arabic became a professional advantage of extreme importance. Culturally, the occupation after 1967 marginalized the Europeans in terms of the linguistic, musical, culinary or family scene, and made their monopoly of power appear more flagrant and more shocking. The existence, within Israel itself, of a minority of Israeli Arabs who had to appear to be being treated as citizens, and whose economic and electoral importance was growing all the time, obliged the ruling classes to watch their language in a way unknown in previous years. While Ben-Gurion's language in the early 1950s, on the danger of "Levantinization" had not disappeared from people's minds, it was no longer expressed openly. Officially, it was the time for the recognition of Arab-Jewish folklore: a year after the appearance of the Black Panthers, the Moroccan-Jewish popular festival at Mimouna was transformed into a national festival, and moved to the gardens in the centre of Jerusalem, with an official opening and ministerial speeches. After three decades of deculturation and Ashkenazi cultural imperialism, the wind of history and demography was beginning to turn.

In order to integrate the Jews "of African and Asian origin" into the nation, however, it was not enough to integrate them economically. And it was there that Zionism began to be caught in its own trap. At the beginning of the 1950s, Ben-Gurion had reached a number of conclusions about the social problematic flowing from the second transfer. After the importation of Arab Jews, originally intended to solve the problems of Zionist colonization, had effected a moral transfer – which today is transferred onto the Jews in the USSR – by which the State of Israel claimed to represent oppressed Jews and in their name perpetuated the state of war, emergency and general mobilization, it became a political end in itself. The massive departure of Arab Jews and their integration into Israel was to cement the historic legitimacy of the Zionist state, which had now become the expression of the self-determination of the Jews of the Arab world. In the argument over the exchange of populations (even recently, the Israeli government, faced with international demands on the subject of Palestinian rights, raised the question of the properties and belongings of the Jewish "refugees" from Arab countries!), the purely colonizing logic of the expulsion was retroactively endowed with the appearances and legitimacy of a "just, honourable and moral solution".

During the Second World War, the same leaders, Ben-Gurion and Sharett, had experienced a foretaste of this reversal of functions: the anti-Semitic persecutions seen solely from the angle of their usefulness for Zionist political ends, whereas Zionism claimed to exist only to solve the problem of persecuted Jews. The wait-and-see policy of the Zionists in the face of the rise of anti-Semitism in Europe – all their efforts being concentrated on the territorial concentration of Jews in Palestine, the securing of independence, the many-sided colonization based on expulsion, and the first transfer – was transmuted after the establishment of the State of Israel into a perverse and murderous mechanism: every means could be used to make the life of the Jews in the Arab countries impossible. Given this, no scruple hindered the Israeli agents from fomenting anti-Semitic provocations: since it was for the good of the victims! In Iraq, Herzl's logic of the convergence of interests with governments took the forms of a secret agreement between the Zionist leadership and the royal prime minister, Nuri al-Said: Israel would take the Jews of Iraq, the Hashemite state established by the British would keep their property. Twenty-five centuries of history thus came to an end. Arriving in Israel, totally destitute, the Arab-Jewish bourgeois of Baghdad saw their children become labourers or delinquents.

In order to shape a still non-existent national unity on this basis, Ben-Gurion felt that the dynamic of national conflict was vital. In a speech to secondary school students in 1953, he contrasted the egotism of civilian society, manifest in the multiplicity of opposing political parties and interest groups, to the grandeur and generosity of military society, in which differences were suppressed in favour of the general interest. In his eyes, Israel was in "danger of peace": the state of war was essential to the "fusion of communities" (*mizug galuioth*). The "history lesson" of the Eichmann trial was designed to serve this end. This new purpose has inspired the deliberately warlike attitude of Israeli governments since 1954. Imposed by Arab resistance to the dispossession of the Palestinians and their expulsion, war became an end in itself, a dynamic value, and Arab hostility a structural necessity of social control within the new entity.

Ben-Gurion had also established that the state could only "safeguard its Jewish character" by basing nationality in law on the ethnocentric criteria of rabbinical Judaism: patriotism on tribalism. Since ultimately it was the Arab Jews who came and peopled the domain previously emptied by the Ashkenazi colonists, Israeli nationalism would have to be based on the synthesis of Zionist territorialism and Oriental confessionalism. This clerical choice by the Labour parties which, by 1949, were presiding over the formation of the bloc of national-religious parties and the concordant between the Labour-Zionist state and the rabbinical hierarchies as a whole, invited to tap the state coffers and strengthen their power thereby in exchange for their loyalty, was to have many consequences: it maintained, during the years preceding the 1967 war, every form of religious coercion and political clientelism; after that date it overflowed the limits assigned to it. With the neo-biblical wave which acted as the ideological support for the annexation of the conquered territories and Jerusalem, the religious right took its independence *vis-à-vis* the Labour bloc and gave rise to escalating extremism, finally engendering the pioneers of colonial neo-rabbinism: from rabbi Levinger, leader of the religious settlers established at Kiryat-Arba on the land of the inhabitants of Hebron, to rabbi Kahana, openly preaching the expulsion of the Arabs; from the National Religious Party to the extremists of Gush Emunim – Bloc of the Faithful – and their new racist theology. The paradox of this victory of ethnocentrism is that it serves to consolidate the annexation of the occupied – and inhabited — territories. Where the discourse on the working class had allowed the expulsion of the Arabs, the discourse on Jewish supremacy puts them back in the picture. It underlies the process of a practical calling into question of the socio-ethnic cohesion of the *Yishuv*, making its structure evolve in the direction of the South African model.

At the same time, the social logic of individual profit was developing, with the integration/exploitation of Arab manpower reaching a peak in 1977 with the electoral victory of the revisionist right under Begin. And this development tended to reduce to nothing what fifty years of struggle for "Jewish labour" had accomplished.

The Oriental Jews participate in this movement without being inhibited by the representations that hinder the acceptance by the Ashkenazi petty bourgeoisie of its dynamic: they are not so ignorant of Arab society, and they did not come to Palestine in order to become peasants or workers. The impulse that had, willy-nilly, brought the Jews of the Arab countries to Israel was ignorant of the social problematic dominating the Ashkenazi world since the end of the 19th century, that of "normality" and redemption through working the land. For the Arab Jews, the move to

Israel was first and foremost conceived of as a movement of the tribe, once protected and vulnerable, to a state of armed sovereignty. This tribal-confessional nationalism today constitutes what may be called the discourse of the man in the street. The efforts to "Europeanize" the Jews from the Third World is being succeeded by the "Levantinization" of Jewish nationalism, whose social aspects are being replaced by chauvinistic bragging: thus, insensibly, Israeli society is moving from colonial socialism to Middle Eastern fascism. Paradoxically, this evolution contains the remote hope of an integration of Israel into the region, of which the separate Egyptian–Israeli peace is but a caricature.

Lot's wife

What comes through the hesitations of vocabulary, between Arab Jews and Oriental Jews, between Sephardim and "those of African and Asian origin" is the imprecision of the subject itself. For we are here dealing with an entity that only begins to exist in the eye of the Western-Other. Before the colonial omnipotence of this vision was invented, the various Jewish groups lumped together under these labels did not recognize any common essence that distinguished them from their co-religionists in Europe or elsewhere. The identity they saw themselves as having did not carve up space at the borders of the Arabic language area, or of some Orient existing only in the mind. One belonged to one's family, the community of one's town, and through that to the kingdom (Turkish, Moroccan, Yemenite, Persian, etc.) and, beyond, one belonged to the "Jewish community": a whole structured by rabbinical Judaism and dispersed by definition. At no time did one identify oneself with Arabness, a concept which – as a cultural concept embracing the Jews – is itself contemporary with the colonial period.

The world of the Sephardim, which on one side touched the mercantile, urban, prosperous and cosmopolitan world of the Levant, which had for three centuries been a staging-post of European expansion, on the other side plunged its roots in a community universe that was plural and sparkling, where the rhythm of rituals and festivals, far from signifying only mourning and contrition, married the human cycle of joy and passion with the apparent unchangingness of village societies.

Here, it is perhaps easier even than in the case of the Polish-Ukrainian *Shtetl*, to fall into the trap of an ahistorical idealization of this community life. To invent for oneself a Judaeo-Arab neo-Hasidism and transform the *mellah*, the Jewish quarter of the towns of the Maghrib, into the place of predilection of an incomparable and lost humanity. The truth, of course, is that all the societies that have disappeared, for one reason or another, were unique, and that the particular life that they at one time sheltered is well and truly lost.

This idealization of traditional life eliminates not only the dimensions of oppression inherent in this life: the external domination of the state over the community mediatized by its internal rabbinical organization. It also proceeds from a reifying and, in the last analysis, colonial vision of Islamic societies. Behind the denunciation of the industrial cataclysm and the mythification of the traditional universe, there is not only romanticization of the past and historico-cultural "ecologism": there is also the false European idea that only Western civilization is historical: only it has classes, events, alienation and boredom. Elsewhere, the so-called "Asiatic mode of production" a Western catch-all, is deemed to determine a structural immobility, at best cyclical, close to the state of nature and paradise lost.

In fact, what one finds at every step in this history is the dual constancy, both structural and theological, of the family, the clan, the tribe, and the confessional community institutionalized by the Ottomans in the *millet* system. Apart from this survival which itself had its ups and downs, there is the history of the Muslim states themselves: the invasions, wars, revolutions and crises, the fortunes and misfortunes of dynasties, populations and classes. There is nothing, in this long chronicle, that is an exclusive privilege or destiny of the Jews. Nothing, except this meeting of rabbinical tribalism and the intertribalism (in the sense that one speaks of internationalism) of Arab Islam. And this meeting occurred in the web of concrete contradictions, not in the abstract sky of theologies.

Throughout the colonial period, that is to say even before the irruption of Zionism into the life of the Jewish communities in the lands of Islam, particularly in the Arab countries, the articulation of the Jewish communal order on the dominant Muslim community was everywhere transformed and sometimes broken. The legal and practical status of the Jews was everywhere strengthened; in some places abruptly, following the military defeat of the Muslim state faced with European conquest, in others, gradually, under the impetus of new economic relations which integrated and subordinated the indigenous markets and their particular rationalities to the sole (Western) logic of Capital.

Is it possible, on paper, to grasp this composite mobility, the transition between the slowness of the traditional community and the speed of the new, and from there go on and conceive the overall movement running through the Mediterranean domain? Is it possible to picture the shift in minds and in the forms of power that made Leghorn and Smyrna centres for the Judaism of the East long before the European conquest? The shift that inspired the intervention of the Jewish notables of Oran, calling, in writing, in 1829, for the imminent French conquest?

In the Maghrib, as in eastern Europe, one may speculate about the variety of the ethnic origins of the Jewish populations. A wholly scholastic distinction can be made between the Berbers first converted to various forms of Karaism – the most rural communities, and particularly the "mountain Jews" of the High Atlas – and the urban strata who had been integrated since Roman times into the Mediterranean trade network.

Summarizing the works of Marcel Simon[11] and the studies by N. Slouschz published in 1905, 1906 and 1908 in *Archives marocaines*, and in his *Voyage d'études*, published in 1909, Simon Szyszman distinguishes the Mediterranean Jews of the coastal regions from the Berbers of the hinterland converted to "biblical beliefs":

> The biblical doctrine probably penetrated into the Maghrib at a very early date, most probably before the Romans, through colonists who came from Palestine following the Phoenician conquest. It began . . . by finding converts among the Punic people on the coast of Africa. That would explain the considerable growth of the communities and the total eclipse of the Phoenicians . . . These conversions were facilitated by the close kinship between Hebrew and Punic, which are in fact only two Canaanite dialects.

In the hinterland, on the contrary, the doctrine based on the Old Testament, which "at the time had no talmudic overtones", underlay the resistance of the Berbers to the Roman empire, Catholicism and then Islam. This was the episode of the Judaeo-Berber queen, the *Kahena*.

> Contrary to a widespread opinion, Slouschz maintains that her religion was not rabbinical Judaism. The role of this warrior woman reminds him of the role played, at the head of the Karaites of Spain, by Al-Ma'alima, who is also said to have been of Berber origin. Slouschz quotes a song collected among the most learned Israelites of Constantine by Cazès, on a mission for the Alliance Israélite Universelle (*Essai sur l'histoire des Israélites de Tunisie*, Paris, 1888). In this, Al-Kahena is cursed for having persecuted the Jews even more cruelly than their greatest enemies in history.[12]

And it is a fact that, after the defeat of the Berbers commanded by the Kahena, it was Coptic and Jewish colonists from Egypt, and then Spain, that Hassan Ben al-Numan settled in Kairouan and elsewhere in the Maghrib.

Thus, some basis exists for the fabrication of a "Khazar theory" in which the Berbers would replace the Turco-Mongols, and the Kahena the Kagan Bulan. The Jews of the Yemen can also be explained by the conversion of the Yemenites under Dhu Nowas, and the migratory history of the Judaeo-Arab diaspora set aside as mythical. However, such a line of theorizing, which is fundamentally racist because it considers only ethnic identity and sweeps aside historical and ideological formations, ignores the essential point: how deep was the mixing that occurred as a result of the internal social reordering of these communities, unified for several centuries through the institutionalization and protection of their rabbinical hierarchies.

It was this system that conferred on the minority of notables their ideological and practical authority over the majority of artisans, workers and small traders in the community.[13] It was this system that enabled the Western-oriented minority to draw the vast majority along in its wake. And this movement sealed the self-exclusion of the Jews (to varying degrees from the Arab national society that was at the same time being forged in the resistance to European conquest and penetration. Long before they came into contact with political Zionism, the Judaeo-Arab world, and, more generally, the Jewish communities of the Muslim world, constituted a complex and composite structure subjected to the whims of the power that protected it and the alliances on which its security was based.

This was first and foremost the effect, and the price, of the intertribal functioning of Islamic society: it was this that put an unbreachable limit on the reordering of clans into classes. Thus, the relationship between the state and communal and tribal liberties was never finally resolved, but was materialized in the endless fluctuation of often violent relations of force. Possession of the land and the armed autonomy of the tribe were the fundamental conditions of this relationship, which has been wrongly identified with feudalism, since its central feature was the liberty of the peasant and even more of the nomad – herdsman and transporter, warrior and trader. Here tax was paid not by the individual (the "citizen") but by the community: it marked not its dissolution in the state but its vitality as an autonomous component of the multi-community state. The rituals of vassalage and protection thus also translated the state's undertaking to confirm the community in its recognized and particular prerogatives and liberties, including the liberty, very foreign to feudalism, to appoint its own chiefs.

When the community in question was Muslim, the free men composing it were armed and could negotiate from strength the modalities of their integration into the Islamic "motherland",[14] as well as the amount of tribute to be paid into the central treasury.

With few exceptions (the most notable being the Maronites of Mount Lebanon) the minority Peoples of the Book, free men and recognized owners of their property, were disarmed: this peculiar status affected the problematic of their relationship with the state. In a construction of this type, the Jewish communities, traditionally unarmed by the convergence of Koranic and Talmudic law, were incapable of ensuring their own security and status by the force of their own guns. They were consequently tied to the protection of the central authority, and perceived, often rightly, as aligned with the state in the masked guerilla war between it and the tribes, the chiefdoms, and generally the periphery of this federation of many societies. Rabbinical Judaism came into being with the renunciation of the power to negotiate or use force to dispute the terms of the protection; and it assumed this dependence by making it into a metaphysical imperative, it sublimated this "voluntary servitude" by seeing in it the inevitable corollary of Exile.

The flaunted humility of this resignation found its compensation in faith in the Coming: moreover, the belief in the imminence of the Last Day, or of the Day of Justice (*Yom ha-Din, Yaum al-Din*) constituted a fundamental tenet of Islam. The abasement of the Jews was thus temporary: kabbalistic mysticism, widely diffused in the Sephardic and Judaeo-Arab world, accounted for this impoverished aristocratism through the theological patterns of exile and redemption, expectation and return. This acute consciousness of its own decline echoed the nostalgia, rife throughout Arab society, for lost greatness and prosperity, which contrasted with its contemporary insignificance (at least before the Second World War). The Arabs are, says Jacques Berque, "fallen Greeks". The Arab Jews, heirs of the Andalusian or Egyptian symbiosis, of the Abbassid one in Iraq or the Ayyubid one in Egypt, even if this were only through the literature of classical Judaism, had experienced this exemplary fall until the end of the last century, which was compensated by an even stronger inner certainty of understanding the higher world.

One can reflect on the role of the minority of Spanish refugees, and that of the Marrano-Sephardic diaspora in the Mediterranean, in the spread of these patterns and the aristocratic consciousness attached to them. But, what was important was that the representation of the world and the Jewish fate, implicit in collective behaviours and explicit in religious activity institutionalized by the rabbinical tribunals recognized by the Muslim state, had ended by being adopted by the Jewish communities in North Africa and the Middle East as a whole.

Added to the taking of power by the Spaniards in the Mediterranean diaspora, from the 16th century onwards, there was the supremacy of the Marrano-Sephardim of Italy and Turkey: the former dominated the world market in Hebrew, Aramaic, Judaeo-Spanish, Judaeo-Arabic and Judaeo-German books by the end of the 15th century. The latter were close to the centre of Ottoman power whose loyal servants they were. Through them, Arab Judaism became articulated on Sephardic Judaism: Spanish, Ladino, European before the letter. Through it, the Arab Jews experienced their first separate contact with the West, and beyond, with the remote world of the Yiddish-speaking Ashkenazim.

At the beginning of the 16th century, in Venice, Reb Capsali, the author of the *Book of Eliabu*, had exalted the providential role of Ottoman tolerance and hospitality. Following the expulsion from Spain, the massive emigration of Jews to the eastern Mediterranean which, as it passed, swelled the communities in northern Italy, had been followed by the creation of new ghettos, as at Venice, Rome or Florence: it was an anti-immigrant policy – the Spanish Jews had come up against the limits of tolerance in the Italian municipalities of the time. And the Italian Jews moved down to Leghorn and Bari as the Jews of Lithuania moved down to the Ukraine. The "divine tolerance" of which the Catholic kings of Poland had boasted two centuries earlier, was nowhere more striking than in Muslim Turkey, opening its doors to the Jewish victims of the Inquisition. And the Marrano-Italian mystics had no hesitation in recognizing in the Sublime Porte the enlightened heir of the Caliphs: the very Caliphs whom Sa'adia al-Fayumi, the *gaon* of Baghdad, and Hasdai Ibn Shaprut, the Cordoban, had served so well.

Two centuries later, the pendulum began to swing the other way, turning the Jews of the Mediterranean Muslim world towards the West. In the West, the Marranos in France, Britain, Holland and Germany formed a tenuous link between the old Sephardic world and the new Atlantic world – and the bourgeois revolution and liberating colonialism. In the East, the endemic revolt of the Slav peasantry, which struck the Jewish communities full blast, did not rest only on the Greek Orthodoxy of the tsars. Very quickly, it linked up with the permanent revolt of the Muslim Tatars backed by the Porte, or by Safavid Persia.

For the Jews of the Arab world, the most cosmopolitan, élitist, commercially oriented and profane central government was always preferable to the popular rule of local military or religious hierarchies, not to mention reformist Islamic movements with a revolutionary social or national content, usually opposed to the tolerance of classical Islam towards Peoples of the Book, or other schismatics. Thus, before the Jews of the Zaidite imamate of the Yemen turned to Britain and later to Zionism, many of them had hoped for the victory of Mohammed Ali's modernizing Egyptians, during the short episode of the conquest. Thus again, they were later accused of aiding the taking of Sana'a by the Turks, in 1872.

Of course, there were areas of community life that had not yet been affected by this attraction to, and fascination with, the West – language and ways of doing things, the dead or living weight of tradition and custom. There was the hinterland, the mountain and village communities in southern Morocco, Yemen, or Kurdistan. The essential thing, however, is not the numbers, but the overall movement: and this was all in one direction.

It is easy of course to draw up a list of special cases that contradict this impulse. To contrast the pro-French notables with Yehuda Ben-Drane, a Jew of Oran, an Algerian national hero and adviser of the emir Abdel-Kader struggling against the colonial conquest. However, the example, which testifies to the tolerance of the still-born Algerian state, remains ambiguous: for Ben-Drane was an ambassador, not a general; but above all, he represented the emir *in dealing with the French*, with whom he had to negotiate his capitulation. A century later, the FLN asked patriotic Algerian Jews ready to join in the liberation struggle to be "the eyes and ears of the Revolution within the colonialist camp".[15] The eyes and the ears, not the arms and the legs.

All through the 18th and 19th centuries, the swing of the pendulum speeded up, with the West, especially Britain and France, becoming the carrier of both the messianic and the secular aspirations of the Jews of the Mediterranean world. The hopes of redemption that Reb Capsali had placed in the Ottoman Porte were transferred to the mission of the West, that is, to European imperialism.

White Jew, Black Jew

The irruption of Zionism into the Judaeo-Arab world, and the impact of Ashkenazi domination on the pieces of it transplanted and concentrated in Palestine, precipitated the reversal of the meaning and sign of words. The creation of Israel had been experienced, simultaneously, as fulfilment of prophecy, return, and response to the Expectation and as the triumph of conquering Western modernity. In Israeli society, which was built on the terrain of the double transfer, a new triangle began to emerge, between the Ashkenazim, the Oriental Jews and the Arabs.

"We are all first class", sang the narrator in the *Couple*, George Amsallem, of Bet-She'an by way of Casablanca. "Only the Arabs are second class!"[16] The common identity of all Jews is the founding myth of the nation and a white lie, daily contradicted by experience and social praxis. Here, the Ashkenazi racist is he who places the frontier of the human between Jew and Jew – whereas it should of course be placed between the Jew and the Other. The racist is thus he who recognizes the Arabness of the Arab Jew, instead of denying it and declaring it null and void. The racist is he who sees in the Arab Jew the Arab, not the Jew: such is the perverse fiction that underpins the unity of the people and the state. While the Jew from Europe can take pride in his European culture, the Arab culture of the Arab Jew must be absolutely rejected, erased in the fiction of exile. (And culture does not mean simply artistic or literary heritage, but above all a way of life and sensitivity, conception of sexuality and aesthetic of behaviour.)

The Arab Jews were Arabic-speaking, engaged in a constant cultural and ideological exchange with their Muslim and Christian neighbours, an integral part of the Arabic-speaking mental world – unlike the Yiddish-speaking Jews of eastern Europe, unlike the Judaeo-Spaniards of the Balkans and Turkey. After the transplantation, the fiction that the Jews had crossed a desert like drops of oil in water, without any interplay or metabolism became obligatory. As a Tunisian jailer at the Abu Kabir prison, in Jaffa, complained to me, in 1969: "It's not our fault if we were born in Arab countries!" Convinced that this was the sole reason for the hostility towards him by the father of his very Ashkenazi fiancée, the young Israeli cop was trying to reduce his forbidden Arabness to a simple matter of chance.

An enormous collective energy was thus scattered, and invested in fruitless mental self-mutilation. The derisive and dramatic mechanisms of this unassuageable denial of the ego is not unlike what Frantz Fanon described in 1952 among West Indians in the French colonies in Black Africa.[17] It is remarkable that the Zionists who, since Dr. Pinsker, have prided themselves on having some intuition in the matter of the psychology of peoples and groups, who consider assimilation as a disease and the glorification of the ethnic ego as the condition of every virtue, who do not hesitate to throw in the face of their Jewish adversaries the ignominious label of "anti-Semitic Jews" and have only the theory of "self-hatred" to denounce them, that these same Zionists should have established in Israel, to integrate the Arab Jews whom they took the trouble to import, a system of ideological control and cultural domination wholly built on the self-denial of Arab Judaism, and on a colonial-style mass psychopathology.

Yet it is this majority, reduced to silence, put through the mill of state Zionism, disinfected and proletarianized, militarized and reordered so as to serve as "people of the land" for the Ashkenazi bourgeoisie, that in fact constitutes the Israeli people today. It is this majority that votes and works, that dies at the front and that kills, that pillages and tortures, that deserts and bears witness. It is even this majority that emigrates in its hundreds of thousands to the United States. From many points of view, Israeli society is today largely Oriental and Orientalized, even though the apparatuses of state power are still, apart from a few symbols, a preserve of the Ashkenazim – and essentially of Ashkenazim born in the country, the offspring of the Zionist pioneers of the turn of the century, a colonial aristocracy, the Mayflower of the *Shtetl*, both panic-stricken and conquering.

Sixty-five per cent of the Jewish population of Israel is "Oriental". The Orientalization of Zionist society transformed the structure of the *Yishuv* into semi-state, semi-private peripheral capitalism, strengthening bourgeois and religious conceptions to the detriment of the social-segregationist ideal of the pioneers of Labour-Zionism. This shift of social model was expressed in the aftermath of the June 1967 war in a rush by civilians into the occupied territories. Ten years later, it brought the nationalist right wing to power.

It was the anti-Labourism of the popular classes, predominantly Oriental, which had precipitated the electoral landslide in which the socialists, for the first time in half a century, lost the exclusive leadership of the affairs of the Zionist movement. It is true that the Moroccan workers of Ashdod and Dimona, the Iraqis of Ramleh, and many of the Orientals who had voted for Begin in 1977, were already regretting it by 1979; that they had voted against Labour more than for Likud: for Begin's liberal economic promises more than for his programme of annexation and war. But it is equally true that the undisguised chauvinism, the open tribalism that inspires the demagogy of the Zionist right are better attuned to their alienated spontaneity than the pseudo-humanist hypocrisy of the "left".

For thirty years, the right, a coalition of liberal bourgeois and fascist petty bourgeois, united by their hatred of state socialism, had capitalized on the bitterness of the Oriental immigrants faced with all the problems they were suffering: urbanization and capitalism, bureaucracy and the racism of Ashkenazi officials assigned to look after their absorption (*qlitta*). Thus, Ashkenazi domination itself was perceived as the corollary of socialism: did not both come from Russia? More or less spontaneously, the Oriental rioters in Jerusalem, in August 1971, mixed their slogans: "Down with Golda!", "Golda to Russia!" and "Golda is a Communist!"

At this time, during public political debates in the popular quarters, it was still being said that Begin was a Moroccan.

Zionist "pioneerism", of both right and left, was generally absent from the behaviour of the Orientals, and limited to a small number of assimilated ones: French-speakers from the Maghrib recently arrived from France, Orientals (above all "Pure Spaniards" of the old *Yishuv*), individually or professionally integrated into Ashkenazi society, spouses in "mixed couples", all more or less cut off from their original milieux. There were few Orientals in the old kibbutzim, and few in the "Peace Now" movement. But there were few too in the new settlements, and practically none at all in the activist or fascist far right – Gush Emunim and the Jewish Defence League – in which the new American and Russian immigrants predominate numerically. And this very absence testifies to the powerlessness and dependence of the Orientals in relation to a political game to which they are subject, and that they only influence unknowingly.

And yet: there is Yitzhak Navon, president of the State of Israel: a Palestinian Jew, a Zionist of the national-socialist wing: Daniel Pinto, a war criminal, found guilty of the murder of four unarmed Lebanese civilians in April 1978, pardoned by the Chief of Staff: a Sephardi of Algerian origin; Moshe Hillel, minister of police at the time of the Oriental riots of 1971–72, who had ordered the Arab mounted police of East Jerusalem against the rioters: an Iraqi Jew; Geula Cohen, a former Irgun girl who is still "violent",[18] a Knesset member of the annexationist far right opposed to peace with Egypt, who opposed the evacuation of Sinai and accused Begin of contributing to the creation of a Palestinian state and selling off the "kingdom": a Yemenite. From top to bottom of Israel society, the list of Orientals could be lengthened, whose position shows the predominance of social and ideological cleavages over communal ones. For the determining contradictions, in the Israeli society that emerged from the double transfer, are social and political: they turn around the profit that Capital – whether private or state, local or foreign – hopes to extract from social labour, and around the control of the machinery, apparatuses and resources of the state. This double source of conflict, typical of capitalist nation-states, underlies all the social, cultural and political tensions in Israel, and subordinates other cleavages. But, because it only exists by virtue of the armed perpetuation of the expulsion and occupation of the Palestinians, it is in turn subjected to the dynamic of the national conflict. Social conflict – the class struggle internal to Israeli-Jewish society – is thus smoothed over, limited and defused by a war whose battlefield is itself the issue. And the very national contradiction (Jewish-Arab or Israeli-Palestinian) that distorts and muffles the clash of classes endlessly gives a new content to the ethno-communal cleavage between the two socio-cultural categories (the Ashkenazim and the others) who are reordered in the new formation.

The Orientals in Israel do not live, or identity themselves, as Arabs of the Jewish faith. Neither do they live in the manner in which they lived for centuries in the Arab world, that is, within the rabbinical communal organization. They live the concrete situations of the new state as Israelis. "If the Zionist domain", writes Ouri Eisenzweig, had been

> hitherto a concept that flowed from the positive need to resolve the problem of Jewish identity – the materialization of this concept, with the advent of Israeli society, heralds a reversal which will increasingly situate identity as dependent on the domain where it is manifested.[19]

Such is the normalizing virtue of state organization. "This state", writes Maxime Rodinson, "can now be defended by the usual means of state structures, diplomacy and war." The social and ideological order can now be ensured in it by the usual means adopted by state structures, the concentration of economic power and the monopoly of violence and repression, through profit and the police.

These facts represent both the historical success of Zionism and its ultimate political failure. The proletarianization of Oriental Jews in Israel like that of the Ashkenazim proletarianized under the Mandate, constitutes a real liberation from the traditional forms of communal protection. In that, the Israeli Zionist bourgeoisie has achieved what no empire had been able, or wanted, to achieve: the abolition of the separate social fate of the Jews, the abolition of Judaism. Is it really paradoxical that this emancipation, that subjects Israeli proletarians to the ordinary, universal forms of capitalist domination, is only being achieved in the teeth of the theocratic pretension and discriminatory legislation of the State of Israel?

The internal contradiction that the impact of the Oriental Jews constitutes for Zionism is not necessarily insurmountable. The distinction between Orientals and Westerners that was flagrant in the beginnings, when the cultural weight of the Ashkenazim of Europe in the *Yishuv* was overwhelming, exacerbated between the 1950s and the 1970s, and glaring at the level of the state apparatuses or statistics on the standard of living, is tending to be transformed among the middle classes. The Israeli commercial bourgeoisie is well aware of this: for several years it has already been modernizing its marketing models in order to "Orientalize" them. For it is to Orientals that jeans and tinned chick-pea purée, furniture and local beer have to be sold. On the look-out, as everywhere, for symbols of social reality, private advertising (the Hebrew worship of goods) is restoring the image of an Israel that is culturally Oriental – and colonized – whereas official Zionist propaganda continues, ridiculously, to distribute photos of blond pilots and rosy-cheeked children.

This shift could be seen when the Americans pulled out of Vietnam in 1975. "Today", the Israeli political class declared, "the Americans are abandoning Vietnam, tomorrow they will abandon us!" In the American press, American Zionists castigated Israeli opinion: could it not see the difference and the sacrilegious and suicidal nature of such a comparison?

There are many signs of this slide into integration into the regional problematic of imperialist designs: from the "peace" made by Begin and Sadat to Israeli protection of the Maronites in southern Lebanon, in whom Zionism has at last found its Cossacks. This orientation is abetted by the great powers, which have made the legal discourse about the equality of peoples the fiction of world order. The myth of the white man's burden, which still inspired the League of Nations in Balfour's time, has been transformed in the West into a Free World crusade, into which the most determinedly barbarian peoples are enrolled. Israeli society, as an exclusive consumer of Western culture, could not long ignore this evolution. Fed by the cultural airlift that binds it to the United States, the Israeli bourgeoisie can see this reorganization of the imperial discourse in which the mission of the West is transmuted into an International of counter-revolutionary nationalisms. Thus, it lays less stress than was the case in Herzl's time on European civilization in its struggle to drive back the frontiers of Asiatic barbarism. Rather, acutely aware of the competition of Asiatic (and especially Arab) bourgeoisies in the global calculations of the great powers, it is tending to withdraw into its own paranoid tribalism, which is expressed in the modern Hebrew ditty, which is scarcely ironical, whose refrain goes:

"The whole world is against us
It's a very old song
That our ancestors taught us!"

The classical colonialist and racist discourse has not disappeared from Israeli society. But the crude racism, omnipresent in the street and the press, in the ideology and cultural production, has almost totally disappeared from the official discourse of the state. When, in 1971, Golda Meir stated that, personally, she found it very hard to understand that Jews should not know Yiddish, most Israelis interpreted her words as a gaffe. But what she was trying to do in this admission was to go beyond the demagogic paternalism that had typified the attitude of her caste towards the Arab Jews, and to establish a dialogue, in the trauma that had followed the explosion of anti-police violence in Jerusalem. She had met the leaders of the Black Panthers in her office, but had been unable to pass the stage of "But why don't you work?" with them. She was now attempting, on the occasion of an interview with a journalist, to show that she "understood": she had only made the admission of her own amazement that one could be Jewish without being Ashkenazi in order to stress her good faith. But, claiming later that she had been misinterpreted, she revealed her unawareness of how deep the gulf was. For throughout the riots of 1971 and 1972 and the demonstration in the following years, one of the slogans chanted by the angry young Orientals was: "Where then is the honour – of the Sephardim?"

Following his resignation as Chief of Staff, General Mordechai ("Motta") Gour gave a long interview to the supplement to the daily *Al Ha-Mishmar* on Independence Day, 10 May 1978, in which he calmly justified the genocides of the Palestinians and the Lebanese, explaining that

> this civilian population was giving asylum to terrorists for over ten years. It is a civilian population known for having actively helped the terrorists. It is a historical fact. It is no use at all being high-minded and nice after the event. I myself, as commander of the front, bombarded them for two and a half years. After the massacre at Avivim [an operation by the PFLP-CG, the Ahmed Jibril faction, against a bus carrying Israeli children in Upper Galilee in the summer of 1969], I bombarded and pounded four villages without formal permission! Do you have any idea of the number of towns and villages we bombarded to protect Beit-Shean?

When the *Mapamnick* journalist, outraged, asked him, "What? Randomly? Without choosing?", he replied:

> Choose what? The people of Irbid did nothing when I machine-gunned and bombarded them. But that was near Beit-Shean, near Maoz Haim, near Beit Alfa ... So people thought it was natural. The air force kept two planes in the air. If someone fired, they bombarded. What's the matter with you, have you forgotten your history?

But our official military statements always spoke of reprisals against the sources of firing or reprisals against only terrorist targets ...

> Oh, please ... Don't you know we emptied the Jordan Valley during the Yom Kippur war?

In other words, when you talk about a bombardment carried out by the Israeli air force, you mean we bombed blindly?

> I haven't got a selective memory. I served in the army for all of thirty years. Do you think I don't know what we were doing all those years? What we did along the Suez Canal? We created a million and a half refugees down there! Really, where do you think we are? You arrange things in your head according to your desires at the time. We bombarded Ismailia, Port Saïd, Port Fuad. A million and a half refugees! What happened all of a sudden? For ten years it was impossible to travel by night along the Lebanese border. How come that this population in southern Lebanon is suddenly transformed into a population of saints? They knew what the terrorists were doing, they helped them before and after their operations and welcomed them as heroes.

So your thesis is that this population can be punished?

> Certainly. I've never had any doubt about it at all.[20]

But, contrary to what one might expect, it was not these admissions that caused the scandal: generals, whether retired or not, are full of them, and one could compile a whole encyclopaedia of horrors displayed in the Israeli press on this point. The real scandal Gour caused was about the Oriental Jews. When the journalist asked him: "The vast majority of senior officers are Ashkenazim, and one may wonder whether the Israeli army is aware of the need to fill the social gaps and accelerate integration", the former Chief of Staff of an army made up of a majority of Orientals replied.

> The army is achievement-oriented. It is a society based on results *par excellence*. You can't appoint a battalion commander on the basis of his ethnic origin. He is leading men in battle. In this area, there are no indulgences or "understanding", but only the ability to fight. And it will be years before the Oriental Jews, even those who get a full education, can successfully master the technological and intellectual mentality of the West.

It is very hard to swallow what you say about mentalities, without taking environmental conditions and factors into account.

> But I do take them into account, very much so! We hope we shall allow them to evolve too. In our schools, they learn how to think, whereas the Arab schools always stress memorizing, and that's a vital difference. That is why I hope that we shall wage our struggle against the Arabs, not only in terms of élites – who *a priori* have the possibility of progress and upward mobility – but also with the broadest strata of society, if we give them the appropriate teaching and education.

It was this passage, highly insulting to Jews, that was Gour's "gaffe" in the eyes of Israeli Jews, and he was obliged to apologize to the very official "Association of Jews from North Africa".

In fact, the open expression of real racism towards Oriental Jews occurs above all among new immigrants: from the USA and the USSR. In 1972, a group of new immigrants from the USSR demonstrated at Nevei-Sharett, in the suburbs of Tel Aviv, to protest against being housed right next to a Yemenite Jewish quarter: "We did not come from the USSR", they said, "to live with Blacks!" In 1973, the Jewish Defence League of the pseudo-rabbi Meir Kahana "declared war" on the Black Panthers of Israel: with a membership made up almost 99 per cent of American Jews, the JDL is allergic to all "Blacks".

Among the eye-witness accounts by Israeli soldiers of the atrocities committed by their units, during the spring of 1980, under cover of the application of prolonged curfews in the towns, villages and refugee camps in the occupied West Bank,[21] there was one by a 40-year-old Ashkenazi reservist who told of a "double session" of "theoretical preparation". It illustrates the two faces – contradictory and complementary – of Israeli racism today:

> At the end of our period of service we were subjected to another lecture. The lecturer, who was introduced to us as "expert psychologist", spoke with a strong American accent, in bad Hebrew, and from time to time had to use an English word. The gist of his lecture was that our task was to train the Arabs like one

trains dogs, and he came back several times to this metaphor of training dogs...

Immediately afterwards, a member of the Gush Emunim arrived, and gave a short lecture in which he said that the world was divided into five categories: the Inert, the Vegetable, the Animal, the Speaking and the Jewish – and that the biggest difference was between the Speaking and the Jewish. He explained that he did not use the term "human being" [in Hebrew, "son of Adam"] which was confusing. "So don't believe", he said, "that you have hurt a human being, since there's no such thing. You have not struck or maltreated Jews, and that's the main thing..."

After the lecture, I had the opportunity of talking privately with this "psychologist". I asked him if he agreed with the remarks made by the Gush Emunim speaker. "Of course not, that's just ... superstition (in English)." I then asked him if some of what he said, about the Arabs, their culture and their education, could not equally apply to Jews from the Arab countries. He looked around to make sure that there was nobody nearby (most of the soldiers in my unit are from Arab countries) and replied: "Indeed, most of them are like the Arabs. But, if we do our work properly, many true Jews will come from the United States." I asked him to explain what he had just said, and he replied that all the American Jews who wanted to beat up Negroes but couldn't do so, would come here and beat up Arabs, and that perhaps then "the Americans would learn from us how to deal with their Negroes".

These were two figures in the service of the military government, both involved in what the previous chief of staff called "appropriate education". This is not fiction: the soldiers who spontaneously came forward to give their harrowing accounts to public opinion, and who felt that in doing so they were running some unnamed risk, were motivated by simple moral and human rejection, not of war on Zionism, but of sadism, cruelty and oppression. These soldiers were often patriots: they wrote to Knesset member Uri Avnery, and declared their readiness to testify before a parliamentary commission of enquiry that their units had been ordered "to strike, frighten and humiliate" the Arab civilian population of the occupied territories. They asserted that, during the traumatic weeks that they had spent assigned to tasks with the military government in the West Bank, "the general atmosphere prevailing among the soldiers reminded us of stories about the acts of cruelty against Jews at the time of the Holocaust".

Witnesses of this quality, like the soldiers who have refused to serve in the territories occupied since 1967, like the anti-Zionist Israeli dissidents, whether pacifists or revolutionaries, socialists or liberals, constitute certainly "another Israel", the focus of hope for the future of this society. But their essential quality, for the time being, remains the testimony. While they are not a force strong enough to reverse the movement, they do make it possible through their action – which is often no more than symbolic – to see its true face.

The "superstitious" language of the spokesman of the Gush Emunim disguised as a military chaplain, and the "scientific" discourse of the American psychologist do indeed refer to two racist systems which, while being complementary and similar, are yet on one point contradictory.

The Jewish racism of the Gush Emunim is clear-cut like that of the slavers of the Nazis: biological, theological and unchallengeable. It seeks the removal of the "Other", and may effectively result, if circumstances require or allow it, in genocide. However, the boundary of this racism goes between the Jew and the non-Jew (the "Speaking"), not between Black and White, between the West and the East, the "true" Jews and the "false" ones. This racism is a synthesis of fascist Israeli state nationalism and rabbinical ethnocentrism: it does not *a priori* exclude Oriental Jews. Quite the contrary, it might be said, since from Warshevsky-Yavni'eli – the "socialist" who dressed up as a rabbi to organize the immigration of the Yemenites – to Ben-Gurion, the only language Ashkenazi Zionism had to integrate the Arab Jews was the language of obscurantist rabbinical ethnocentrism.

Whereas the American version, on the other hand, proceeds from Western racism: "socio-cultural" racism, with theories about the "education" of the Arabs, as with Motta Gour or Ezer Weizmann in 1968.[22] It will have nothing to do with all these "superstitions": there are Blacks and Whites, in Palestine as in America. The only concession it is ready to make to the idea of a world mission of Judaism relates to its dream of a State of Israel as the leader of the anti-popular war, selling its repressive know-how to the White racists of the whole world: "Perhaps the Americans might learn from us..." – a complete caricature of the prophecy: "And Israel shall be a light unto the Nations!"

Whatever the current power and influence of this latter system, it paradoxically has less future than the former within Israeli society, because it divides it as much as the other unites it. This imported racism, which survives in the behaviour of new American or Russian immigrants is doomed to disappear with the generation that brought it – whereas the superstitious mediaeval discourse of the neo-rabbi may endure, survive and take root.

While the most virulent racism is often expressed openly with regard to Arabs, the contempt for Oriental Jews is almost always confined to private exchanges. The Ashkenazi *Sabras*, as soon as they enter into the area of "civil" social relations – at work, in the street – know the subtlety of communal categories, and their shift along the social scale. For here, class comes into play, and, as the Haitian proverb says, "a rich Negro is a Mulatto". This evolution, of which the choice of Navon as president is a sign, just as is the choice of a Black to represent the United States at the UN, is inscribed in the material circumstances of international society, as well as in those of Israeli society. It is also strengthened by the nationalist ideological dynamic that feeds on the permanent state of war with the Arab world.

Such an integrationist dynamic could only weaken or diverge if the cohesion of the factors that engender it fell apart. Peace, or a total Arab victory, both of which are unlikely in the medium term, might, each in its own way, be such a moment of crisis. But, as the war goes unendingly on, the "fusion of communities", through crisis and gaffe, revolt and scandal, will continue to operate in the inegalitarian reordering of communities into classes. So long as the confrontation continues to be perceived in Israel by the mass of Oriental Jews as a global vertical clash between two opposed and mutually exclusive peoples, the Palestinian question will continue to deepen the integration of the various Jewish communities into the inegalitarian structure of the new nation-state.

Despite everything, the overlapping of social and ethnic cleavages, together with the fact that Israeli capitalism has been built under the label of socialism, has created a situation in which the pacifism of the privileged classes strengthens popular chauvinism. The Israeli satirical chronicler Kobbi Niv illustrated this configuration three years ago.[23] Analysing the terms of a letter published in *Al Ha-Mishmar*, in which a Peace Now activist related how he had been maltreated by a group of young layabouts in a cafe in Beersheba, Kobbi Niv showed the racism, both ethnic and class, in it and concluded that the blows received by the "fine soul" had not been received for nothing.

In the present state of the conflict, there is almost no link between the political crisis engulfing the highest echelons of the state, the moral crisis affecting petty-bourgeois youth, and the structural social crisis of the Israeli formation; no articulation between the political and reasoned opposition of some, and the individual and deviant desertion of others. Light years separate the educated young Ashkenazi Israeli who expresses his moral outrage before the excesses of the occupation, and the uneducated young Oriental Israeli who, in his practice and in his behaviour, disrupts the national social and ideological consensus.

In the one case, a young reservist, a technician and programmer, informs the army's central computer of the new information that he thinks is relevant. And when the chief of staff's daughter – after the latter had pardoned the war criminal Daniel Pinto – comes to consult the computer to obtain some administrative information about her father, the machine replies: "Rafael Eytan, chief of staff born . . ., etc. Pardons murderers." In the other, there are the young recruits assigned to the maintenance of tanks who sabotage 18 of them to slow them down. Israeli society is thus riven by a chasm which, far from disintegrating it or deepening the polarization within it, is leading it to chase its own tail and contributing to its impasse. This relates to the Zionist blocking of any peaceful solution – the refusal to recognize the Palestinian national fact in the heart of the colonized domain.

Notes

1. Ya'acoub Daoud Eskandarany, "Egyptian Jewry – why it declined", *Khamsin* no. 5 1978 (London); Daniel Cohen, *Le colonialisme français et les Juifs au Maroc* (Paris Colloquium on "Racism, anti-Semitism and Zionism", March 1980).

2. Gérard Nahon, "Pour une histoire globale", *"Le second Israël"*, special issue of *Les Temps Modernes*, May 1979.

3. *Sefer Ha-Haganah* (Defence Book), official military history of the Zionist movement in Palestine, by the Maarakhoth Publishing House, the Israeli Army Publishing House, Tel Aviv.

4. This refers to the pro-German revolt by Rashid Ali El Kilani: "national", it certainly was, but anti-imperialist? In any case, it is not certain that the anti-Jewish incidents were the work of British agents alone.

5. Eliav, a Zionist leader since the days of the Mandate, was, during the 1950s, one of the organizers of the clandestine immigration of the Jews of the Maghrib to Israel. In 1956, at the time of the tripartite aggression against Egypt, he was parachuted into Port-Said wearing a French army uniform, with the task of sounding out the possibilities of counting on Egyptian Jews in the hoped-for eventuality of the fall of the *raïs*. As a Labour party member of the Knesset, Eliav stood out in 1967 for this dovish stand, and, after the 1973 war, he allied with Uri Avnery to form the *Sheli*, a faction advocating dialogue with the PLO and withdrawal from the territories occupied in 1967. But he remains firmly Zionist, and his language about the Oriental Jews, an example of which appears in the special issue of *Les Temps Modernes, Le Second Israël,* strikingly illustrates this fact.

6. I.S.R.A.C., no. 6 (Paris, Maspéro, December 1971) *Khamsin* no. 5 (London, March 1978).

7. *Panthères Noires d'Israël*, presented by Mony Elkaïm, (Paris, Maspéro, 1972).

8. Aharon Abu Hatzera was accused of corruption, and, on the eve of the 1981 elections, created an Oriental "party", causing a "communal" split in the National Religious Party to which he belonged.

9. The film does not actually live up to its title: its director, Yigal Niddam, a Moroccan Jew from Israel who lives in Switzerland, is a "left" Zionist, moderate and well-meaning, and the Israelis interviewed in the film are all patriots of the Zionist state.

10. *Le Monde,* 15 November 1977.

11. Marcel Simon, *Le judaïsme berbère* (Recherches d'histoire judéo-chrétienne) (Paris – The Hague, 1962).

12. Simon Szyszman, op. cit.

13. S.D. Goitein's works on the Cairo *Geniza* show how old this articulation was.

14. *Ummat al-Mo'minun:* "motherland" of the Believers. The word *Umma*, from the root *Um*, "mother", is usually translated by "nation", but it rather indicates the community in the broad sense. On the semantic ambiguities of this concept, see Amr I. Ibrahim, "La 'Oumma ou la 'Communauté' d'une langue à l'autre", *Peuples méditerranéens*, no. 15, April 1981.

15. FLN Appeal to the Jewish community of Algeria (1956), quoted by F. Faron, *Studies in a Dying Colonialism*, tr. H. Chevalier (New York, Monthly Review Press, 1965).

16. Rami Rozen, *Fashkolnik,* a satire staged in 1976 at the Khan Theatre in Jerusalem, published by Galileo, Jerusalem, 1978.

17. Frantz Fanon, *Black Skins, White Masks*, tr. C.L. Markman (New York, Grove Press, 1967), and "West Indians and Africans" in *Towards the African Revolution*, tr. H. Chevalier (New York, Monthly Review Press, 1967).

18. A shock-fighter in the National Armed Organization (*Irgun Tsvi Leumi*), known in the West as the Irgun, Geula Cohen has recorded her exploits in *Women of Violence. Memoirs of a Young Terrorist,* tr. H. Halken (London, Rupert Hart-Davis, 1960). She became a Knesset member in Begin's party, and in 1978 created a new extremist party, *Ha-Tehiyya*, the Renaissance.

19. Ouri Eisenzweig, *Territoires occupés*, p. 88.

20. Interview with "Motta" Gour, *Al Ha-Mishmar*, 10 May 1978; French translation in *Nouvelles de l'intérieur*, no. 6, June 1978.

21. Accounts published in Hebrew in *Zo Ha-derekh*, selections of which were disseminated by Knesset member Uri Avnery in an open letter to members of the Knesset. French translation in "Frapper, faire peur et humilier – des soldats israéliens témoignent", *Nouvelles de l'intérieur*, special issue, May 1980.

22. In July 1968, Ezer Weizmann, then commander of the air force, gave an interview to the daily paper *Ha-aretz*, in which he asserted that "the Arabs are not up to" modern warfare. Quoted by Eli Lobel, "Les Juifs et la Palestine".

23. Kobbi Niv, "The Good have problems", *Ha-olam Hazeh*, 24 May 1978.

8   By Way of Conclusion

It would be nice not to conclude. What is the point of constructing paper epilogues that history has not yet imagined? We should end with the frustration of this impasse in which the peoples of the Middle East are exhausting themselves; show that this lack of movement, of which sporadic warfare is part and parcel and changes nothing, is laden with decay and threats; and reassert that history is not fate, but a series of contingencies and freedoms.

Peaceful and democratic solutions are always preferable to violent and imposed solutions. But the content of projects does not prejudge the means used to implement them. So it was with the transfer, that the Labour-Zionists deemed "a programme that was logical and just, moral and humane in every respect": violent in its content, it unfolded over a long period, as S.H. Bergman used to say on the eve of the First World War, "under the sign of the money given to the effendi more than under that of the sword". It was, in the end to be accomplished amid massive armed violence. Conversely, the violence of a national or social struggle does not imply the absence of liberating content, even though it harbours within its organization the embryo of a different order.

There are no peaceful or violent solutions. There are projects, which usually claim to be peaceful, and put the responsibility for violence on to their opponents. There is, as always, the "peacefulness" of the victor and the "violence" of the defeated. There are projects of violence that are advanced by diplomacy and there are projects of freedom that are forged in violence. There are also cases where violence bears its flag openly, and others, much less common, where freedom grows for a time as if without resistance. It is difficult in any case to see why, in the Middle East and about the Middle East, men in power should be more open to reason than men in power elsewhere. That is why consideration must be given, in actual confrontations, to the content of the projects proposed, and the arithmetic and the configuation of the material and moral forces: the field of this battle, open to the winds of every imperialism.

The State of Israel, having emerged victorious from its wars with the Arab world, has appropriated to itself the means of making or not making peace.

Of course, the State of Israel does not have the power to resolve instantaneously, by governmental decision, all the problems created, over decades, by its creation; any more than it has the power to decree its own disappearance. But the Israeli leaders, because they are the victors, can, in theory, push the conflict at every stage towards escalation or towards compromise. After each of the two great military Israeli victories, in 1948 and 1967, they chose escalation.

The practical choice in favour of escalation was based on the very dynamic of the Zionist colonialist enterprise. At each stage of this century-old trajectory, faithfulness to the initial choice has inspired concrete strategy. In 1911, when the sheikh of Sullam, in Galilee, offered his protection to the settlers at Merhavia, the leaders of the Jewish Agency gave the order to refuse. They even gave the settlers instructions

> to provoke violent clashes with the policemen in Nazareth . . . so that the matter should become public knowledge, and that it be used as evidence against the prefect of Nazareth. A strong complaint was sent to the governor at Acre, the *wali* of Beirut and even to Istanbul. The prefect was ordered to stop persecuting the Jews.[1]

Here the intransigence flowed from the need to empty the domain in which the Zionist project was to take form. So long as the project – a constitutionally Jewish state in place of Arab Palestine – is neither re-examined nor revised, escalation is only one of the names of the very dynamic of the conflict.

Following the creation of Israel, after the admission of the Zionist state to the UN which had given it birth, such an option seemed open, and even briefly to have materialized, in 1952-53, with the hesitations of Moshe Sharett's government and the proposals for negotiation between Sharett and Nasser. Ben-Gurion and his lieutenants Peres and Dayan, like his right-hand man at the time, Arik [Ariel] Sharon,[2] were absolutely opposed to such dealings: from the murderous "reprisal" operations in 1953 to the raids on Gaza in 1954 and '55, which led directly to the escalation of the autumn of 1956 and the joint Israeli–French–British aggression against Egypt, they had set out in actions but also in their speeches, the broad outlines of their position. A central theme became established in Israeli propaganda and diplomacy, which is summed up in one phrase: "Not a single refugee will return."

Translated into concrete language, on the ground abandoned by the Arab villagers and city-dwellers driven out during the war, for the refugees massed beyond the allegedly provisional ceasefire lines provided for in 1949 by the Rhodes agreements, this policy principle was an order given by the Israel high command, which was equally terse: "Fire on infiltrators." An infiltrator was any Palestinian attempting, even peacefully, to return to his home. But this Zionist choice in favour of escalation concerned what, for the Israeli leaders of the time, that is Ben-Gurion, constituted the main thing, what was "not negotiable", what was irreversible: the miracle of the transfer. When Yossef Weitz heard that, at the end of 1948, Israel had undertaken to take back a few tens of thousands of Arab refugees (out of 800,000!), he tore his hair out in despair. Following 1948, for Ben-Gurion and his followers, everything was negotiable, everything could be re-examined, except the disappearance of political Palestine, the expulsion of the Arabs outside the territory of Israel....

Following the Israeli evacuation of Sinai and the Gaza Strip in 1957, Ben-Gurion justified himself: the essential thing was not to keep the territories, but to re-establish the historical relations of force with the whole Arab world. In a pamphlet which he wrote and distributed at the time, he wrote:

> Another aim of the Sinai campaign was to reduce the standing of the Egyptian dictator, and the importance of that should not be underestimated. As the person in charge of security, even before the foundation of the state, a serious worry had always lodged in my heart: we know the lamentable situation and corruption of Arab leaders, which is one of the essential features of their military weakness. But I have always apprehended that an outstanding man might arise, in the manner of such a man who arose among the Arab tribes in the 7th century, or in the manner in which Mustafa Kemal arose for the Turks after their defeat in the First World War, galvanizing the people's spirit and restoring its self-confidence, turning it into a fighting people ... And it was beginning to appear that Nasser might be that man. It is significant that children wear his picture in various Arabic-speaking countries ... And to have reduced the standing of that Nasser is not a small political act.[3]

The choice of escalation displaced and extended the front. From being a conflict between Palestinians and Zionists, it was to become one between Jews and Arabs, then between Europeans and Arabs and then Americans and Soviets. As early as 1953, Ben-Gurion was explaining to anyone who would listen that it was too soon to be satisfied with ensuring the existence of Little Israel, like "an Albania": while he was organizing the importation of Arab Jews, he was talking of saving the Jews of the USSR and of making room for the Jews of the West when the storm came, and was preparing new escalations, new provocations, and new conquests to this end. Speaking at Kfar Ruppin, in 1970, to the students of a school of agriculture, Moshe Dayan – who was to say a little later, brilliantly summarizing the meaning of the whole Zionist enterprise, "we took an Arab country and made it a Jewish one"[4] – asked them to contemplate the distance travelled by Jewish colonization in a hundred years: "Do not say, the journey is over! It is still long..."

After July 1967, a new working principle of escalation was established in "policy". It consisted in asserting that the occupation of some areas (such as Jerusalem) was irreversible and non-negotiable. After the 1973 war, Rabin's (Labour) government solemnly undertook never to recognize the PLO, never to accept the creation of a Palestinian state alongside Israel, never to accept a return to the frontiers of 4 June 1967. In 1975, when the

General Assembly of the United Nations adopted a resolution describing Zionism as "a form of racism and racial discrimination", the Israeli government reacted by renaming "Zionism Boulevard" all the "United Nations Avenues" and deciding on the creation of new settlements in the occupied West Bank. And, after his election in 1977, the new prime minister Menachem Begin explained to anyone who cared to listen that the Palestinians in the occupied territories, which he called liberated, had to get used to living under Jewish rule, as the "Israeli Arabs" in Galilee and the other areas incorporated into the Jewish state in 1948 had become used to it.

Yet, this Israeli intransigence is not unanimous at the popular level: the October 1973 war, growing international pressure and the resulting isolation of Israel, Sadat's initiative itself, together with the resistance of the Palestinians in the occupied territories and abroad, the economic crisis, the loss of legitimacy by the leaders and concern about the future, have all begun to undermine the determination not to yield an inch of territory in an area where – except for the city of Jerusalem – only some 20,000 Israeli settlers live, scattered in their armed forts in the midst of a million and a half Palestinians.

Such a state of mind, though still a minority one, is certainly important: it could greatly favour the type of territorial compromise envisaged by the international community, consecrating the existence of two states. But it would be surprising if the Palestinians considered as anything but their due the restoration of 22 per cent of the territory of their homeland, and saw this solution as the achievement of their aspirations and demands.

The coexistence of two states could only be transformed into reconciliation, that is, a truly peaceful solution, if the imposed cohabitation of the apparatuses gave way to the voluntary and freely accepted coexistence of the two peoples. That supposes a complete transformation of the present values and ideological functioning of Israeli society, a reconsideration of the relationship between ethnic group, confession, nationality and state – between the tribe, the domain and the law. It is this transformation that we usually call "de-Zionization". It does not, or at least not necessarily, imply the dismantling of the Israeli social formation, any more than the denial of the national rights of the Israeli people. It implies only the ending of apartheid and the establishment of a democracy for the two communities. It is not even incompatible with the continued existence of a state structure peculiar to each, provided that such a partition of the domain is made by negotiation and not by coercion.

Both of these possible stages are matters of struggle and negotiation: they are being worked out elsewhere than simply in the field of debate. Our intention here has been to make people understand and feel, not to promote a magic formula in which history would give up the ghost.

The few certainties that emerge from the still vague portrait of this tragedy are negative: the need to disaggregate the false cohesion of the mythical categories of Nation, Race and Religion, and even of Class, and replace them with the particular knowledge of contents and forms.

I have endeavoured to show what, at each stage, changed and remained of the Jewish subject, of Judaism as an actor in the history of the Jews. I have tried to bring out the movement by which this subject survived, in two distinct cultural areas (the Arab-Muslim world and Latin Europe), and how in eastern Europe this subject became consolidated, while in the West Judaism became a mere religious denomination. How the Zionist ideological and political movement, born in the crisis of the Jewish society of eastern Europe, based itself on the rise of an anti-Semitism in western Europe which was itself the product of the massive emigration of Jews from eastern Europe to the far west. How Zionism and its establishment in Palestine – violently transformed into the State of Israel – are avatars, the latest in time if not the final ones, of this subject. How illusory it is then to want to construct analyses and solutions that ignore this subjectivity.

In the 6th century BC, in Assyrian Babylon that had fallen under the sway of the Persians, a particular model of imperial protection of the dispersed Jewish ethnic group had been introduced. It rested on the civil – including fiscal – autonomy of the community, and on the domestic power of the priests, ranked in a hierarchy around the central administration of the Temple. This system, which was the foundation of Judaism, radically transformed the old religion of Israel which had been conceived in the conquest and sedentarization of the Israelite tribes in Canaan. This Judaism, arising after the completion of both the state cycle – the kingdom of David and Solomon, divided into the rival kingdoms of Israel and Judah – and the prophetic cycle was designed for an ethnic group which had lost its territory, and responded to a twofold necessity. The first was imperial, and Persian, which ensured for itself the loyalty of the Judaean diaspora by relying on a minority group; the second was Judaean, and more particularly priestly-clerical: the party of the priests, whom the "ungodly" aristocrats of the kingdoms of Israel and Judah had driven from power, recovered it with the help of Persian protection, in exile, and before long in the rebuilding of the temple in Jerusalem by imperial decree.

In the succession of empires – Persian, Macedonian, Seleucid, Roman – this protection underwent some ups and downs: either the empire ended its protection, or the war party which was constantly re-surfacing wanted to reject it in order to restore a sovereign kingdom. This revival of monarchism, often articulated on the social contradictions exacerbated by the succession of foreign occupations (Maccabees, Zealots, Bar-Kokhba), fuelled a myriad sectarian and messianic currents. The nationalist revolts led the Romans to draw up a new contract of protection with the Jewish ethnic group scattered to the four corners of the empire. The Temple, the priesthood and sacrifice were past. The intellectual opposition of the sages, the exegetists (pharisees) opposed to the Temple administration, became

235

the rabbis: scholars, lawmakers and judges, new ethnarchs benefiting from Roman and Byzantine protection, rising up from the defeat of the kingdom.

Under Byzantium, this protection reached considerable proportions, recreating contradictions and new oppositions between the rabbinical hierarchy – the "patriarchate" – and the society subjected to its authority: the Judaean ethnic group. By the 4th century, with the rise of Christian groups in the east of the Byzantine empire, the centre of gravity of the rabbinical system was displaced towards Mesopotamia and Persia, where the Sassanid emperors renewed with the Sages the contract of protection made a thousand years before by Darius and Cyrus with the Scribes and the Priests.

Such protection – whose survival enabled several centuries of rabbinical legislation to be codified in the enormous talmudic literature – ensured victory for rabbinical Judaism (often obtained with the help of the secular arm of the non-Jewish state) over the various missionary and universalist dissident groups that emerged from the disintegration of the priestly organization. These dissident groups, which were to produce Christianity directly and Islam indirectly, were the source of massive conversions to biblical doctrine among the peoples on the periphery of the Roman world (Arabs, Berbers, Khazars): these were later to be absorbed by Christianity and Islam, and in some cases, reabsorbed into non-missionary, ethnocentric and protected rabbinical Judaism.

For a whole set of practical and ideological reasons, the Islamic states, under whose sway most Jews soon found themselves, offered the rabbinical-Judaic system unparalleled conditions of protection, in the shadow of which, from the gardens of Andalusia to the shores of the Gulf, from Fez to Aleppo and from Cairo to Sana'a, classical Judaeo-Arab civilization flourished. Culturally transformed by the massive and absolute adoption of the Arabic language, through which they came into contact with the Greek heritage, and socially reintegrated by their participation in the commercial growth of the new civilization, the Jews of the mediaeval Arab world were now recognized, united, ordered in a hierarchy and locked up in their new confessional identity. The Law updated by the new lawmakers and scholars no longer concerned only an ethnic group that had lost its territory and was dispersed among kingdoms and states: this mobile, portable Law reflected also the disappearance of the agrarian relations that had underlain the talmudic law, and the transformation of the community into a society caught up in an economic order that embraced it and went beyond it.

For this time, when the whole of Jewish life was ordered by the jurisdiction of the rabbinical tribunals, the identity of national group and religion, tribe and Law was affirmed to be constitutive of the community. The foreign elements that attached themselves to it, either by collective conversion or, more often, by individual assimilation – by marriage or by enslavement – were forced to subject themselves to the ethnic fiction that formed the basis of both the Law and the rationality of the protection: thus, the considerable ethnic mixing was constantly obscured by the insistence on the tribal story.

To each of these phases in which the forms of autonomy and protection shifted there corresponds a corpus of texts: to the restoration of the Temple, the rewriting of the ancient Scriptures (the Christians' Old Testament); to the establishment of the rabbinical order, the compilation of the Talmud, etc.

In the Christian West, imperial or royal protection stood up badly to the pressures of the Church, and the emerging nation-states no longer tolerated any autonomy. From the Crusades onwards, Jewish community life there became narrower and atrophied, for lack of protection, under the repeated and combined attacks of the clergy, the nobility and the "populace". Watched, humiliated, vulnerable and persecuted, Judaism in the West became secret; it declined. Prohibited, it went into exile. The Jews were expelled from country after country, from France and most of the German states, from England and Spain, from Portugal and Spanish Italy. The once flourishing rabbinical Judaism of these countries moved eastward: to southern Italy and the Ottoman empire; to central and eastern Europe.

For several centuries, there only remained in the West small Jewish communities protected by their status as "treasury slaves", enclosed in their economic roles as bankers and usurers, and in their social function as allies of the king in his fight against the feudal order. With no other right than the favour of the prince which could be revoked at any moment, these communities did not enjoy any recognized autonomy: Jewish community life was reduced to worship in the synagogue and family and private festivals. Linguistically and culturally integrated into society, these Jews were to be transformed, with legal emancipation, into full citizens of their respective countries.

As the centre of gravity of rabbinical Judaism had moved, in the 3rd and 4th centuries, from Palestine to Mesopotamia, so it was displaced, with the expulsions that accompanied the Crusades and the wars against the Muslim states, epidemics and heresies, peasant revolts and the Inquisition, towards the countries of the new European periphery: beyond the German states and the Holy Roman Empire, on the lands of the Slavs and the Tartars.

While, in the Mediterranean, the successive waves of expellees from Christian Spain were integrated from the top into the Jewish communities protected by Islam, from Saladin "the Kurd" to the Ottomans, an exceptionally cohesive Jewish community, enjoying an unprecedented autonomy and degree of protection, took shape in north-eastern Europe, on the moving eastern fringes of the German language area: from the Baltic to Bohemia and the Danube.

This society's rabbinism – in which German played the role of Aramaic in talmudic literature, as Arabic had played this role in classical Judaism – crystallized autarkically and separately, in ignorance of the separate fate of the Jews of the Muslim world.

This Judaeo-German society structured on the talmudic model, protected on the marches of the Holy Roman Empire not by the strength of the state but by its division and fragmentation, only found the protection it needed from the 13th-14th centuries onwards: in the principality of Halich, and later in the kingdom of Poland, soon to be united with the grand duchy of Lithuania.

There, faced with the invisible and moving frontier of the Golden Horde which had only just fallen back, and whose columns still held the shores of the Black Sea, the separate Jewish society was consolidated from which three-quarters of today's Jews descend. Under the Piast and, later, Jagellon kings, this society enjoyed an autonomy unparalleled since talmudic times. The union with Lithuania and the extension of Poland to the marches of the Crimea enlarged the field of this freedom. They also brought Yiddish-speaking rabbinical Judaism into contact with the pre-existing Jewish elements and groups in this area, notably a significant proportion of Turcoman Khazars, Karaites or partly Judaized, a section of whom was then culturally and socially absorbed into the new organization.

While the internal model of the community organization thus established conformed to the legal and ideological categories of rabbinism, the institutional model of autonomy already existed. The successive "Constitutions" of Polish Judaism, which culminated, in the 16th century, with the establishment of a Jewish parliament represented in the Polish Diet, were a pendant to the "Magdeburg law" granted to the German merchants who were also called upon by the Piasts to rebuild Silesia which had been ravaged by the Mongols. The occupation of the domain by a third ethnic group faced with the twofold enemy – internal and external, social and national – was here a classic technique of government, numerous examples of which are to be found in the history of Lithuania, the Ukraine and Russia.

For almost four centuries, rabbinism managed the separate social organization of the Jews in Poland with the backing of the executive power of the state: just as the despotism imposed uniformly on the community masked the internal stratification – the existence of rich and poor within it – so it mediatized the external power of the protecting state.

With the development of mercantile relations and the rise of Christian bourgeoisies from German trade in the Baltic, the exchange function of Polish-Lithuanian Judaism lost its importance, and clashed variously with Protestant competition, or the Lithuanian admirers of the Inquisition. As the Polish monarchy weakened in the face of the assaults of its neighbours and its subjects, protection became more uncertain and less effective. From the 16th century, Polish Judaism began to be displaced towards the rural Ukraine where a feudalism prevailed that was all the more brutal because its protagonists were people-classes at the same time as religious communities: the lords Polish and Catholic, the serfs Ukrainian and Orthodox. While the rabbinical hierarchy remained in the towns in the north and west, the main part of community life took shelter under the protection and on the lands of the Catholic lords of subjected Ukraine. There the Jews, sovereigns over the domain of their mini-city, the *Shtetl,* were artisans and traders, horse-dealers and wine-sellers, and even small-scale chicken rearers: but they were also the direct intermediaries of feudal exploitation: tax farmers, tithe and rent collectors, stewards of estates at the same time as usurers.

After 1637, the anti-Polish and anti-feudal – and anti-Catholic and anti-Jewish – revolt of the Orthodox Ukrainian peasantry heralded for the formerly protected Jewry of Poland the era of massacres and destructions. The revolting serfs who established their fortified areas on the edge of the steppes where the nomad Tartars roamed became Cossack military republics, and were soon protected by the Muscovite princes who turned them into autonomous military orders in their pay. Thus, the expansion of Russia into the formerly Polish Ukraine took the structural anti-Judaism of the Ukrainian peasantry as a fundamental political fact.

The Swedish conquest that followed Chmielniczki's revolt (1648-58) and the subsequent annexations of the Polish territories to Russia, Austria and Prussia led to the successive partitions of Poland. What territory remained was finally carved up in 1815 among the three crowns, and Poland as a state disappeared for a century.

The ruin of the Polish monarchy signified the end of the protection that it granted the Jews and the rabbinical legal organization.

From the 17th century to the dawn of the 19th, small numbers of Jews were continually fleeing the massacres, harrassment and impoverishment that accompanied this decline. The legal emancipation of Jews in the West, whose effects were felt in a slow process of emancipation in Austria and the German states that coincided with the exacerbation of the crisis of the *Shtetl,* transformed this human trickle into a massive displacement as the 19th century went on: several hundred thousand Yiddish-speaking "Jews from the east" *(Östjuden)* moved westward.

While, in Russia, the community life that subsisted in the "Pale of Settlement" found in messianic pietism a compensation for the oppression weighing on it, the migratory movement westward often proceeded from a deep-seated desire for assimilation (especially in Germany), and full participation in the new democratic order. Paradoxically, this aspiration to liquidate the rabbinical social order fuelled ideological integration as much as Jewish cultural, and later political, nationalism of which Zionism was at first an avatar.

In the West to which Jews emigrated, as in Russia where they stayed, industrialization and the crisis of feudal relations posed the question of emancipation, while at the same time disrupting the sociological unity and ideological consensus that formed the basis of the Jewish community. The diaspora of the Yiddish-speaking Jews of eastern Europe all over the West telescoped regional sub-problematics, and gave rise to a new geography in which the western capitals were one pole, and the small towns of the

Ukraine the other.It also precipitated, almost at once, the appearance in western Europe – that is, in France and more particularly, although later, in Germany – anti-Semitic political and ideological currents which hindered the emancipation of the Jews even before it was legally achieved.

It was against this background that there developed, simultaneously, the racist and conservative anti-Semitism of the Holy Alliance, and the anti-clerical and anti-capitalist anti-Judaism of various currents within the Labour movement, essentially anarchist currents, victims of this "socialism of fools". It was to be their coming together and alliance that created the ideological consensus behind which the Nazis annihilated several million European Jews.

In an underground and unacknowledged symbiosis with notions abroad throughout the region, various Jewish nationalist currents had come into being in the meeting of the European movement of the Enlightenment and the east European *Shtetl*. Divided by Yiddish-Hebrew bilingualism, they were articulated on popular messianism as much as they expressed the emancipationist, and even socialist, aspirations born of the new economic relationships.

At the same time, the rise of anti-Semitism in Western countries held up the process of assimilation already underway and engendered a violent reaction: a complete reconsideration of their past and present. In this withdrawal of Jews recently assimilated into secularized tribalism political Zionism was born. It was to articulate the cultural nationalism of the Pale of Settlement on the strategic interests of the great powers: on their desire to get rid of the Jews and divert the flood of refugees from the *Shtetl* in flames to Palestine, as much as on their will to use them in the service of their own imperial domination over the region where their protection would settle them.

Thus, the Zionist movement, which claimed to provide a foundation for the normality of the Jews by giving them a state of their own, was to reproduce, at the level of several continents, the pattern of imperial protection and settlement imposed on the local population by force of foreign arms.

However, the social content of autonomy, and then of the independence thus guaranteed, differed basically from the traditional Jewish social organization. The Jewish social entity formed in Palestine during the colonial process, although still constituting, in its own way, a ghetto, was now an armed ghetto. This was a key difference, and from it flowed the normal state organization of Israel, and the dynamic of another relationship with the domain; a key difference because in this domain emptied of its Arab population by an expulsion that lasted a hundred years, it was a system of capitalist production – peripheral, dependent and subsidized, but capitalist – which was built up, and it is from its organization that the contradictions of the new society flow.

This restructuring of Jewish society in Palestine was essentially the effect of the autonomous action of the Zionist settlers of Palestine, from the beginning of this century, to establish their exclusive hegemony over the Palestinian domain, a domination that was not only military and economic, but also social, and demographic. The conquest, at first peaceful, then violent, of Arab lands, in order to establish a peasantry composed of Jewish settlers on them, was extended in the exclusion of indigenous manpower from the new labour market, and ended in the project, achieved in the 1948 war, of transfer: the displacement of the Arab population.

The vacuum thus created was to be filled by the massive immigration of Arab Jews to the new state, a result of the side-effects of the Palestine war on the life of the Jews of the Arab world and the Zionist efforts to uproot the Jewish communities of the Muslim countries. The structure of Israeli capitalism was forged in the proletarianization of these so-called "Oriental" Jews by the state and private bourgeoisie of the European Jewish colony of Palestine, now become the State of Israel: it was a national society whose concrete identity flowed from its own organization, in contradiction with the mythical and mystical identity that its leaders imposed on it, and inconsistent with the religious and tribal ideology that holds sway there.

The existence of this society is an immediate fact of the consciousness of Israelis. Paradoxically, it is nowhere more striking than in the United States, where half a million Israeli emigrés constitute a separate community quite distinct from American Jews, with whom relations are often even strained. In Israel, it merges with the identity of the *Sabra*, which has become all the more deep-rooted since, in the last twenty years, Israelis born in Palestine have become the majority and, above all, an Oriental majority. The profound and irreversible Hebraization of everyday social life has produced an official, but also popular and sometimes dissident, modern Israeli culture – literature, music, cinema – which testifies to its depth.

Yet, for reasons that are at once ideological and tactical, the Zionists continue to proclaim the unity of a world-wide "Jewish nation", that history has long since divided, in some places dissolved and everywhere transformed, and in so doing they deny the specific reality of Israeli society. Symbolically, it was Itamar Ben-Avi, the son of Eliezer Ben-Yehuda – the author of the first modern Hebrew dictionary, a Lover of Zion and a Hierosolomitan in the 1870s – who was the first to call for what he called "Canaanism": considering himself the first Ashkenazi *Sabra* whose mother tongue was Hebrew, he decreed that this linguistic identity made him the first member of a new Hebrew-Canaanite nationality, distinct from the European "Jews". However, the Canaanite current, above all based on the desire to secularize Zionist nationalism, at the time of the Mandate, at the same time as being the expression of the nationalism of the petty bourgeoisie settled for several generations in the *Yishuv,* was to decline with the years of massacres in Europe, followed by the years of massive immigration.

The reality of Israeli society has steadily grown stronger. It impregnates the pan-Judaic fiction of Zionism at the same time as it is immersed in it, a real society in the pores of official society, a Hebrew capitalism between the lines of Jewish nationalist discourse.

This reality does not justify the state: for it is not the basis of it, but result of it. That is no doubt why the Israeli leaders prefer to invoke, as the basis of the state, the biblical promise, the persecutions in Europe, the 1947 partition resolution or the fear of "mixed marriages" – anything but the national rights of the Israeli people, which, like all rights, are limited by the rights of others, notably of the Palestinian people.

This national society is not only real unbeknownst to its leaders. Based – in principle and in practice – on the dispossession, expulsion, dispersion, occupation and oppression of the Palestinian people, it is also, to a large extent, not conceptualized, invisible and denied by the victims themselves. To the moral refusal to endorse the injustice accomplished was added the ideological refusal that declared the society being formed on the usurped land a sham.

In the Arab, and particularly Palestinian, refusal to recognize Israel, the West seeks to see the manifestation of an irrational, outdated irredentism obsessed by the determination to "drive the Jews into the sea". In reality, following the humiliating defeat of 1948, which sealed the loss of Palestine and the dispersion of almost a million refugees on the road of exile, this refusal proceeded first of all from a reassertion that they existed and the simple refusal to disappear. A straightforward rejection of occupation, dispossession and deportation: nothing could be less enigmatic than this human will, proclaimed in defeat, to continue to live in order to hope to win. For Zionism, emerging from a universe quite foreign to the Arabs of Palestine, had taken on for them the impersonal face of adversity. Had the settlers been Chinese, Amerindian, Bantu, Norwegian or extra-terrestrial, the refusal would have been fuelled by the same concrete sources of spoliation and uprooting: since no society accepts freely to commit suicide on the altar of the subjective needs of another human group. On the contrary, it is the non-existence of such a refusal which would have been surprising: only the Zionists and some Westerners could, out of contempt for the Arabs, imagine that a people that has been expelled could resign itself to its own dissolution, or that its revolt would not assume the dimensions of a true problem for the society that had taken its place.

For the "Palestinian without a homeland",[5] dumped at the door of his forbidden land, it is, more than anything, the hope of return that inspires this refusal, indissociable from his own humanity. But this return is not only an unrealistic and consoling utopia (in the manner of the metaphysical return to Jerusalem that the Jews had wished each other year after year during fifteen centuries of Protection). It is also the simple and suicidal act that has consisted, since 1949, in walking straight ahead, towards the barbed wire that separates the refugee camp from the house, the field, the orchard, the goat abandoned during the exodus – an act so simple that it too is devoid of mystery, with no particular cultural pattern. Suicidal, because of the order to "fire on the infiltrators". This Israeli choice punishes the will to return with death. It thus, quite naturally, engenders the "heroes of the return" and other isolated semi-commandos who made the simple attempt to penetrate into the usurped land a slogan and then a strategy.

All colonizations of settlement have experienced the physical and exterminating confrontation with indigenous civilizations that resisted. For the young Palestinian kamikaze born in the camps, the murder of settlers who hope to live in peace without him on his land is as normal as attacking the wagon trains of American settlers was for the Indians during the conquest of the West, or of the South African Trek was for the Bantu nations; as normal as the Kalmuk and Kirghiz resistance to Russian colonization along the Volga in the 18th century. It is in the quantities and methods that the specificity of this conflict lies, at least as much as in the peculiarities of the peoples concerned. Morally, the ignorance and the denial of the humanity of the natives is no less reasonable in Palestine than in North America. The difference, therefore, lies elsewhere: in the timing and in the impact, in the relations of force. In the 20th century, in an awakening Arab world in which "the whistle of the locomotive" accompanies the rise of nationalism, and in a context marked, after October 1917, by an unprecedented international polarization, a movement as weak as Zionism, in terms of its human and material resources, could not, in such a short period, erase the Arabness of Palestine and inculcate in the survivors of colonization, as the Whites of America had succeeded in doing there, a post-defeat logic. Even the fleetingly demoralized Palestinians, the "Israeli Arabs", at the darkest hours of their isolation and prostration, had been enthused by the Nasserite wave of the years 1956-58,[6] precisely because it incarnated in their eyes the hope of the Arab national renaissance – and of the liberation of Palestine. And, for most Palestinians, for the refugees in the camps in Gaza and the West Bank as for those in exile in Lebanon or Kuwait, the hope of return has never died. Better, it was this "unrealistic" hope that was to galvanize the energy of the refugees and make them the spearhead of the new Palestinian nationalism.

Thus, the determination to return and the refusal to endorse the colonial *fait accompli* constitute the two sides of the same determination to fight against what many Zionists had themselves identified as "an injustice".

The Palestinian refusal to see the occupied domain as the occupying society had transformed it, which was absolute up to 1967 (except, of course, for the Arabs of Israel, whose very life within the Zionist entity constituted a sort of treason daily underlined by the collaboration and denunciation used as a method of policing by the Israeli military government), certainly reflects, first of all, a necessity of a quasi-effective sort: it is an ideological defence mechanism. But this blindness was also, until 1967, reinforced and encouraged by the official Arab consensus, in which the anti-Israeli, and often anti-Jewish, verbal escalation demagogically accompanied passivity and inaction, if not hidden complicity with the Zionists. The official Palestinian and Arab theses of the time (except for the discordant notes sounded at the time, very isolatedly by the Arab communist parties which had supported the 1947 partition plan, and Habib Bourguiba) were set out in 1964, in the first covenant of the PLO, patronized and controlled by Nasser, and led by Ahmed Shukairy until the aftermath of the 1967 defeat. They are very well set out in the special issue of *Les Temps Modernes* on the Israeli–Arab conflict which appeared just as the Six-Day War was breaking out; and they were articulated around key arguments that are not always crystal clear.

In the traditional Arab argument – the one that existed before the Palestinian argumentation of Fatah and the January 1969 programme – the luminous and indisputable demonstrations of the historic Arabness of Palestine, of the imperialist alliances and immoral methods of Israel, of the acts of aggression against, and oppression of, the Arab minority that remained within the new state, were mixed with another order of justificative discourse. And that is where everything becomes complicated.

In order to justify, in theory, the programme "in all points humane, moral and just" of the "repatriation of the Jews to their country of origin", the defenders of the Arab cause started from the postulate that a Jewish people did not exist, from which they quite naturally argued that an Israeli people did not exist. Paradoxically, this position led them to outbid each other on the Jewishness of the settlers, envisaged both in the Western perspective of a mere religious denomination and in the traditional Islamic one of a protected confessional minority.

These theses often started out from conciliatory intentions towards the Jews themselves, invited to free themselves of their "chimaerical nationality", to use Marx's expression. They were, moreover, inspired by Western thinking about the question: since the invaders had come from Europe, what could be more scientific than an approach that involved seeking advice from Europeans? But, in Europe, precisely, apart from the Nazis, whose anti-Semitism the Arabs realized belatedly would cause great harm to the Palestinian people, no one recognized the Jews as a nation. They were loved or hated, sometimes as a religion, sometimes as a class. They were said to be a caste, a church or a corporation depending on whether theology or economics was being invoked to lambast or defend and even praise them. The non-Zionist Jews in the West themselves, whether religious people faithful to the pattern of Expectation and submission to the "law of the kingdom", or supporters of assimilation, either bourgeois or socialist, whom the Arabs had every reason to prefer to the supporters of colonization, repeated it to them tirelessly: the Jewish nation is a heresy, Judaism is a religion, the Jews belong to the various countries where they were born, etc.

Thus, there was a shift from the assertion that the dispersed Jews did not constitute a single nation in the 19th century, to the assertion, presented as a corollary of the previous one, that the Jews brought together and organized by Zionism in Palestine could not constitute a society, but only an aggressive military base, void of social relations, and having only hierarchical relations. Somewhat inconsistently, the political and ideological needs of Arab nationalism here linked up with the language of emancipation that aspired, following in the steps of the abbé Grégoire and Marx, to the abolition of Judaism as the double incarnation of alienation, both religious and economic: but this line of argument was turned on its head when its Arab defenders began to speak of the generosity with which they intended, after the defeat of Zionism and the repatriation of the European Jews to Europe, to extend to the Jews of the old *Yishuv* and the Arab Jews repatriated to Morocco and Yemen, the Islamic protection that would preserve and protect the community. For, more than any other factor put forward from time to time in the debates, it was the actual experience and memory of the participation of Arab Jews in their society that inspired the certainty and good faith of the Arabs in their refusal to see, to "recognize", Israeli society.

Religious anti-Judaism, from the Mufti of Jerusalem Hajj Amin al-Husseini to the Muslim Brothers, is not, contrary to the notion circulating in the West, a key, or basic, factor in this refusal. The relations of the Mufti of Jerusalem with the British, then with the Nazis, show very clearly the secular, and scarcely Islamic, nature of his alliances. Sheikh Ezzedin al-Qassim, who in 1935 was preaching in the mosques of Haifa, summoned the Arab peasantry of Palestine to anti-imperialist armed revolution: "Not against Jewish women and children, but against British imperialism", as tracts distributed in 1937 by the "rebels" declared.[7] In Palestine, especially, where there was a high proportion of Christians among the urban dwellers, and even more among sectors that had come into contact with Western culture through European missions, it was essentially Orthodox Christian minorities that, as in neighbouring Syria to which Beirut still belonged, constituted the intellectual vanguard of the *Nahda,* the Renaissance to which Arab nationalism claimed allegiance. Thus, while Islamic traditionalism, faithful to its vocation as protector, denounced "the atheist Zionist bands" and not Judaism, the modernist neo-Jacobinism of the heralds of the Arab awakening preferred the national myth to the confessional tradition: the former integrated them, the latter marginalized them.

That does not mean that European-style anti-Semitism has never had any impact among the Arabs: the success that periodic new editions of the *Protocols of the Elders of Zion* encounter in various Arab countries, and especially Egypt, indicates the persistence of a certain receptiveness to the anti-Jewish languages of Europe, at the same time as a tendency to treat the enemy as the devil.

But the deepest ideological current, which bears and expresses in the most extreme way the Palestinian and Arab rejection of the *fait accompli*, is that of radical Arab nationalism – modernist, often socialist, and above all unitary. The organicism of the Arab nationalists (Ba'ath, Arab National Movement, Nasserites) hits against the reality of the Zionist occupation of Palestine, and sees in it the main impediment to the geographical and political unity of the Arab world. Here, the virulent antipathy of the unitary nationalists for any regionalism, and even more for any nationalitarian separatism (*Shu'ubiyya*), whether linguistic or ethnic, confessional or territorial, is grafted on to the juridical and moral legitimacy of rejection. This antipathy, transformed in a series of states into a principle of hegemony and authoritarian repression of all the old forms of social organization, flows from a centralizing conception of the nation inspired by the European, especially French, model of the state. This, in the expression of the Nazi Rosenberg speaking of political Zionism, is "a contamination by the national spirit and the state conception of the peoples of Europe". The Arab nationalist refusal to recognize Israel as a non-Arab national fact and independently of any question of structure, is here on a par with the denial of Kurdish rights in Iraq or Azanian ones in the southern Sudan, once again in a global approach in which the Israeli Jews are not the only targets.

The Zionists, in any case, are the last ones in a position to denounce Arab blindness to facts whose significance they constantly distort: for what Maxime Rodinson rightly calls "the Arab myths of anti-Zionism" are often no more than the obverse or even the reverse of Zionist myths themselves. After all, it is the Zionist discourse that dissolves Israeli specificity in Jewish generality, and claims to represent the interests of the West as a whole.

The Palestinian and Arab rejection of the *fait accompli* thus constitutes the ransom of the Zionist logic of the transfer, nurtured in the century-old refusal of the Zionists to recognize the human and national rights of the people of the country, and of the Zionist proclamation of the incompatibility of Israel and Palestine. If, in their definition of nationality, the Zionists assert that religion, ethnic origin and citizenship are indissociable; if they assert the Jewish character of the state created, in the terms of its own declaration of independence, "as a Jewish state on the Land of Israel", then it is difficult to criticize the Arabs for having long stood by these terms. When the Israeli Zionists, right or left, justify discrimination, apartheid or religious coercion with "Zionist" arguments along the lines "without it, the state of Israel would disappear", they not only testify to their own inability to perceive the material sources of Israeli identity. They also justify the Arab illusion that Israeli society exists only by violent virtue of Zionist laws and apparatuses, and that these only have to be abolished for the society to disappear. They certainly encourage the Arab hopes of a reversal of the military relations of force, endowed, in this shared fantasy, with the metaphysical omnipotence of making social formations appear or disappear.

The morality of a cause is not, however, a guarantee of its success. The Indians of America, who had not asked anybody for anything, before all but disappearing under the successive waves of European colonization, are evidence of this, as are all the innocent victims of injustices with which human history is replete.

The year when Israel was created froze for twenty years and more the redivision of the world: from Yalta to Teheran, the broad outlines of this division had been settled. The balkanized colonial empires would come to independence in ragged order and the often absurd frontiers that they inherited from colonialism would be sacred. The territorial *status quo* became the watchword of international competition, and the only recognized foundation of peace in the world. By getting the international community, in 1949, to accept its annexation of half the territory allocated to the Arab state of Palestine by the UN in 1947, Israel benefited from an exceptional obligingness, and went on to barricade itself inside the extended limits of its annexation, behind the inviolability of borders. The guilt-laden sympathy of the industrialized world for the Jews of Europe, transformed by the Zionists into political and economic support for the State of Israel, as much as the social autonomy of the *Yishuv* over the domain cleared, gave the Israeli entity an economic, demographic, cultural and, of course, military anchorage in the soil of Palestine, that the mere Word of rejection proved quite incapable of dislodging.

By giving concrete form to the Palestinian autonomy of rejection, the action of the commandos of the new Palestinian nationalism, Fatah, led from 1964 onwards to the Israeli–Arab military escalation, as if in a replay of 1954–56. Caught in the trap of their verbal, although passive, rejection, the main Arab states let themselves be led down the road to the defeat of June 1967, after which a new regional configuration took shape, and from which, in conformity with the strategy of the emerging national liberation movement, the Palestinian question was once again on the agenda: of the great powers and the UN, of the world and the Arab world, of the Zionist state and the Israeli people.

With the occupation by Israel of Arab territories – whether placed under Jordanian and Egyptian administration like the West Bank and the Gaza Strip, or an integral part of the Egyptian and Syrian national territories, like Sinai and the Golan Heights – and the reunification of Mandatory Palestine by the occupying army, the Palestinian Resistance was invested with a new legitimacy, both popular and institutional, Palestinian and Arab, and then international.

In the strategic alliance that was forged between the exiles and the people in the occupied areas, between the return and the resistance, between the exterior and the interior, a genuine historical mutation occurred, which transformed a nationalist vanguard into a national movement, an armed party into a spokesman and government of a whole fragmented and dispersed society. After 1970, and the military collapse of the PLO before the Jordanian army in Amman, the multi-faceted resistance of the

Palestinians inside the occupied territories began to become a qualitatively new factor in the relations of force, the importance of which was growing all the time. Gradually, the rejection became a project, doubly confronted with the real world: with the unbearable refusal of the real world to conform to the ideology, and with the often bloody price of theoretical illusions.

The project is Palestinian, as the rejection was, and remains Arab. And, as the Palestinians are also Arabs, the rejection is not absent from the project. But the project is nurtured not only by the despair at having lost and the abstract hope of a revenge, but also by the concrete hopes of men and social sectors directly confronted with occupation and exile. A double realism in the way the Palestinian peasant or worker in the occupied West Bank sees the occupier: the occupier, the harsh reality of whom can no longer be decreed a sham, and the Arab language of solidarity and commitment. As for the refugees, they had felt this dialectic from the very earliest years of their exile: the bitter and secret determination to reject the Arab tutelage linked to the desire to mobilize the Arab popular consciousness for Palestine.[8]

As an armed materialization of the rejection and at the same time a measure of its limits, the Palestinian project of 1969 was entitled "secular and democratic Palestine" and called for the creation, on the whole of the territory of Mandatory Palestine, of a unitary state in which Jews, Christians and Muslims would enjoy absolute equality of rights and duties. The significance of this slogan must be appreciated: in 1974 Yasser Arafat, speaking from the podium of the UN, set out its implications, stressing (in contrast to Shukairy's covenant in 1964) that all the Jews in Palestine were invited to stay and "live with the Palestinians".[9] And, when Eric Rouleau asked him whether such a demand did not appear exorbitant in the present situation, Arafat opposed his right to dream.

"The dreams of some are the nightmares of others", declared the Knesset member Uri Avnery in September 1977 in London, at an Israeli–Palestinian Seminar, in response to the late Saïd Hammami who was reaffirming the legitimacy of this dream.[10] For this slogan, revolutionary in many respects, which translated a generosity – or a realism – unprecedented in the history of resistance movements to settler colonization, overlooked the radical transformation that has taken place within the Zionist entity. Since the Israelis are not, structurally, a community, nor Jewish communities, but a social formation of a national type, the status of religious community protected in its civil rights within an Arab state is as unattractive in the eyes of the exploited Oriental masses as it is in the eyes of the Ashkenazi bourgeoisie and petty bourgeoisie. So that the slogan of a secular and democratic Palestine, inspired by analysis of the "Jewish question" in the West, the perception of the Jews as a confessional community and the lessons of the Lebanese situation, is perceived in diametrically opposite ways by the two sides.

The slogan of a secular and democratic Palestine, conceived so as to eradicate the mechanism of the vertical confrontation between the communities – as well as in order to propose a "constructive solution" to the Palestine question – was rapidly transformed, by the Zionists themselves, into a new version of the old rejection.

In fact the Israeli leaders are well aware of the danger, for them, of a Palestinian proposal based on the principle of coexistence and partition of the domain, which would make possible a reversal of the moral relations of force at the international level, and might eventually take root in Israeli society. The Palestinian formula was thus declared to be identical in its content to the slogan of Arab Palestine. A new branch of Israeli Orientalism, Palestinology, developed among Israeli generals and military experts: while the disciples of Gush Emunim were taking up a new theology of race and land, these "scientists" delved into the exegesis of Arab documents and statements. One of them, professor-general Yehoshaphat Harkavi, a great expert on the Palestinian Covenant, succeeded in getting teaching of it made compulsory in Israel. The Covenant! Everything is in the Covenant, these national educators explain, in writing and in speeches, in public and in private. This Covenant that they know by heart – whereas the majority of Palestinians are unaware of it – means the dismantling of Israel and the repatriation of the Jews to their countries of origin, and talk of anything else, they decree, is hypocritical and a smokescreen. Arguing from the formulation reducing the Jews of Palestine to a mere religious community, they challenge the PLO to contradict (more recently, to amend) the Covenant, that is, to disrupt the institutional Arab front that integrates the PLO into the Arab League, and to take the risk of disrupting the Palestinian front.

The Marxist factions of the Palestinian movement that emerged from the acceptance by the Arab Nationalists of the slogan of the liberation of Palestine in the aftermath of 1967, did indeed attempt, during the summer of 1968, to raise the idea of a bi-national state. The attempt was still-born: a text submitted to the Palestine National Council, a tract distributed at Athens airport when some hostages were taken, and an article by Naif Hawatmeh in *Le Monde* [reprinted in *The Times*]. The accusation of defeatism and treason, easily brandished in intra-Palestinian factional struggles, and always available for use by the brother-states in their ceaseless attempts to subordinate the Resistance, made advocating such analyses unpopular and dangerous.

The defeat of Black September in Jordan, in 1970, which strengthened the Palestinian dependence on the Arab regimes, made them even more out-dated. However, a rethinking began following the commitment of the Arab states to the path of a negotiated settlement: launched by the acceptance by Nasser of UN Security Council Resolution 242 of 22 November 1967, and confirmed with the acceptance by the new Syrian regime of the same position in 1970, this commitment was to become more serious after the October 1973 war, leading to the demand for a Palestinian state in the West Bank and Gaza, that is, alongside Israel and not in place of it, as the first stage in a settlement.

The rise of this new realism, after 1974, which has inspired all the decisions taken since by the Palestine National Council, has considerably strengthened the international authority of the PLO, but has not succeeded in altering Western, or Israeli, opinion. It has happened in a context in which Palestinian nationalism is vulnerable to Arab pressures and the more or less manipulated "hard factions": by presenting the coexistence of two states as a purely tactical stage, without going into details of what the next stage would be beyond the "tri-confessional" formula of 1969, the Palestinian Resistance lost, in the eyes of Israelis, the credibility that it intended by so doing to retain in the eyes of the Palestinian and Arab masses.

Ben-Gurion knew this, and he counted on the permanence of the conflict to consolidate the laager mentality: it is vital for Zionism that the Arab war aims can be interpreted as signifying the extermination of the Jews of Palestine, their being driven into the sea, their expulsion. Sadat, too, moreover, had understood it, in an initiative that the Israeli chief of staff Gour immediately described as a "war strategem".

Thus, isolated words and acts are never innocent of their symbolic implications. The discourse of coexistence undermines the monolithic character of the Israeli denial of Arab rights just as the discourse of the armed destruction of the state strengthens it. But in both cases, it is only a matter of discourses which do not prejudge the practice that may underlie them: one can perfectly well fight with a peace programme, just as one may not fight while talking of great massacres. An operation such as that of 2 May 1980 in Hebron, in the occupied West Bank, where an armed Palestinian group executed six fascist activists in broad daylight, carefully and systematically sparing the women and children among the designated victims, such an operation does not have the same symbolic meaning and hence not the same repercussions, as a hostage seizure in a working-class suburb or in the nursery of a border kibbutz.

In the vicious circle of overlapping negations, there is, of course, no symmetry between oppressors and oppressed, between strong and weak, between the one who defends the *fait accompli* and the one who disputes it. There is no comparison between the suicidal terrorism of the desperate and the reasoned terrorism of an overarmed state. But there is this blockage in which we are living, where, in the interstices of the latest defeats and the space of the rare victories, the outlines of a few escape routes, and the hope of a break appears. The recognition of the character of Israeli society by the Palestinians, from the embraces between Israelis and Palestinians at Sofia in 1980 to those at Brussels in February 1981, the signs of which are multiplying at both the popular level and the fighting level, under the occupation as in exile, constitutes a historical breach in the spiral of expulsion. One cannot but observe the weakness, in Israel, of an equivalent conceptual revolution.

History has prepared an imbroglio in Palestine that is unlike any other, even if each of its ingredients can be found elsewhere.

> All the classic patterns on the subject of national and colonial problems run up here against a single fact: the Palestinian people – although part of the Arab nation – has no other homeland than the one the Zionists have taken over; and the Israeli people, although composed of various communities, has no other homeland than the one it stole from the Palestinians.[11]

In this challenge, the peoples of the region must either sink – into war, poverty, tyranny and foreign intervention – or discover a response that meets the seriousness of the question. Such a creation, by which Palestinians and Israelis, Arabs and Jews, would work out novel, and today unimaginable, forms of coexistence, is not only the only alternative to war and new slaughters: it would integrate in practice the rights of peoples and the rights of man; it would define new approaches for groups and communities, and would contribute to making the world intelligible.

The Middle East conflict does not involve only the Israelis and the Palestinians: all the peoples of the region, where it has become a running sore creating many impasses, have their lives poisoned by it. The involvement of great and small powers (international order and disorder) in the use, arming, financing and protection of the direct protagonists in the conflict has made it into a crucial feature of the crisis of humanity. Certainly not its centre, as some people in various quarters tend arrogantly to claim, but certainly one of the areas of the world where the permanence of war and occupation, repression and hatred, may at any moment upset the balance of terror that takes the place of world peace.

This involvement of local and global interests and problematics is no doubt universal: but here the network of connections and ramifications cuts across indirect correlations: while Palestine moves the Arab world and the whole of Islam, and behind them virtually the whole Afro-Asian bloc and the so-called socialist states, in the West it sets off passionate reactions that betray the depth of the involvement of Westerners in this affair.

Western societies have a double stake in the genesis of this conflict: because, historically it is part of the area of European colonial rule; and because it has its source in the European circumstance of persecution of the Jews. The war of figments awakened in the European imagination by the simultaneous appearance, as actors, of Arabs and Jews silences or sterilizes dialectical reason, as Sartre personally testified in 1967: here it lapses into apologetics, recrimination and sentimentality.

Thus, the Judaeo-Arab impasse is articulated on the inability of Western opinion (and thus states) to think the problem through: to consider this tragic and banal picture moved only by the desire to understand before acting. What a utopian and archaic demand of philosophy! Americans, Europeans and Russians are for numerous reasons responsible for this mess: and that risks making them, at some point, its first victims if it should get out of hand. Is this not a sufficient reason to take the time to analyse its causes and effects?

The Jewish problem dressed up to suit every taste, of which the consumer of culture is today so fond in the West, is not, alas, only a historical problem. Not only because the Palestinian question has inherited it, but because it continues to be posed, and because its Middle-Eastern dimension, far from solving it, maintains it and complicates it. It is posed in the Eastern bloc countries, its homeland, where anti-Semitism, for a while disguised as militant atheism, has long since become, under cover of anti-Zionism, state policy: less intended to strike the Jews than to turn aside and divert political oppositions, anti-bureaucratic revolts and nationalitarian demands, which is nothing other than the traditional role assigned to anti-Semitism by the policies of tsarist Russia in the good old days. It was posed in Argentina, where the fascists armed by Israel protected the Nazi killers of Argentine Jews. It is posed in the United States, where the most numerous, the most prosperous and the best organized Jewish community in the world lives, in a symbiosis with the Zionist movement and the State of Israel which makes it a protagonist in the conflict and a vital element in the relations of force: a position which might, in the twin framework of a social crisis in the United States and a contradiction between the interests of American imperialism and those of Zionism, become explosive. It is posed everywhere that the identification of Israel, Zionism and the Jews is imposed: a few months before the victory of the Sandinistas in Nicaragua, a revolutionary commando group attacked the synagogue in Managua... to protest against Israeli military support for the dictator Somoza's National Guard!

In Europe itself, especially in France, for several years the signs have been growing of an ill-defined desire, made up of objective and paradoxical convergences – from the interview given by the French Nazi Darquier de Pellepoix to the *Express* in 1978 to the mysterious murderous attack in the rue Copernic in Paris in October 1980 – to reintroduce into the violent culture of popular racism, which is essentially anti-Arab, the language of anti-Judaism.

The dialectic of the ideological movements that I have attempted to describe in the particular case of the Jews proceeds, in my opinion, from the ordinary mechanisms of the history of societies. It is up to others to bring it out in their own area. This reduction to the commonplace is not an abandonment: for anyone who wants to count in the scales of resistance to death, clear thinking is the condition of rationality in action.

There must be a way out of this sad history. A way of neither remaining prisoners of its ancient parameters, nor remaining entranced by the turn of phrases, the echo of visions, the texture of the paper. The page must be turned.

Notes

1. "The conquest of the lands of Merhavia", in the *Defence Book*.

2. Moshe Sharett's diary, and Livia Rokach's book, *Israel's Sacred Terrorism*, reveal their complicity in the campaigns to assassinate Jordanian civilians in 1953–54, which at the time were presented as "reprisal operations" carried out by "civilian" settlers who were out of control.

3. David Ben-Gurion, *Why We Fought, Why We Evacuated, What We Have Obtained* [in Hebrew] (Tel-Aviv, Mapai Central Publishing House, 1957).

4. Moshe Dayan, speaking to the students of the Haifa Technion, July 1972.

5. This is the translation of the French title *(Palestinien sans patrie)* of the autobiography of the Palestinian leader Saleh Khalaf (Abu Iyad), (Paris, Editions Fayolle, 1978). English translation, *My Home, My Land* (New York, Times Books, 1981).

6. Borhan Allauié's film, *Kafr Kassem,* describes the massacre of 44 unarmed Arab villagers, on 29 October 1956, by a border guard unit charged with enforcing a curfew "pitilessly" on the eve of the aggression against Egypt. The scenes of life in the village show the prostration, and the hope, then symbolized by speeches broadcast by Arab radio stations, which is epitomized in the voice of Nasser announcing the nationalization of the Suez Canal.

7. Private archives of Mordechai Stein, an independent anti-Zionist lawyer since the 1930s, Tel-Aviv.

8. Cf. Fouad Raouf, *L'analyse historique de la révolution palestinienne* (Paris, Department of Economic Sciences, University of Paris – VIII, 1974).

9. In the words that serve as the title of the Hebrew edition of a collection of texts by Eliahu Eliachar, an old Arab-Jewish activist of peaceful coexistence, close to the Peace Alliance at the time of the Mandate, still active today in the Israeli peace camp.

10. Saïd Hammami, one of the first Palestinian leaders to have spoken openly, in 1974, of peaceful coexistence between Palestinians and Israelis, was assassinated in London, in January 1978, by the group led by Abu Nidal, a Palestinian "dissident" at that time armed, financed, trained and manipulated by Iraq. A few months later, it was the turn of the PLO representative in Paris, Ezzedin Kalak, to die.

11. Manifesto – programme of the *Maavak-an Nidal* (Struggle) group (Jerusalem), February 1974. Mostly reprinted in *Khamsin* no. 1 (Paris, Maspéro, 1974).

Index